Leisure and Society in Britain

Leisure and Society
in Britain

edited by Michael A. Smith,
Stanley Parker and Cyril S. Smith

Allen Lane

Published in 1973

Allen Lane
A Division of Penguin Books Ltd
21 John Street, London WC1N 2BT

Hardback edition ISBN 0 7139 0225 6
Paperback edition ISBN 0 7139 0528 X

Printed in Great Britain by
Lowe & Brydone (Printers) Ltd., Thetford, Norfolk

Contents

Acknowledgements

In the course of bringing together the various articles and writing the editorial material which together compose this volume, we have had critical and helpful advice from a number of friends and colleagues. Even though we did not always take their advice, we wish nevertheless to thank them cordially for the interest they took in the project. Our thanks are due to those who gave secretarial support, and in particular Mrs Pat Leavey. Above all we should like to express our appreciation to the contributors, who have shown patience and understanding in negotiations with us about their articles, and who in some cases have had to wait a very long time to see their efforts in print.

We should like to express our thanks to the publishers for allowing us to reprint the following articles: Chatto and Windus for Raymond Williams' *Culture and Society*, pp. 307-14, and the original version of *The Long Revolution* (pp. 363-74 of the Penguin Books edition), and for Richard Hoggart's *Speaking to Each Other*, volume 1, pp. 45-61; and the Department of Education and Science, publishers of *Trends in Education*, for J. A. Simpson's 'Education for Leisure', January 1967, pp. 16-23.

The general introduction and the introduction to Part 1 were drafted by Michael A. Smith, the introductions to Parts 2 and 4 by Stanley Parker, and the introductions to Parts 3 and 5 by Cyril S. Smith. Each subsequently had the benefit of joint editorial discussion and criticism.

M.A.S. S.R.P. C.S.S.

General introduction

A book about society and leisure involves certain risks. It may not appeal to the expert who knows a great deal about his particular leisure enthusiasm and would find it ignored here. It may not appeal either to the individual who sees himself as having very little time or energy to read about the leisure he could pursue if he had the time to do so. This is the dilemma and fascination of the subject. It compels examination of the reasons we give for the choices we make in how we spend our time and resources.

The title of this book indicates that we are concerned not just with reviewing leisure as a sphere of activity in its own right but with understanding it in the context of the kind of society in which we live. At the outset, then, it is desirable to sketch, however briefly, some of the ways in which leisure in Britain is shaped and influenced by various social factors. Chief among these is perhaps the growth of science in enabling man to have greater control over the means of producing material wealth; so far society has used the benefits of science mainly to increase production of goods and services rather than to develop the potentialities of individuals and of improving the 'quality of life'.

Since leisure is a sphere of life which is, by its very nature, supposed to be free and uncommitted, there are certain difficulties about applying scientific techniques to the study or the planning of leisure behaviour. If we want to understand the complex mechanisms of our society — perhaps with a view to changing them in desired directions — then we need to ask what social science can offer by way of insight into social processes and patterns of human behaviour. This applies to leisure no less than to other fields.

We live in an industrial society in which organizations of various kinds shape our experiences and in which differences of income and status are built into the economic system. Success is measured by profitability and individual achievement: it is often identified with possession of the appropriate status symbols. It is a 'class' society in which differences in income and opportunity for achievement are related to the existence of distinct cultures and ways of life, to different values and standards. Inevitably these features of our society have a pervasive influence on the opportunities open to us to enjoy leisure and even on the meaning that leisure experiences have for us.

A book about leisure should tell us something about ourselves. It should also tell us something about our society, in particular something about the influence of technology and social class on the ways in which human choices and social relationships are patterned. Leisure is thus an important and fascinating subject for the individual and the planner, for the informed public and the expert, for the politician and the administrator, for the escapist and the entrepreneur. The discussion of leisure cannot easily be separated from the other important issues which occupy a significant place in public debate, especially since these issues relate to the problem of the quality of life possible in our society. People are no longer satisfied with a way of life in which the opportunities for leisure are restricted. This book examines the sources of this discontent and seeks to answer a number of relevant questions. What are the leisure patterns and trends in our society? How far is it possible for everyone to pursue his own leisure interests in a society of limited resources? How is work related to leisure? Should we educate for leisure? In what way does the 'life cycle' influence leisure pursuits and values? Do there exist different leisure cultures and if so do they conflict? Is it possible to plan for leisure?

Leisure is such a varied phenomenon, it has so many facets and guises, that it can be regarded as a very debatable subject. Part of any such debate is in *describing* the variety of human behaviour; part is in *ascribing* values and standards to what is described. Social science certainly concerns itself with categorizing and defining the motives underlying people's choices; the norms or expectations which regulate social relationships; the organizational framework within which different kinds of behaviour occur. These concerns are central to a science of man in society. Also important, but more contentious, is how to evaluate the behaviour described by social science. Ethics is part of human choice; it is not possible for social science to escape from the responsibility of making judgements about what aims are worth while and what values worth pursuing, especially in relation to leisure. This dualistic role of social science, to describe and explain human behaviour, and express judgements about human values and aims, creates many tensions. Some social scientists sharply distinguish the two spheres, claiming that they are incompatible. Others see social science as having a humanizing role of helping in the pursuit of socially desirable objectives.

Why social science has neglected the subject of leisure and how this situation might be remedied are basic questions to be answered: this is a *social science debate* about the importance of describing and understanding leisure. There is also the question of the ethical and moral standards by which to judge what leisure people should have, its quality and scope: this is a *policy and planning debate* about the priorities which determine the allocation of resources in society and the social control processes which exist to regulate human behaviour. These two debates — the social science one about understanding the content and patterns of leisure in Britain; the policy and planning one about the ethics and values inherent in the economic and political choices which have to be made in relation to the development of leisure in Britain — are the organizing themes in the rest of this introduction and they are intertwined throughout the book.

1. The contribution of social science to describing and understanding leisure

Every discipline has its great men, the theorists from the past who have laid the foundations and defined the scope of the subject. In social science the great men have been more concerned with the pathology of industrial life than its virtues, more concerned with the restrictions resulting from new forms of the division of labour than the content of the freedoms possible. It would be false to say that they were not concerned with leisure; they were, but only negatively in terms of the problems of societal disintegration or loss of personal freedom. *Karl Marx* with his focus on the 'disease' of capitalism, its exploitation and reduction of human beings to factors of production, its inherent and self-destructive tendency towards individual alienation and social crisis, saw the solution in the classless society where men could be autonomous and creative. *Max Weber* conceived the problem somewhat differently. Western society was distinctly a rational society and capitalism the specific expression of such rationalism. The danger was in the restrictions, both organizational and political, created by rationalism; bureaucracy would permeate all spheres of life and political choice with the consequent loss of personal freedom. Weber summed up the growth of legal-rationalism in terms of industrial capitalism with the phrase 'the disenchantment of the western world'; the secularization of values and the loss of individual freedom through the growth of science and its application to economic and social life. *Émile Durkheim* was more concerned with ways in which industrialization led to the breakdown of social order. People were no longer part of close-knit communities but were subject to a variety of conflicting values and standards of behaviour. The result could be a loss of any sense of integration with society, the loss of significance and identity. Suicide was one indication of an anomic social order in which people lost their sense of belonging, their significance and meaning for the groups to which they belonged.

Social science, particularly sociology, has developed this tradition of examining the impact of industrialization on society. Thus, very little attention has been paid to leisure in its own right, and this is a reflection of the impact of the classical theorists who saw leisure as dependent and residual rather than autonomous and central. Other commentators on the social scene, however, have approached the study of leisure through the study of culture, for example, Raymond Williams and Richard Hoggart, who have contributed chapters to Part 1.

There are good reasons for resisting the view that leisure values and behaviour are only explicable through some more 'important' aspect of society and only merit attention as the residue of social life. One such reason may be that people do not experience it in this way — leisure itself may be a central life interest and merit urgent attention for that reason alone. It is also quite clear that a framework of understanding which claims to examine man and society and ignores leisure omits a considerable part of social life. Leisure behaviour and organization cut across family patterns and work commitments and to a large extent may be independent of both.

Perhaps the most important reason for making leisure a subject of analysis is found in the part social knowledge plays in the development of our own society. Man has turned upon himself and his society the quest for knowledge. The attempt to analyse, predict and control physical phenomena has extended to an attempt to explore the patterns and trends of social behaviour. The principles upon which society is based are now increasingly challenged and inspired guesswork is being replaced by accurate knowledge about human behaviour. This is what makes social science so frightening for some people and fascinating for others. It is not just a technique for uncovering the patterns of behaviour and social relationships of people — it also leads to a radical appraisal of the causes of such behaviour and relationships. In applying the methods of science to man in society, social science, and sociology in particular, points up the tension between stability and change, tradition and innovation, between freedom of choice and a planned society. An analysis of leisure, the patterns of social organization and human choice, is a probing and questioning by man of himself as the creator of his own society, it is a recognition that what is accidental need not be the best that can exist; it is asking what are the underlying trends in the social organization of leisure and the possibilities of further development.

What is leisure?

The way we define our own behaviour, the meaning we give to the relationships we have with others, are rooted in individual life experiences. By asking the question 'what is leisure?' these experiences become clear. For some people the question is answered by saying that leisure is *freedom from* the necessity of work; it is time in which those things which are interesting and enjoyable can be pursued. Leisure in this sense is a sharp contrast to the demands imposed by the constraints and pressures of those things which have to be done. For many people leisure is this *negative experience of freedom,* freedom *from* the pressures of everyday life. For some it takes the form of an escape, an adventure into a fantasy world of illusion and reality. The scientist can become the fanatical football supporter, totally identified with his team. The bank clerk can lose himself in the romance of amateur dramatics. The factory worker can escape from the noise and boredom of his job by going fishing and experiencing the freedom denied by his work. The housewife can escape from the triviality of being a domestic servant by taking an Open University degree. Leisure, then, in this sense is a feeling of escape from obligations which give little freedom. Lack of freedom is experienced as having to spend a great deal of time and effort in activities and relationships which are unrewarding, if not physically, intellectually or emotionally damaging. This suggests that for many people the experience of leisure is freedom *from* unrewarding life experiences, from the necessity of unavoidable obligations.

The question 'what is leisure' can be answered very differently. For some people it is answered by saying that life is very much of a whole, that obligations and enjoyments are so much part of each other that it is not meaningful to refer to separate times and activities as distinctly work or leisure. Life is very much a mixture of the two and if anything the experience of leisure is a qualitative one in which the individual can manage the constraints upon him. He can manage them in such a way as to maintain his integrity as an individual and can express himself through the choices he makes. Leisure in this sense is a *positive experience of freedom*; of freedom *to* enter into obligations and relationships, to pursue interests and opportunities. Such freedom is never total, just as constraints are never completely compelling. Freedom is relative to the kinds of limits being imposed on people. How far they are self-imposed seems the qualitative distinction which the positive experience of freedom involves. The negative experience of freedom is where constraints are external to the individual and he is seeking some form of compensation or escape. The positive experience is where any imposition is internal, self-chosen and intrinsically meaningful.

The significance of work
Everyone has to make a living. For some their work is a pleasure, a chance to pursue what they find interesting and intrinsically rewarding. It is the positive experience of freedom. Work is the challenge of the new, the chance to wield power, the excitement of risk-taking, the satisfaction of work well done. For other people work is less rewarding and a necessity based squarely on the need to survive. It involves a

negative experience of freedom, a denial of autonomy: the monotony and boredom of much mass-production work, the 'money in my pay-packet' approach, the necessity of 'labour'. Much work of this kind is dehumanizing, alienative, destroying human dignity and personality. It is often said that we become like the things we do, and this is especially true of the kind of work in which people engage. Work may afford purpose and fulfilment or it may not. Many people thus find their work absorbing and satisfying; it has the characteristic of 'paid leisure', and in their free time they may take up interests and skills similar to those of their work. Others find work boring and dissatisfying and seek leisure which sharply contrasts with their work — their free time is an escape from the tedium and drudgery of labour. In short, types of work differ in the freedom they allow and the constraints they impose and can predispose people to see and use their leisure in particular ways.

The problem with such an assertion about the interdependence of work and leisure is that it rests upon an assumption that work is important to people, that it radically shapes their self-image. This is not always true. People bring their self-images into their work situations as well as being influenced by them. Such self-images are closely tied to the kinds of things people enjoy and the experiences they consider important. Work may afford neither enjoyment nor importance and thus may have a marginal significance for personality and social needs. Many writers have referred to the decline in work as 'a central life interest', and have suggested that work is just something to be done in between the more important things in life. It may be that most people in industrial society have never considered work important — just that social scientists think they ought to.

However, there is evidence that people are increasingly, consciously, looking for alternative sources of significance to that offered by work. The quest is for new sensations, new experiences, new leisure identities; the process involves the questioning of traditional behaviour, codes of ethics and sexual norms. The fashion revolution, the growth of minority cultures, the cult of the eccentric and the exotic, the acceptance of rebellion as a way of life, each involves a rejection of the traditional view that work is the most important reference point, that whether it be enjoyed or endured, work is a way of life and the centre of existence. It may well be that people are seeking a new focus, given that work may have been a 'central life interest', and that they are seeking this through leisure. If so it could mean that work will decline as a source of enjoyment and self-evaluation. This may explain why leisure is becoming such an important social issue for planners, educationalists and social scientists. And it may also explain the increasing diversity in the form and content of leisure values and behaviour.

Leisure and work
It has been suggested that in answer to the question 'what is leisure?' many would reply that it is *freedom from* obligations imposed on them. Some would express this positively and claim that leisure is *freedom to* develop one's own interests and capacities. The work people do may be important in explaining the quality of the leisure they experience and in influencing how they choose to use their 'free time'. The different kinds of work in which people engage is not itself a total explanation for the diversity of leisure pursuits and values. Leisure may be seen as a compensation for work or in some sense its extension, but leisure cannot be explained simply in those terms. It involves exploring what people find important and enjoyable, some measure of what is significant for their self-image. Work may be declining as a source of such significance, being replaced by a search for leisure identities. The relative meanings of work and leisure, and some of the ways in which empirical research is being undertaken to test tentative theories of leisure, are some of the major themes in Part 2.

The important point from which to begin an explanation of leisure is in the way people themselves define the experience. Such an approach avoids the spurious position of those who want to impose some *implicit* ethical standard on leisure activities, in some sense for the good of others. There may well be ethical issues, questions about public control and private morality, but these issues should be part of an *explicit* discussion in relation to particular problems. The view that leisure consists of the content and quality of people's experience has other advantages. It avoids the tendency to regard leisure exclusively as a type of activity, as a sport or hobby, or as a particular segment of time, such as free time or non-work time. Leisure is all of these things but not reducible to them. It is rather like the classical definition of God in that its circumference is everywhere and centre nowhere. Leisure is closely linked to people's sense of enjoyment and freedom, their capacity for self-realization and self-expression, the process of recreation and renewal, the possibility of choice and opportunity.

The growth of individualism
There is a trend, with the growth of a mass-consumer market and a strong youth culture, towards ego-conscious rather than class-conscious symbolism. Status symbols and life styles are becoming *expressions of individual taste* rather than *reflections of economic position* or social

class. The growth of individuated self-awareness underpins the movement towards ego-conscious symbolism. As people become more aware of themselves as separate individuals the process of choice becomes a conscious one and they are less guided by what is 'appropriate' than what expresses their own self-image and style of life. The result is a loosening of the social fabric in which class consciousness is tied to recognized class symbols and life styles. The growth of mass communication is one of the important factors involved in such a loosening process.

Part of the increasing diversity and variety of leisure values may be due to the declining significance of social class as a basis of people's behaviour. One indication of such a decline may be in the decreasing centrality of work to which reference has already been made. Another may be found in the break-up of traditional working-class communities brought about by slum clearance and re-housing policy. The break-up of such communities has tended to be associated with a reduction of single-industry areas. It is also possible that there is some truth in the image of the 'affluent worker' aspiring to be middle-class, but the extent of such affluence and aspiration is doubtful. Although different levels of income give access to different styles of life and status symbols, people may be becoming less class-conscious in the way they express themselves and the choices they make. There are some things that only money can buy, but they are becoming fewer and more people are able to buy them.

The development of verbal and visual media is as profound and revolutionary in its way as the evolution of language itself. The social world people inhabit is not co-extensive with their face-to-face relationships or the general network of the relationships they have. The world of the media makes possible a range of personalities, information, ideas, each of which may constitute another dimension of an individual's social reality, though the media are also a powerful influence making for social integration in the sense of conformity and standardization. There is a large amount of data on the time people spend and the resources they use in connection with the media. What is more difficult to assess is the qualitative impact of such interaction. The general finding is that people tend to watch, read and listen to those things with which they agree and which reflect their own values and life styles. Such selective perception cannot, however, be total or complete, particularly when the long-term effects of the media are considered. One such long-term effect may be the growth of individualism and self-awareness within a society. It may well be that the growth of a leisure-conscious society is a consequence of the spread of the media and that ego-conscious symbolism is a reflection of the self-awareness generated by such a process of diffusion. It may also be that this process is only just starting, that class consciousness is fragmenting and that class behaviour patterns are yielding to a more diverse and complex situation.

Social science debate – conclusions
Although the study of leisure has so far been relatively neglected by sociologists and other social scientists in Britain, there are signs that this situation is changing. Although it would, in our view, be wrong to seek to divert attention from other pressing areas of social concern in order to study leisure, there is a strong case for seeing the facts, values and problems of leisure in social context and dealing with them accordingly. In various countries there has been some attempt to develop testable hypotheses about leisure – the first few steps on the road to theory building. In Britain there is a need both to encourage research into leisure and to do so on a basis which recognizes that various social science disciplines are involved. Part 3 of this book deals with one important context of the study of leisure – the stages in the life cycle – while Part 4 spans economic and sociological considerations in the study of the leisure industries.

2. The policy and planning debate
The idea that there are policy decisions to be made about leisure, that leisure involves allocating resources and 'planning for freedom', may seem an impertinent one. It suggests an invasion of personal freedom by some well-meaning, largely unaccountable, authority. Looked at in another way the question is less threatening; it is asking what are the principles underlying control over leisure, its expression and development. What leisure ought to mean in an industrial society is a complex question of social policy, of the cultural values and political principles underpinning such policy, of the criteria for reconciling individual freedoms with collective or public good. The issues dealt with in this debate are covered at considerable length in Part 5.

Values and social organization
The analysis of leisure poses the question of 'who should control and for whose good?'. This general debate is one aspect of the discussion of the 'quality of life' which concerns the degree of control which should exist over various aspects of social life. Some people want a society in which minimal control exists over individual choice and where freedom of expression is the most important organizing principle of life. Other people consider this dangerous because the consequence could be cultural anarchy or unlimited commercial exploitation. Advocates of a

middle way suggest that there should be some controls for vulnerable groups, while encouragement through education and public discussion should be given to the development of personal responsibility and discrimination.

The dispute over censorship is one area where there is conflict about what is 'good' and what is 'bad' leisure, especially in terms of the cultural differences between 'élite' and 'mass' culture and the kind of social controls which should exist. The conflict is largely about the distinction between pornography and art; how far to control bias and the portrayal of violence in the media; the balance between personal choice and public order, between human dignity and commercial exploitation.

Another area where the question of leisure values and choices leads to public debate is that of social planning. Assuming that we are not going to leave it entirely to the market to satisfy people's leisure needs, we must inevitably accept some degree of planning. Planning is not new, although it is only relatively recently that planners have begun to ask the consumers, those they plan for, what is important for them rather than what is supposed to be good for them. Planning involves political decisions about the use of resources and touches most aspects of social organization. Planning in the public sector is primarily decided according to the political priorities and views of those who control local, regional and national levels of decision making and policy formation. In the private sector the ethical problems of leisure provision are less important than the criterion of profitability. It is perhaps where public provision and profitability conflict that acute questions about personal freedom and public good arise. The preservation of green belt areas, the control of the motor car, the use of national parks, finance of the arts and sport, each of these is an issue about which there is fierce dispute. And such dispute is important because it affects people's opportunities for leisure, their quality of life in industrial society.

Nowhere is the dispute more intense than in the area of educational provision; the basis upon which education should be organized, the criteria of organizational selection and the aims of educational policy are subjects of intense political debate. Should education be organized on egalitarian lines, compensating for emotional and environmental deprivation? Should Britain have a 'democratic' or an 'élitist' system, one which is open to all or one which selects the most able for the best provision? Should educational aims and content be tied closely to the economic system or should there be 'education for leisure'? Such questions involve ethical choices, decisions about social provision and planning, and at centre suggest that there are different views about what kind of society Britain should create.

What kind of society?

Britain is an industrial society; economic organization and technology shape the work experiences and social fabric of the lives of its members. Britain also is an unequal society in which differences of income and status are built into the economic system. Success is measured by profitability, and individual achievement is assessed by possession of the appropriate status symbols. Thus our society is a 'class' society in which differences of income and opportunity for achievement are related to the existence of distinct cultures and ways of life, to different values and standards. The differences between people are not random but linked to the economic basis of social opportunity and cultural diversity.

Our society is also a rational society in which social objectives, communication systems, ways of thinking about ourselves, are open to critical examination. The right to question is not simply a scientific principle, but the social basis of political democracy. The rational society is one in which freedom of expression is the consequence of making those who have economic and political power accountable for their decisions. The right of the individual to express his views is contingent upon the right to question the aims and decisions which affect his own and other people's lives.

The social organization of leisure, the values which underpin social policy and planning are ultimately a question of the kind of society considered worth striving for. Some have argued for the *classless society* on the basis of the inequalities of capitalism. Inequalities of income and opportunity give rise to different patterns of choices and relationships; leisure reflects such inequalities; only when changes have occurred in the ownership and control of economic resources will a society of leisure be possible. Until then leisure simply reflects and perpetuates inequality. The unemployed and the poor are the victims, as are the educationally and culturally deprived. The criticism of the divisiveness of class is usually accompanied by some ideal of the planned society where human needs will not be subject to market manipulation. Such a society could be one of freedom and equality, or perhaps one of total boredom and total terror.

Others have argued for the *participant society* which will give the individual a sense of identity and integration in the face of mass society. The mass society theory brings together a variety of features and deserves attention as the most pervasive criticism of industrial society next to that of Marxism. It seems to be a combination of the kinds of problems Weber and Durkheim described. Mass society is one in which men have become estranged from each other even though they have become much more interdependent through changes in transport, communication and changes in the division of labour. Individuals have become separated from any core values, and any critical standards of taste and culture have been lost. Spatial and social mobility have created a world of 'lonely crowds' susceptible to political manipulation. Bureaucracy, mass media, mechanization, alienation from work and the degeneration of culture are taken as symptoms of decline of social and political life. Populism and cultural uniformity are generated within such a framework. These kinds of criticism unite existentialists, high-culture exponents, critics of representative democracy and others. At the heart of the criticism are several assumptions: that the members of pre-industrial society were meaningfully integrated with their society; that diversity of values and the freedom of choice encourage moral decline and cultural degeneration; that 'mass' characterizes the heterogeneous membership of groups and organizations mediating between the individual and society; that work is totally alienative and self-destructive. These assumptions are rather extreme; it is doubtful if mass society theory describes society, rather it is an ideology of romantic protest against change.

How far it is a romantic protest can be debated. What seems important, however, is to accept that the participant society is one which generates genuine individual involvement in all levels of decision making. Leisure and its social organization may be important as one aspect of such involvement. In this sense knowledge about leisure becomes part of the question of what leisure ought to mean to people in industrial society.

Policy and planning debate − conclusions

How far there exists 'good' and 'bad' leisure; the degree of control which should exist over leisure values and activities; and the importance of the part to be played by social science in explaining the social organization of leisure; these are the significant questions raised in this discussion. Leisure is not a dependent and residual area of life. Social science has the task of exploring leisure patterns not just in the sense of analysis and prediction but also control. Man is the creator of his own society. Censorship and planning pose conflict of values and methods and such conflict may only be resolved by asking what kind of society is worth pursuing. A society of equality and participation may be an alternative to one in which social class or loss of self-identity are the dominant features.

The policy and planning debate in relation to leisure is assuming growing importance in Britain. With scarce resources, rising expectations and worsening environmental problems, the issues are becoming more acute, requiring us urgently to find solutions. It is now agreed by all sections of the community that the state has a role to play − only the extent and form of that role is contentious. Various quasi-public corporations have been set up, such as the Arts and Sports Councils, which appear to be working reasonably well. In a period of rising demand for social and welfare services, there is great pressure to satisfy basic needs before seeking to satisfy needs associated with leisure. But to assign a low priority to leisure would leave us in danger of failing adequately to provide for that sphere of life in which man may most fully realize himself, his hopes and his creative abilities.

Part 1

Culture

Introduction

The analysis of culture opens many questions and directions of interest for social science. In essence such an analysis involves exploring the diversity of human experience and its expression. Such an exploration involves problems and risks. It means adopting *categories* for explaining human diversity and its symbolic expression. It means recognizing the *values* by which different forms of behaviour are judged. It means searching for the points of consensus and conflict in terms of which *shared meanings* form the framework of social reality. The analysis of culture suggests that some decisions need to be considered in relation to the categories used to analyse, the values used to judge and the meanings people share. Much of the discussion about culture focuses on these three issues.

There are different ways of categorizing or defining the cultural component of human behaviour. One such definition is to regard culture as the attempt by man to realize some state of human perfection, the attainment of some ideal. Culture is the expression of the most perfect aspects of creative imagination in all its variety and force. Such a view usually embodies a developmental approach to explaining culture. Some societies are more advanced than others because they adopt and express cultural forms which are separate and even opposed to man's human − animal − nature. In fact there is a close relationship between viewing culture as an ideal towards which man strives and claiming that such striving must be rational and the product of human reason. According to this view, then, the growth of human culture is conditional upon the growth of rational forms in art, music, drama, and such a link expresses an ideal towards which man is moving.

A second definition of culture is the substantive one which consists of the content of man's intellectual and imaginative efforts. Such content is a record of thought and experience, as well as criticism of the substance of man's efforts. Analysis and criticism itself has been regarded as one of the essential components of which culture itself consists. The expression of thought and imagination cannot be held to be distinct from such criticism and analysis, since for many theorists it is *the* relationship which gives culture its substantive and conscious social content.

A third definition of culture is that it consists of the everyday experiences shared by people and fed into the life-stream of social meaning. It is not a separate and necessarily rational activity, it does not take distinct and conscious forms, but arises from the relationships in which people engage and the characteristics of the structures through which they communicate. Culture is a rational or ethical ideal; it is the critical social comment and content of thought and imagination; it is the everyday experience of shared meaning. Categorized in this way it is clear that as a subject for discussion culture is not something which can be neatly packaged. It penetrates all areas of human activity. The genuine complexity of culture constitutes something of a problem, since each of the definitions presented contains an element of truth. One of the purposes of this first section in the book is to discuss these ways of viewing culture in relation to leisure. Such a discussion runs the risk of being over-simple in its conception of cultural diversity, its form and content. It is also exposed to the danger of viewing culture as determined by the structures and processes of society. Both risks are avoided to a large extent, culture being viewed by the contributory as semi-autonomous and complex.

The problem of categorizing or defining culture has a parallel in the problem of defining leisure. It is almost the same problem, for leisure forms are expressions of the symbolic significance and diversity of human experience as part of human culture. They are also expressions of human values and standards of behaviour. It is to be expected, therefore, that there would be different claims about what in culture is worthwhile, what values are worth upholding, what important principles are at stake. Interestingly enough, the kinds of criticism made of some forms of leisure are the same as those of some forms of culture.

One way of stating this difference of value is the distinction between minority and popular culture. Minority culture is usually that which rests its appeal upon intellectual or artistic taste, upon specialist interest and knowledge. Popular culture usually consists of fairly standardized forms with an appeal to mass taste. It has been claimed that different ethics underpin each expression of culture; minority tastes are somehow 'better', involve a greater degree of creative or intellectual effort and comprise the standard from which culture as a whole is to be judged. On the other hand, popular culture tends to appeal less to the intellect than the emotions, involves very little creative or artistic merit and is closely tied to the degeneration of 'real' culture. The mass media are the mechanism for the spread of such a mass culture and are instrumental in what is held to be the devaluation of language, music, drama, in fact the general social life of man.

The existence of different social classes has been used as part of the explanation for the conflict between 'élite' and 'mass' culture. There is little doubt that different groups do develop different standards of taste and opinion. Such groups may enshrine the most important aspects of their life experience in their culture. In so far as economic opportunity and work provide a fundamental anchorage for the different life experiences of social groups, it would seem reasonable to assume that the values enshrined in the culture may be 'class' based. It may be true, therefore, that minority culture tends to be élitist in nature and derives its claim to excellence from the advantage the 'bourgeoisie' have in the economic system. In so far as the 'proletarian' or working-class experience is one of exploitation and manipulation, it may be that 'mass' culture is a compensatory extension of economic opportunities and the values attributed to different kinds of work. It may also be true that the content of culture itself does not reflect in such a deterministic way the values generated by the economic system. Both of these claims find expression in the chapters in this section. It is suggested that culture and its leisure correlates may be autonomous and cut across the major economic and social structures of industrial society. It is also possible to contest the view that there is any neat link of élite culture to 'middle classness' and that intellectual activities are any 'better' than any other kinds of activity. There is a classlessness about much of the leisure pursued by different people and the discovery of individual identity may be a much more significant process than class position or values.

Human beings are not passive recipients of the external world but actively shape its social significance for themselves. This shaping process is made possible by the existence of language and common sets of symbols which create a framework of shared meaning. The development and use of symbols is the basic characteristic which distinguishes conscious from instinctual activity. The nature of symbolism and its significance in human activity is a central feature in explaining the origin of culture, its diversity and development. Where symbols have a shared meaning cultural forms tend to embody the significant individual and group experiences which have been shared. It is from the sharing of life chances and their importance that ritual develops, often through a repetition by a group of the central features in the struggle to survive, historically and socially, as it seeks to affirm its identity and its symbols of shared significance.

The part played by language in this process is one of being both a transmission and a differentiation agent. It is through language that a written and oral tradition develops; it is through language that a sense of identity is developed and fostered. Language embodies similes and pictures based upon the historical and social significance of culture; language transmits this significance, but in the process becomes also an agent of differentiation. Not everybody receives the same images or has the same experiences. It is somewhat ironic but true that the creation of cultural differences is bound closely with different conceptions of social reality. Communication is never perfect or complete and forms a partly open system in which important features of individual or group experience are reflected in different conceptions of social life. To some these differences are viewed as class-based, in the economic sense of opportunity and status; to others they are much broader and encompass symbolism, ritual and language in a subtle and complex pattern of shared meaning in which the communication process itself provides the focus for cultural integration and conflict.

Raymond Williams first examines the question of how far working-class culture is an 'alternative' culture. It is not useful to think of culture as a product simply of one class, or, indeed, to assume that class and culture are co-terminous. Rather, Williams suggests, the area of a culture tends to be proportionate to the area of a language rather than the area of a class. A selective filtering process exists, but often culture emerges in opposition to the influence of economic factors on this process. It is not enough to claim that the working class possess material affluence and are therefore becoming 'bourgeois'. Language, dress, leisure, these may become standardized; and 'bourgeois' may be a differentiation based on the nature of social relationships rather than external indicators. Individualism as a basis for social relationships contrasts with the idea of society as a positive means for all kinds of development, as some form of collectivism. Class certainly exists, but as a collective mode rather than as a rigid framework for the interpretation of individuals, their possessions and relationships.

Richard Hoggart is concerned to describe the physical and social changes which have resulted from the increased affluence of the working class. The setting of battered pubs, tiny corner shops, cheap little houses, nonconformist chapels; these are rapidly giving way to a new kind of community. New municipal housing areas have been created and changes in consumption – clothes, television, cars – have emerged. Recreation itself has become more 'glossy, streamlined and centralized' – bigger and better. Changes in styles of life have filtered through to the way people define themselves and their relationships. Individualism has been fostered at the same time as conformism – the car and the television tend to produce contradictory tendencies. Age is an important factor – the teenager is almost autonomous and classless. The most important changes are seen in the family itself, the balancing of responsibilities and the sharing of power. The weakening of 'community' and the post-war reduction of economic distress and insecurity are leading to new possibilities and choices.

Tom Burns' contribution is to set the question of the relationship between class and leisure within a broad framework. With industrialization work has become less dehumanizing and yet it would be untrue to claim that leisure choices simply reflect economic opportunities and values. In the early industrial period working-class leisure may have been a reflection of brutalizing labour, but new leisure forms have developed which are autonomous. Just how autonomous is a question Burns links to the whole issue of the changing meaning and impact of work on people's lives.

Ralph Glasser takes a somewhat different approach. He is concerned to explore the importance of identity-seeking for leisure choices. The individual has a need for certainty, both personal and social. The consumer market, the process of emulation and the importance of success for the individual form key elements in the pursuit of a satisfactory identity. Understanding leisure choices is a question of understanding identity aspirations. The cultural framework has changed from one of stability and certainty to one where it may be realized that beneficial choices in the use of leisure are by no means self-determining. The individual exists 'isolated in an eroded culture' in which neither work or material rewards provide security of purpose. Recreation is not leisure, rather it is 'sugared aimlessness'. What is needed is for social institutions to reflect human purpose, a social ethic to foster a secure personal ethic. This is the question posed by leisure and the meaning of the good life.

The contributions to this section on culture and leisure raise and attempt to answer some central issues. Cultural content is discussed in terms of the development of a distinct working-class culture somewhat opposed to an élite or minority culture. Changes in the material and social conditions of industrial life are explored in terms of leisure forms and life styles. The extent to which such forms and life styles are separate and discrete rather than dependent and homogeneous is a fundamental concern. Equally important and pervasive as a focus is the problem of the values which are implicit in and attach themselves to different cultural *mores*. Are these class values or are they rather more complex and varied? Is there a general movement away from class as a basis of leisure activities and cultural patterns? The feeling is that there may be and that the rigid strait-jacket of cultural conformity is breaking down in the face of new values and new behavioural forms. One basic source of such a breakdown is in the part played by the importance of identity-seeking for people. The search for a satisfactory identity is part of the process of making human choice a conscious action. The growth of self-awareness has become the central element in culture, and thus leisure can be related to the growing diversity of individual and social choices made possible through such self-awareness.

1 Minority and popular culture

Raymond Williams

We live in a transitional society, and the idea of culture, too often, has been identified with one or other of the forces which the transition contains. Culture is the product of the old leisured classes who seek now to defend it against new and destructive forces. Culture is the inheritance of the new rising class, which contains the humanity of the future; this class seeks, now, to free it from its restrictions. We say things like this to each other, and glower. The one good thing, it seems, is that all the contending parties are keen enough on culture to want to be identified with it. But then, we are none of us referees in this; we are all in the game, and playing in one or other direction.

I want to say something about the idea of 'working-class culture', because this seems to me to be a key issue in our own time, and one in which there is a considerable element of misunderstanding . . . We cannot fairly or usefully describe the bulk of the material produced by the new means of communication as 'working-class culture'. For neither is it by any means produced exclusively for this class, nor, in any important degree, is it produced by them. To this negative definition we must add another: that 'working-class culture', in our society, is not to be understood as the small amount of 'proletarian' writing and art which exists. The appearance of such work has been useful, not only in its more self-conscious forms, but also in such material as the post-Industrial ballads, which were worth collecting. We need to be aware of this work, but it is to be seen as a valuable dissident element rather than as a culture. The traditional popular culture of England was, if not annihilated, at least fragmented and weakened by the dislocations of the Industrial Revolution. What is left, with what in the new conditions has been newly made, is small in quantity and narrow in range. It exacts respect, but it is in no sense an alternative culture.

This very point of an alternative is extremely difficult, in terms of theory. If the major part of our culture, in the sense of intellectual and imaginative work, is to be called, as the Marxists call it, bourgeois, it is natural to look for an alternative culture, and to call it proletarian. Yet it is very doubtful whether 'bourgeois culture' is a useful term. The body of intellectual and imaginative work which each generation receives as its traditional culture is always, and necessarily, something more than the product of a single class. It is not only that a considerable part of it will have survived from much earlier periods than the immediately pre-existing form of society; so that, for instance, literature, philosophy, and other work surviving from before, say, 1600, cannot be taken as 'bourgeois'. It is also that, even within a society in which a particular class is dominant, it is evidently possible both for members of other classes to contribute to the common stock, and for such contributions to be unaffected by or in opposition to the ideas and values of the dominant class. The area of a culture, it would seem, is usually proportionate to the area of a language rather than to the area of a class. It is true that a dominant class can to a large extent control the transmission and distribution of the whole common inheritance; such control, where it exists, needs to be noted as a fact about that class. It is true also that a tradition is always selective, and that there will always be a tendency for this process of selection to be related to and even governed by the interests of the class that is dominant. These factors make it likely that there will be qualitative changes in the traditional culture when there is a shift of class power, even before a newly ascendant class makes its own contributions.

Points of this kind need to be stressed, but the particular stress given by describing our existent culture as bourgeois culture is in several ways misleading. It can, for example, seriously mislead those who would now consider themselves as belonging to the dominant class. If they are encouraged, even by their opponents, to think of the existing culture (in the narrow sense) as their particular product and legacy, they will deceive themselves and others. For they will be encouraged to argue that, if their class position goes, the culture goes too; that standards depend on the restriction of a culture to the class which, since it has produced it, alone understands it. On the other hand, those who believe themselves to be representatives of a new rising class will, if they accept the proposition of 'bourgeois culture', either be tempted to neglect a common human inheritance, or, more intelligently, be perplexed as to how, and how much of, this bourgeois culture is to be taken over. The categories are crude and mechanical in either position. Men who share a common language share the inheritance of an intellectual and literary tradition which is necessarily and constantly revalued with every shift in experience. The manufacture of an artificial 'working-class culture', in opposition to this common tradition, is merely foolish. A society in which the working class had become dominant would, of course, produce new valuations and new contributions. But the process would be extremely complex, because of the complexity of the inheritance, and nothing is now to be gained by diminishing this complexity to a crude diagram.

The contrast between a minority and a popular culture cannot be absolute. It is not even a matter of levels, for such a term implies distinct and discontinuous stages, and this is by no means always the case. In Russian society in the nineteenth century one finds perhaps the clearest example of a discontinuous culture within recent history; this is marked, it should be noted, by a substantial degree of rejection of even the common language by the ruling minority. But in English society there has never been this degree of separation, since English emerged as the common language. There has been marked unevenness of distribution, amounting at times to virtual exclusion of the majority, and there has been some unevenness of contribution, although in no period has this approached the restriction of contribution to members of any one class. Further, since the beginning of the nineteenth century it has been difficult for any observer to feel that the care of intellectual and imaginative work could be safely entrusted to, or identified with, any existing social or economic class. It was in relation to this situation that the very idea of culture was developed.

A culture can never be reduced to its artifacts while it is being lived. Yet the temptation to attend only to external evidence is always strong. It is argued, for instance, that the working class is becoming 'bourgeois', because it is dressing like the middle class, living in semi-detached houses, acquiring cars and washing-machines and television sets. But it is not 'bourgeois' to possess objects of utility, nor to enjoy a high material standard of living. The working class does not become bourgeois by owning the new products, any more than the bourgeois ceases to be bourgeois as the objects he owns change in kind. Those who regret such a development among members of the working class are the victims of a prejudice. An admiration of the 'simple poor' is no new thing, but it has rarely been found, except as a desperate rationalization, among the poor themselves. It is the product either of satiety or of a judgement that the material advantages are purchased at too high a human cost. The first ground must be left to those who are sated; the second, which is more important, is capable of a false transference.

If the advantages were 'bourgeois' because they rested on economic exploitation, they do not continue to be 'bourgeois' if they can be assured without such exploitation or by its diminution. The worker's envy of the middle-class man is not a desire to be that man, but to have the same kind of possessions. We all like to think of ourselves as a standard, and I can see that it is genuinely difficult for the English middle class to suppose that the working class is not desperately anxious to become just like itself. I am afraid this must be unlearned. The great majority of English working people want only the middle-class material standard and for the rest want to go on being themselves. One should not be too quick to call this vulgar materialism. It is wholly reasonable to want the means of life in such abundance as is possible.

This is the materialism of material provision, to which we are all, quite rightly, attentive. The working people, who have felt themselves long deprived of such means in any adequacy, intend to get them and to keep them if they can. It would need more evidence than this to show that they are becoming vulgar materialists, or that they are becoming 'bourgeois'.

The question then, perhaps, is whether there is any meaning left in 'bourgeois'? Is there any point, indeed, in continuing to think in class terms at all? Is not industrialism, by its own momentum, producing a culture that is best described as classless? Such questions, today, command a significant measure of assent, but again, while drawing support from the crudities of certain kinds of class interpretation, they rest, essentially, on an external attitude alike to culture and to class. If we think of culture, as it is important to do, in terms of a body of intellectual and imaginative work, we can see that with the extension of education the distribution of this culture is becoming more even, and, at the same time, new work is being addressed to a public wider than a single class. Yet a culture is not only a body of intellectual and imaginative work; it is also and essentially a whole way of life. The basis of a distinction between bourgeois and working-class culture is only secondarily in the field of intellectual and imaginative work, and even here it is complicated, as we have seen, by the common elements resting on a common language. The primary distinction is to be sought in the whole way of life, and here, again, we must not confine ourselves to such evidence as housing, dress and modes of leisure. Industrial production tends to produce uniformity in such matters, but the vital distinction lies at a different level. The crucial distinguishing element in English life since the Industrial Revolution is not language, not dress, not leisure — for these indeed will tend to uniformity. The crucial distinction is between alternative ideas of the nature of social relationship.

'Bourgeois' is a significant term because it marks that version of social relationship which we usually call individualism: that is to say, an idea of society as a neutral area within which each individual is free to pursue his own development and his own advantage as a natural right. The course of recent history is marked by a long fighting retreat from this idea in its purest form, and the latest defenders would seem to the earliest to have lost almost the entire field. Yet the interpretation is still dominant: the exertion of social power is thought necessary only in so far as it will protect individuals in this basic right to set their own course. The classical formula of the retreat is that, in certain defined ways, no individual has a right to harm others. But, characteristically, this harm has been primarily interpreted in relation to the individual pursuit — no individual has a right to prevent others from doing this kind of thing.

The reforming bourgeois modification of this version of society is the idea of service (to which I shall return). But both this idea and the individualist idea can be sharply contrasted with the idea that we properly associate with the working class: an idea which, whether it is called communism, socialism, or cooperation, regards society neither as neutral nor as protective, but as the positive means for all kinds of development, including individual development. Development and advantage are not individually but commonly interpreted. The provision of the means of life will, alike in production and distribution, be collective and mutual. Improvement is sought, not in the opportunity to escape from one's class, or to make a career, but in the general and controlled advance of all. The human fund is regarded as in all respects common, and freedom of access to it as a right constituted by one's humanity; yet such access, in whatever kind, is common or it is nothing. Not the individual, but the whole society, will move.

The distinction between these versions of society has been blurred by two factors: the idea of service, which is the great achievement of the Victorian middle class, and is deeply inherited by its successors; and the complication of the working-class idea by the fact that England's position as an imperial power has tended to limit the sense of community to national (and, in the context, imperialist) lines. Further, the versions are blurred by a misunderstanding of the nature of class. The contending ideas, and the actions which follow from them, are the property of that part of a group of people, similarly circumstanced, which has become conscious of its position and of its own attitude to this position. Class feeling is a mode, rather than a uniform possession of all the individuals who might, objectively, be assigned to that class. When we speak, for instance, of a working-class idea, we do not mean that all working people possess it, or even approve of it. We mean, rather, that this is the essential idea embodied in the organizations and institutions which that class creates: the working-class movement as a tendency, rather than all working-class people as individuals. It is foolish to interpret individuals in rigid class terms, because class is a collective mode and not a person. At the same time, in the interpretation of ideas and institutions, we can speak properly in class terms. It depends, at any time, on which kind of fact we are considering. To dismiss an individual because of his class, or to judge a relationship with him solely in class terms, is to reduce humanity to an abstraction. But, also, to pretend that there are no collective modes is to deny the plain facts.

We may now see what is properly meant by 'working-class culture'. It is not proletarian art, or council houses, or a particular use of language; it is, rather, the basic collective idea, and the institutions, manners, habits of thought, and intentions which proceed from this.

Bourgeois culture, similarly, is the basic individualist idea and the institutions, manners, habits of thought, and intentions which proceed from that. In our culture as a whole, there is both a constant interaction between these ways of life and an area which can properly be described as common to or underlying both. The working class, because of its position, has not, since the Industrial Revolution, produced a culture in the narrower sense. The culture which it has produced, and which it is important to recognize, is the collective democratic institution, whether in the trade unions, the cooperative movement, or a political party. Working-class culture, in the stage through which it has been passing, is primarily social (in that it has created institutions) rather than individual (in particular intellectual or imaginative work). When it is considered in context, it can be seen as a very remarkable creative achievement.

To those whose meaning of culture is intellectual or imaginative work, such an achievement may be meaningless. The values which are properly attached to such work can, at times, seem overriding. On this, I would only point out that while it may have seemed reasonable to Burke to anticipate the trampling down of learning by the irruption of the 'swinish multitude', this has not in fact happened, and the swinish multitude itself has done much to prevent it happening. The record of the working-class movement in its attitudes to education, to learning, and to art is on the whole a good record. It has sometimes wrongly interpreted, often neglected where it did not know. But it has never sought to destroy the institutions of this kind of culture; it has, on the contrary, pressed for their extension, for their wider social recognition, and in our own time, for the application of a larger part of our material resources to their maintenance and development. Such a record will do more than stand comparison with that of the class by which the working class has been most actively and explicitly opposed. This, indeed, is the curious incident of the swine in the night. As the light came, and we could look around, it appeared that the trampling, which we had all heard, did not after all come from them.

2 Changes in working-class life

Richard Hoggart

I should guess that it is a long time since British people as a whole, and working-class people in particular, felt so sharply the sense of change in their lives. The conversation below was recorded in a public-house in a Northern working-class district at the beginning of the 1960s. I do not think one would have heard it five years before. It indicates with economy, and vividly, the main cause and effect of the changes in British life today. The speaker is a middle-aged working-man:

'Everyone's bloody-upside-down if you ask me,' said Freddy. 'They're bound to be happier,' went on Owd Jem, 'because they've got a bit of cash to play with!' He stared at us to let his words sink in. 'Before the war money was that tight every penny was spoken for! But today folk have a bit of choice. And they feel better for it. You go out and you can see it on their faces. They're no longer frightened. They feel freer. It stands to reason!' (1)*

Prosperity – to make generalizations out of what he is saying – removes old fears and increases confidence; it increases the power to make choices of one's own, because the straight-jacket of poverty has been loosened. It increases the feeling of individuality, of being a person with idiosyncratic wishes and decisions. Of course, to feel more of an individual is not necessarily to be more of an individual; there are plenty of agencies which aim to take money from working people by encouraging their feelings of individuality whilst, in fact, encouraging them to think and choose exactly like millions of others.

You can begin to see the main physical changes by making a simple tour through, for instance, one of those massive working-class districts – in the North, the Midlands or London – which are monuments to the energy and toughness of the Industrial Revolution. Most of them were established in the early and middle years of the nineteenth century. It has always surprised me that they remained so little changed for so long. I was a working-class boy in the 1920s and 30s and my physical setting was substantially late-Victorian. Nonconformist chapels, battered pubs, tiny corner-shops, cheap little houses, even the uneven cobble-stones in the road, all had been there

* Figures in parentheses refer to notes and references at the end of each chapter.

since about 1870 and framed a way of life which, in many of its essentials, had not greatly changed. Look at those districts today or, if they have been cleared, go outside to the new municipal housing areas. Many of the old areas still do exist, because rehousing is slow; but the late twentieth century is emerging in a thousand details: in the wider range of goods in the corner-shop's window (the shop itself may well have become a small supermarket), in the forests of television aerials, in the scatter of cars — usually second-hand — outside the doors. You can see it in people's clothes, and especially in the clothes of younger people. The clothing which identified a class, the clothing which says that you are and expect to remain a worker, has almost gone. In Lancashire twenty-five years ago clogs were still often worn and the women draped black shawls round their heads and shoulders; today they can hardly be found and in their place are a variety of relatively cheap and usually attractive clothes. Some day a study will be written about the contribution of one firm — Marks and Spencer's — to this change. Women's drinking cannot now be identified by the old music-hall jokes about stout and port-and-lemon. The new drinks look sophisticated, are not heavy or befuddling and are reasonably cheap. Showerings of Somerset estimated this need precisely a few years ago and produced Babycham, perry (pear cider) which has been aerated and vaguely suggests champagne. Packed so as to increase this suggestion, it sells enormously. Even the fish-and-chip shops sell roast chicken and chips; and Chinese restaurants exist in towns so solidly Northern working-class that the conjunction seems at first against nature. Recreations are becoming more glossy, streamlined and centralized — bigger Bingo saloons open week after week and indoor bowling alleys on the American pattern, large and bright and electronic, are taking hold.

To a quick or biased observer prosperity may seem to encourage chiefly 'materialism', by which is meant the wish to have certain large consumer goods. More important, as we saw earlier, prosperity can increase the sense of individual choice; and it can lengthen perspectives. It not only gives immediate opportunities but, since work is more secure, encourages a longer view, the ability to plan ahead. If you fear unemployment without warning you will not, when extra money becomes available, be likely to plough it into some future project; you will be more likely to spend it at once and enjoy a brief liberation from the grind of week after week. Now working people can begin to plan ahead and, inevitably, younger people are leading the way — especially young married couples. Such an adjustment is not easy; it requires a point by point change in old outlooks, old habits, old customs.

Then there are the changes in housing. Those tightly-packed working-class communities — 'the barracks of industry', the Hammonds called them — are being cleared. But they were not simply row upon row of shabby dwellings for masses of workers. They were more like interlocking villages, with their own close and embracing ways of life. They had developed these ways partly — perhaps primarily — in response to the social and economic situation of their inhabitants. You were, for example, a 'neighbourly' person and hoped those around you were good neighbours too. This neighbourliness was fed by your Christian background (which was probably Nonconformist) and by your feeling that, if you did not help one another, no one outside in the larger and more prosperous world would much help you. Nor could you, as the middle classes could, often buy service for money. A particular economic situation helped nurture a specific way of life.

Now those districts are being cleared. More and more people are moving into the architect-designed new towns, or on to suburban housing-estates on the far outskirts of the cities. These estates are improving but many of them look inorganic and are inorganic; they have no natural centres and their layout does not encourage the emergence of centres for social life — 'a graveyard with lights' said a teenager of the main street in one such brick and concrete estate. Or people are moving back into the old districts after they have been cleared, and after towering blocks of flats have risen on the ground which before contained hundreds of two-storied little houses in a horizontal vista for as far as one could see. Again, people have to learn to live in their new settings, to find contacts, to establish habitual routines, to identify their relationships with their neighbours, their estate, the larger town life — and with themselves as a family, since that too changes as its setting changes. It is not easy now to maintain, for instance, one of the strongest characteristics of the old districts: the extraordinarily complicated interweaving of visits between members of the 'extended families'. Grandmother was likely to be around the corner in the next street, available to help and be helped; whatever they may have lacked, children grew up with a sense of the interdependence and continuity of generations within a family. Cousins, aunts, uncles all were likely to be within hailing distance and to be constantly 'bobbing in' for a word.

Even more, people are becoming readier to move as the locations of work change. In my childhood a man belonged first to a district and if his job came to an end he — being probably a general labourer — looked for another job in another works in the same area. He hardly thought of moving from that area. Today his son is likely to pack his suitcase and move where new work and bigger money are to be found — to the Midlands and the complex of motor-car industries; or to the outskirts of London and one of the new electronics factories. Similarly, the nature of work is itself changing and will go on changing. The

Lancashire cotton-belt is, as a cotton-belt, almost dead. But the big mills are not all of them silent. Some are on new kinds of work, which their skilled men can do as well as anyone. But the old 'general labourer' seems likely to be less and less in demand; training of some kind is more and more needed. The pattern of relationships at work itself is changing – the old pattern of men-on-the-bench, with the foreman between them and the lower echelons of management, is giving way to more elaborate, more professionally 'lubricated' forms of industrial relationship. Functions are defined in more complex ways. More married women are appearing in the factories as work becomes physically less heavy and increasingly demands precision and patience. All these industrial changes challenge older habits and assumptions.

As the changes increase the style of life has to alter or absorb. It is difficult to live in a society which is changing so quickly, and perhaps especially difficult if much in your way of life was previously decided by the customs of the group, if the range of deliberate, planned, conscious, individual decisions was limited by custom as well as by lack of cash. Here a whole new feature of British life comes in strongly: mass communications. Mass communications – advertising, the press, television, magazines (especially women's magazines, which are flourishing since women decide on major purchases and lead the movement towards new social styles) – all these do more than pass idle hours. They are helping people to come to terms with, to live with, their new world and new opportunities. Older working-class habits are being eroded and working people – whatever some observers may say to the contrary – do not on the whole wish to imitate the manners of the traditionally 'higher' groups: they want a new style, a new picture of life. The new men, the classless men – the advertisers, their artists and copywriters, television personalities, magazine columnists – are creating an image of a new way of life which does not belong to the old class-defined society of the past. All these are socially educative forces. Their aims are not usually disinterested and we may suspect the sort of life they promote. But we must recognize that they are social teachers, are replying to an unspoken but powerful need for directions within a more open society. As one of their spokesmen has said, grand as ever: 'Advertising may play a large part, perhaps a leading part, in teaching the art of living.'

But this is going ahead too quickly, claiming too much change too soon. In some important respects working-class life is still much as it always was. I remember noting this power in the middle-fifties – the power not only to resist change but to assimilate, modify and adapt to traditional ends, things which looked at first like major agents of change. Professor Zweig makes the same point in the early sixties, and will not be the last to do so. There is a strong thrust, or drag, to keep things recognizably as they have usually been, especially in those parts of life which are most personal and near to us. Of course, change is going on even here; but it will be a long time before major breaches are made in some areas.

Supporting this capacity is the assumption that home and family life are the most important things in life. In some sense this may be true of working people in other countries, but comparisons like that would not have much point in this essay. In some sense this may be true of other classes in England, but a working-man's feeling for home and for his family life is not quite the same as that of a man from another class. Home means both a refuge and a place of free-standing independence against an outside world which is rough or which holds you of little account. Here you can 'go your own way' once the door is shut; and here there should be, it is felt, love and affection. One gets above all, listening to people talking about their ideal of 'a good home', the impression of a warm and cherishing security. The ideal is not always attained, of course, but ideals are illuminating. Behind this assumption one can see again, as behind the belief in 'neighbourliness', a creative response to economic and social hardships.

Is the sense of family, then, unaffected by the new movements in society? Not quite. Leaving aside metaphysical relationships, a sense of powers outside man, we can say that all of us have to try to establish working relationships in four areas: with our own personality, with our family, with our immediate neighbours and locality and — last — with some larger groups. Traditionally, working-class people put most emphasis on establishing relationships in the second and third categories; and most of all in the second category, in relationships within the family.

By the first area, 'personality', I'm thinking of the extent to which the assumptions of one's group encourage one to be individualistic, to think of oneself as a separate personality. These distinctions are bound to be rough, but one may say that the older forms of working-class life did not much encourage the development of strong individual 'personality'; to have done so would have worked against the emphasis on the importance of the family and the neighbourhood-group. It may well be that 'personality' in this sense becomes stronger as you move into the middle classes or aspire to do so (e.g. the individual desire to 'get on' in life, or the individual acceptance of larger social responsibilities — the self-made business man or the devoted colonial official). It seems likely that the sense of 'personality', of individuality, will appear to become stronger among working people — partly because it will be encouraged in its own right, partly because it will grow as the sense of neighbourhood weakens. Yet it will have to co-exist with strong pressures towards mass conformity. So it may actually not be stronger at all. One might see emerging a massive pseudo-individualism.

As to our second area of relationships, those within the family: here the power to adapt and assimilate the objects of the early sixties is remarkably illustrated. The two most obvious products are the television set and the motor-car. Most working-class families now have a television set; many have a car and within a decade most are likely to own one. The television set is quite obviously keeping the family together. It cuts down attendance at cinemas and even at public-houses. It dominates the living-room, as a sort of substitute-hearth; and the family group around it. It can, we always tell ourselves, suggest wider horizons, different ways of life, new ranges of outside activities. But primarily it is a cohesive force. Most working-class families have it on for three to four hours a night, as a sort of unifying noise and moving picture, whatever the actual content of individual programmes. It does not much appeal to teenagers; it is too enclosed, too much of the family hearth, for them; they are beginning to find their own way, in the town's coffee-bars. They are moving into the almost autonomous and classless world of the European teenager. More, the circle round the television set tends to keep out odd members of the 'extended family' who used to drop in for a gossip. All in all, we may say, the set encloses the single family more and more within itself, the family of father, mother and the younger children. Here, it cooperates with the new forms of housing, which tend to isolate individual family-units.

So some people say that television reinforces the family. But what does this mean? The old family hearth was a gregarious and garrulous place (as any studious scholarship-boy knew better than most); it was all-embracing and assumed that people hardly ever wanted to be alone or silent. You heard all night the gossip of work and neighbourhood and school, with the chirp of a pet-bird or the yawning of a family cat in the background. Is watching television — though it is often broken by talk — really strengthening the same sort of relationship as existed round the living-room fire? In many respects that life goes on; people can carry on the traditional life of the family against the most persistent background. But for how long? It is likely that as the years pass the relationships within such family groups will change. Visions of the future tend always to project at unreal speed and without enough checks and balances; but the tendency is towards holding millions of disparate individuals each umbilically linked to the one quasi-personal centre.

By contrast, with the television set, the motor-car might seem likely to break up the cohesion of the family. It takes people away from the hearth, introduces them to new areas and new ways of behaving. There is some evidence that working-class people with motor-cars are beginning to desert their local 'pubs' and go out to different kinds of public-houses, houses not so identified with one social class and its manners. But in spite of such exceptions the most striking characteristic of the working-class adoption of the motor-car is that they have assimilated it to their own uses, their own older values and attitudes. Middle-class observers have remarked, with regret or amusement, that most working-class people do not know how to take advantage of a car. When they get to the countryside or the sea-front they do not always go for a good walk or a swim. They are just as likely to sit in the crowded and fuggy machine, surrounded by food and newspapers, with the window steamed-up and a transistor blaring out the Light Programme. But this, as Dr Mark Abrams was the first to point out, is one form of adaptation; the car has been taken over, made to fit, made into an extension of the family living-room. It has become for many people 'a mobile living-room'.

Old habits die hard. Hobbies, for example, have always been a major interest of working-men. Some of them, such as fishing or pigeon-fancying, may take men outside the home. Many more keep them pottering about in the house or yard. There seems no evidence that this interest has weakened, in spite of the attraction of television. Here, prosperity is bringing the sophistications of technology into old routines; many working-class handymen get sets of home-power-tools for Christmas from their wives.

It is increasingly common among young married couples for the wives to stay at work for a few years. Both husband and wife tend to accept overtime willingly, and to put their spare money into purchases which will help establish their new style, that style so often taught by the women's magazines.

A subtler change lies behind this, a change in the relative positions of the father and mother within the family. Traditionally, the father was the boss whether he was in or out of work. This is not to say that the mother was necessarily a drudge and feeble creature. She had her sources of power and authority and, to the children (as many a novel by an ex-working-class boy shows), was the heart and centre of the hearth. Still, the husband was regarded as and referred to as 'the master' and enjoyed a kind of deference or respect. He was the one who every day and for long hours toiled in a not particularly friendly outside world and brought back the money which gave shelter and food to the mother and children. In both father and mother this relationship produced strengths and weaknesses, both in quite large measure — at the extremes the domineering but careless father and the protective but smothering mother. Now the trend seems to be towards a more even balance of power and responsibility between the parents. Two purses, two people going out daily into the outside world, make as much difference to the internal relations of a family as they do to its capacity to buy goods. At the moment women seem to work until children begin to appear, to start again when the last child (probably of two or three) has begun to go to school, and to give up finally at about the age of fifty.

As the nature of work changes, so men's work is not so often heavy, back-breaking; his wife may be doing a job physically no less demanding than his and perhaps more demanding in skill. So the tired-out husband sitting at his sacred seat by the fire, plied with mugs of tea by his home-bound wife, is becoming less and less typical. We are more likely to come upon a husband and wife, each quite tired, but each doing a share of that work about the house which has had to wait until they both returned from work. More and more husbands help with the occasional chores such as washing-up; more and more take shares with the basic housework. Among younger couples, more and more make joint decisions about the spending of the family's spare money; and more and more young husbands can be seen pushing prams around the streets on shopping expeditions.

The third area of relationship I suggested is the immediately social: relationships within the locality or neighbourhood. These are 'face-to-face' relationships outside the family. Here, I think, the trend is towards a weakening. We have seen that the old form of life – in its physical setting and economic background – helped encourage a remarkably strong sense of neighbourliness. Wives talked regularly over backyard fences, slipped into one another's houses, helped one another in times of stress (childbirth, illness and so on). Husbands did not take so active or pervasive a part in maintaining the neighbourly network; but they lived within it through listening to their wives and contributed to it at the local pub or working-men's club, and by helping one another with odd jobs at nights and weekends (two men would decorate a room or put up a hen-hut). Much of this still goes on, naturally, even in the most individualized-looking suburban estate. But it is easy to see how some present tendencies are combining to weaken the sense of belonging to one's immediate neighbourhood. One can buy things or services which hitherto one had to rely on neighbours to lend or give. Wives are not so likely to be at home all day and, when they do get back from work at night, are too busy cleaning the house to have much time for gossip. When a wife and her husband relax they are likely not to go out but to stay in watching television. So the older sense of neighbourliness is likely to be transformed. New groupings will emerge; young wives with babies, for instance, do need help from each other and the reassurance of one another, and on even the most unpromisingly agoraphobic estate they will create ways of satisfying these needs – at the Clinics or Launderettes, for a start. But they will have to act, to take thought, to learn some of the arts of social intercourse to do so; they will not be immersed within a neighbourhood and an extended family like fish in a deep pool.

The last of the four areas of relationship was the largest and most varied; it covers larger, public groups, relationships wider and less immediately intimate than those of a neighbourhood or locality. (But not, in this essay, relationships at work. They are very important, but I'm not qualified to talk about them.) They can cover a wide range — from clubs and societies which people join because they have common interests, not simply because they happen to live in the same street or area (e.g., advanced hobby clubs, cultural clubs), to those which imply a larger than local sense of one's rights and responsibilities (local government or party political activities, for instance). Understandably, this kind of activity has not hitherto attracted more than a tiny minority of working-class people (though that minority has exercised an influence out of proportion to its numbers). But for most the character of their lives and especially of their assumed relation to the public world outside did not encourage this 'civic' awareness. Just as certainly, more working-class people need to acquire this sense or we could end with a society which would look freer than the old but would really be less free (since most of its citizens would be sitting, mildly content, among their possessions in the enclosed family lounge).

Working people are likely to begin to move outwards, but rather slowly. I do not think mixed or general-purpose social clubs in the new areas will be the main sources of strength here. Working people will probably move outwards by means of those specialist skills and hobbies which prosperity is encouraging them to develop even further. Most British hobbies and recreations have been identified by social class (our kind of people do this kind of thing, not that kind of thing), but these divisions are crumbling. In one town, for example, the local education authority claims to have some of the most successful classless groups in Britain — of teenagers bound together by common specialist interests in such pursuits as advanced photography and boat-building. As that generation marries and sets up its homes it is more likely to want to retain centres of association for these specialist or 'highbrow' interests than feel drawn to recreating neighbourhood centres of the old general kind.

Some people are content to sum up all this change in the phrase: 'The working classes are becoming middle-class.' What does that mean?

If it means that many working people, being rather more prosperous and secure, are acquiring the longer perspectives described earlier, the statement might seem partially true. The fact that previously most working people did not dream of buying their own homes was not usually due to indolence or a desire to live for the day. They knew enough about their lack of prospects, the uncertainty of their jobs, their incapacity to obtain credit from a Building Society, not to cry for the moon. But now they are beginning to look forward longer, are taking out bank accounts (often in the Post Office Savings Bank which seems 'homely' — the main banks still look formidable though they are now making big efforts to convince newly affluent groups, especially young married couples, that a cheque book is as much part of a normal man's equipment as is the key to his front door); or people are planning their children's education as a long-term matter; and they are becoming more ready to think of buying their own houses. To buy a house is an act of confidence, based on a long steady look down a vista of twenty years. It is only within the last year or two that more than an occasional member of my family, those of us who became teachers, chiefly — have made this considerably imaginative leap. This sort of thing may be called middle-class. But it does not necessarily indicate that working people wish to assume the *mores* of the middle class; it is a form of parellelism, a sign that more and more working people have reached that stage of security at which they too can adopt some of the more useful practical arrangements long common to middle-class people.

And of course most working people are anxious to own more of the larger consumer goods. Many of them are keen to work overtime; they have a lot of leeway to make up. As more goods come on to the market and as wage-rates rise rather more quickly than the prices of many of the more attractive mass-produced consumer goods, so extra money is spent on things man and wife jointly want. If you put in the extra hours the goods are available, are within reach.

Will all this and much else — increased eating in restaurants, the spread of wine-drinking, the increase in telephone installations, foreign holidays — make working-class people middle-class? Not in any useful sense of the words. The essence of belonging to the middle class was to hold a certain range of attitudes, attitudes chiefly decided by that class's sense of its own position within society, and its relation to the other classes within it. From this its characteristics — its snobberies as much as its sense of responsibilities — flowed. These attitudes are not brought into play merely by possessing certain objects or adopting some practical notions from the middle class.

New kinds of social stratification may be developing, but they will not correlate exactly with the old social orders and gradings. And they will have to mesh, somehow, with a partial classlessness. Here one comes back to the world of mass communications, to those agencies which are helping to educate people socially for life in a changing society. The voices from the older order — the public and 'establishment' voices, the voices of the Guardians — find it increasingly difficult to make themselves heard. The new voices of the mass persuaders are more friendly and gregarious and consumer-conscious; in many respects they are more attractive than the old, slightly hierarchical voices. They are also, very often, callow and cheap. But they have their ears to the ground and are likely to register major successes for years ahead. In a puzzling open society the voices of popular mass communications are bound to be ingratiating. In all this teenagers are, as usual, the best barometers. They have taken over much of the new commercial world (after all, it isn't drab); but many of them make their own criticism of this world. They know when they are being 'got at' and make themselves some space for living in their own way. As they marry they are beginning to constitute the first generation of working-class families which has not known economic distress and insecurity. They belong to a more prosperous world and have either assimilated themselves to its persuasions or — whilst taking advantage of its opportunities — have learned how to make their own choices. They have then become more self-aware as individuals, more used to making decisions, than their parents were usually required to be.

So there is a tension between the movement towards a kind of openness and the movement towards a narrowing or stratifying. The openness I have already sufficiently described, and its origins in increased prosperity and security, in industrial changes and the erosion of older class-forms. And I have suggested that to live in so much more open a society requires a degree of self-awareness, of critical choice-making, greater than we have been accustomed to, and from many more people. The narrowing and stratifying is being assisted by two groups of forces not naturally allied, since one is commercial and the other a product of social good intentions.

The commercially-inspired movement towards narrowing is a result of the tendency of a prosperous commercial democracy to weld its consumers — its customers; its readers — into large single blocks. This process of concentration can be seen in any technologically advanced country but is particularly well advanced in Britain. Look at the press. In the last twenty years we have taken to reading more and more newspapers. Yet — and this is the evidence of concentration — we publish fewer different newspapers today than we published twenty years ago. More and more of us are reading the same newspaper. This is economically more profitable to those newspapers which remain; it can be a convenience to advertisers; it can be assisted by persuasion. Look also at the energy and skill which are used every week to make teenagers turn their attention only to a very few popular songs on gramophone records, buy them in great numbers and forget them as soon as the next batch has appeared.

We commonly underestimate the capacities of working people. It was easy to think in this way when workers looked — and probably sounded, since British speech is so much defined by class — like members of a 'lower order'. Yet a kind of contempt for people can be found in the friendly but condescendingly shallow approach of many 'democratic' mass persuaders today. It would be better if we could combine some of the strengths of the old life (tolerance, nonconformity, neighbourliness, responsibility) and some of the new (flexibility, greater emotional and intellectual disinterestedness). Otherwise, we could move from the inarticulate 'lower classes' to the conformist classless mass in one easy stage. It really depends, at bottom, in how we look at one another.

Reference
1 Quoted in *Britain Revisited*, Tom Harrisson, Gollancz, 1961.

3 Leisure in industrial society

Tom Burns

I want to make this chapter serve two purposes. First, I shall discuss and, to some extent, develop explanations of the nature of leisure, and do so by relating what can be said about it to our understanding of industrialism, and to the implications of both leisure and work in the organization of society. Secondly, I shall arrange this account so as to exemplify a particular strategy for sociological explanation (or 'theory') in general.

1

Much of the earlier research into leisure was directly concerned with the significances – the meanings – which were variously attached to leisure. The most obvious of these seemed to be afforded by the contrast with work, and empirical studies and discussion of fifteen years ago were preoccupied with the connection and the contrast between leisure and work. Was it to be regarded as in effect a pursuit of compensatory activities for the fatigue, the boredom, the alienation endured at work? Or did it provide for the free exercise of the skills and energy that workers sold to gain a livelihood? Or was it rather a re-affirmation in games and gambling of the sense of autonomous decision-making of which submission to the constraints of work organizations had deprived the industrial masses?

One can read the record of research in the sociology of leisure over the past ten or fifteen years as an exploration, to begin with, of the implications of this kind of interpretation and then an escape from them. Dumazedier, whose name more than anyone else's is associated with the sociology of leisure, mirrors this theoretical development in a sentence: 'Just as labour is more than the negation of idleness, leisure is more than the negation of labour. Leisure is also the negation of yet other obligations: familial, social, civic, religious.' (1) Leisure is seen as a reaction from the combined pressures of traditional institutions and the social forces of contemporary organization, or more fundamentally, as a kind of delinquent escape from the impossible dilemmas of a situation midway between the Marxian view of man's destiny as a worker and a 'post-industrialism' image of him as a learning animal.

Some of the simplicities in this elementary interpretation we can now dismiss. A good deal of survey research in France, particularly, has been concerned to test and disprove the hypothesis that the form taken by leisure activities is determined by the need to compensate for the deprivation or constraints or demands of work, and the alternative hypothesis that leisure activities tend to reflect the direction and level of work performance. Both Dumazedier's Annecy studies and Crozier's survey of office workers (2) reach the same conclusion – that there is no evidence of either a direct or an inverse relationship between work and leisure.

These studies, and a large number of others, follow the main methodological convention of survey research and seek to enumerate leisure pursuits or to compare 'profiles' of leisure as whole or part of the description of communities, groups, or categories of people. Inevitably, the development of 'social characteristics' research is governed by the need to account for more and more of the variance left unexplained, or to rope in more and more recalcitrant individuals left in minority or mixed categories by previous research; quite properly, this leads to an increasing refinement of characteristics, cannier (if not exactly more rigorous) sampling frames, and smaller parcelling of categories. Also – and much more important – interpretations of data, explanation, theory are all couched more and more in terms of the extent to which each social characteristic combines with others (the 'predictive value' or characteristics). Lastly, the most important of all, the sociologist finds himself peopling the world with what Hans Paul Bahrdt has called 'sociological men' – crude identikit characters labelled 'the conservative working-class voter', 'the spiralist', 'the empty nester', 'the affluent worker' and so on. If the most significant task of contemporary sociology is, as Edward Shils claimed, 'the theorization of empirical research', then it is one which will have to be accomplished not by buttering survey research with theory but by the reconsideration of the elementary relationship between the goals of sociological explanation and the methods to be used for attaining them.

Survey research, the almost exclusive research method for the empirical study of leisure, does not in fact make it easy either to develop hypotheses of a sociological kind or to develop theoretical explanations, since it is applied to individuals and their responses and presumes the possibility of inducing social characteristics from the study of populations. The task of obtaining causal connections and of developing explanatory categories is, as Durkheim has shown us, something which has to be done, not so much 'at another level', perhaps, as from a different, broader set of premises contextual to the always tiny assortment of firsthand facts empirical researchers can collect for themselves. If this is not done as itself an exercise in sociological explanation, as Durkheim did, then sociological explanation lapses into description by numbers (which gets us nowhere, except perhaps into market research, or into providing ammunition for those academic friends and neighbours who insist that 'those who count, don't') or into interpretation according to ideological slant.

Those who have followed the same research convention but used the strategic point of departure of the audience or public for a particular kind of entertainment or recreation (e.g., all audience research and the outdoor recreation studies commissioned by the U.S. Department of Agriculture) have not fared better in the search for connections between leisure pursuits and social characteristics. Wilensky, in the paper which did so much to refine the treatment of the subject and relate it in a reasonably satisfactory way to some of the main preoccupations of sociology, concludes that 'Television, the most "massified" of the mass media, the one with the largest and most heterogeneous audience, has become central to the leisure routines of majorities at every level. The usual differences in media exposure and response among age, sex and class categories – easy to exaggerate in any case – have virtually disappeared in the case of television.' (3)

Even for the very earliest students it was clear that leisure was not simply non-work; unemployment was also non-work, and to describe an unemployed worker as leisured is a very tired piece of journalistic irony. The key to the concept of leisure which seems to underlie these earlier studies is, I think, that leisure in industrial society is somehow the counterpart of industrial labour. This is put in its simplest form by Riesman, in his introduction to Chinoy's *Automobile Workers and the American Dream*. 'Chinoy's interviews,' he says, 'show work to be part-time imprisonment, through which one pays off the fines incurred by one's pursuit of the good – or rather the good time – life at home and on vacation.' (4) The converse of this, or its fuller meaning, is that adequate work performances and successful endeavour cannot be maintained in terms of aspirations and goals relevant to the work situation or the occupational career; these essential aspirations and goals have had to be transformed into values which can be realized in leisure activities. In this reading of the meaning of leisure there is a parallel (the implications of which we shall explore later) between the relationship of leisure and work and that between consumption and production.

2

I want now to give some consideration to the origin and implications of the simple contrast notions of leisure as time free from work and as a counterpart of work (and, by intention, a complement to it) – notions which sociologists may simply have seen as demonstrably appropriate within their academic niche in industrial society and treated as 'litmus-test' hypotheses for other milieux much as they did with notions like job-satisfaction and alienation.

First and most obvious is the significance which attaches to its being free time which has been won from the working day. Guy Chapman, in a book which anticipated an uncomfortable proportion of later sociological work, called 'the Ten Hours Act by far the most important landmark in nineteenth-century social history' (5). There are two significant aspects of the agitation for this particular reform. First, it came from factory workers, mainly, of course, textile workers; secondly, it was the first legislative reform carried through by popular agitation among industrial workers, and formulated in direct response to their demands.

In pre-industrial society work was part and parcel of everyday life; and there was no sense in which leisure was a separate section of the day. Work was something which caught up and included a good deal more than work. It was carried on in the fields within sight of the home or within the home itself along with the cooking, child minding, the friendly conversations and quarrels, and the business of village life. It is only when work came to be done in a special place, at a special separate time and under special conditions that leisure came to be demanded as a right. This demand, moreover, seems to have taken precedence over any demand for increased earnings. Increases in prices were the usual occasion for demands for higher earnings, which were related to a fairly specific norm of working-class living standards. In any case, apart from negotiations about piece rates, it occurs that workers were, in the earlier decades of the nineteenth century, more concerned with prices than with wages. Chapman argues this point at some length and, I think, convincingly. In the earlier part of the nineteenth century, so far as earnings were concerned, demand seems to have been limited to 'the wages which will pay for the cost of living and a little more', among factory workers and non-factory workers alike. For instance,

> Leonard Horner, the factory inspector, examined a large number of workers in 1848 and found that 70% of them were in favour of the ten hour day ... The opinions of several men working 12 hours were taken ... many of them said they would prefer working ten hours for less wages, but they had no choice (6).

The unprecedented demand for leisure time was a response to unprecedented conditions. The working week for factory workers in the mid nineteenth century was over seventy hours. This applied not only to this country but to France and America. Yet what evidence there is suggests that the pre-industrial urban proletariat had at least as much leisure as exists at the present day, when industrial workers throughout Western Europe and America work between forty and forty-six hours a week, and even less in Eastern Europe. Rudé remarks that saints days and holidays were so frequent (111 in the year) as to have reduced the ordinary Parisian workers' average working week to something less than four days (7). The change to a full working week must have occurred much earlier in England, well before the Industrial Revolution, along with the general change to wage-labour in the seventeenth century (8). Under pressure from that peculiar combination of business acumen and high moral tone which we have learned to call the Protestant ethic, the ordinary working week was considerably expanded by the suppression of saints' days and church festivals. It was this longer — or fuller — English working week which was taken over as a prescriptive right by factory owners.

The achievement registered by the working-class movement which can be said to have 'created' leisure — in the manifest, historical, political, sense — was threefold. It was the first successful challenge to the immersion of everyday life in industrial work. Secondly, it was a major episode in the development of a strategy of collective bargaining for improved conditions of work and, as it proved, earnings. The connection was soon learned. Very clearly, pressure for a shorter working week maintains the character of a tactical device which can, if successfully employed, result in increased earnings as well; although the preference for increases in leisure over increases in earnings still prevails among industrial communities (e.g., miners) whose institutional life was formed in the early years of industrialism. Thirdly, however much the Parliamentary success of the movement was due to chance political combinations of the time, the working class did score a specifically political gain in face of the power of industrial capital. And since then the most striking *political* successes of organized labour versus organized capital in this country have been in terms of restriction of hours of work much more than of increased earnings.

We thus have the spectacle of everyday life being swamped by the tide of capitalist industry, and subsequently of this tide receding under pressure from workers, to leave an increasing number of hours of freely disposable time.

The second aspect of leisure regarded in terms of its historical development is logically connected with the first. There is a qualitative difference between the popular social pursuits which formed everyday life along with work before the Industrial Revolution, and what later emerged as leisure. Release from work was demanded or excused only on church and civic festivals, and took on always the guise of a sacred occasion, however secular or mundane the actual pursuits were. (It was one of the more often repeated, as well as more serious, charges against the theatres in London that they drew apprentices and journeymen from their work, and one of the substantial reasons for their eventual closure.) Time out from work not only had to have its own particular justification and sanction in public ritual or celebration, but the kind of pursuits appropriate to each occasion were defined and organized in terms of meaning and significance attached to the occasion.

Leisure, under industrialism, was sanctioned, defined and organized in entirely different terms. The new leisure of the working classes represented a vacuum which was largely filled, even to begin with, by amusement industries. The new middle classes of bureaucratized industry and commerce, and government obtained their release later than the textile workers. Lloyds closed on Saturday afternoons from 1854 on, but the Stock Exchange remained open for another twenty years. The Civil Service gained its Saturday half-day in the sixties. Shop assistants, of course, had to wait until the end of the century before they were allowed some remission of their eighty-four hour week. Nevertheless, 'by the end of the sixties, amusement for leisure has become an undertaking worthy of commercial exploitation' (9).

Drinking was the first and most general pursuit to be commercialized. During the last quarter of the nineteenth century an increasing amount of the profits of the brewing trade were invested in building licensed premises where evenings could be spent; the drink shop was replaced by the gin palace and the public house. Racing, a disreputable racket in the 1850s, was reconstituted, heavily capitalized, and a popular mass entertainment by the 1880s. Professional football and boxing followed the same path even more rapidly. Absorbing more time than either, the popular press cashed in on a public formed earlier by cheap prints and broadsheet reports of criminal cases.

Just as organized working-class demand for improved working conditions was first successfully articulated in terms of leisure, so the commercial response to improved living standards made itself apparent first in the provision of new services. Increase in the supply and variety of consumer goods, which meant so much to the new middle classes and to the ways in which the system of social stratification worked itself out in the twentieth century, was a subsequent development. But in both cases there is a complementary relationship between the growing subdivision, specialization and organization of labour on the one hand, and the increased hourly earnings and pressure for a shorter working week on the other which the selfsame industrial development generated and facilitated. There is also a parallel relationship between the increasing constraints which larger and more elaborate structures of industrial organization imposed on the work situation, and the increasing definition of leisure pursuits in terms of the organized provision of services and goods by new forms of commercial and industrial enterprise.

The force of Chapman's remark, 'The Ten Hours Act effected the greatest change in the work situation of ordinary people since Moses brought the six-day week down from Mount Sinai' lies not merely in the separation of leisure and labour which it began. Besides initiating this crucial stage in the differentiation of everyday life, the Act also made way for the development of commercial, industrial and other organizations which would provide a structure of activities ordered for individual choice and preference, individual satisfactions and rewards. The range of possible pursuits out of working time is arguably much wider than it was for any previous generation than ours. The point to be made is that these pursuits are wholly secular, organized for a commercial market, or at least for a user public, and, by and large, limited to what can be so organized.

This puts a new light on the thesis, which has gained some currency, of the increasing dissociation of social stratification from social class. Individual consumption has had to be expanded to become the necessary prime mover of economic expansion; secondly, this replaces the directly exploitative relationship between capital and labour by a relationship which involves the fostering of the propensity to consume among the masses of the population in the self-interests of the industrialist entrepreneur; thirdly, both the development of modern industrial organization and of new ways of organizing the spending of disposable means and time led to the evolution of new stratification systems and the blunting of the structural definition of classes through conflict.

I have dwelt on the implication of the elementary idea of leisure as contrasted with labour because it has seemed to me that sociologists have been in rather too great a hurry to dismiss this interpretation as *simpliste* and to hurry on to more rewarding data and interpretations; they have thus ignored some of the more profound and durable contributions to our knowledge of the social structure, and especially of recent changes in it, which this notion has made. The thesis argued in this section is that the swamping of everyday life by industrialism has not been succeeded by a mere ebbing, or forcing back, of the flood. Social life outside the work situation has not re-emerged; it has been created afresh, in forms which are themselves the creatures of industrialism, which derive from it *and which contribute to its development, growth and further articulation.*

3

When the elementary idea of leisure as contrasted with work is set in the context of a straightforward, even superficial, account of the historical developments of the relationship, there is an immediate expansion of the explanatory force of the contrast. Together they make more sense than does either singly; but this is not to say that one *illuminates* the other. If the first orientation of study springs from a particular consensual view of some symmetry obtaining between the two halves of everyday life which has a peculiar force for contemporaries, then the second derives from an equally consensual apprehension of history as development. A third perspective is afforded by the appreciation that there are limits to the shared meanings action can have. Groups and categories of people standing in some asymmetrical relationship to one another may ascribe *different* significances to *similar* patterns of behaviour.

The connection between the second and this third orientation to the theme lies in the political significance which attaches to the movement for the reduction of the working week during the nineteenth century. The historical circumstances of the movement itself, and its later incorporation in the strategies of organized labour, give some support to the speculative remarks of Pizzorno (also applied to nineteenth-century development) about the ideological function of leisure (10). In a society devoted increasingly to the values of leisure and consumption rather than to those of production, leisure presents itself as an alternative source of ethical values to those founded in production and work, and which are identified with the middle class. But the choice between the alternatives is not open and individual. Pizzorno suggests that, during the earlier period industrialization, the bourgeois values of thrift, austerity and production were adopted by (or it could be more plausibly said 'wished on to') the working class, but became obviously incompatible with their situation in industrial society. Further, leisure values developed as a counter-system in much the same way, he suggests, as the virtues of bourgeois capitalist society developed as an alternative counter-system to those of the aristocracy and gentry.

There is some parallel between this suggestion, with its Orwellian overtones, and the findings of Alberoni, another Italian student of leisure and consumer behaviour (11). His point of departure is the assumption, which American economists and sociologists have taken over from Veblen, of social differentiation as uni-dimensional — that there is unanimity about the value of having more goods, or more leisure, for use and display than others.

The Veblenesque view, current in America and reflected in the later 'embourgeoisement' thesis of European social commentators, of what happens when traditional orientations to other values are eroded by mobility and rapid rises in living standards, is that such values are slowly replaced by those directed towards emulation and imitation of the better-off. For Alberoni, the radical change is in the frame of reference. The effect of mobility and improved living standards on the traditional leisure class is that it loses its definition as a *Stand*: the effect on lower-class families is that they look beyond the local community as a reference style of life and adopt what they see as the national society's. The national community differs from the earlier, local community as a reference style in that it possesses two élites - one a political, economic (and, in Italy, religious) power élite; the other an élite without power made up of all those personages who are the object of imitation, admiration and collective attachment – the '*divi*', who are the protagonists of the mass media and who suggest ways of behaviour and influence popular values without making decisions about them. The '*divi*' in modern society take the place of the collectivity of traditional small-scale societies in that they become the collective objects of gossip, now a conversational traffic involving millions of people. Although they are few and privileged, they are not at the summit of the social system, neither do they constitute a social group or class. As such, they are not the object of envy or class resentment. Any person, rich or poor, can 'adopt' or become identified with one or other individual in one or other category, or in one or other social identity, which means that they act as a kind of structural solvent; in fact of the '*divi*', the members of society become a populace, a mass (12).

In adopting leisure pursuits and individual purchasable items from the powerless élite, people are not involved in emulating them or each other. 'The girl who dresses like Elizabeth Taylor is not trying to display wealth or to testify to her membership of the leisure classes. She is expressing her membership, along with that of innumerable other girls all over the country, of a world to which Elizabeth Taylor also belongs.' Hence, Alberoni goes on, the familiar preference of a television set to a sewing machine, and to other mundane and useful consumer durables among those confronted for the first time with the actual possibility of choice between the two. The television set is an escape hatch from the local community as well as from immediate social pressures, and an entrance to the larger world in which one can now participate, to which one is welcomed, and in which one can, in a new, oblique, but meaningful sense, consort with the '*divi*'.

When we move, with Pizzorno and Alberoni, to this new plane of analysis, a good deal more is changed than merely the scope of considerations relevant to the study of leisure and consumer behaviour. What they have done is to demonstrate, once again, that sociological explanation has to be sought in bringing structural connections to bear on individual connections; to exploit the basic assumption of sociology – which is that social structure influences the behaviour of individuals – one has to do more than merely invoke it.

At all events, at the level of the considerations drawn in from Pizzorno and Alberoni, there is a direct regard for the implications for each other of changes in the social structure and in the development of leisure. There are two ways in which, for example, their findings and comments challenge orthodox concepts of social stratification.

It is now common ground that in leisure and consumption, no less than in other respects, it is difficult to regard the stratification system in unilinear terms; i.e. as a continuous gradient of status differences which is produced by the deflection of a principle of distributive justice by another principle, effecting an asymmetrical ordering of power and rewards. Pizzorno's and Alberoni's work raises again and suggests possible solutions to the old unanswered questions about why there is still no direct challenge to the power and authority of capitalists and managers, why Chinoy's and Andrieux and Lignon's and Popitz' workers direct their aspirations to acquisitions and 'fun' and independence instead of towards promotion or a redistribution of power and rewards within the enterprise, why production committees and *Mitbestimmung* failed and were not succeeded by other devices and other claims for a share in management.

Secondly, their work rescues the concept of 'style of life' from the status to which it seems to have been relegated, of a dependent variable, an extra and perhaps superfluous appendage of class or occupational status. The way in which people spend their disposable money and time is a mode of organizing their lives and, therefore, one of the concrete forms in which the social structure is manifest in action. The appropriate sociological cliché, one could perhaps say, becomes 'way of life' rather than 'style of life'.

One is not, therefore, arguing for a simple class-determined view of leisure to replace an occupationally-determined one, still less following Henri Raymond's tentative suggestion that 'affiliation to one social stratum is determined by choice of leisure' (13). Rather, one is confronted on this third plane of analysis with the appearance of different, autonomous, even rival structures which pertain to the ordering of social behaviour and of society in terms of stratification, occupational system, and styles of life, and which are certainly interrelated, or even 'multi-bonded' or 'crystallized', if you like, but between which the causal flow of dependence is not easy to determine. For example, from some of Dumazedier's work it seems that the organizing principles at work in the articulation of leisure activities extend beyond leisure itself. Occupational choices may be made not so much to provide the income which will support the highest standard of living as to consort with a preferred style of life. Preference for particular forms of leisure impose constraints on choices made in the rest of life and especially in terms of hours of work, opportunities for supplementary earnings, and the social milieu offered by the workplace.

In addition, of course, such preferences affect actual decisions (in the case, for example, of married women, about whether or not to seek employment) and they affect location and mobility.

4

One can leave the matter here, at the point at which a strong case has been made for the implication of leisure in the system, or systems, of social stratification in industrial society, and for increasing the weight to be attached to characteristic leisure activities when considering the structural location of individuals.

If one remains unsatisfied, one does not *solve* the residual problem by adopting a new perspective, moving to yet another plane of analysis. What one has to attempt is explanation in *contextual* terms, too, as a necessary conclusion to the various levels of considerations already invoked. This context concerns the relationship between the way in which social facts are defined for the individual by himself and by sociologists. In Bendix and Berger's terms, we have to 'consider not only the social conditioning of the individual but also his capacity for independent action for which that conditioning is only the necessary basis' (14).

In his study, *Le Monde des employées de bureau,* Michel Crozier ends by insisting on the plurality of the office-worker's world, on the variety of ways in which he can select and arrange and organize his life in terms of work situation, of commitment to the organization, of collective action, of social groupings, and of differentiation of leisure pursuits. In fact, he points out the strategic advantage to the individual of the very lack of correspondence between sections of the structure to which Marshall has referred (15). In a sense, perhaps, this choice of a hand from the cards one is dealt is no more than a choice among an array of alienated positions, but, he says, 'The multiplicity of the kinds of alienation possible, and the consequent incoherence (of the systems of social ordering and of values obtainable) tend to liberate the individual' (16).

This is more than a restatement of the basic Simmelian position, in which 'The member of different social groups in which the individual participates is one of the landmarks of culture' (17). It is nearer, perhaps, to Simmel's development of the same notion:

As individuals, we form the personality out of particular elements of life, each of which has arisen from, or is interwoven with, society. This personality is subjective *par excellence* in the sense that it combines the elements of culture in an individual manner. There is here a reciprocal relationship between the subjective and the objective. As the person becomes affiliated with a social group, he surrenders himself to it. A synthesis of such objective affiliations creates a group in an objective sense. But the person also regains his individuality because his pattern of participation is unique (18).

The implication of Crozier's conclusion is that, in a world of organization and organized activities, while it renders self-realization (or autonomy) through identification of the individual with his work and its product impossible, a kind of second-order self-realization and autonomy is available in the ability to choose both *which* commitments of all those preferred him by work, associations and cultural pursuits he will engage in, and also *how much* 'psycho-social capital' he will invest in those he chooses.

A similar strategic inversion of the notion of alienation has been developed by Touraine in the concept of *projet*. For Touraine, the total apparatus of industrial society, in work, in leisure, in the political order and in the cultural world, representing the detritus of the total historical development of society, constitutes the inescapable datum of existence for the individual, who must live within the constraints imposed by the apparatus on the several status positions he occupies. But the same apparatus is also *data for* existence, in that he orders his life in terms of the commitments he enters into each status, and can, from that position, view the apparatus of society as means whereby he can realize his *projet*.

There are many other forms taken by this perception of an analytical component representing the individual as interacting positively with the social order. Raymond Firth, in his essays on social organization, expands the limited play allowed for truly individual choice in Crozier's and Touraine's formulations and affirms the connection with analysis in terms of structure for which Bendix and Berger argued.

> One may describe social organization, then, as the working arrangements of society. It is the processes of ordering of action and of relations in reference to given social ends, in terms of adjustments resulting from the exercise of choices by the members of society. This is not the same as describing social action as the working *rules* of the society, which implies a conformity and an imperative in the ordering of the activities of the society which may be only partly true (19).

A clearer lead still is given by Goffman in his earlier treatment of the notion of the styling of activities, as of demeanour and choice of furnishings and accessories, as an element in the individual's purpose of conveying to others the impression of himself he wishes to convey, and by this means to control the social situation into which he enters.

Styling is thus the overt expression of the positive aspects of the self-image – it displays the upper frequencies of an oscillating self-consciousness forever rebounding between self-doubt and aspiration. In its most articulate and successful form, it is encountered among individuals who have modelled their behaviour on a specific social identity which overrides both occupational position and the organized apparatus of leisure and consumption, and fixes an appropriate 'distance' (again in Goffman's terms) between this identity and the several roles they occupy. Youth culture provides the more familiar styles but, at a more sophisticated level, it is possible for identities to be developed which do not merely override but manipulate and exploit the apparatus of the organized world of work and leisure.

This behaviour process presented is most clearly visible in the world of the powerless élite itself – at least, to take one representative milieu, in the social territory of television studies. The styles cultivated there derive from the implication of the whole occupational community (of television) in the world of the theatre and of social sophistication in the commonly accepted sense. So people are divided into professionals and amateurs, and, more significantly, into camp, butch (terms now used without any hint of their nineteenth-century origins as homosexual cant) and square. Individuals can be camp – i.e., act habitually with an edgy elegance or sophisticated charm, or 'play it camp' for a social occasion; groups, occasions, or whole departments can be 'campish'. 'Butch', which carries an equal connotation of being sophisticated and on the inside, allows of an alternative mode – plain or coarse-spoken cynicism or directness. Both terms clearly denote not personality types but manners and styles of conduct which can be assumed, and which relate to traditional 'characters' or even 'humours' in the English theatre as old as the seventeenth-century stage, where both types are clearly discernible and, indeed, explicitly portrayed. To reject both, and to be square, is, in this milieu, an equally positive choice, equally a style which has to be cultivated from models and consciously maintained.

The sense of purposed fabrication which runs through the notions of *projet*, or strategy, or the organization of commitments, or the presentation of self, or – at a more conscious level – styling, relates to the individual's attempt to organize his behaviour in everyday life so as to give it significance and meaning. Analytically, the concepts seem to allow for the construction of and connections between work and leisure and social structure which can contain the otherwise confusing two-way flow of causal relationships that survey research has shown to exist between the world of work and that of leisure, and also to round out the more general explanatory theses of Pizzorno and Alberoni, which invoke larger considerations of a structural kind but which also suffer from both a bias towards sociological reductionism and a still sizeable weight of variance unaccounted for. It also seems to me both to be in line with Wilensky's findings and also to offer a more satisfactory solution than the elaborate structural interpretation he rather tentatively advances. At least it avoids the decline into determinism in the manner of Whyte's *Organization Man* with which Wilensky concludes:

> As rich countries grow richer, harmonizing structures in politics, education and mass communications combine with an already high level of cultural uniformity to reduce the hold of differentiating structure of age, religion, work and locality, and bring about greater consistency of structure and culture – a new combination of 'mass society' and 'industrial society', mass culture and high culture (20).

One is sometimes tempted to regard congruence theory as an occupational disease of sociologists.

5

Finally, one has to ask what human purposes are involved in the projects, strategies and stylizations of life which organize the worlds of work and leisure for individuals?

There is a fundamental contrast suggested by the historical origin of contemporary leisure in industrialism, and what stood in pre-industrial life in place of leisure now. Everyday life, in so far as it was explicitly freed from work, was organized in terms of religious and civic festivals. It derived meaningfulness from permanent (sacred, as Weber says) and ritualistic elements in human life. There is a sense in which leisure activity in contemporary society represents an attempt to recapture the same quality of meaningfulness for everyday life now. This is certainly the thesis which runs through the work of Henri Lefebvre; leisure, he suggests, is an attempt to break away from everyday life, which is characterized throughout by frustration, into a factitious world which will endow everyday life with meaning and worthwhileness (21). In a somewhat similar sense, Edgar Morin's social criticism of the cultural role of the cinema confers on it the function of an experimental, innovative composition of the potentialities of life for industrial man, a composition which remains, however, imaginary and unrealized (22).

Leisure, and the games and entertainments which fill so much of it, may therefore be a substitute for ritual. The significance of the connection between ritual and, if I am right, the displaced behaviour which serves as its modern counterpart is indicated in Lévi-Strauss' brief analysis:

> Games thus appear to have a *disjunctive* effect: they end in the establishment of a difference between players or teams where originally there was no indication of inequality. And at the end of

the game they are distinguished into winners and losers. Ritual, on the other hand, is the exact inverse: it *conjoins,* for it brings about a union (one might even say communion in this context) between two initially separated groups . . . In the case of games the symmetry is therefore preordained and it is of a structural kind since it follows from the principle that the rules are the same for both sides. Asymmetry is engendered: it follows inevitably from the contingent nature of events, themselves due to intention, chance or talent. The reverse is true of ritual. There is an asymmetry which is postulated in advance between profane and sacred, faithful and officiating, dead and living, initiated and uninitiated, etc., and the 'game' consists in making all the participants pass to the winning side by means of events, the nature and ordering of which is genuinely structural. Like science (though here again on both the theoretical and practical plane) the game produces events by means of a structure; and we can therefore understand why competitive games should flourish in our industrial societies. Rites and myths, on the other hand, . . . take to pieces and reconstruct sets of events (on a psychical, socio-historical or technical plane) and use them as so many indestructible pieces for structural patterns in which they serve alternatively as ends or means (23).

Mass entertainment now offers the same re-composition of events and action so as to provide initiation into secrets, inclusion among the survivors, and acceptance by the officiating élite, for all. And there is a sense, known to all of us, in which events and places remain 'unreal' (i.e., unattached to our ordered knowledge of things, and therefore unmeaningful) until they have been recorded, processed, and presented on television, in films, or in the newspapers. Just as games re-enact both the constraints of the social structure ('the rules of the game') and the latitude still left the individual (who exercises autonomy in exploiting the rules of the game), so entertainment, on the other side of organized leisure, can be construed as contemporary society's response to the enduring need to ritualize the unfamiliar and disconnected, the unattainable and the threatening, to reduce the increasing range and strangeness of the individual's world to the synthesized and safely repeatable form of a composed story, or documentary, or performance. The structures of leisure exist to serve as repositories of meaning and value for everyday life.

Notes and References
1 J. Dumazedier, *Toward a Society of Leisure*, Collier-Macmillan, 1967.
2 M. Crozier, *Le Monde des employés de bureau*, Paris, Seuil, 1965.
3 H. L. Wilensky, 'Mass Society and Mass Culture', *American Journal of Sociology*, April 1964.
4 E. Chinoy, *Automobile Workers and the American Dream*, New York, Doubleday, 1955.
5 G. Chapman, *Culture and Survival*, Cape, 1940.
6 ibid.
7 G. Rudé, *The Crowds in the French Revolution*, Oxford University Press, 1959.
8 C. B. Macpherson, *The Political Theory of Possessive Individualism*, Oxford University Press, 1962.
9 Chapman, op. cit.
10 A. Pizzorno, 'Accumulation, loisirs et rapports du classe', *Esprit*, 1959.
11 F. Alberoni, *Consumi e società*, Bologna, Mulino, 1964.
12 This rendering of Alberoni's conclusions is largely that of Dr Gianfranco Poggi, to whom I am indebted for introducing me to Alberoni's work.
13 H. Raymond, 'La Sociologie du loisir en France – résultats et perspectives', *Information*, 1964.
14 R. Bendix and B. Berger, 'Images of Society and Problems of Concept Formation in Sociology', in L. Gross (ed.), *Symposium on Sociological Theory*, New York Harper and Row, 1959.
15 T. H. Marshall, 'Changes in Social Stratification in the Twentieth Century', in *Sociology at the Crossroads*, Heinemann, 1963.
16 Crozier, op. cit.
17 G. Simmel, *Conflict, and the Web of Group Affiliations*, Glencoe, Free Press, 1955.
18 ibid.
19 R. Firth, 'Social Organization and Social Change', in *Essays on Social Organization and Values*, Athlone Press, 1964.
20 Wilensky, op. cit.
21 H. Lefebvre, *Everyday Life in the Modern World*, Allen Lane The Penguin Press, 1971.
22 E. Morin, *Le Cinéma, ou l'homuve imaginaire*, Éditions de Minuit, 1956.
23 C. Lévi-Strauss, *The Savage Mind*, Weidenfeld and Nicolson, 1966.

4 Leisure and the search for a satisfying identity[1]

Ralph Glasser

Many people greet the mention of leisure with a snigger of denial that they have any. Others profess amazement that leisure can present problems that merit discussion. The latter group includes a few old-fashioned sociologists who prefer to count heads rather than to see what is in them. The former group are in some ways more interesting. Their nervy snigger reveals to the discerning social analyst a furtive awareness that some of the ways in which they do use their time might not bear examination in terms of the purpose of life. Such an awareness is at least a good start. But their response also shows, in common with the myopic sociologists referred to, a difficulty in perceiving what leisure is and the personality problems its use poses.

The people who pretend they have no leisure must surely either be wrong or are misusing the word. Do they mean by leisure a final residue of time after all other obligations have been met? If so what do these obligations include? Work? Yes, let us agree that work is unavoidable though we shall see presently that this apparently self-evident truth has qualifications. What about drinks with colleagues or business associates – obligatory for career reasons? Possibly, but an element of choice does creep in here. Attending a boys' club committee meeting or a cricket club meeting? Quite a lot of choice must exist here despite the strength of communal and other group loyalties. You do not have to go to the meeting. You go because you believe participation is meaningful to you in various important ways so that to do so amounts to a debit against the credit balance of your freely disposable time. And so we could go down the scale of weaker obligation until an activity has no emotional pull or only a marginal one. Can it be, then, that the people who claim to have no leisure have their time so fully debited with such obligations that 'true' leisure has only one meaning, namely time literally hanging on their hands with no claim on it of any kind and for the use of which the available choices of activity present no attraction? This must be a truly desperate situation, one might think, driving one to fill such dead time almost at any price? Having to face the fact of such dead time carries with it the admission of a bankruptcy of feeling, a thought that most people would prefer not to have. Imposed boredom is bad enough but at least one can blame it on someone else for depriving us of choice. A self-imposed dead end is not tolerable. So it is quite natural for people to say, with the facetiousness that exposes doubt, that they have *no* leisure, meaning that they have taken steps to avoid the uncertainty about ends that dead time would reveal.

Choice, therefore, is a deciding factor in defining leisure. It is also a key to understanding the sociology of leisure, for it leads us to regard the use of time as a medium for achieving personal goals. In my Identity Theory of Leisure (2) these goals are to be analysed in terms of the search for a satisfactory identity that is central to each person's decisions about the pattern of life to pursue.

It has become customary in recent years when one is propounding a new concept or theory to explain carefully to the audience or readers that really it is not new but merely a continuation of something already known. Heaven preserve us from a new idea! The fear of the unknown is less terrible if one can share it with others who have gone before. So also with the theory of identity. Of course the theory has a genealogy. People have talked of it in many ways without realizing it – of *amour propre*, of having a proper conceit of oneself, awareness of personality and so on. Literature in the modern period has been full of it, especially in the neo-Romantic genre ushered in by Wyndham Lewis's *Tarr,* upholding a view that what the person meant or represented in himself was important above all else. It is significant that this theme of the identity of the individual grew into a paramount pre-occupation in literature and the arts with the decline of the influence of religion as a guide for behaviour. Poetic insight is always far ahead of rational exposition. As James Stephens says:

'I have learned' said the Philosopher, 'that the head does not hear anything until the heart has listened, and what the heart knows today the head will understand tomorrow.' (3)

People tend to be impressed when some mundane field of inquiry supports perceptions from the humanities, an interesting comment on how far the technocratic age has weaned us from respect for the things of the spirit. Market research is not therefore so strange a field from which to get insights into what used to be the sole preserve of social philosophy. Sophisticated techniques of consumer research have confirmed some truths that insight and reflection had perceived long ago. Some little time ago I was concerned with a depth survey into shopping motivations on whose results I have developed my Identity Theory of Leisure and of choice in patterns of living. This theory is a key to unlock a number of hitherto difficult problems in personal goal fixing and social policy. The primary aim in shopping expeditions is not to purchase but to perceive and to reaffirm a satisfactory identity. People go out shopping to redefine their own identity to themselves as well as to amend their perception of what should be the ideal to aim at. They do this by a process rather like a radar system plots out a map by sending out signals and recording the contours made by the returning echoes. In this case the echoes are of themselves. They are reflected back from other people, what they are wearing and saying, from the environment, fashions; other people's responses expressed in tones of voice, degree of interest or indifference – all the nuances of reaction also help to fill out the picture of their own identity. They combine these echoes with their own responses to them. The resulting composite picture of themselves is then compared with a view they possess of an identity which the culture inculcates as desirable, both personally and for the group or series of groups to which they are related in the various contexts of their lives – the work group, the family, the street, the neighbourhood, the club, the professional association, etc.

The identity in this sense is like a personal work of art, a positive version of the situation in *The Picture of Dorian Grey* where the individual monitors his success, not his failure, in building his personality according to the twin requirement of acceptability to himself and to the group. He craves certainty and this imposes a need to affirm and to reaffirm again and again that this composite two-level identity is one that fits his understanding of what is desirable. He is unhappy when he cannot perform this monitoring and adapting process. This is why people who are isolated by special circumstances, solitary confinement, a lonely job or a long solitary voyage, often undergo severe psychological strain, the consequence of difficulty in monitoring the progress of their identity.

Identity will vary in different contexts. A woman doing window shopping is testing her perception of her identity in different projected roles, what it should be and what it is – as she perceives it and as she fancies other people do – evaluating, confirming, and perhaps amending it and making decisions about purchases or other actions which will outwardly express this assessment. This outward expression is itself important. To this extent we are all still in the grip of the primitive faith in sympathetic magic. If we feel we want to have the attributes, say, of a current folk hero we are impelled to underline this, to pin it down by means of an action characteristic of the attributes concerned; in this way we hope the change will be brought about. This is the basis of all fashion, in speech, clothes, leisure patterns and personal goals in general. Thus the woman in her window shopping considers her identity, focusing her fantasy on certain objects that for the moment represent the attributes she feels the need to re-emphasize or to change, a piece of furniture, a set of china, a piece of curtain material. These are the symbols only, chosen to sustain the identity aimed at in different situations. Always, however, there are the two levels, the personal one — the identity fitting as nearly as possible to the private perception of that ideal model to be aimed at — and the one acceptable to the social group. The combination nearest to fulfilling all these requirements is the one used as a yardstick in making a particular choice, whether it is a job, a product, a food, a restaurant, a club, a holiday, a friend, a lover.

Most of the power of the modern persuasion process, whether for business or other propaganda purposes, derives from the fact that it provides answers of a kind to this insatiable need for reassurance as to what is the desirable identity to pursue, and gives guidance in redefining it and in making the choices likely to bring about desirable modifications in it. The whole of consumer demand can be specifically identified in terms of this identity principle. All behaviour, manners, and patterns of living can be seen in this way too. One has only to analyse any piece of consumer goods advertising to see this principle in action. Best of all one sees this in the willingness to identify with particular people who seem to wear the aura of identity success, folk heroes from show business, pop music, sport — a trusting urge towards identity improvement by emulation, freely exploited by the marketing persuasion process. Whether this urge to identity improvement by emulation is on the right lines or not is beside the point. The marketing process is not concerned with that in human terms, only with its aptness or otherwise for product development policy and promotional success. This willingness to identify with symbols of identity success provides the medium for fashion change, whether in clothes or in anything else. By this means is leadership exercised, consciously or not, over the standards that people need for emotional security.

That the persuasion process does work requires no proof, assuming that it is based on accurate perception of the identities being sought by the people or the market segment aimed at, and assuming also that the products being promoted are correctly designed to fit that identity. One could say that the very existence of the persuasion process, and its success in such aims as the creation and maintenance of brand loyalties, provide objective models of the ways in which human fulfilment is pursued through the search for an acceptable identity. Satisfaction is offered and bought on this basis. Fulfilment is bought too, whether in the form of a product to help one to present a slim figure to the world, a tanned skin, or an outfit of clothes that echoes some folk hero whose qualities one accepts as desirable to possess.

In symbolic terms such behaviour is comparable to primitive man's efforts to identify with a totem figure, to endow himself by sympathetic magic with the powers of the totem and so to obtain an identity desirable on personal and social grounds. In each case, primitive and sophisticated, fulfilment is sought through the pursuit of an acceptable identity.

The decisive element in this behaviour is the frame of reference used to decide what identity should be aimed at. What gives us the idea on which we secretly construct inside ourselves the ideal archetype of a person, the model with which we compare our real-life perceptions of ourselves? We can think of life as if we were all student artists sitting copying a master work; but each time we close our eyes and open them again the model looks slightly different and we have to check anxiously to see that our own copy is following the model faithfully or not. So also our lives, looked at as works of art, are never complete and likewise never true to our mental model of what it is we want to resemble. We forever pursue and refine the desirable identity; the complete model always eludes us. We can hold the image only for a moment.

Because our perception of identity changes with time and with context, we must constantly monitor it and make needed adjustments. We need guidance in what to aim at, which explains why, with religious influence weaker than at any time in the Christian era, there is a guidance gap that the marketing persuasion process has rushed in to fill. It provides an appearance of certainty, as well as transient emotional props, presenting deceptively easy methods whereby people may redefine and reassert a desirable identity with temporary confidence. That the confidence cannot be other than temporary is the reason why a basic emotional doubt and weariness is the key social feature of our time and why the persuasion process must constantly renew the fading confidence, ever devising new identity models and new encouragements in pursuing them, just as people in a leaking boat must never stop baling.

Because leisure is the area of life where more or less free choices are available we must see leisure choices as reflecting the stages that the search for a desirable identity has reached in people or groups. The kinds of identity people choose reflect their view of the aims of life itself. This view is chosen or at least profoundly shaped by the persuasion process working upon the deeper influences derived from the inherited culture. Accordingly, just as the study of identity aspirations is the prime key in understanding the consumer in the interests of marketing strategy, so also is it the key determinant in the sociology of leisure. One could go further and see it as a means of obtaining a new perspective in social philosophy.

I must now examine how the present confusion of thought about leisure happened. It surprises many people to be reminded that we are still very much under the influence of the Romantic Movement of the end of the eighteenth century and the beginning of the nineteenth.

Leisure as society now regards it is a comparatively new concept, with life seen as a dichotomy: one part obligatory, work, and the other part a period of time at one's free disposal, leisure, with little or no connection between the two. This modern view of life dates roughly from the Romantic Movement with its emphasis on the primacy of the individual *vis-à-vis* society, and its rejection of his long submergence in the Classical view of an ordered harmony. The Classical order had crumbled long before. The religious frame of reference for behaviour and social structuring, so long a bulwark of Classical order, had also lost its sharpness of outline. In spite of all its deviations and frequent inhumanities, it had at least provided people with a set of standards against which even deviations could be perceived and provided for. The Romantics in their search for a new human perspective were attracted to the idea of natural man as a frame of reference, meaning by this the parcel of attributes with which each man was endowed and which they believed it was his destiny to attempt to fulfil as completely as possible. Here, they felt, was a new touchstone for behaviour and institutions. The aim of social policy must be to facilitate this natural fulfilment. Its extent was the measure of personal and social success. No one attempted to define fulfilment. The need to do so was neatly evaded by a curious piece of Romantic naiveté. Natural man, they said — meaning a man as nearly as possible in the state of nature, a state of minimal constraint — possessed a built-in mechanism for ensuring that his nature would automatically take him towards maximum fulfilment. There was, therefore, no need to ask what that fulfilment was. If it was determined by his nature that was guarantee enough that the fulfilment was right for him. The circular reasoning contained in this approach appears to have escaped the Romantics. The concept of natural man seemed a perfect key to all situations. Free him from constraints and all would be well. His parcel of attributes would automatically steer him to the fulfilment that was right for him. What prevented him was the burden of work. Give him leisure and his nature would automatically swing him to fulfilment as unerringly as the compass needle reaches out to the north.

That the leisured class, who did have both time and means, did not enjoy automatic fulfilment but were just as prone to the discontents of life as anyone else, was dismissed as mere decadence. Why this decadence would not attack others just as fast as *they* obtained leisure was never considered a valid question. We in our age, faced with a barnacle growth of leisure decadence that would have appalled the sincere social reformers of the Romantic period, may smile grimly at this insouciance. So long as leisure was scarce most people in the social reform movement probably felt that such contradictions, if they saw them at all, could be safely ignored, that the question of purpose could be shelved. So effectively did they obscure this issue that only in the last two or three decades has awareness spread that beneficial choices in the use of leisure are by no means self-determining. It is not *yet* accepted that the employment of leisure raises the most fundamental questions about the purpose of life.

I have already mentioned the erosion of the influence of the great religions in the maintenance of a frame of reference for conduct. This erosion, sometimes called permissiveness, has now gone so far that there is a virtual vacuum of belief. The consequence is a pervading emotional insecurity comparable to that which children feel when deprived or unsure of parental certainty. There is a massive irony in this. Progress was expected to simplify the pursuit of the good life. Now there seems no longer any common certainty as to what the good life is. Nevertheless, most people do have a hazy, evanescent mental image of the good life as a personal goal, seldom thought of consciously. Generally it is a set of latent hopes and longings composing a vision of what it is desirable to aim at, what sort of person one should try to be, a perception of a desirable identity.

Choices in activity and the identity search are therefore so closely linked as to be inseparable parts of a set of aims continuing with amendments through life, a strategic policy whose success is measured by the degree to which the identity actually achieved approaches the ideal image. Whereas formerly this was judged on a combination of traditional social approbation and a reference to the ethical standards derived from religion, for contemporary man the reference is to social approbation alone, itself at the whim of the caprices, the transient fads by which people comfort their insecurity.

I said earlier that leisure as we now know it is a new concept. In tribal cultures we can study the unitary society, as I call it, ordered by a view of life as a pattern of changing activity — each type of activity being essential to the rest, as in a mosaic. The idea of dead time to be filled up at any price, or a period of free choice bought with one's obligatory labour, is unknown in the total commitment of the unitary society. With all activities obligatory in contributing to the common pattern of life, in a bonding together of individual and social identity, floating choices only existed, if at all, within very narrow limits. Individual identity in the unitary society had little meaning outside the communal pattern. In fact extrusion from the communal identity meant total isolation and death. Now, with the persisting Romantic emphasis on the individual isolated in an eroded culture, man seems to have chosen precisely the opposite course, forced to make choices with none of the secure guidelines once provided for us by the compulsory frame of reference of the unitary society.

For the majority of people in modern society the working out of an independent identity strategy is too great a task and must be assisted, and in most cases completely guided, by the persuasion process.

A major factor in the evolution of our present *déraciné* society has been the steady elimination of craft skill and therefore of personal involvement in the paid occupations with which leisure is purchased. In modern technology-based production there still remain isolated pockets where there is a direct craft relationship with materials and with the environment. The carpenter, the high-price furniture maker and the interior decorator are examples of such outposts of personal involvement, where the worker leaves a part of himself in the finished task and where the work itself is recognizably his. But this personal identification, inseparable from pursuing identity through work, is becoming increasingly rare. For many people, indeed, their part in the production process is difficult if not impossible to perceive. Work motivation has for many generations depended on this factor of personal identification, more so than the social reformers with their basic belief in material rewards have cared to admit. With work satisfaction increasingly attenuated by technology, management's urgent task is to find other ways of motivating the labour force. So far material reward alone has been the spur, more leisure and more purchasing power with which to fill it. But as leisure becomes less and less satisfying in identity terms, material rewards become progressively less motivating too. Mankind faces an apparently intractable dilemma: on the one hand work provides less and less emotional satisfaction and, on the other, man finds that in his increased leisure a satisfying identity continues to elude him. The resulting stress is already making itself felt in the form of aimless permissiveness, disruption of social institutions, capricious violence and − basic to society − a lowered work incentive.

This stress is the result of thwarted hopes, of the shattered Romantic dream of fulfilment through the realization of a satisfying identity in leisure. Since technology has closed most of the fulfilment avenues in paid work *society must seek solutions to work motivation outside the work environment.* It will have to evolve methods of guiding people into using leisure in ways leading to a desirable identity. It is difficult to see how these methods can take any other route than a re-knitting together of society, breaking down the isolation of the individual and restoring the links between personal and communal identity. This could not be on any other basis than that of building a renewed ethical framework. Religion grew from man's need to clothe his insecurity with purpose, from his search for a meaningful unity with the natural forces. It could revive for the same reason, but the spiritual thesis and ethical codes will have to be reshaped to win over the contemporary spirit.

It is worth looking at the word recreation, so often used as a synonym for leisure. Literally it refers to the apparent purpose of leisure activity, a therapeutic process of repairing the wear and tear resulting from work and its stresses. By recreate we must mean to restore, to re-establish, to return to an original or ideal state. What is that ideal state? Religion offered an answer to this in the idea of Grace, a spiritual unity with the Divine Will, inseparable from a certain kind of conduct. Separated from this spiritual view, the idea of recreation is less easy to understand. Is the aim merely to be restored to a state in which we can best continue our work? Such aimless circularity is part of the reason for the contemporary movement of unrest, a perception that the newly-won volition of the advanced societies and the new scope that technology and permissiveness have made available for experiment does not lead to an enriched identity. People may accept the message and the sweet appeals of the marketing/persuasion process offering transient comforts, but the basic stress creeps through. Clinical evidence shows that frustration of a person's need to grasp and hold a desirable identity produces severe emotional stress, and stress is coming to be recognized as the most dangerous killer of all. It is cumulative and it is contagious. It feeds on that rejection of traditional values which has been a feature of modern times. One symptom of this rejection is the drop-out. There are many more ways of dropping-out than taking drugs. It is no coincidence that the words escape and escapism have figured so prominently in the literature and folklore of our time as to become almost its trade mark. If leisure is used, as it largely has been, as a means of escape it must inevitably increase stress, not relieve it, since no person continues for very long to deceive himself deep down in his heart. He merely blurs his perception for a time. Even the drop-outs demonstrate beyond anything else that they seek something secure to believe in. This seems to me one of the most hopeful signs that society is tired of wrecking its inherited institutions, of permissive isolation of the individual, frightened of its *déraciné* state, of the vacuum of belief that it has brought about. There are signs that people are getting tired of mere negation of former values and of the use of leisure to forget the vacuum thus created, and that they are beginning to grope towards stable values once more.

Even by its transient reassurances the marketing/persuasion process underlines man's hunger for a desirable and enduring identity; in fact most advertising turns on this theme. In spite of temporary blurring of perception, the principal occupation of increasing leisure and volition will be the drive to explore and refine the personality. Society at present is still following the deceptively easy route of merely providing facilities for killing time. The current boom in building recreation centres with their bars, ten-pin alleys and coin-operated *rôtisseries* is merely providing a glossy version of the old Victorian remedy of 'keeping idlers off the streets'. Gradually, as growth points of perceptive opinion develop, there will be an increasing demand for a more fundamental approach than this sugared aimlessness. Social institutions must once more reflect a sense of human purpose, a social ethic helping to nurture a secure personal ethic. It is interesting that the idea of voluntary communal service has become stronger in recent years, especially among the young. There are some bodies of opinion who go so far as to advocate for school-leavers a form of compulsory national service consisting of various kinds of communally beneficial work. There will probably be considerable resistance to this, perhaps especially from the trade union movement. Properly organized, however, such a scheme could easily avoid any encroachment on union interests.

There are and always will be economic shortages, for human demands are insatiable. Housing, old-age and invalid welfare services, amenity preservation, help for the blind and handicapped, counteracting pollution are examples of unsatisfied social needs. The age of technology has blunted many people's perception of what are the sinews of society, its organic nature, the fragile interdependence of people and institutions. For a young person in the critically sensitive period between school and either further education or an industrial commitment, before life becomes an impersonal maze of pushing buttons or turning levers, it would be a vitalizing experience to come to grips with the building blocks of society, necessarily at the delicate frontiers of communal life, and to understand how to make a constructive personal contribution to the quality of life in general – discovering himself and his responsibilities more clearly in the process. Personal involvement in the work of social institutions could counteract the starvation of the personality that materialism and individual isolation has produced. This could be an important way for society to guide the individual to use his leisure to refine his identity in terms ethically desirable both to himself and to the group, and to understand that the good life can only be pursued in these terms.

Notes and References

1 Most of the ideas explored in this chapter are pursued in greater depth in my book *Leisure – Penalty or Prize?* (Macmillan, 1970) but some of the material reflects development in my thinking since that book was written.
2 cf. my 1970 book; also 'The Sociology of the Leisure Age Society', my opening address to the Biennale Européene du Loisir, Geneva, May 1970.
3 *The Crock of Gold.*

Part 2

Work and leisure

Introduction

Having dealt in Part 1 with matters related to the role of leisure in culture in the wide sense, we turn now to a set of topics the linking theme of which might well be described as 'occupational culture'. In addition to being an integral part of culture, leisure is intimately, if often subtly, connected with the world of work. It is not difficult to see the ways in which leisure and work are related, and direct contrasts clearly do not exhaust the range of possibilities. The meanings and values attached to work and leisure are inextricably tied both to each other and to the cultural norms of a particular society. The chief aim in this part of the book is to trace some of the ways in which the two spheres interpenetrate.

The relations between work and leisure involve economic, philosophical and social science considerations. The work people do affects how much time they have for leisure, when they can have this time, and how much they can spend on those leisure pursuits which cost money. It is commonly believed that in recent years the trend has been towards shorter working hours and hence more time for leisure, and that this trend will continue and even accelerate in the future. While it is true that the length of the *standard* working week has been reduced for many categories of employees, overtime working has been increasing, so that actual hours worked have fallen only slightly in recent years. Furthermore, there is evidence that some types of employees – particularly managerial and professional – are working longer hours than hitherto. In a few firms workers have been put on a four-day and even a three-day week, and 'flexible hours' have been introduced elsewhere. All of these developments have implications for leisure, but so far they have significantly affected only a tiny minority of all employees. This is not, however, to underestimate the potential for change in the future.

The core of the philosophical debate about work and leisure concerns the extent to which society has moved from being work-centred to leisure-centred. In the heyday of the Industrial Revolution the 'Protestant ethic' held sway: not only was work conceived to be the path to worldly success but also to other-worldly salvation. Today vestiges of this ethic remain, but it has been strongly challenged by a more leisure-based ethic: that work is a means to the end of enjoying oneself in leisure. Earlier, work gave a man his sense of identity; today, it is claimed, his leisure style is more likely to supply it. Each of these ethics has special implications for the way the relationship between work and leisure is conceived. The Protestant ethic saw leisure as something earned by work and to be used as 'wholesome recreation' to enable work to be tackled with fresh vigour. The leisure ethic sees no such instrumentality in leisure: it is a part of life in its own right, to be enjoyed without guilt and not to be mortgaged to work.

The social science interest in work and leisure is in their inter-relationship as two spheres of society and of individuals' lives. One debate is summed up as 'fusion' versus 'polarity' − are work and leisure becoming more alike, or more clearly demarcated from each other? Are there leisure-like elements in the work which people do, and to what extent do they choose to engage in work-like activities during their free time? Answers to these questions can be found as a result of research within a framework of sociological theory, though relatively little such research has so far been carried out. Sociologists and social psychologists are also interested in other facets of the work-leisure relationship, notably the functions served by various forms of leisure in the lives of individuals in different circumstances or with different needs.

Let us try to draw some of the strands of the three debates together by noting some points on a more individual level. Leisure, in the modern sense, emerged in Western society where men have traditionally been committed to work. They created leisure without intending to, and must now find ways of living easily with it. There are several types of answer to the question of what to do with free time, and contemporary society provides the means (more or less) for individuals to pursue the leisure path of their choice. One way is to 'buy a good time', to let the leisure industries supply you with entertainment, diversion, or excitement. The connection with work is here twofold: to get the money to pay for fun one must normally earn it, and to enjoy it to the full one must feel that it really is different from the *workaday* world.

A second answer to the problem of what to do with leisure is to spend it with the family − to become 'privatized' (which has a negative connotation of withdrawing from the world outside) or to 'break down role segregation' (which has a more positive meaning of husband and wife spending leisure time together as equal partners). Work intrudes into this answer, too, in the form of do-it-yourself, drive-it-yourself, and dig-it-yourself. Perhaps watching television is now the most popular leisure pastime because it combines two very powerful ingredients: the purchase of a good, relaxing time yet within the context of home and family.

But there is a third answer to the problem of what to do with leisure — an answer which, paradoxically, is often made by people who claim to have no time for leisure. It can be used for 'creative' or 'active' pursuits of one kind or another. Again, work is lurking behind this answer, in at least two guises. The first is that creative leisure is frequently associated with voluntarily assumed duties or commitments. Thus one can join an 'issue' organization or engage in a wide range of social or civic activities in one's spare time and find that, though freely chosen, these involve a lot of hard work. The second guise in which work features in leisure is with active pursuits. These are often devoted to the production of an amateur 'work' of some kind. Examples of music, drama and the arts spring most readily to mind, but the 'work' may also be in other fields such as sport or hobbies. A good round of golf or a prize collection of something or other may be the very satisfying end product of active leisure.

It may seem to the reader that the argument so far is tantamount to what might be called a 'work' theory of leisure. This is not intended. The treatment of leisure in this part of the volume *is* in the context of work, but it aims to probe the complex relations between the two spheres and the paradoxes to which these relations sometimes give rise, rather than to offer an explanation of leisure *in terms of* work. Leisure may, as is often claimed, be the child of work (or, more particularly, of our industrial system), but the child has now grown up. The general theme of the chapters which follow is that there is still quite a degree of family resemblance — and a curious kind of ageless generation gap — between leisure and work.

Much of the theorizing about the nature of the relationships between leisure and work — and much of the small amount of empirical work that has been done in this field — has been based on the assumption that there can be discerned *patterns* of such relationships, made up of the typical work-leisure behaviour and attitudes of people in similar circumstances. This is an example of the interplay between theory and research which characterizes the growth of social science generally, though there is every reason to be cautious and tentative about the progress that has so far been made in the field under consideration. As a result of an extensive survey of the literature and of his own fieldwork, Stanley Parker suggests that there are three main patterns, which he calls extension, opposition and neutrality. Extension is when at least some leisure activities are similar to work and when no sharp demarcation is made between work and leisure. Opposition denotes a deliberate choice of leisure activities different from those of work and a rigid separation of the two spheres. Neutrality, although in some ways a middling pattern between the first two, is characterized by detachment from, and lack of involvement in, both work and leisure.

One or more of these hypothesized patterns are apparent in the leisure behaviour of groups of people examined in the following chapters. James Mott's study of the role that pigeon racing plays in the lives of miners and weavers shows that it can perform different functions for, and be related in different ways to, the working lives of people in various occupations. With miners the keeping of pigeons seems more often to be a kind of oppositional compensation for the repression of human potentialities in mine work. With weavers, however, it is more a matter of extending the skill and industry of the work into a leisure activity 'grateful and natural to their tastes and habitudes'. In their study of the occupational culture of ship-building workers, Richard Brown and his colleagues point to a way of life in which leisure can extend into the world of work. Some of the leisure activities of these workers take place in work time and in a work location, and the authors show that the opportunity for such leisure is inherent in the work processes of the shipyard. There is a pattern of social contacts in the work situation, and these contacts result in sociable groupings that retain identities over time and constitute an important element in work satisfaction. Finally, we have a comparative view of the leisure of British and American managers which suggests that the former are generally closer to a 'neutrality' pattern and the latter to an 'extension' pattern. John Child and Brenda Macmillan compare the typical British manager, who prefers to compartmentalize his life so that the job is forgotten during leisure time, with the typical American manager, whose leisure time (such as it is) is infused by considerations relating to his work, which represents his dominant interest in life.

Although these attempts to describe the work and leisure patterns of occupational groups in the context of theoretical considerations are perceptive and thought-provoking, they raise certain questions about our present state of understanding. Ignoring for the moment the 'neutrality' hypothesis that work and leisure can have, as it were, lives of their own, we can see that most of the 'explanations' which have been offered for the work-leisure relationships found have been after the event rather than predictive in the scientific sense. This applies particularly to what are often called the 'spillover' and 'compensatory' hypotheses. For example, if we find isolation at work associated with solitary leisure patterns this can be explained as resulting from a style of work behaviour spilling over into non-work settings. If, on the other hand, we find the same isolation at work associated with a high degree of sociability in leisure, we can 'account' for this by compensation. To make further progress we may need, as Kando and Summers suggest, to make a systematic distinction between the form and meaning of both work and leisure (1). By taking into account the fact that the same work or leisure activity may have *different* meanings to people, and that different forms of work or leisure may have essentially *the same* meaning, we may be able to reach a better understanding of this extremely subtle relationship.

The opening chapter by Parker takes up the theme of work-leisure relationships at the individual level, and goes on to describe two contrasting models of society and the policies for work and leisure which flow from these models. The segmentalist view is that the lives of individuals and the spheres of society are segmented, and that social policies should deal with the problems of work and leisure separately. The holist view (favoured by the author) is that society is essentially an integrated whole and that therefore long-term, integrated policies for work and leisure are needed. Parker anticipates, in relation to work and leisure, some of the questions of planning and education which will be discussed more fully in relation to leisure itself later in this volume. The ways in which sociologists can influence policy makers are discussed, and it is suggested that the central problem is not one of maximizing work values or leisure values but of integrating the two. The question is not whether leisure is 'free' or 'engineered'; it is more a matter of which agency does the engineering and with what motives. Collective intervention may be necessary to encourage people to develop their potentialities in work *and* leisure, but whether they take advantage of the opportunities offered should remain their own choice.

The ways in which pigeon racing can be linked both historically and currently to particular occupational sub-cultures are central concerns in the chapter by Mott. Weavers and miners are the main groups traditionally associated with pigeon racing. Mott's analysis leans heavily, though not exclusively, on a piece of research carried out by French sociologists in a mining area. This research provides a sensitive analysis of the various types of compensation offered by pigeon racing. In his chosen leisure pursuit the miner can be autonomous and responsible — 'he plans and calculates, he acquires complete knowledge of a complex question'. He can participate in the organizational side of the sport, being on committees and helping to formulate rules in a sociable atmosphere. And he has the chance of winning fame through competitive success, either as an individual or for his group as a whole. The author concludes with a comparison of the French with the English pigeon racing scene, and he notes the shift of the sport in England away from the textile and mining areas and towards the middle classes and 'new working class'.

In their study of shipbuilding workers, Brown and his colleagues first note home- and family-based activities predominate in the leisure of these workers. But some of their leisure activities take place in work time. Very often the social meeting places at work are more fixed and permanent than the places in the yard where the work is actually done.

These sociable groups have common interests in recreational and sexual activities. The authors maintain that these and other leisure-like group activities are part of a set of social relations which extend much beyond what is necessary to do the job — they provide an essential element in the occupational culture. Shipyard workers talk about their 'leisure-at-work' and this has become an important foundation for wider loyalties to trade groups and the unions that represent them. As leisure taking at work comes less and less to be regarded as illicit and improper, it may be part of a move away from rational-bureaucratic work values and towards a rival system of values based on defiance of restriction, leisure taking and camaraderie.

In the final chapter Child and Macmillan take a comparative look at the leisure of managers in Britain and other countries, notably America. They examine three aspects: the amount of leisure taken by managers, the content of this leisure (particularly as it relates to work interests), and the subjective meaning of the leisure activities to managers. Unlike their American counterparts, few British managers appear to devote an appreciable part of their leisure time to activities that in any way directly further their work and career. The authors consider the implications of the prediction that within twelve years many British managers are likely to find themselves working for American-controlled corporations. Such managers may face a personal conflict between two value-systems: to opt out of the more rewarding and demanding levels of managerial employment, or to meet American expectations and possibly face domestic strains and conflict as a result.

Reference
1 T. M. Kando and W. C. Summers, 'The Impact of Work on Leisure', *Pacific Sociological Review*, July 1971.

5 Relations between work and leisure

Stanley Parker

To consider every facet of the relationship between work and leisure would take much longer than one chapter. Here I propose to restrict the discussion to three topics: (a) the different ways in which work and leisure are related in the lives of individuals, (b) alternative policies for work and leisure based on different philosophies concerning the relationship of life spheres, and (c) the role of planning and education in helping to realize human potentialities in work *and* leisure.

Types of work–leisure relationship

First, there is work that still provides an occasion for primary self-identification and self-commitment of the individual – for his 'fulfilment', if one prefers. *Thirdly*, there is work that is apprehended as a direct threat to self-identification, an indignity, an oppression. And secondly, between these two poles, is work that is *neither* fulfilment nor oppression, a sort of grey, neutral region in which one neither rejoices nor suffers, but with which one puts up with more or less grace for the sake of other things that are supposed to be important (1).

Or, to summarize Peter Berger's remarks, there are three types of work: fulfilling, damaging and boring. Drawing on accumulated research findings in this field, plus my own studies of the work and leisure patterns of various occupational groups, I shall outline three proposed patterns: extension, opposition and neutrality. But I would stress that these are only the first few faltering steps towards an adequate theory of work-leisure relationships.

Some fortunate people have jobs from which they derive a high degree of satisfaction, which give them freedom to make their own decisions, the chance to use their abilities fully, and the feeling that they are expressing themselves in the work rather than just earning money. Such people tend to have leisure activities which are often similar to their working activities – they find work pleasurable and absorbing, and are willing, even eager, to devote at least some of their own time to the same sort of thing. Thus a social worker will often do voluntary work in the same field as his paid duties, or a chemist may experiment with fertilizers and fungicides to change the colours of flowers in his garden. Such people make no sharp distinction between what they consider work and what they consider leisure — indeed, they may claim that they simply do not see their lives as divided in this way.

For people in absorbing and creative jobs it is probable that work will be a more central interest in their lives than either leisure or family life. In saying that work for them is the centre of life, they will not necessarily be denying the integrated role that leisure plays in it. This is because work, to someone who sees a continuity between work and leisure, is a much more embracing concept that just 'the job' or even 'the occupation'. Also, because of deep involvement in their kind of work, it leaves a relatively great imprint on the rest of their lives — it is often an influence from which they are never really free.

In sharp contrast to people with the 'extension' pattern, others have jobs from which they derive little or no satisfaction, jobs in which other people make all the decisions, in which they use only a narrow range of their abilities, and which they experience as a kind of 'forced labour' imposed on them by the need to earn a living. Such people usually want in their leisure to forget anything even remotely connected with their jobs. But paradoxically they may not in one sense get away from work at all: so deeply are they marked by the hated experience of work that they measure the delights of leisure according to how much unlike work they are. For example, an unskilled factory worker or a distant-water fisherman may seek 'explosive compensation' for the physically or psychologically damaging work he does in wild and exaggerated leisure activities.

People in these kinds of jobs often have a love-hate attitude to work. They may hate it because of the feeling of oppression it gives them, but love it because they are fascinated by its arduousness or by its dangers (it is 'real man's work'). If work is viewed with unmixed hatred then presumably some aspect of non-work is seen as the centre of life. But if there is a love-hate relationship to work then either work or leisure could be seen as central, or perhaps the very opposition and dissimilarity of the spheres makes comparative judgement impossible.

Thirdly, there are the neutral jobs, bringing 'neither fulfilment nor oppression' — jobs which are experienced as vaguely 'all right' rather than either definitely satisfying or dissatisfying, and in which the involvement is calculative (experienced as a transaction to earn a living) rather than moral or alienative (2). As with 'opposition' pattern, people in neutral jobs tend to have little freedom to make their own decisions and to use few of their abilities in the work. In some ways the pattern of neutrality appears to be a kind of watered-down opposition. Thus work and leisure activities are 'usually different' rather than 'intention-ally different'. But the neutrality pattern is *not* intermediate between those of extension and opposition.

The crucial difference between extension and opposition on the one hand, and neutrality on the other, is that the first two denote respectively a positive and negative affective *attachment* to work, while neutrality denotes a *detachment* from work. In the first two cases the imprint left by work on leisure is relatively marked, in either a positive or negative way. But people showing the neutrality pattern are neither so engrossed in their work that they want to carry it over into non-work nor so damaged by it that they develop a hostile or love-hate relationship to it. Instead, work leaves them comparatively unmarked and free to carry over into leisure the non-involvement and passivity which characterizes their attitude to work. In other words, detachment from any real responsibility for and interest in work is matched by detachment from any active and constructive leisure pursuits – the tendency is to sit back and wait to be entertained.

These three patterns of work-leisure relationship are offered as systematic explanations of differences found in the work and leisure behaviour and attitudes of individuals and groups. But they should be thought of as tendencies and probabilities rather than as rigid categories. A given individual's behaviour and attitudes may generally correspond to one of the patterns but in some respects be more like one of the other patterns. Thus a social worker may fight against too much extension of work into leisure by deliberately choosing some 'oppositional' leisure activities; and exceptional individuals may combine neutral work with a rich and creative leisure life. Elsewhere the probable implications of these patterns for other work variables and for non-work variables such as educational level, duration and main function of leisure are discussed (3). To some extent, analysis of this kind enables us to understand social behaviour more fully. But it also connects with a wider analysis having policy implications, to which we now turn.

Alternative policies for work and leisure

Below I shall now consider two contrasting social policies for dealing with problems of work and leisure. These policies are based on alternative models or views of society. One view – sometimes referred to as atomistic but perhaps more accurately described as *segmentalist* – holds that people's lives are split into different areas of activity and interest, with each social segment lived out more or less independently from the rest. Work is said to be separated from leisure, production from consumption, workplace from residence, education from religion, politics from recreation, and so on. The second view – a *holist* one – maintains that society is essentially an integrated whole, every part of which affects and is affected to some degree by every other part. Attitudes and practices developed in one sphere of life, it is said, can spill over into another — thus killing time at work can become killing time in leisure.

Our choice between these two schools of thought has important implications for the kind of policies that we support with regard to work and leisure. Alternative philosophies lead on to the proposal of qualitatively different solutions to problems. The choice has significance both for leisure and for work. In the field of leisure, planning for the allocation of scarce resources — and to some extent the *creation* of resources — is determined by the general philosophy we have of leisure in relation to work. Also, the priorities we give to man as producer and man as consumer are bound up with our view of work in relation to leisure.

It is possible to examine the segmentalist proposals for work and leisure in relative isolation from each other, although it may be useful to distinguish the 'neutrality' from the 'opposition' approach. As a starting point we may consider the three 'solutions to the problem of stultifying labour' outlined by Wilensky:

1 develop patterns of creative, challenging leisure to compensate for an inevitable spread in dehumanized labour;
2 offer vastly better compensation to those condemned to alienating work situations (the trade-union solution of more money for less working-time . . .);
3 redesign the workplace and the technology to invest work with more meaning, and hence enhance the quality of leisure (4).

Although the first solution includes the word 'compensation', and to that extent implies a recognition of some kind of relationship between work and leisure, it suggests that 'dehumanized' labour can be tolerated if it is kept separate from a creative, challenging leisure. The second solution is a more straightforward acceptance that leisure is the opposite of work. The difference between these two segmentalist solutions may be expressed as the collective voice of society making two compensatory propositions to those whose work it recognizes to be intrinsically unpleasant or unsatisfying: (a) 'We know it's boring, but put up with it and we shall make it up to you in leisure', or (b) 'We know it's damaging, but you need only do it for a short time and we shall pay you well for it'. Only the third solution is an example of holist thinking (to be considered below).

The reasons for the greater popularity of segmentalist solutions to problems of work are not hard to find. They have the obvious merit of being applicable on a small scale and do not require the amount of research and education of public opinion that would be entailed in holist solutions. Segmentalist solutions aim at limited goals which are therefore more easily achieved, and their programmes tend to flow from obvious rather than imaginative comparisons. Thus the goal that workers usually set themselves (or that is set for them by their representatives) is to obtain the best possible income and working conditions which any comparable group of workers has achieved. The 'differentials' are the subject of much concern, but they are *actual* differentials between groups of workers – not the differential between present conditions and potential ones given a possible re-structuring of society and its values.

The segmentalist approach to leisure is parallel with the approach to work. Since the influence on leisure of other spheres of life is discounted, attempts are made to change it as a more or less self-contained sphere. The aim to 'develop patterns of creative, challenging leisure' does not depend on the individual bringing to it values and experiences gained in other spheres of life, and so the question of *how* these new patterns of leisure are to be developed becomes important. In a society in which the provision of leisure goods and services has become a major industry, there is no great problem of access to the means of spending leisure time, assuming that one has also money to spend. For the segmentalist, a greater problem may be how to encourage people to spend their leisure time in ways which are socially or at least subculturally acceptable, because segmentalism rarely extends to a complete unconcern with the effects on society (or, for that matter, on the individual) of 'undesirable' activities.

In contrast to the kind of policies considered above, *holist* policies are concerned with the patterning of society as a whole. Although they may embody specific proposals for dealing with work or leisure problems, they do so within a framework of thought that recognizes the interdependence of spheres. Indeed, their advocates may go further in suggesting that part of the problem may lie in the very split between spheres, and, unlike the advocates of segmentalism, may point to the costs rather than the gains to the individual of such a split. Inevitably their policies are longer-term than segmentalist ones, since they involve wider repercussions on established standards of behaviour and values. In their effect on the social structure they are revolutionary rather than reformist, and hence are open to the pros and cons that are generally put forward in connection with these alternative ways of changing society.

Most holist policies for dealing with work and leisure have a basis in work, since those who put them forward tend to share Dumazedier's view that 'leisure is itself a creation of our industrial system.' (5) With this proviso, concepts that apply to both work and leisure spheres have a special value to holist policies. One such concept is the 'productive orientation' put forward by Fromm (6). This refers to the active and creative relatedness of man to his fellow man, to himself and to nature, and is expressed in the realms of thought, feeling and action. The productive orientation is set against both the exploitative and hoarding orientation (the exploitation of man by man and the pleasure in possession and property, dominant in the nineteenth century) and the receptive and marketing orientation (the passive 'drinking in' of commodities and the experience of oneself as a thing to be employed successfully on the market, dominant today). The receptive and marketing orientation sums up a situation of alienation from both work and leisure. By contrast, the productive orientation sums up a situation in which people *participate* in what they do, whether it is called work or leisure. Such an orientation is implicit in Harrington's belief that 'there could be a new kind of leisure and a new kind of work, or more precisely, a range of activities that would partake of the nature of both leisure and work' (7).

A number of writers have suggested that one of the chief barriers to a closer integration of work and leisure is the preoccupation of our society with production at the expense of other values, and the individual preference for more income at the expense of more leisure time. The economist Alan Day has pointed out that much the greater part of the benefit of rising productivity has been taken out in the form of more money to buy more goods, and very little in the form of increased leisure through shorter working hours (8). Bearing in mind the growth of hire purchase and the power of the mass media to stimulate wants which need higher incomes to satisfy them, there is no reason to look for an early reversal of this trend. Also, many workers in America who lack definite ideas about what to do with increased leisure time seem to prefer the same number of working days rather than more days in which they are expected by their wives to do small tasks around the home. Day notes that some of the benefits of automation and mechanization are now enjoyed not in the form of higher productivity but of more pleasant working conditions. Easing off on the job so as to have more time for a smoke or a gossip may constitute a 'restrictive practice' from a purely economic point of view but may, from the worker's point of view, be a reduction in the split between work (which is something unpleasant and has to be tolerated) and leisure (which is isolated and pleasurable).

What do holist policies imply for the actual content and conditions of work and leisure? Apart from deliberately introducing leisure-like experiences into the working day (thereby somewhat blurring the distinction between work and leisure), certain policies with regard to management are also relevant. After pointing out that work and leisure in our society are antagonistic and that leisure is largely an escape from the unfree, irresponsible work situation, Gillespie advocates shared responsibility in and for work and democratic participation: '... if shared responsibility of a reasonable and economically effective kind can be initiated in work; the problem of leisure will be less acute for, instead of leisure activity being a substitute for work, it will complement work activity' (9). Giving people greater autonomy in their work should help in this process, since this is a feature of jobs that has been shown to be associated with a tendency to have a pattern of life in which work interests extend into leisure time.

It is possible to approach the twin problems of work and leisure from the angle of leisure as well as from that of work. Instead of starting with concepts such as the 'productive orientation' or 'shared responsibilities', which stem mainly from work, we can inquire what is the optimum role of leisure in life and society and then seek to integrate this with other spheres, including work. Leisure as the opposite of work, that is, leisure as comfort, passivity, and general absence of effort is not reconcilable with work, but leisure as interest, pleasurable activity, and a general sense of creative self-expression can be seen as continuous with some aspects of work. Our aim can thus include the growth of leisure time in which to do the work we wish (10). The integration of work and leisure means more than just introducing a few bits of leisure-like activity into certain restricted parts of the working day − it means a whole new pattern of daily activities.

Planning and education for work and leisure

If the realization of human potentialities in work and leisure is to be pursued as a social aim, there arises the question of how the relevant policies may be shaped and administered and what part sociologists can play in this. It is true, as Bressler points out, that 'sociologists *qua* sociologists have no special gifts as definers of public welfare' (11). However, this does not mean that sociological theory and research has nothing to contribute to policy making. Within industry sociologists can convey to management, unions and employees the results and conclusions of investigations into the effects on workers' attitudes of variables in the work situation such as authority structure, type of technology and style of supervision. Those in a position to initiate or press for changes in such variables may do so in the reasonable expectation that corresponding changes in attitudes will be likely to result. In the realm of leisure, sociologists can obtain and convey information to both the consumers and the providers of leisure goods and services concerning the needs of people in various situations and the factors which have combined to produce these needs. Even more importantly, sociologists can join with psychologists, philosophers, historians, administrators and others in making the general public aware of the possibilities of *social* development that technological development is opening up. The special 'publics' of students and organized workers are showing increasing militancy in seeking some degree of control over their educational and working lives. These campaigns may be seen as the spearhead of a wider movement towards a type of society which not only allows but encourages democratic participation by all its members.

Any programme for the realization of human potentialities must be based on the satisfaction of need, but the concept of need may be interpreted in various ways. We may posit a hierarchy of needs from the purely physiological to the most socially determined (12). Some needs are basic to life itself and their satisfaction occupies an irreducible minimum of any individual's time budget. At the other end of the scale are needs which are least basic to life itself but are said most fully to express the character of civilized man. Just as individual man has to satisfy his basic needs before he can concern himself with 'higher things', so society has first to meet the basic needs of all its members before it can provide leisure to even a section of them. But to see a straight-line progression from all labour (distinguished both from work and leisure, in Arendt's sense (13)) to all leisure is to distort the picture. The weight of historical, anthropological and contemporary empirical evidence is that, whatever their expressed desires, men in all societies *need* to have work as well as leisure. Further, in cases where their work embodies many of the values normally associated with leisure, a separate period of time labelled leisure appears to be necessary neither to their own happiness nor to their creative function in society.

The central problem, then, is not one of maximizing some values (i.e. those associated with leisure) and minimizing others (associated with work) but of achieving an integration of both sets of values. Integration of another kind is also necessary: that between the needs of individuals and those of society. It is this latter kind of integration that causes the most problems to those concerned with planning for work and leisure, since it is only in a metaphorical sense that society has 'needs' apart from those of its individual members. Neither the needs for work nor for leisure are easy to determine on a societal scale, and the latter are particularly difficult. It is fairly easy to see what kinds of work are consonant with expressive needs, because the kinds of work that are not are undertaken only instrumentally. But with leisure there is no such criterion to employ − it is *all* supposed to be expressive.

Willener writes that 'true leisure ought to be free, "natural", it cannot be engineered' (14). This is the *laissez-faire* doctrine of leisure as free time, ostensibly undetermined by anyone other than the leisure user himself but in fact quite markedly mediated by various social influences, for example, those of the mass media and of advertisers. It is true that the person who is sufficiently self-contained may resist these influences and, provided he has resources developed in other spheres of life, may create for himself an autonomous leisure. But for the mass of people who play no greater part in determining the conditions of their leisure than tney play in determining the conditions of their work, the choice is not between having the use of leisure engineered or not engineered; it is between having it engineered by various agencies, with various degrees of persuasive power and with various motives of those doing the persuading. At present we appear to be content to let the provision of leisure facilities, and even the very ideas about how leisure should be spent, be guided by a kind of 'invisible hand', which produces results in the leisure field comparable to those produced by the same *laissez-faire* doctrine in the industrial field.

There is surely a parallel to be drawn between planning in the industrial sphere and planning in the leisure sphere. The recognition that complete *laissez-faire* is not the best way to reconcile supply and demand, even within a market economy, led to the intervention of the state and its increasingly important role as supreme planner. However, in Western countries the role of the state is limited, and decisions at a lower level than those of national policy are left in the hands of individuals or groups, though these decisions are to a large extent shaped by the interplay of economic factors and not by individual will. The parallel with leisure lies in the possibility of state, or other, collective intervention in decisions which affect the facilities provided for leisure, but in such a way that individual autonomy and development is promoted rather than diminished. Most people would agree that we should not try to direct people's energies into channels specified in advance. We should rather aim to nourish the individual's potentialities so that each, according to his capacity, can find his own solution.

The key institution in this process of collective planning for individual development is that of education. The idea has recently been gaining ground that the schools should teach leisure subjects to young people who are probably going into kinds of work that they will not make their central life interest. Faunce predicts, as one of the social consequences of automation, that 'in the long run the primary responsibility of the schools may well become that of instilling certain kinds of values and interests which permit the creative use of leisure and, in general, the teaching not of vocational but of leisure skills' (15). This is an example of the segmentalist approach, though if the subjects are taught in such a way that they generate needs and values which react on what is expected from and achieved in work it can be valuable. More importantly, from a holist point of view there is the possibility of teaching subjects in such a way that they are instrumental neither to work nor to leisure but are expressive in both spheres.

Conclusion

It may be helpful to recapitulate and draw together the main points made in this chapter. Research suggests that there are three different ways in which work and leisure may be related in the lives of individuals – extension, opposition and neutrality – though these should be thought of as tendencies rather than rigid categories. The choice between two main schools of thought about the relation of life spheres in urban-industrial society is important and connects with individual work-leisure patterns. Segmentalists will want to tackle the problems of work and leisure in relative isolation from each other, on the assumption that differentiation of spheres makes this possible; holists will want to pursue a more difficult and longer-term policy of integration, on the assumption that the interdependence of spheres makes this necessary. So far as planning is concerned, any specific changes in the content, organization and environment of work and leisure will depend for their success on accompanying changes in the relevant social values. The key institution in any process of revaluation, and hence of individual development, is that of education, both in the schools and in adult life.

Despite more active policies of planning and education, it may be that some people will still choose to invest relatively little of themselves in their work and may see it only as a means of enjoying leisure. But at least the options will have been open. Collective action to achieve, beyond better pay and conditions, more rewarding work for all would reinforce the process of critical evaluation started in the schools. In the field of leisure provision, people would be treated more as participants than as consumers, though passive entertainment will no doubt continue to be needed and supplied. The important thing is to make opportunities for rewarding work and for the various kinds of leisure that complement rewarding work. The extent to which advantage is taken of such opportunities must, of course, remain the choice of the individual.

Notes and References

1 P. L. Berger, *The Human Shape of Work,* New York, Macmillan, 1964, pp. 218-19.

2 cf. A. Etzioni, *A Comparative Analysis of Complex Organizations,* Glencoe, Free Press, 1961, pp. 9-11.

3 S. R. Parker, *The Future of Work and Leisure,* MacGibbon and Kee, 1971, especially chapter 8.

4 H. L. Wilensky, 'Work, Careers, and Social Integration', *International Social Science Journal,* no. 4, 1960, p. 546.

5 J. Dumazedier, *Toward a Society of Leisure,* Collier-Macmillan, 1967, p. 33.

6 E. Fromm, *The Sane Society,* Routledge, 1956, pp. 32, 361.

7 M. Harrington, *The Accidental Century,* Weidenfeld and Nicolson, 1966, p. 264.

8 A. Day, 'Leisure for Living', *Observer,* 17 May 1964. But in America workers 'determinedly chose, and collectively bargained for, more time away from the job'. (G. Soule, *What Automation Does to Human Beings,* Sidgwick, 1956, p. 94.)

9 J. J. Gillespie, *Free Expression in Industry,* Pilot Press, 1948, p. 14.

10 A. Comfort, *Nature and Human Nature,* Weidenfeld and Nicolson, 1966.

11 M. Bressler, 'Some Selected Aspects of American Sociology, Sept. 1959 to Dec. 1960', *Annals of the American Academy of Political and Social Science,* September 1961.

12 This is similar to the hierarchy of needs suggested by A. H. Maslow (*Motivation and Personality,* New York, Harper, 1954, ch. 5), except that the progression from satisfaction of lower to higher needs may be seen more clearly as a function of varying degrees of interaction between individuals and social influences, rather than as a function of personality development.

13 H. Arendt, *The Human Condition,* Chicago University Press, 1958.

14 A. Willener, 'French Sociology and the Problem of Social Engineering', paper presented to the British Sociological Association Conference, London, 1967.

15 W. A. Faunce, 'Automation and Leisure', in H. B. Jacobson and J. S. Roucek (eds.), *Automation and Society,* New York, Philosophical Library, 1959, p. 305.

6 Miners, weavers and pigeon racing

James Mott

Pigeon racing and breeding has been until fairly recently a very clearly defined pursuit in social terms, and is therefore an especially rewarding field of inquiry for the sociologist of leisure and the historian of popular recreations. In this chapter I shall briefly discuss the influence of industrialization on popular amusements including pigeon racing, look at its practice in two specific occupational milieux – weaving and mining – and conclude with an account of the organization of the sport in Britain and its place in popular culture.

The rural basis of the sports and amusements of the factory workers was evident until well after the 1830s, although by this time many of these same pursuits were more strongly established in urban areas than in the countryside itself. The relationship of pigeon racing to these social and economic changes is very clear, as the sport depends on a high degree of concentration of population combined with some mobility, and the extinction of the Lord of the Manor's exclusive rights over pigeons.

Although the more vicious amusements had become less widespread by the 1830s, they survived as occasional brutalities in most areas. In fact their survival into the 1880s can be linked to the depression and the emergence of unemployment as an alternative to short-time working. These more brutal amusements included cock fights and cock shies (throwing billets at a tethered cock), dog fights, Lancashire purring (kicking fights in clogs), badger baiting, hare coursing and boxing. Among the more gentle amusements attracting very strong followings as the century advanced were whippet racing, fishing, bowling and pigeon racing. And they gained support in mining villages, among navvies on the railway works, and in the semi-rural industrial areas of 'overgrown villages', rather than in the great urban manufacturing centres.

Pigeon racing itself has two distinct histories: short-distance racing, intensely communal, disreputable and associated with gambling, which virtually perished in the last war; and long-distance racing, intensely competitive, national and very respectable. The latter emerged towards the end of the last century and has increased its strength ever since. Virtually all pigeon racers also breed birds in the attempt to create a champion strain, and the racing and breeding together constitute the activity under discussion. However, the breeding and exhibiting of fancy pigeons, for the sake of their forms, colours and patterns of flight, is very much a separate activity, bearing no relation to pigeon racing today. In the past carrier pigeons were bred for exhibition purposes, and the bird was considered to be the king of the fancy pigeons.

In Belgium long-distance pigeon racing emerged at the beginning of the last century as the major national pastime, calling forth the same reactions that horse racing did in this country, and being intensely pursued by all classes and occupations. In France and Germany the sport attracted the devotion of the miners, while in England a more representative cross-section of the manufacturing population was originally drawn to it. In Belgium the *petite bourgeoisie* played a large part in developing the sport and pigeons are still kept in lofts above factories and workshops today. These historical differences in occupational and class support for the pursuit remain essentially mysterious.

In Britain the training of fast and reliable long-distance pigeons was closely bound up with transport, commerce and finance. The owners of stage-coach and (later) railway companies were well placed to train birds over long distances, and did so. Bankers, like Rothschild, maintained large and well-staffed lofts, and pigeons flew in relays from the commercial centres of Europe with early news vital to stockjobbing. They followed the route: Calais, Dover, Sittingbourne, Blackheath, the City (1).

It was through pigeons that Rothschilds benefited greatly from the fluctuations in Spanish funds in 1825. They were used by newspapers to get the results of horse races round London until the 1860s and were, of course, vital to military intelligence throughout Europe. Most governments centralized the control of pigeons for this reason, and introduced subsidies for citizens who bred reliable pigeons. This system spread, and in the 1880s, for instance, Hanoi was building up a centralized system of military lofts. Similarly the birds were used by the Customs to catch smugglers, and all south-eastern sea ports held large concentrations of pigeons.

With the development of the electric telegraph the commercial lofts declined; the birds came on to the open market and so fell into the hands of amateurs. In fact it was this expansion of the electric telegraph and the railways that made training for long-distance flights possible on a large scale. Before the railways Gravesend was an important place for pigeon tossing because of the easy passage down the Thames for East Enders and others.

The weavers
We have the evidence which enables us to link the birds to specific

trades, mainly colliers and weavers. But this also applies to dockers, printers and the Billingsgate porters, who by virtue of their contacts with Dutch fishermen were one of the first groups to import 'Antwerps' into the country (Antwerps or 'Twerps being the correct name of the long-distance homing pigeon) (2). Printers and dockers may have originally inherited the sport from their neighbours in the East End of London, the Spitalfields weavers and, as mentioned above, all newspapers kept pigeons.

Huguenot weavers in Spitalfields, and later Bethnal Green and neighbouring districts, formed a metropolitan base for pigeon racing, which complemented its support in the semi-rural industrial areas and mining villages. Weavers all over the country supported learned societies, musical activities and horticultural organizations until well into the 1830s. By then the severe depression of their living standards had begun to destroy this way of life. The Assistant Commissioners for the Hand Loom Weavers, in their report on the Spitalfields weavers of 1840, point out that they could no longer afford to keep their birds in the bad conditions of trade. Nor were they able to keep up their allotments and summer houses on the northern outskirts of the city.

Henry Mayhew commented on this connection between an occupational milieu and the pursuits associated with it.

> The fondness of a whole body of artificers for any particular bird, animal or flower is remarkable. No better instance need be cited than that of the Spitalfields weavers. In the days of their prosperity they were the cultivators of choice tulips, afterwards, though not in so full a degree, of dahlias, and their pigeons were the best 'fliers' in England. These things were accomplished with little cost, comparatively, for the weavers were engaged in tasks, grateful and natural to their tastes and habitudes . . . the exercise of skill and industry. To such things the Spitalfields man did not devote his time but his leisure (3).

Mayhew observed in the 1840s that the bird lover was a more domestic, prosperous and contented man, and that the bird trades had a refining influence. But the dog lover was more away from home, which he neglected, and was more likely to be a slaughterer, drover or coachman. With the silk weavers, Mayhew says, 'it was all flowers and birds'. And Mayhew credits these weavers and other operatives with humanizing the popular culture, brutalized by the upper classes, and he dwells on the thought of 'a man going home from . . . an examination to satisfy himself that his birds were "all right" ', in contrast to the man interested in rat hunts (4).

By the end of the century the pursuits of the weavers had spread more widely through the East End, and Booth gives us a less favourable description of the crowded geniality and criminal ambience of the Sunday morning bird fair in Sclater Street, Bethnal Green. In the 1930s the New London Survey found 11,000 racing pigeon fanciers in Greater London attached to the Homing Pigeon Union (i.e. long-distance racers), belonging to all social classes. 'Working men home their pigeons in sugar boxes, and race them from small lofts in their backyards.' (5)

In 1946 Ruth Glass found that the recreations of the Huguenots were still popular with Bethnal Greeners, and Peter Townsend, writing in the late fifties, notes an almost universal attachment to birds and flowers, mentioning, like Mayhew a hundred years before, the dahlias (6).

The miners

Around the middle of the last century pigeon flying was associated with the hard and dangerous life of the miners, lumped together with more brutal sports, and seen as a part of the Sunday riots (7). By the 1930s short-distance pigeon racing had in its turn become more organized, although at that time it was suffering from the unemployment in industrial areas, never to recover — a pattern identical to that of the Spitalfields weavers a hundred years before. This pursuit was skilled, active and cooperative, and was centred on the local pub. The club had rules and a number of offices and specialized technical roles: mappers, timers, tappers and tossers. The distance being relatively short (a few miles), the birds were separated on arrival by fractions of a second and the distances, like the times, had to be very precisely calculated. There were prizes, pools and betting on the side. This was usually for cash, but sometimes in kind: for black puddings and tripe (8). Many publicans themselves bred pigeons in mining areas.

My discussion of miners is, however, mainly based on a French study, *La Colombophilie chez les mineurs du nord*. I take *La Colombophilie* to be a germinal work for French sociology, and for the sociology of leisure, and am surprised that it is not translated and better known (9). It is interesting that French scholars have always taken popular culture very seriously, and since the eighteenth century have provided us with wonderful studies of pageants, street literature and the fairground.

La Colombophilie is based on 185 questionnaires and 56 interviews obtained in the mining area around Bruay-en-Artois. In France pigeon racing is most highly concentrated in this area, far more so than in any part of England. The authors of the study basically interpret this relationship between mining and pigeon racing in terms of *compensation* for the experience of coercive, fragmented and repetitive work in the mine. The loft provides the opportunity for quiet reflection alone; in his racing and breeding activities the miner is autonomous and responsible, he plans and calculates, he acquires complete knowledge of a complex question. In the club he participates in an organization, formulates rules, holds office and develops a means of class defence.

The poverty of the miner's work itself is offset by the many skills necessary to the successful pigeon racer: architect and carpenter, breeder, accountant, vet and psychologist. It is hard to express *bricolage* (do-it-yourself?) and *dada* (hobby-horse?) in English. Similarly, he finds compensation for his inferior social position in the mine through winning fame, as an individual or for his group as a whole. And through the range of social activities centred on the club and exhibitions he achieves a direct emotional satisfaction. Considerable sums of money can also be won, but not earned.

The guiding concept here is *revanche,* assertion of the human potentialities which have been repressed or 'bullied' in the mine. The authors of the study bring out the implications of three main themes in the involvement of the miners with pigeon racing: attachment to the loft and the birds, striving after success and involvement in exhibitions.

Some miners take great pleasure in isolating themselves in the loft, and do not participate much in the collective aspects of the sport. Others do not repudiate these collective aspects, but do spend a lot of time in the loft: they seek the calm and security which the loft offers, or some strong emotional tie to the birds as a uniquely personal possession, which may be sensual or lean to a keen appreciation of their lively and friendly nature. The less qualified or less skilled miner was more likely to turn to the loft as a refuge.

The search for fame and glory does have a highly individualistic character for some miners, especially the younger pigeon racers. They work hard at developing training methods, keep these methods secret and aim to win the money. For the older miner this striving takes on a collective character: he does not distinguish his own worth from that of his group.

Less than half the pigeon racers were interested in attending exhibitions. Those who were interested were well integrated, felt they had 'arrived', and went to the exhibitions to argue and dispute with other fanciers. Although this attendance definitely takes second place to racing, in a sense the miner who does attend the exhibitions is the complete or perfect pigeon fancier.

In the course of writing their work the authors, one of whom had raced pigeons in Bruay for many years and the other had worked in a factory for two years, develop the converse guiding theme to compensation: conditioning. The more skilled workers in the mines carry over capacities and abilities, encouraged at work, into their leisure. They have a more rational and organized approach to the whole business: *'ils bricolent pour améliorer leur pigeonnier'*. As we have seen, the less skilled seek out the security of the loft and rely on *trucs* (dodges and devices) to win, which take on the character of magic.

Historically pigeons have symbolized purity, peace, grace, fidelity, simplicity, sacrifice, guidance. We can also see them as symbols of communication, freedom, community (10) and the bearing of burdens. In *La Colombophilie* the miners spoke of their attachment to the pigeons and the qualities they looked for and found in them: faithfulness, and the sense of being chosen by the pigeon, who always returns to *me*; sagacity and adroitness in overcoming obstacles to a safe return; the sensuality of power and beauty. The return of a bird after travelling hundreds of miles is an intensely emotional moment, almost overwhelming; and there are well-authenticated accounts of this powerful emotion killing the owner. The authors of the French study argue that the intensity is only explicable in terms of the human needs which are not satisfied in daily working life.

The study at Bruay-en-Artois is completed by looking at one club, *Le Ramier du Mineur,* formed after the Liberation and having 500 members, a large majority of whom are miners. The club is very well organized and has a democratic ethos, where the overriding value is attachment to the pigeon for its own sake.

The club is the expression of a class solidarity: an essentially collective system of opposition to *le gros* (the big guy, the bosses) (11). These mining clubs may withdraw from the larger federations of clubs, and often do not attempt to make their views known in the pigeon racing world: *d'être contre* is enough. The miners are at home in this homogeneous milieu, traditionally permeated by *colombophilie,* an expression of their solidarity in the face of outsiders and injustice. The names of some of the clubs express this: Le Sans Peur. Fifty out of the 186 pigeon racers questioned associated *only* with other pigeon fanciers.

Before giving my assessment of *La Colombophilie* it is interesting to see what its authors have to say about England, which one of them (M. Louchet) visited in an effort to understand the miners' devotion to the sport.

The English pigeon racing scene puzzled M. Louchet, and I have exchanged letters with him on the subject. He argues that the French miner has his loft on top of the house or immediately to the rear of it, whereas the British miner has a loft, adjacent to many others, on an allotment site (as in Durham). Therefore, the pigeons do not constitute a 'complete world always present' or 'an important universe' for the English miner. The collectivity of lofts in the Durham area and parts of Scotland may indicate the overriding importance of the social side of the sport. But most British pigeon racers do have their lofts in the garden, although there has admittedly been a prejudice for a long time against having them in the house itself, as is common in Belgium.

The weakness of *La Colombophilie* lies in its positivistic method and associated empirical social psychology. Pigeon racing is seen in terms of a powerful linkage between work and leisure: the frustrations of work leading to the aggressive *revanche* through individual emotions (refuge, sensuality) and collective activities (the club, glory). The study has the great virtue of insisting on a social account and interpretation of the sport.

However, the brief discussion of the weavers above makes it very clear that it was precisely their autonomy, status and unchallenged solidarity that formed the basis of their successful development of the sport in Spitalfields and elsewhere (12). The concept of 'conditioning' in *La Colombophilie* alludes to this, but it is a modification of a basic situation explicable in other terms. The authors sacrificed too readily the historical, cultural and comparative approach touched on in the first part of their book.

Organization in Great Britain

The 3,000 local clubs in this country are affiliated to the Homing Unions, who enforce a rather rigorous code of conduct, and combine in the Confederation of British Homing Unions. For the purposes of organizing races in the season, the clubs get together locally in federations and combines. These are called 'North Road' or 'South Road', denoting the direction in which the pigeons are sent off in vast road transporters, with convoyers to protect the birds and tend to them. Individuals may also belong to national clubs (such as the National Flying Club with 4,000 members), which organize races with very valuable prizes.

There are about a quarter of a million pigeon racers in the United Kingdom, with some eight million birds. Below is a table of membership figures, which are approximate:

	Membership			
	1890s	1930s	1940s	1970
Welsh Homing Union	—	1,311	—	5,700
North of England Homing Union	—	4,254	—	8,643
Irish Homing Union	—	2,000	—	3,800
Royal National Homing Union	2,518	40,000	20,000	100,000

Double and triple club membership makes the figures to some extent suspect, and of course they refer only to long-distance pigeon racing, which began to be organized in this country around the middle of the last century, and clearly emerged in the 1890s. As organized and unorganized short-distance pigeon racing has almost totally disappeared, the total number of pigeon racers and owners has in fact declined. The drop in the figures for the 1940s was due to strict rationing of bird food, and a limit on the number of pigeons each owner was allowed.

The regional distribution of the membership of the R.N.H.U. considered with that of the independent Unions, shows a decline in the textile and mining areas (except Wales), indicating a shift of the sport to the middle classes and 'new working class'. It has become, in fact, rather an expensive pastime. Of course, the original organizers of the long-distance form of the sport in the last century were drawn from the middle classes.

	1,000s		1,000s
London	20	North Western	4
West Midland	17	Irish	3
East Midland	14	Westmorland & Cumberland	2
Western	10	N.W. counties	2
Derbyshire & S. Yorks	9	N.E. Lancs	2
Yorkshire & Northern	8	Welsh	1
South Western	7		

Membership is expanding yearly in all regions of the R.N.H.U. except those competing with the independent Unions, such as the North of England Homing Union. Three periodicals serve the sport today, and the leading one claims a circulation of 60,000. The *News of the World* is the only national paper to print the results of races, and the sport has lost the space it once had in the press. There is an international organization, with an Olympiad, decided through exhibition.

Prizes of £40,000 can be won in one race, with a single maximum prize of perhaps £1,500, and a champion pigeon can change hands for over £3,000. The pigeon racer can back his own pigeon in a system of pools run by the local clubs and federations. In 1953 the gross turnover of the sport was reckoned to be £10m., and British Rail were said to have lost £2m. per year when Beeching closed the branch lines and forced the pigeons to reach their release points by road.

The birds can fly at about 40 m.p.h. in windless conditions, and South Road flights may be from as far away as Barcelona. The season is from May to September, with the 'squeakers' (or young birds) flying in August and September. Prosperous pigeon racers will buy houses near to the main flight paths from the Continent, as the birds return in large groups in a general direction, branching off to individual lofts at various points.

I visited some enthusiasts, printers in the East End of London, holding a club meeting in the large upper room of a pub near Bow. Nearby a lively Pentecostal service was in progress, and two small bingo halls were open. The sound of a piano and drums came up through the floor from the bar room below, and there was a general atmosphere of gaiety as the men brought their clocks in to be synchronized and completed forms of entry. In a corner was a large trunk containing the club's cups and shields. The birds are brought in on Friday to be ringed, and visits paid on Saturday and Sunday evening as the results come in.

These men spoke of the decline of enthusiasm for short-distance racing in their youth, and were dismayed at the influence of television and commercial entertainment. They all bred their own birds, and some of the pedigrees can be clearly traced back to the 1870s. Each racer has his own 'dodges', shared with a favoured few, but they generally involve the use of such substances as salt, sulphur, linseed, quinine, and alcohol, stopping short of doping. The sexual jealousies (*veuvage*) and maternal instincts ('cheating') of the pigeons are also exploited.

Some members of the club, rehoused in tower blocks, had had to purchase shares in the lofts of those who had not been rehoused; and some councils have put a ban on pigeon racing among their tenants. Jealousy was expressed of the 'dockies' (dockers) at nearby Custom House, who could celebrate Saint Monday when weather delayed the return of the pigeons. Many of the birds in this club were registered in the name of the man and his wife, or the man and his brother, or the man and his son. This family nature of the sport and its home location is certainly compatible with the observed shift in pigeon racing to the better-paid 'privatized' worker.

Pigeon racing and popular culture

Pigeon racing was bound up with the development of industrial and metropolitan communities: I have failed to find any early description of it in a rural setting. It reflected the gentle and communal nature of English popular culture; also its private and unofficial character – its intransigence. It must be compared to the fairs and feasts which provided the break with routine in the more distant past: the opportunity to be something other than what work made one. Indeed, we find the carrier pigeon at Tyburn fair, the heart of eighteenth-century London's popular culture: 'it was the custom to let a homing pigeon loose at Tyburn at the moment the fatal cord is drawn away, to notify distant friends of the shameful exit of the unhappy criminal.' (13) The pigeon fancy was also a kind of freemasonry, with its secrets, ritual practices and strong tradition of mutual aid. Some observers have compared it to an addiction: and *La Colombophilie* shows how it provides a perpetual opportunity to dream while carrying out routine work, through a sort of anthropomorphic identification with the pigeon.

We have seen that it can be a family pursuit based on the home, rather than an all-male preserve constituting an escape from the home — the traditional picture of working-class pursuits. So there is a natural link to the life pattern of the 'privatized' worker, and those writers who still see pigeon racing as a vital expression of the working-class community as such, and a key to entering it for outsiders, may be mistaken (14). *La Colombophilie* shows that even in the conditions of solidarity which it describes there is an ambivalence in the miners' attitudes: the feeling *contre,* but also the feeling of some that they had 'arrived'.

Some nineteenth-century observers saw pigeon racing as an index of the corruption and immorality of the working classes ('the fancy'); others as an index of their amelioration and humanity; the Chartists saw it as evidence of passivity. Winston Churchill asked in 1938 'How many people know, for instance, that, even before the War, six or seven special trains left Lancashire and Newcastle every Friday, all filled with homing pigeons, to be released at distant points in elaborately-organized races?' when he wished to emphasize the width and variegation of the tastes and talents of the people (15). The rail transport has now been replaced by road, but in other respects the essence and functions of the sport remain.

Notes and References

1 *Collected Works of 'Old Hand',* vol. 1, p. 3. I have prepared an extensive social history of this branch of 'the fancy' to appear elsewhere.
2 J. M. Eaton, *A Treatise on the Art of Breeding and Managing Tame, Domesticated, Foreign and Fancy Pigeons,* 1858, p. 112.
3 Henry Mayhew, *London Labour and the London Poor,* 1865, vol. II (*London Street Folk*), 'Of the Street Sellers of Live Birds', p. 73.
4 Mayhew, op. cit., p. 74.
5 Sir Hubert Llewellyn Smith, *The New Survey of London Life and Labour,* vol. IX (*Life and Leisure*), 1935, p. 10.
6 R. Glass and M. Frenkel, *A Profile of Bethnal Green,* report no. 39, Association for Planning and Regional Reconstruction, February 1946, p. 2; Constance Harris, *The Use of Leisure in Bethnal Green,* Lindsay Press, 1927, pp. 21, 60.

7 T. C. Barker and J. R. Harris, *A Merseyside Town in the Industrial Revolution: St. Helens, 1750-1900,* Frank Cass, 1959, pp. 278, 418.

8 Mass Observation, *The Pub and the People: A Worktown Study,* Seven Dials Press, 1970 (first edition reprinted with a new preface by Tom Harrisson), p. 288.

9 J. Frisch-Gauthier and P. Louchet, *La Colombophilie chez les mineurs du nord,* Paris, C.N.R.S., 1961.

10 Some of these meanings are expressed in a poem by the Welsh poet Gwenallt: 'People were still a community, if a community of suffering, and in asserting their humanity they asserted their divinity. The pigeons released at the bottom of the gardens in the evenings after the slavery of the day,

> Circle the pillars of smoke in the sky,
> Colouring the curve of grey
> A mass of beauty amid the fog
> The shape of the holy spirit above the valley.'

(Review of Gwenallt's *Y Coed,* Llandysul, in *Times Literary Supplement,* 11 September, 1969.)

11 Class feeling comes out in the headline of a national paper when a coal-face worker from the Rhondda Valley won the pigeon championships: 'A Welsh Miner Beats the Queen'. The reference is to entries from the royal lofts near Sandringham. The idea of 'social revenge', of beating someone of superior social status and resources (*le gros*), who then (ideally) loses self-control, is very attractive to some groups of pigeon racers. Class values are expressed in the bourgeois preference for a 'working bird', to be judged by performance, rather than an exhibition bird, to be judged by appearance in the aristocratic tradition. Pigeon racers still agitate against the depredations of peregrine falcons kept by some landowners.

12 The accounts given by unskilled workers of their pleasure in the pigeons are extraordinarily similar to accounts given by the gentry in the last century. 'A solace and consolation impossible to describe . . . when nervous and tense almost to breaking point . . . a stabiliser . . . one is brought back to the norm . . . a temperer.' Rev. J. Lucas, *The Pleasures of a Pigeon-Fancier,* 1886, p. 13.

13 Daniel Girton, *The New and Complete Fancyer,* 1799, p. 133.

14 Brian Jackson, *Working Class Community,* 1968, pp. 174-5.

15 Winston Churchill, 'The Effect of Modern Amusements on Life and Character: Sport as a Stimulant in our Workaday World', *News of the World,* 4 September 1938. George Orwell makes many interesting comments on pigeon racing in *The Road to Wigan Pier* and *The Lion and the Unicorn.*

7 Leisure in work: the 'occupational culture' of shipbuilding workers[1]

Richard Brown, Peter Brannen, Jim Cousins, Michael Samphier

In sociological writing a key point of reference for the relationship of work and leisure is the idea of 'occupational community' (2). This in turn is seen as being a feature of 'traditional' workers in 'traditional' industries (3). We are critical both of the use made of these concepts themselves, and of the way they are commonly associated. We hope to show that, even in a reputed *locus classicus* of working-class traditionalism, workers are neither so 'traditional' in their leisure patterns nor so commonly members of 'occupational communities' as is usually suggested. Instead we find in the concept of an occupational or industrial culture *at work* a more satisfactory explanation of our evidence, and a more useful tool for analysing current industrial problems.

In its classical form the concept of 'occupational community' refers to the situations where those who work together also spend their leisure time together so that social relations at work are reinforced and overlaid by relations outside work. The concept also implies a degree of segregation from the outside world, the sort of situation where there is a distinct set of norms and values, a separate hierarchy of status which would not necessarily be recognized or accepted by others. Indeed 'occupational communities' are thought likely to develop where those who work in a particular industry or occupation are isolated from others either physically, as in the mining village or in dockland, or temporally, as with shiftworkers in printing or the steel industry (4).

With a high degree of segregation of the sexes in most industries, and particularly the traditional industries with which 'occupational communities' are frequently associated, sexual segregation is expected in leisure activities as well. In fact it has been suggested that the man spends his time with workmates in the pub or club, and the woman has a separate set of companions among her relatives and neighbours. When 'workmates are normally leisure-time companions, often neighbours, and not infrequently kinsmen', then a high degree of solidarity would be expected, with a common culture and an emphasis on activities which reinforce the sense of belonging. To be different is to risk censure in a situation where there is little choice available of an alternative network of social relations.

Shipbuilding has frequently been referred to as one such 'traditional' industry (5). We do not doubt that there may be a 'community' of shipbuilding workers, but it is more varied and more open to choice by its members than has normally been recognized in discussions of the 'occupational communities' outlined above. This is reflected in the variety of leisure activities undertaken by workers in this industry and in the complexity of the networks of social relations of which they are members.

The leisure-time activities of shipbuilding workers do not conform to the pattern suggested by the concept of occupational community (6). Home- and family-based activities predominate. It is true that, compared to 'affluent workers', an active gregarious social life is more common, though far from universal. But even in the life of the pubs and clubs there is an important family element of wives accompanying husbands. Nearly all the working men's clubs in the district studied had a strong family entertainment appeal: groups and concert parties for the three nights of the weekend and usually dances during the week. Masculine drinking is of course common, particularly amongst single men and the traditionally rougher but better-paid boilermaker tradesmen. Even so, drinking with workmates is not the predominant pattern of masculine drinking. Indeed drinking with workmates tends to be confined to the dinner hours or after 'half shifts' or Sunday overtime when, of course, it is a natural extension of work-place sociability.

However we do not doubt that work-place social relations form an important part of shipyard workers' lives (if only because of the long hours of overtime worked). And our interviews strongly suggest not merely a considerable density of social relations at work but also that considerable intrinsic value is placed on them. In exploring this situation we have found the concept of an 'occupational culture' to be helpful and important; shipbuilding workers do share a culture, which is made of elements from the sub-cultures of the different occupational and other groups in the shipyard and in turn contributes in important ways to the wider working-class culture (7).

The production process and technology of shipbuilding permit manipulation to allow 'unofficial' sociable relations on the job, yet that same technology operates more effectively as a result of such a pattern of friendly relations. More important than any specific activities, however, is the common culture, which can be shared by men with preferences for quite different patterns of leisure activity and social life outside the yard. This work-based culture of play, 'being one of the lads', has important consequences for work in a shipyard. With change in both the organization of shipbuilding and social relations in the wider society this culture is also changing in nature and significance.

Leisure-time activities

It is important to make a distinction between the 'time' and 'activity' dimensions of work and leisure (8). In shipbuilding leisure activities most definitely take place in work time and in ways which are significant for work activities and leisure time. Considering first the leisure-time activities of the shipbuilding workers in our sample, however, these do not fall neatly into any one stereotyped pattern. They are neither 'traditional working-class', nor 'privatized', nor 'middle-class', as these terms have been used in the literature (9). The picture we can give is not a very surprising one; a similar picture might well emerge from investigation of other working-class areas. Our data do not allow us to say whether this is the result of marked. changes in leisure activities in the area we studied nor in what direction such changes are going, if any might be taking place. So far as their spare time is concerned, however, at present shipbuilding workers appear to engage in a wide variety of activities; the pattern of these activities is not uniquely associated with their type of work.

Table 1 shows that a good deal of the spare time of these shipbuilding workers is centred on the family and the home. Many of the most frequently mentioned activities outside the home were family-centred – visiting relatives and friends, shopping, working on an allotment, family outings and so on. Activities at home, whether watching television, reading or listening to the radio, or doing jobs in the house, gardening, doing things with the children, hobbies or car maintenance, were all mentioned by considerable numbers of our respondents. In addition, of the married men a fifth normally entertained friends or relatives at home each week and two fifths once a month. Thus a 'neglect' of the home which has been suggested in some studies of 'traditional' industries is not to be found among these workers.

The Working Men's Club is nevertheless an important institution for many shipbuilding workers; visiting the club or the pub for a drink (and the conversation and so on which goes with it) is the most frequently mentioned pastime outside the home. Substantial numbers, too, are involved in sport, mostly as spectators. These are reportedly the leisure activities of the 'traditional' working class. Their importance must not be exaggerated however; only 57% of those interviewed were members of a Working Men's Club and 27% of them said that they did not go out to a pub or a club in a normal week. In contrast to most ideas about leisure activity amongst 'traditional' workers, few of these activities appear to have involved marked segregation of the sexes. Of the married men who went to the club nearly half were accompanied by their wives at least on occasions, though significantly it was a smaller proportion when visiting the pub. Otherwise with the exception of working on an

Table 1 Normal, weekly leisure-time activities of shipbuilding workers

The figures show the percentage taking part in each activity
n = number of workers interviewed

Leisure-time activities	Total n = 266	Steelworking trades n = 108	Outfitting trades n = 100	Semi-skilled n = 26	Unskilled n = 32	Those normally accompanied by n = 222
a Outside the home						
Visit pub	50	53	50	42	44	37
Visit working men's club	49	59	43	42	37	49
Visit relatives	45	50	44	50	31	78
Shopping	39	39	49	31	22	79
Work on allotment	33	31	34	23	41	17
Watch sport	32	40	29	23	22	3
Family outings	27	29	31	31	9	80
Visit friends	20	22	24	12	9	81
Walking	18	12	29	15	16	53
Cinema	14	12	22	4	3	58
Play sport	11	12	10	12	6	—
Bingo	9	12	9	4	3	78
Church services	7	8	8	4	—	50
Other social clubs	6	6	8	4	3	57
Trade union activities	5	6	5	4	3	—
'Other' activities	14	12	17	19	3	57
b At home						
Watch TV	78	77	83	73	72	
Jobs in the house	64	66	68	65	41	
Reading	45	40	44	50	59	
Garden	42	42	43	50	38	
Activities with children	30	34	32	19	19	
Hobbies	21	23	20	23	19	
Car maintenance	18	25	18	19	—	
Listen to radio	18	17	19	15	19	
'Other'	4	4	3	4	6	

allotment and sporting activities wives and husbands spent their leisure outside the home together more often than not.

Although strictly comparable data are difficult to obtain, it would appear that these workers have more varied and more home and family centred leisure-time activities than has been reported in most studies on the 'traditional' working class. On the other hand they differ too from the 'affluent' workers studied by Goldthorpe and his colleagues. They are more likely to belong to Working Men's Clubs and less likely to belong to other associations or to serve as officers for any formal associations (Table 2). They entertain less often at home; 48% of the sample said they entertained neither friends nor relatives; and their friends and social contacts are much more frequently associated with work than was the case with the 'affluent' workers (10).

Table 2 Membership of clubs and associations (excluding trade unions)

The figures show the percentage of workers who belong to each club or association
n = number of workers interviewed

Clubs and associations	Total n = 266	Steelworking trades n = 108	Outfitting trades n = 100	Semi-skilled n = 26	Unskilled n = 32
None	32	23	30	50	53
One	52	56	51	46	47
Two or more	16	21	19	4	—
As official	6	8	6	4	—
Working men's club	57	68	54	42	41
Sports club	7	10	8	—	3
Church group	5	5	7	—	—
Political party	2	5	1	—	—
Tenants' association	2	3	1	—	—
Parent–teacher association	1	1	1	—	—
Other clubs and associations	7	5	9	12	3

Yet, though work as a source of friends was valued and important, the leisure-time companions of these workers were by no means exclusively men from the same industry or occupation. This is an important point in view of the current sociological conception of the 'traditional' worker. Three-quarters of the men we interviewed had 'good friends' in the yard; 55% of them met one or more of these friends fairly frequently outside the yard. In contrast to the 'affluent' workers, many shipbuilding workers do meet each other socially outside work; 50% of them consider shipyard workers 'a pretty tight knit group'; and about the same proportion talk about their work when they are with other shipbuilding workers. But only 13% prefer the company of shipbuilding workers to that of others and the majority of their spare-time companions are not men from the same industry. Therefore in terms of one of Blauner's main criteria these shipbuilding workers were not unambiguously members of an 'occupational community' (11).

Finally, it is noticeable that the unskilled workers, and to some extent the semi-skilled workers, are less active in their leisure time than the skilled steel working and outfitting tradesmen. We have emphasized elsewhere that the labour force in shipbuilding is highly differentiated (12), but on the whole this differentiation is not reflected in leisure-time activities. Those in the steelworking or 'black' trades, which are more shipbuilding specific, tend to participate more than average in so-called 'traditional' working-class activities – pub and club, visiting relatives, sport; those in the outfitting trades mention more frequently family centred activities such as shopping and walking, but also go to the cinema more often. In general, however, skill-level differences are more important than occupational ones, with the non-skilled less likely to join associations or 'entertain' at home.

Leisure at work

The concept of 'leisure' is obviously not exhausted by reference to specific activities, hobbies or pastimes. Indeed one important aspect of leisure is the presence of periods of time which cannot be allocated to any single simple descriptive category. Leisure as it exists within the work situation is obviously largely, though not exclusively, of this kind. As we shall try to show, the opportunity for such leisure is inherent in the work processes of the shipyard.

Shipbuilding can be described as a craft industry under a craft-based style of administration (13). Inherent in the production process of such an industry is the difficulty of close managerial control of work. Shipbuilding was until recently, and in many instances still is, an industry of one-off production. It is a very complex assembly industry where detailed planning is difficult or impossible and subject to the vagaries of climate and outside suppliers. Production control of the individual worker is therefore loose: 56% of workers in our sample claimed they had never been told how long a job must take; 72% said the time they took on a job was never checked. This is fully confirmed by our own detailed observations.

Since discipline by the production process is weak control of workers' movements about the shipyard is weaker still. Delays on the job are frequent; 78% of our sample said that they suffered hold-ups due to other workers. Workers can legitimately move about to seek information from other workers before they can start their job, to seek tools or equipment that may be required, to obtain access to a job or the removal of obstructions, or to seek any servicing their job may require such as drilling, burning or welding. Over 80% of our sample said that they depended on other occupational groups to be able to do their job. Before fitting a pipe on a ship, for example, a tradesman may have to contact an electrician (so that neither's work blocks the other's), his foreman (for extra labour on a heavy job), the stores (for valves or flanges), a burner (to cut a bracket to shape), a welder and stagers (to build up or remove scaffolding to gain access to the job). Thus a shipyard worker is constantly on the move, and the layout of shipyards and ships ensures that quiet corners out of the eye of authority abound. Many opportunities exist for the making or taking of leisure at work.

Obviously the possibility of informal social contacts does not establish a workplace culture. Our evidence, however, suggests that there is a pattern and continuity in social contacts at work and, further, that these contacts result in sociable groupings that retain indentities over time and become an important 'work satisfaction' in their own right. 'Occupational culture' does not merely mean leisure-taking at work; it means that the social relations at work come to have a link with workers' values, attitudes and actions. This is what is posited in the concept of 'occupational community' as the outcome of an overlap between social relations at work and social relations outside work. Even though this overlap is only of marginal significance in the shipyard we believe that the relationship between sociability and social values is still of importance.

Firstly, the immediate work-group is itself a social group. Only 29% of our sample worked alone; 34% had no regular 'mate', while 29% claimed to have at least three regular mates. Given the constant shifting of work locations, and the rapid building up or decline of workers' numbers in any one location as the flow of work varies with a ship's construction this is a very remarkable degree of work-group stability. In our own experience we have seen workers planning and plotting to keep these work-groups in being as work on a particular ship tails off before launch or before completion. Even when the work-group is split up it can re-form months or years later, being kept alive meanwhile in the constant social contacts that are possible in the yards.

Beyond the immediate work-groups further and wider social groups exist. There are few status barriers in the shipyard. Only 17·4% of the work force in the industry in 1969 was composed of clerical, administrative or professional employees (14), and in any yard these are geographically isolated from the manual workers. There are negligible numbers of female employees outside the offices. Most of the manual workers have 'served their time' as apprentices for five years during which friendships can be made. Given the limited number of yards on the Tyne and the relative stability of the labour force in the industry, these friendships and contacts are constantly renewed in later life. Three quarters of the 208 tradesmen were still in touch with men with whom they had served their time.

These social groupings beyond the immediate work-group are not all of one type, nor are they merely dependent on casual contacts. They can serve as, and be described as, elements in a culture because there is range and diversity in their nature and because they are based on certain locations, however temporary, that enable a worker both to make deliberate social choices and to build them in to his social life at work in a planful and deliberate way. Very often, in a reversal of normal industrial practice, the social meeting-places at work are more fixed and permanent than the work-places.

Two of the most important types of social group are the apprentices and the younger tradesmen. Certain obvious common interests of a general nature bind these groups together such as recreational interests and sexual activity (though these interests can take on a very different style of expression in each of these groups). But each group has certain common interests specific to the work situation that give it an identity. The younger journeymen are more concerned with assertions of independence against foremen, and discussions of the shop stewards and job opportunities. The apprentices try to prevent themselves being taken advantage of by the journeymen or the foremen; knowledge as to who is good to work for and with, and standardized methods of coping with particular individuals can be shared. The apprentices' work-groups are also more varied – some work with journeymen, some on their own, some with labourers, some with another apprentice. This marks their progress and is an important source of discussion in its own right. The apprentices and the younger tradesmen generally have their own meeting-places. For example, on a ship building a certain area under the keel may be a meeting place at break or at start and finishing times; on a ship fitting out it may be a certain cabin. In 'cabins' (mess-rooms) a corner is usually taken over by one such group.

Not all apprentices or young tradesmen always form part of these groupings, but the groupings always exist with their own flavour, their own perspective on yard gossip, their own 'business' that can be entered into. In the very nature of such groups they generate their own gossip, their own activities and provide the basis for friendship. Very common amongst these groups are lunchtime drinking after pay-days and 'bachelor parties' before weddings. In some trades these 'bachelor parties' are institutionalized.

Other social groups that may, and commonly do, exist are groups from a particular town. Not merely do they have their own particular news to share but, since yards traditionally have taken their labour from the area immediately adjacent, those from other areas tend to form minority identities for protection against what is normally harmless or even banal ragging, but what could be and has been active discrimination in employment. These men, as 'travellers', will often use the same gate out of the yard or the same transport home.

Another type of sociable group more closely related to conventional leisure activity is the group which exists for a definite and specified purpose: regular groups for cards, dominoes or crosswords exist in a number of different places in the yard. Generally such groups exist outside working time but on days when the weather makes work difficult or impossible (the building berth is most vulnerable to this) these groups re-form in a convenient place. Some workers even return to their trade's store or mess-room at teabreaks. A group playing cards can thus exist off and on throughout the day. In two groups of workers we observed, numbering about a hundred men in all, at least seven such groups existed on a regular basis.

We have described four main types of group – the apprentices, the younger men, the residential and the specific activity groups. In addition many foremen and chargehands have their own 'squad' – a particular group of men that has been selected or acquired through getting to know their particular skills or quirks, or whom they find particularly reliable. These men may get any one of a number of little extra privileges that the foreman can bestow. They may sometimes be hostilely regarded as 'blue-eyes', though under another foreman the same men may be underprivileged and form a focus of opposition. In normal circumstances these groups are an important source of information about the foremen and chargehands – their rivalries, conflicts and personalities – and also about the future pattern of work. They ensure that the yard even in its daily organizational work remains an open social community. If few things are hidden from the foreman because these groups exist, equally the foreman can hide few things from the men. The foreman's past history as a worker, his social life, his quirks, his position with the other foremen are made known to the men. The foreman, whether he chooses or not, is exposed to the social gaze and the social approval of his men. One foreman who persistently made some of his men work in the snow, was informally sent to Coventry by them. The mediation of the foreman's favoured men restored social relations.

These types do not exhaust the range of patterned groupings that could be described. They are sufficient, however, to justify our contention that a work-place social life and culture exists within the shipyard gates. The concept of member may, indeed, be a very misleading one. Apart from a very few most 'members' are in fact absent at any given time. All shipyard workers are, actually or potentially, a 'member' of a variety of such groups. From these groups it is possible to construct a varied social life of one's own whim and choosing.

Now it would be perfectly possible to consider what we have been describing as minor social distractions functional perhaps either as a compensation for what is very often physically hard work in poor conditions, or facilitating the work process in an indirect way, or enabling occupational or trade union groups to develop an effective 'charge' to their identity. There may indeed be functional consequences of this kind, but we would argue that these consequences (particularly the second) are of declining importance.

In the past these patterns of sociable grouping and friendship may have played an important functional part in employment and production. Traditionally the 'black' or steelwork trades were pieceworking. Piecework was often worked on a squad basis with several tradesmen and their helpers sharing a 'bill'. This was particularly so amongst platers, caulkers and the near defunct trade of riveting. These squads would be picked out at a 'market' in the yard each morning by the foreman. The financial incentives, and the need to maximize output to impress management, were so great that squads tended to become tightly-knit *social* groups that were mutually competitive. Friendship patterns were important in getting, keeping and functioning in jobs. One shipyard plater told us

> It was tough . . . You depended on knowhow and ability. Some call it craftsmanship but it isn't. It's more the ability to bully, fight and cajole. I told a manager once that the squads were fighting each other — yes, physically fighting — for the use of derricks to get their stuff aboard. It was purely initiative.

However important this 'squad' system was it has now disappeared. Indeed all piecework in the main yards on the Tyne ceased in 1968. 'Squads' as groups of regular workmates of course continue to exist. The granting of 'favours' based on social groups and social contacts at the yard also continues: for example shipwrights share their jacks on the berth: joiners can lend stools to other workers on the ship to work from; welders and burners may lend their services or their gear to someone they know for a quick small job out of the line of strict duty. To be actively part of the social life of the yard, to be known widely as 'a character', can make work easier and reduce delays. But we do not feel this is more than a minor aspect of the work-culture of the yard. Indeed the decline of squad work has probably led to a far greater social homogeneity in the yard. Decreased fear of redundancies, and a widening of the work role of tradesmen by new training schemes, union amalgamations and relaxation of demarcation have strengthened the wider, public and open culture of work that we have been describing.

Thus the social relations and interaction of shipbuilding workers at work extend considerably beyond what is necessary for the performance of their roles in production, though the nature of these roles makes such an extension easier. The pattern of interaction we have described provides an essential element in the occupational culture of workers in shipbuilding.

What runs through all of these groups, and, from our observation manifests itself in most social contact at the yard, is a certain style of conduct. Certain topics of conversation constantly recur: current affairs, sport and sex. Persistent awkwardness or ignorance incurs a social penalty. The possession of a wide range of knowledge and the ability to handle well the style of conversation with its emphasis on quick wit, quick verbal reactions and rapid changes of tack, carry a social reward. To be regarded as a 'character' or a 'patter merchant' with a witty, caustic and self-mocking style and a wide variety of interests and stories is to have a welcome, and an acknowledgement, in all parts of the yard and often outside it as well. This style of conduct commonly involves an element of horseplay as well: mock fighting, mock kissing, mock embracing.

There was also a high degree of social activity by the various departments and occupational groups in the yard such as outings, 'smokers' (15) and socials. Only 6% of our sample said there were no department activities; 45% said there were more than four such activities. Of those who had activities they could participate in, only 13% did not participate in any.

This sociability is an important intrinsic work satisfaction. When asked about the things they liked most about working in the shipyard about 25% of both our shipyard worker sample and our shipyard apprentice sample mentioned first their social relations at the yard with workmates and friends. This complex of social practices and activities, and the high value placed upon them, is summed up in the perpetually used phrase 'just one of the lads'.

In view of the unattractiveness of the yard surroundings, the nearness of many workers to their homes, and the easy access on foot to the town centre from the shipyard, it is remarkable that 71% of workers stay in the yard for their dinner hour. The labour force in the yard is extremely dispersed, and the high proportion of workers using the dinner hour and teabreaks for regular and sustained social contacts with other workers is evidence of a strong desire for such contacts. These contacts are not confined to the yard; a third of those interviewed met members of their dinner group socially outside the yard.

Indeed the yard is both a place where most workers have 'friends' and a place for making friends. Only 24% of our sample said they had no 'good friends' in the yard, and 30% said they had six or more. Four out of every five shipbuilding workers thought that the yard was 'a good place for making friends'; two thirds of them had first met friends there.

Conclusion

It is not possible to claim that there is a specifically shipbuilding workers' life style. Our evidence is that there is a great deal of diversity of activities among shipbuilding workers and no pattern which clearly differentiates them from other workers. However, there exists a particularly strong occupational or workplace culture in the shipyards. No doubt this culture is part of, and a forming factor in, the distinctive working-class culture of Tyneside, and the North East generally. However we feel that the concept of occupational culture, of leisure and social life at work, has a significance wider than a specific industry or region. Sociological research has uncovered evidence of occupational cultures (or of what at least could be elements in an occupational culture) in a wide variety of regions and industries.

The concept of 'occupational community' was born out of attempts to account for workers' values and workers' actions. It is our belief that the concept of 'occupational culture' would have a similar explanatory potential. Certainly shipbuilding workers talk about their 'leisure-at-work'; they take great pleasure in the social relations at the yard, and this clearly emerges in the yard. But as the basis for action this culture has been weakened by the past diversity of the shipyard labour force — the different trades and other groups and the different unions that represent them. This is shown in the traditional status hierarchy amongst the workers based on some boilermaker trades' centrality to the production process and high piecework earnings. These dividing factors are being broken down by such factors as union amalgamations, the relaxation of demarcation lines and productivity bargaining, all of which have developed very rapidly in the last five years. The basic cultural unity of the shipyard labour force based on social relations and leisure-taking at work has become a more and more important foundation for newer and wider loyalties (16). The course of industrial relations in shipbuilding seems clearly set against the older sectional and local identities.

Moreover we would suggest that the 'occupational culture' of workers will become stronger, or at least be made more public, as leisure-taking at work comes less and less to be regarded as illicit or improper, and as the Protestant ethic loses its force in our society as a system of values. Work situations are normally thought of as dominated by rational-bureaucratic or Protestant ethic values. We can see that they are also the site of an alternative, rival system of values including an emphasis on play, defiance of restriction, leisure-taking and camaraderie (17). It is these that are represented in the occupational culture we have described. Their potential as a basis for action may even now not be fully exercised.

Notes and References

1 This chapter has been prepared in the course of a research project entitled 'Orientation to work and industrial behaviour of shipbuilding workers on Tyneside' carried out in the Department of Social Theory and Institutions, University of Durham, from 1968 to 1970, and supported by a grant from the Social Science Research Council. A full report of this project is in preparation.

2 The most systematic discussion of this concept is to be found in R. Blauner, 'Work Satisfaction and Industrial Trends in Modern Society', in W. Galenson and S. M. Lipset, *Labour and Trade Unionism,* New York, Wiley, 1960, especially pp.350-52.

3 The most sophisticated discussion of 'traditionalism' is to be found in D. Lockwood, 'Sources of Variation in Working Class Images of Society', *Sociological Review,* 14, 3, Nov. 1966, especially pp. 250-56.

4 See, for example, N. Dennis, F. Henriques and C. Slaughter, *Coal is our Life,* Eyre and Spottiswoode, 1969; University of Liverpool, *The Dock Worker,* Liverpool University Press, 1954; G. W. Horobin, 'Community and Occupation in the Hull Fishing Industry', *British Journal of Sociology,* 8, 4, Dec. 1957. S. M. Lipset, M. Trow and J. Coleman, *Union Democracy,* Glencoe, The Free Press, 1956; Peter G. Hollowell, *The Lorry Driver,* Routledge, 1968, especially ch. 7.

5 See the discussion in *Shipbuilding Inquiry Committee 1965-6 Report,* H.M.S.O., Cmnd. 2937, 1966 ('The Geddes Report'), especially p. 12.

6 In addition to the interviews with a stratified random sample of 266 shipbuilding workers from one Tyneside shipyard, several members of the research team spent lengthy periods in intensive observation in the yard. We are grateful to all those who made our research possible.

7 Some writers have used the term 'occupational community' in a similar way to our use of 'occupational culture'; see I. C. Cannon, 'Ideology and Occupational Community: a Study of Compositors', *Sociology,* 1, 2, May 1967.

8 S. R. Parker, *The Future of Work and Leisure,* MacGibbon & Kee, 1971.

9 See, for example, F. Zweig, *The British Worker,* Penguin, 1952; Michael Young and Peter Willmott, *Family and Kinship in East London,* Routledge, 1957; Josephine Klein, *Samples from English Cultures,* Routledge, 1965; John H. Goldthorpe and others, *The Affluent Worker in the Class Structure,* Cambridge University Press, 1969, especially ch. 5, 'Aspirations and Social Perspectives'.

10 Although our data are not directly comparable, 45% of the 'affluent workers' reported having no 'close friends' among workmates, as compared to 24% of our sample who had no 'good friends' in the yard; J. H. Goldthorpe and others, *The*

Affluent Worker: Industrial Attitudes and Behaviour, Cambridge University Press, 1968, p. 57.

11 Blauner, op. cit., p. 351: 'The essential feature of an occupational community is that workers in their off-hours socialize more with persons in their own line of work than with a cross section of occupational types.'

12 See R. K. Brown, P. Brannen, J. M. Cousins and M. L. Samphier, 'The Contours of Solidarity: social stratification and industrial relations in shipbuilding', in *British Journal of Industrial Relations,* vol. 10, no. 1, March 1972.

13 Richard Brown and Peter Brannen, 'Social Relations and Social Perspectives among Shipbuilding Workers – a preliminary statement, Part 2', *Sociology,* 4, 2, May 1970, especially pp. 197-9.

14 Department of Employment and Productivity, *Gazette,* Jan. 1970, p. 18.

15 'Smokers' are all-male departmental parties normally taking place in a hired room in a pub or club.

16 Brown, Brannen, Cousins and Samphier, op. cit.

17 These values were also of importance to workers in earlier stages of industrialization; see for example E. P. Thompson, 'Time, Work-discipline and Industrial Capitalism', *Past and Present,* Dec. 1967.

8 Managers and their leisure

John Child and Brenda Macmillan

It is perhaps surprising to find a chapter on the leisure of managers in the light of Dubin's comment that 'in the folk-lore of managerial literature much is made of the need for total immersion of the individual in his organization'. Whyte's portrayal of the 'organization man', which has so captured our imagination of managerial life, seems to confirm the view that managers hardly possess any leisure worth writing about, if by leisure we have in mind non-obligatory activity (1).

These impressions of the unleisured business manager come, however, from the American scene, as does most research on managers. It is still not very clear just how different is the pattern of work and leisure experienced by British managers. Most studies comparing British and American managers have concentrated on attitudes. Some of these have concluded that British managers are closer in outlook to American managers than they are even to managers in other European countries, while other commentators have made the point that substantial differences still remain between the British and American scenes. Most comparisons of managerial activities and behaviour between Britain and America rely upon purely impressionistic evidence. It is in any case extremely difficult to generalize about managers even within one country because they do not comprise a homogeneous occupational group.

Nevertheless, since our stereotypes of management are heavily influenced by American evidence, it is important when considering leisure among British managers to attempt some comparison with American data. Indeed, any differences emerging between the two countries in the relationship of managers' leisure and work would provide an illustration of how life-styles are influenced by the different value systems which serve as a point of reference for social behaviour in the two countries. Also if we look ahead, the rapid spread of multi-national corporations, which are mostly American controlled, portends a powerful force for change which may have a substantial influence on the way in which British managers are free to look upon and enjoy their leisure time. For reasons such as these it is important when examining the leisure of British managers not to adopt a purely insular perspective.

This chapter examines three aspects of managerial leisure in Britain. First, the amount of leisure taken by managers; secondly, the content of their leisure activities with particular attention to how closely these relate to their work interests; and thirdly, the subjective meaning of leisure activities to managers. No systematic studies have been made of British managers' leisure activities, or indeed of their life-styles in general, and this chapter therefore proceeds by piecing together bits and pieces from scattered sources of evidence. Most of the available data in this field is from samples of American managers and it is therefore possible to compare British findings with those from American (and occasionally other European) sources.

How much leisure?

Studies of British managers suggest that they are able to enjoy quite as much free time as other occupational groups. British managers may, as the Pahls claim, work hard, but this does not generally take the form of exceptionally long hours. Stewart asked a sample of 160 managers to keep a diary of their working time over four weeks. She found that their hours of work varied from 30 to over 60 hours a week, with an average of 42 hours. A slightly longer average total working week for British managers has been found by Burns (43½ hours), and by Horne and Lupton (44 hours). Another study of executives working for a firm of consultants suggests that British top managers may have less leisure time than their subordinates (2).

Top managers in America also show a more extended devotion to work than their subordinates, although the most striking conclusion is that managers as a whole in the United States work very much longer hours than their British counterparts. *Business Week* reported that the 335 corporation presidents in its sample worked for up to 75% of their waking time, that is, 80 to 90 hours a week. These presidents claimed that lack of time was one of their biggest problems, but they wanted the extra time for work, not for leisure! Elliott claims that top American executives are among the world's hardest working men, sleeping little and working most of their waking hours. He found that such executives were ashamed of the small amount of time they spent with their families, but they did nothing to change the situation. Heckscher and De Grazia report an average working week of 62 hours, including business entertaining and business travel, among their large sample of 3,000 managers. American managers in general appear to have less leisure than do the members of other occupational groups. The American Bureau of Census figures report an average 53-hour week for managers and proprietors, the longest work week recorded (3).

Some economists have speculated that the marginal utility of leisure to managers will influence the extent to which they strive towards maximizing company performance. The lower their marginal utility of leisure, so the argument goes, the more managers will seek to maximize company profits through harder and longer working hours (4). While sampling differences between available studies do not allow for precise comparison, it does seem clear that British managers tend to work shorter hours than their counterparts in the United States. Indeed, there are indications that managers in many other industrialized countries such as Russia, Japan and members of the E.E.C. also tend to give more time to work (5). The British manager's shorter hours of work presumably reflect a higher marginal utility of leisure and a lower level of commitment to the job. While these shorter hours may avoid decreased performance through fatigue, the lower level of commitment which they probably reflect could account for a good deal of the British manager's supposedly inferior business effectiveness. Certainly the American manager's life tends to be more work-related, and lived at a higher pitch of activity, as the following studies on the content of leisure indicate.

The content of managerial leisure

The British manager, as we have seen, has appreciably more leisure time than his American equivalent during his normal working week. But is his pattern of interests correspondingly more varied and active? And is his longer time away from work reflected in a set of leisure-time activities which suggest that the job represents less of a central life interest for him?

Unfortunately, data which would allow one to compare in detail British top managers with their American equivalents are not available. The main British source for this level of management is a survey carried out by the *Director* early in 1966 of 2,400 British company directors which gives a very limited amount of information. By and large, the British company directors surveyed did not seem to be particularly active during their leisure time. For example, 57% watched television for at least an hour each weekday evening, while 25% of the sample never took any exercise, even walking! However, 57% of the sample belonged to committees or boards devoted to public service, a commitment which is also shared by senior American executives (6).

The main sources of information on British managers' leisure are four studies, by Leigh, Humblet, Macmillan and the Pahls, which were not confined to top managers. Leigh looked at just over 1,000 British managers under 50 years of age who were 'known to be ambitious and concerned about their careers' and who had at least 'some form of training'. Humblet reports on a sample of 110 British managers of various organizational ranks as part of a comparative study involving British, French and Belgian managers. Macmillan collected data from a sample of 964 members of the British Institute of Management as part of a wider study into managerial mobility in Britain. The Pahls studied eighty-six British managers and their wives, and they provide some qualitative data on leisure activities (7).

Leigh found that 34% of his sample spent over 5 hours a week on organized activities after working hours. These organized activities included business and professional matters to which as many as four out of every five managers in the whole sample devoted some of their leisure time. It is not clear to what extent these business and professional activities were directly connected with the managers' jobs, in that one in four of the sample claimed under this heading to teach or to write regularly or occasionally. As Leigh himself comments, teaching and writing may represent a second string to the manager's bow rather than any extra commitment to his main employment. Humblet found that a very high proportion of his sample (99 out of 110 British managers) belonged to at least one association; professional organizations and company clubs were the types which the managers considered most important. However, some of the company clubs were purely sporting clubs, and most managers who held any position of responsibility in their associations were top managers. There is little suggestion in Humblet's data that managers at other levels took a particularly active part. In their study the Pahls comment that 'among our managers it seemed as though voluntary associations were more important for the women (i.e. the wives) than for the men'. These managers mentioned membership of sporting clubs far more frequently than other kinds of clubs.

Leigh's data indicate that the managers in his sample spent most of their uncommitted leisure time at home. Only 27% of his respondents gave pressure from work as the reason for not participating further in outside activities, and these tended to be the executives who were already spending a large amount of their leisure time on organized activities. The larger, relatively inactive, part of the sample tended to give home and family commitments as the reason for reserving leisure time to purely private activities.

Further results suggest quite strongly that for British managers work-related activities do not constitute a major part of their leisure time. Humblet asked his managers to mention their most frequent leisure pursuit, and in their answers sport ranked most highly (37·6% of the sample cited this as a principal activity) followed by family (15·8%), gardening (14·8%) and cultural pursuits (6·9%). Only 2% of the sample claimed to have no leisure interest outside their work, a figure which is somewhat lower than for the French and Belgian managers. Macmillan asked her sample of managers to say what they did in their leisure time and her results (Table 1) show agreement with

Humblet's findings in that taking part in or watching sport was mentioned most frequently, along with home-centred activities, and cultural pursuits were given relatively low emphasis. A negligible proportion of the sample appeared to have no leisure interests, while the only category of activity which could be related to the job – self-improvement – appears to be of modest and not overwhelming importance. In fact, many of the activities categorized as 'self-improvement' (reading literature, general study, etc.) do not necessarily have a bearing on a manager's work.

Table 1 Leisure activities among British managers

Sample of 964 British Institute of Management members, 1970

Leisure activity	Percentage of sample engaging in activity
Sport 1. Taking part	57·8
2. Watching	9·3
Home improvement	55·9
Hobbies (including motoring and travel 16%, and photography 11%)	54·3
Self improvement	43·0
Attending cultural activities, as a spectator only	23·5
Civic and political affairs	20·3
Family life in general	13·7

No other type of leisure activity was mentioned by more than 10% of the sample. Active participation in cultural pursuits as well as watching TV were each mentioned by 10% of the sample.

It is also evident from the material presented by the Pahls in their book that sport tended to be given most emphasis by managers when asked about their non-work pursuits. Writing of Saturdays, the Pahls conclude that

in the afternoon, typically, sport dominated the men's lives. Some still played, others watched on television or at the stadium or local playing fields. Fathers sometimes took young children out, but not always (8).

Thus all the studies which have been made so far agree on the importance of sport in most British managers' leisure time, a finding which almost certainly reflects more of their nationality than of their particular occupational position.

The Pahls assert that the managers they studied 'worked very hard', but the statistics we have presented appear to question this, especially when compared to data on American managers. In the United States, the picture emerges of top executives devoted almost wholly to their work, without much time for their family and with little variety in their leisure pursuits. Although in America middle managers appear to have more time to spend with their families than top managers, this is still far less than the average for British middle managers. The story is still one of a man who typically has a limited range of leisure pursuits or outside interests. For instance, Guzzardi found his sample of young aspiring executives to be completely job-oriented, intellectually narrow and rarely interested in the humanities or liberal arts. Most of their leisure activities were non-intellectual, and sometimes these were 'discussed at such great length and with such eagerness as to permit the inference that they were pastimes chosen and treasured precisely because they are so devoid of intellectual content' (9).

The attachment of American managers to their jobs is further indicated by the finding that only 47% of Heckscher and De Grazia's sample allowed themselves a day off 'now and then', even though they would normally have the authority to do this. In fact, Heckscher and De Grazia conclude that the American executive enjoys his work, and that his way of life permits no clear-cut distinction between work and leisure. Indeed, 'his work is penetrated by qualities which we would ordinarily associate with voluntary, carefree, and leisurely pursuits' (10). A study by England of the value systems of 1,072 American managers listed in Poors 1965 Directory lends additional credence to this picture of the highly work-oriented American manager. He found that satisfaction in the job was listed as highly important by more managers (88% of the sample) than was any other out of thirteen personal goals, with leisure being given the least weighting (listed as highly important by only 11%). Other job performance goals such as achievement, success and creativity, came high on the list (11).

The conclusion that can be drawn so far from the available evidence is that work and the job represent less of a central life interest for British managers than is the case in the United States. The difference in the total number of hours given to the job itself appears to be further reflected by the findings that many British managers devote no appreciable part of their leisure time to activities that in any way directly further their work and career. The heavy burden of work faced by American managers is not a problem for their equivalents in Britain, or indeed in France and Belgium. It is difficult to say from the evidence available whether British managers engage in a wider *range* of leisure activities, though the impression is that they do at least have more hobbies and spend much longer pursuing them.

The purpose of managerial leisure

Macmillan collected information on the purposes that managers saw their leisure time as fulfilling for them. These data further confirm the impression gained already that British managers prefer to compartmentalize their lives so that the job is forgotten during their leisure time. Only 2·3% of a sample of nearly 1,000 B.I.M. members mentioned that their leisure time was used to improve their careers and performance in their jobs, while in contrast almost ten times as many managers specifically mentioned that a major function of leisure time for them was in fact to escape from and to forget their jobs. It could be supposed that these results are all the more indicative of a British value-system that contrasts sharply with that of American managers, in that this sample was exclusively of B.I.M. members, whose membership of the Institute presumably means that they have a somewhat above average interest in the problems of their occupation. The most frequent purpose of leisure-time which these managers mentioned was enjoyment and self-fulfilment in one form or another, while self-development and a broadening of outlook through educational participation was given relatively infrequent mention (see Table 2).

Although a direct comparison is not possible, these findings on a sample of British managers may be set in contrast to Heckscher and De Grazia's results from their study of 3,000 American managers. In this latter survey managers were asked what they considered to be valid end-purposes for the use of leisure time. The largest number of these executives cited self-improvement and cultural pursuits (79%). Almost as many (72%) mentioned the use of 'leisure time as a refresher to enable you to do better work', while leisure as an end in itself for one's own amusement and pleasure came third in the list. Although in this instance these American managers were replying not just for themselves but also with reference to their employees, the different weighting given to the use of leisure as a means to performing better work is quite remarkable, as is also the different emphasis given to self-improvement. There would seem to be a noticeable cultural difference here between American and British managers, with the mantle of the Protestant work ethic now being almost exclusively assumed by the former.

Cultural versus other influences

Some noticeable differences have appeared between the leisure-work relationships of managers in Britain and the United States. The way in which available studies have fairly consistently pointed to these

Table 2 The purpose of leisure

Sample of 964 British Institute of Management members, 1970

Purpose of leisure	Percentage of sample answering
Enjoyment, self-fulfilment	45·8
(Enjoyment mentioned specifically as a change from work)	(27·8)
Escape from the job	21·4
Family life	19·6
Keeping fit	17·1
Social contact	14·2
Relaxation and resting	12·7
Recuperation for the job	5·9
Self-development, broadening of outlook	5·7
Improving career and performance in the job	2·3

Other purposes of leisure were mentioned by 2·8% of the sample, while 0·7% replied 'none' or 'not much'.

differences suggests that they are more than just a product of sampling, even though the available survey data do not allow for precise comparisons. Rather, these results point to the influence of two contrasting value systems which comprise cultural reference points for the meaning that non-work time has for the manager and for his consequent choice of leisure behaviour. However, to conclude the analysis at this point would be a misleading over-simplification, for we have also already come across indications that *within* particular cultures other factors, such as the manager's hierarchical rank, may be associated at least with his hours of work and his total length of leisure time. There have, further, been indications that senior managers are the more likely to hold positions of responsibility within their local communities.

Within the context of American society, Heckscher and De Grazia's survey provides further clues on non-cultural associations with variation in managerial leisure patterns. They compared managers' leisure preferences with their level of annual income (which in most cases reflects hierarchical rank), their age and their educational level. One would expect managers' income levels to rise with their age and in fact many preferences displayed a similar pattern for both increasing income and increasing age. Thus increasing age and income were both associated with a lessening interest in self-improvement, in cultural activities and in watching sports. However, managers who were both young *and* highly paid formed an interesting group. For they tended to emphasize that leisure should be an end in itself for the fun it provides, and it may be that this is the group of American managers who show least acceptance of the otherwise dominant Protestant ethic. The levels of education which the American managers had attained were closely associated with only one leisure preference, and in a not unexpected manner. As their levels of education rose, so did their interest in using any extra leisure time for cultural activities.

In Macmillan's sample of British managers, age appeared to have a more important effect than other factors both upon the degree of participation in different activities and upon the importance of different purposes that managers saw their leisure time as meeting. Table 3 lists the instances where age seemed to have some association, and they do not by any means entirely support Heckscher and De Grazia's results. For although there is a slight tendency for interest in cultural activities to be less among older managers, watching sport tends to increase with age while self-improvement showed no apparent association with age at all. One has to treat the question of cultural interests with some caution because, as in the American survey, Macmillan found some tendency for managers with a higher level of education to participate more in cultural activities, and younger managers are the more likely in both countries to possess a degree or superior education (12). Level of education and level of income did not assume any strong pattern of relationship with other leisure pursuits of British managers. The conclusion for these managers, and one which is not refuted by data on American managers, is that age appears to be the major non-cultural determinant of leisure activities.

This is perhaps hardly a surprising conclusion, but there is one age-related characteristic among the British managers which is less obvious. Among older managers 'escaping from the job' appears to assume less importance as a purpose of leisure time. This could be due partly to the fact that as managers become older they assume responsibilities and status which increase their attachment to and interest in the job. Older managers may also in some cases adjust their expectations downwards and hence feel less frustrated with the positions they are occupying. At the same time the fact that almost one third of managers under 35 years of age in the British sample, without prompting, attached importance to escaping from the job, and the apparent absence of this sentiment from any of the data reported on American managers, is food for serious thought. It certainly appears to lend indirect support to Dubin's conclusion that many young and able

Table 3 Age and managerial leisure

Sample of 964 B.I.M. members. Figures give percentage within age groups answering in each category

a Activities where age appears to affect participation

	Percentage participating according to age		
Leisure activity	Under 35 years (n = 172)	35-49 years (n = 562)	Over 50 years (n = 230)
Sport 1. Taking part	65·1	57·8	50·8
2. Watching	4·7	8·4	15·2
Family life	15·7	15·4	7·8
Home improvement	46·5	55·3	64·4
Hobbies	30·8	38·7	44·2
Travel/motoring	13·4	14·8	20·2
Cultural (participating and spectating)	36·6	34·0	30·4

b Purposes of leisure showing variation with age

	Percentage according to age		
Purpose of leisure	Under 35 years	35-49 years	Over 50 years
Escape from the job	30·8	20·3	17·0
Social contact	8·1	13·9	19·6
Keeping fit	14·0	16·5	20·9
Relaxation and resting	9·9	11·0	18·7

managers in British industry are frustrated by the high value placed on age, experience and status, and by the consequent lack of scope given to younger men to demonstrate the performance and to assume the position their ability and expertise warrant.

Discussion

We have collected together evidence which suggests that the relationship between work and leisure tends to be of a different order for most

British managers than it is for their American counterparts. British managers are likely to devote more time to home and family, and their leisure would seem to assume more of what Parker has called a 'neutral' relationship to their work (13). Although many of the organized activities in which they may engage during their leisure time have some connection with their work, these organized pursuits do not, in most cases, appear to take up much of British managers' relatively generous time off from work.

In contrast, the American manager to an important degree uses leisure as an 'extension of work', and the top level American executive provides an extreme instance of this pattern. His leisure time, such that remains, is infused by considerations relating to his work, which represents his dominant interest in life. It is difficult to draw any line between his work and his leisure. Studies of American middle managers have also shown them to be largely job-oriented. The conclusion that this 'extension' pattern is most evident among top American executives is consistent with other findings that senior managers in American business derive greater satisfaction from their jobs than do managers lower down in the hierarchy (14). One would expect managers who were highly satisfied with their jobs to extend work interests into their leisure time.

It is worth considering for a moment what may lie behind the marked differences in managerial leisure between Britain and the United States, in anticipation of our conclusion that American conditions may become far more prevalent in British industry. We have already mentioned the possibility that such differences reflect what Dubin claims to have observed, namely that British managers have far less opportunity for creative self-fulfilment in their jobs than their American equivalents. However, a different explanation has also been advanced to account at least for the fact that American managers devote a substantial amount of ostensibly free time to activity on behalf of their companies. This argument maintains that it is not so much positive motivation deriving from a challenging and absorbing job which stimulates this leisure activity, but pressures emanating from top management which are reinforced by the ethos it establishes and by the criteria for advancement it operates.

Interest in the so-called 'organization man' syndrome has to a large extent been stimulated by a concern not only that aspiring American business managers have to work long hours, but also that their leisure activities are not freely chosen. Whyte, in his classic portrayal of organization man, has provided the example of corporation programmes designed to mould behaviour of executive wives, and American business writers urge in all seriousness that such programmes aimed at harnessing wives' activities towards the corporate well-being should be adopted more extensively (15). The Pahls, noting how in the United States a wife may sometimes be expected to join certain clubs because of her husband's position in the firm, found no such expectations of the British managers' wives they studied. There is also a widespread belief in the United States that business leaders expect their executives to represent corporate interests within the local environment through an active participation in political and other community affairs. American political liberals have been greatly alarmed by this apparent attempt to extend business influence, especially as it smacks of 'behind the scenes' activity (16). If these fears are justified, this would represent a particularly important encroachment on the voluntary nature of managerial leisure in the United States.

Thus American managers do appear to differ from British managers in regard to the role of political involvement, *but* the explanation for this difference is unlikely to be as sinister as the 'organization man' stereotype implies. In fact, rather than being pushed into political and community activities by top management, the aspiring American manager probably seeks such involvement quite actively as a further extension of his job interest and expression of his talents. A survey in 1968 of over 2,500 American managers of varying rank suggests that company pressures on managers to undertake political activities is not so great as is sometimes feared. Although 27% of the respondents stated that their companies urged managers to serve as elected officials in their local cities, a mere 5% said that political activities were considered in recommendations for promotion within their company (17). In short, it seems more likely that the association between career success and political involvement among American managers is the product of their own positive motivations towards work in general. We are thus returned to our original explanation for Anglo-American differences in managerial leisure, which points to contrasting orientations to work and corporate policies concerning the opportunities for and evaluation of personal achievement.

Although ours has often been hailed as an age of increasing leisure, there is some reason for expecting that British managers may be increasingly obliged to offer the same degree of commitment to work as today characterizes managers in America and in dynamic growth economies such as Japan. The pressures of international business competition are likely to promote an equalization of managerial job performance between different countries, at least in larger enterprises which have to sell beyond highly specialized or localized markets in order to survive. A major force behind this equalization of expectations placed upon managers will be the multi-national corporation. Professor Perlmutter has recently predicted that by 1985 some 300 giant corporations will dominate the world economy and of these some 200 will be American-controlled. If this prediction proves to be correct, many British managers are likely to find themselves within twelve years working for American-controlled corporations. These will probably impose upon any executive occupying a senior position the level of expectations concerning commitment to work and the use of leisure time that we already see reflected in the contemporary American scene.

In this event, British managers will face a sharpened personal conflict between two value-systems. They will be presented with a choice which amounts on the one hand to opting out of the more rewarding levels of executive employment and remaining rooted in the British home-oriented value-system, or opting to meet American expectations of commitment to work but quite possibly facing considerable domestic strains and conflicts as a result. The Pahls found that there was in any case some degree of tension between the competing values of work and home among the managerial families they studied. The dilemma we have predicted is already becoming a serious one for some British managers working in American-controlled companies. Even though managerial work may become more challenging, creative and absorbing with the development of more sophisticated techniques and computer information technologies, most British managers are unlikely to see this as adequate compensation for the sacrifice of more home life. It has often been argued that the very advance of managerial technology will render middle management superfluous; perhaps for many British managers an enforced move into other employment will eventually be the means to preserving the type of leisure they currently enjoy.

Notes and References

1 R. Dubin, 'Business Behavior *Behaviorally* Viewed', in G. B. Strother (ed.), *Social Science Approaches to Business Behavior,* Tavistock, 1962, p. 27; W. H. Whyte, *The Organization Man,* Penguin Books, 1960.

2 J. M. Pahl and R. E. Pahl, *Managers and their Wives,* Allen Lane The Penguin Press, 1971; R. Stewart, *Managers and their Jobs,* Macmillan, 1967; T. Burns, 'What Managers Do', *New Society,* 17 Dec. 1964; J. H. Horne and T. Lupton, 'The Work Activities of Middle Managers', *Journal of Management Studies,* 2, 1965; 'Longer Hours for Executives', *Financial Times,* 9 Dec. 1969. These British studies include all time spent in work activities wherever the location, although there are minor differences in definition between them. Stewart, in particular, has attempted to exclude non-working activities engaged in during office hours. This presumably accounts for her lower figure.

3 'At Top, It's All Work, No Play', *Business Week,* 24 Aug. 1957; O. Eliott, *Men at the Top,* Weidenfeld and Nicolson, 1960; A. Heckscher and S. De Grazia, 'Executive Leisure', *Harvard Business Review,* July-August 1959; R. Denney, 'The Leisure Society', *Harvard Business Review,* May-June 1959.

4 e.g., E. E. Hoogstraat, 'Attacks on the Value of the Profit Motive in Theories of Business Behavior', in J. W. McGuire (ed.), *Interdisciplinary Studies in Business Behavior,* Cincinnati, South-Western Pub. Co., 1962.

5 D. Granick, *The Red Executive,* New York, Doubleday, 1961; P. Scott-Stokes, 'Why Japan's Executives Take No Holidays, Thank You', *Financial Times,* 21 July 1970; A. Rowley, 'Europe Leads the Pay Stakes', *The Times,* 18 August 1970.

6 'The Director Observed Away from the Desk', *The Director,* May 1966.

7 A. Leigh, 'The Executive Unleashed', *Business Management,* Aug. 1967; J. E. Humblet, *Les Cadres d'entreprises,* Paris, Éditions Universitaires, 1966, Part IV; Unpublished survey in 1970 by B. Macmillan with the collaboration of S. Birch, *British Institute of Management.*

8 J. M. Pahl and R. E. Pahl, op. cit., p. 258.

9 W. Guzzardi, Jnr, *The Young Executives,* New York, New American Library, 1964.

10 'Executive Leisure', op. cit., p. 12.

11 G. W. England, 'Personal Value Systems of American Managers', *Academy of Management Journal,* 10, March 1967.

12 cf. H. B. Rose, *Management Education in the 1970s,* H.M.S.O., 1970; W. L. Warner and J. C. Abegglen, *Big Business Leaders in America,* New York, Harper, 1955.

13 S. R. Parker and others, *The Sociology of Industry,* Allen & Unwin 1972, 2nd ed., ch. 14.

14 L. L. Cummings and A. M. El Salmi, 'Empirical Research on the Bases and Correlates of Managerial Motivation', *Psychological Bulletin,* 70, 1968.

15 e.g., B. Kimmelmann, 'Executives' Wives – the Need for a Positive Company-Sponsored Approach', *California Management Review,* Spring 1969.

16 cf. A. Hacker (ed.), *The Corporation Take-Over,* New York, Doubleday, 1965.

17 S. A. Greyser, 'Business and Politics', *Harvard Business Review,* Nov.-Dec., 1968.

Part 3

Leisure in the life cycle

Introduction

It is often assumed in the sociological analysis of modern societies like Britain that status is achieved rather than ascribed, and that therefore the biological fact of age is much less important than the social achievements of education and occupation in determining positions in the social structure. This assumption may have led us to underestimate the pervasive influence of age, and it does not square with the common practice in empirical research of using age as a key variable. Age is certainly relevant to an understanding of leisure behaviour, for it is clear that the content of leisure shifts throughout the life span, and that this shift in content is related to the general social status ascribed to age, and to the specific roles which are performed by each age group. It is also related to the changes in membership of different social groups, beginning with the narrow horizons of childhood, widening in adulthood and returning again to the limited parameters of the family in old age. It is also clear that the content of leisure changes historically with changes in social values, and the expectations attached to an age group such as adolescence have changed considerably in the last three generations.

It is useful, first of all, to establish the typical content of leisure in each stage of the life cycle; in childhood, in adolescence, in the family-building stage of married life, in middle age, and in old age. This will be easier to do for childhood and old age, as the pattern tends to be more homogeneous. In childhood the distinction between work and leisure is not always clear for, while going to school approximates to going to work, the activities within school may be very similar to play. Here a significant difference may be the close adult supervision of play in school. Children's play, as Elizabeth Child makes clear in her contribution, has many functions in the child's development. It enables the child to assimilate the environment within his own experience, usually through fantasy, and to accommodate himself to that environment. In infancy the child creates his own world through toys and has to accommodate to the demands of the family. In later childhood he joins in constructive play with other children and has to accommodate himself to the demands of his peers. The traditional pastimes of childhood are now, of course, overlaid with a daily infusion of television.

In adolescence the individual identity of each person emerges and with it a widening range of personal interests. Some adolescents become interested in reading, others in music, still others in team sports and so on. Nevertheless, it is clear that there are certain typical adaptations in adolescence to the opportunities which leisure presents. One is to spend much more time in the company of one's peers but often doing nothing except talk. Another is to become more interested in the company of the opposite sex, and this presumes making oneself attractive to them. Within this matrix of personal relationships certain interests such as music and sport are highly valued, and certain activities such as visiting the cinema and watching sport, are given preference. This age group still watches a lot of television, but less than children do.

In early married life leisure becomes more home-centred and geared to building a home and raising a family. The husband, on return from work, will share in the household chores, add improvements to his house and tinker with his car. The wife, whose day is not so clearly divided into work and leisure, may chat with the neighbours in between her various duties, or visit her relatives or friends, and then later prepare herself for the return home of her husband and children. In the evening she will rarely go out and her leisure interests may still be connected with her children, for example the magazines she reads will educate her about childrearing and cooking. Both husband and wife will spend long periods together watching television.

In later married life, when the children are growing up and are beginning to leave the parent household, the pattern of interests changes again. By this time the wife is already back at work, or if she is not working she will be spending much more time with her friends and relatives during the day. Both man and wife will take more interest in joining organizations. Both are now able to spend more money pursuing their own interests and those interests will be drawn from a very wide spectrum, from the Mother's Union to racing pigeons. But despite this activity and interest the overwhelming majority are usually at home watching television.

In old age the onset of infirmity inevitably means a restriction of physical activities, although as Amelia Harris and Stanley Parker make clear, a great many people still have a very active social life. Old people go out less, are unwilling to risk the hazards of bad weather or dark nights, and are more dependent upon people coming to see them. Failing eyesight or hearing may also place a limit upon the range of interests they may pursue at home. For the woman this adaptation of leisure interests to the onset of old age may be a very gradual process, but for the man it is dominated by the social fact of retirement. He now has to fill the void created by the loss of his working day, and he may still feel the need to regulate his day by spending time out of the home, as though he were going to work.

This brief picture of the changing content of leisure in the life cycle does not do justice to the very great variety of individual pursuits which exists, and it overemphasizes the influence of certain mass leisure pastimes such as watching television. In any case it is misleading to think of watching television as having the same meaning to all age groups, for not only does the choice of programmes differ but the response to a particular programme may also vary. Nevertheless it is already clear that the content of leisure behaviour appears to be a function of age and we must examine more closely what is the nature of this function.

The first relationship to be examined is how the general social status assigned to age affects leisure behaviour. This social status may carry with it certain legal sanctions or more usually the force of social disapproval, which proscribe certain activities for specific age groups. Children and adolescents may be prohibited from seeing certain films or they may just be discouraged by their parents from watching certain television programmes. But such sanctions are not only negative, for the child may receive positive encouragement to spend his time (and money) in one activity rather than another. Here, if the parents are the source of income, their influence may be greater in the consequent expenditure. On the other hand if the child earns money he also earns the right to spend it in his own way. The withdrawal of children from economic activity over the last century has, therefore, been a critical factor in relations between the generations, enhancing the control exercised by parents. This has, however, been counterbalanced by the obligations which society now places upon parents to help their children fulfil themselves as individuals.

The general social status attached to adulthood allows right of access to the whole range of permitted leisure activities within the society, but actual access may be limited to those who have the resources and this will be linked to a man's occupation (or in the case of a wife to her husband's). It may be linked to his occupation in two ways. If he has a career it will often indicate the stage he has reached within an ascending scale of income. If he is a manual worker his earnings will often sharply fall as his physical strength declines. Increasingly, however, it is not sufficient to consider the man's income alone in order to appreciate the style of living he enjoys. His wife's work and income, and possibly that of his wage-earning children, must also be considered.

Old people enjoy the legal status of adults but in terms of social status their position is diminished by their retirement from the labour force, and their consequent poor command over resources. It is characteristic of those with low incomes that a higher proportion of their income is spent on essentials like food and shelter, and proportionally less on luxuries such as entertainment. Nevertheless, old people expect to share in some degree in the rise in standards of living, and this has been recognized by the state in the level of pensions and supplementary benefits. Smoking, drinking, visiting children and watching television are all now regarded by the state in social security provision as part of a normal pattern of expenditure in old age.

General social status in our society is directly dependent on age, but it is also an indirect function of age through participation in the labour force. Both functions have their effects on leisure. But general social status is composed of many partial statuses, and though occupation may be the most important of these, because of its control over income, there are other statuses and associated roles which have a bearing on leisure. For example, part of the status of child is contained in the status of school pupil, part of the status of adult is contained in the status of parent. Each of these shapes and constrains the leisure which may be enjoyed at different points in the life cycle.

The central task assigned to children and adolescents by adults is learning, and they set aside part of each day for this purpose. This controls not only the time available for leisure but it also reduces the possibilities for earning. The demands of education spill over into leisure time and in the case of adolescents preparing for examinations, may leave little time for their own interests. But education not only marks out certain time for effort devoted to learning, it is also meant to prepare (as some of our contributors show in Part 5) the young to enjoy their leisure.

The status of student usually ends with adulthood except for the minority who participate in adult education, but other statuses are now assumed which greatly affect participation in leisure activity. These are associated with marriage and the family. As Colin Bell and Patrick Healey show in their chapter, the type of conjugal role within marriage will greatly affect the character of leisure for both man and wife. They show how in the traditional marriage leisure for the woman was very limited, and generally spent with female kin. They stress how the changing norms in non-traditional marriage not only allow more time for leisure but so define the role of woman in the marriage that she has the right to be an individual within it and that this individuality can be found in leisure.

Bell and Healey do not extend their analysis in depth to parental and filial roles, but much of what they have to say has relevance there too. The reduction of the number of children in a family has made it much easier for the mother to assert her own individuality independent of her children. On the other hand, this change has also been accompanied by a much greater respect for children as individuals. Whatever opportunities the smaller family does present to parents and children, it is clear that most adults still choose to find their satisfactions in their relationships with their children rather than with other people outside the family, and that the modern small family makes greater demands on the father than did the traditional large family.

The disintegration of the family as the children leave home to start their own families means that the man and wife have to adjust the level of intimacy of their own relationship, and the degree to which they share their leisure activities. Eventually with the death of one of the partners, usually the man first, this new pattern has itself to give place to a further adjustment which may mean a greater closeness to married children, or a resumption of relationships with the survivor's own siblings.

We have seen that the general social status accorded to each age group, and the particular statuses attached to occupational and familial roles, all have their bearing upon the way in which people choose to spend their leisure. Each of these statuses and their obligations cannot be easily avoided. If you live in this society you have to obey its laws, follow its practices with regard to earning your living and raising your family. There are, however, other statuses which are optional for some; whether to take part in politics or to support a church are examples. Involvement in these activities may produce very different patterns of leisure.

The evidence suggests that membership of groups outside of work and the family and kin group is fairly widespread. Almost everybody has belonged to some organization at some time during their lives and about 40% of the adult population currently belong to one. If we exclude trades unions where membership is nominal and makes relatively little demand on leisure time, the proportion is somewhat lower. It would appear that the first peak in membership is reached at the age of sixteen and that membership declines until the thirties are reached. A new peak is reached in the forties. This is followed by a further slow decline into old age. This overall pattern masks a number of important changes in type of membership throughout the life cycle. In adolescence membership tends to be in youth organizations, most frequently of the club variety where physical activities dominate the club programme. Membership in early adulthood tends to be of a single-purpose type, with sport still being important. Organizations which appeal to the middle-aged are either social clubs, or single purpose in character, political and welfare organizations being especially important. In late middle and old age membership of churches becomes highly important.

There is one remaining dimension to our discussion of leisure in the life cycle and this examines the changes which are taking place over time as a result of changing ideas about work and leisure. Old people may no longer be productive but this does not stop them having views about the work habits of those who still work, and these views may have been formed a half century ago. It does not prevent some of them from feeling that they would like to have continued working but have been forced to retire. The value they may place on work is still shared by their sons for whom the experience of unemployment in the 1930s served to strengthen their demands for the right to work. It is doubtful whether it is shared to the same degree by their grandchildren, particularly those in manual occupations.

As attitudes to work are linked to age, so are attitudes to leisure. The valuation placed on leisure by the young is higher than for other age groups and this emphasis may be expected to remain with them as they age, though its particular form of expression may alter. Youth culture is after all a novel phenomenon and its pioneers are only just entering their thirties. There is no comparable 'elders culture' deriving from the new leisure situation of the elderly. This may be because it would not have the same strategic role which youth culture has for commercial interests who want to form and change patterns of consumption. Its most fertile ground in the future may be in the resorts to which the wealthy retire and where a new style of life appears to be emerging.

It is not only the youth culture which has made its claims for the self-expression and fulfilment of the individual outside work. The educational system has increasingly widened its objectives in the curriculum from the basic skills needed for work – the three Rs – to producing rounded people. Although the examination system and the pressures induced by competition for university entry have limited progress towards this objective for some children, the dangers of specialization are widely appreciated among teachers. Nor is it only changes in the curriculum which have contributed towards this interest in the all-round development of the individual child. The newer methods of teaching which stress the consent and participation of the child have also encouraged the child to believe that he must nurture his own development as a person. There is, of course, a bitter debate among educationalists as to what have been the consequences of such 'activity methods' for educational standards.

In this introduction we have tried to show that age is relevant to an understanding of leisure behaviour, as it is to social behaviour in general. At a commonsense level we all appreciate that the biological and physical process of ageing makes certain activities more or less attractive to us than others, but age may also set up social expectations as to what people think is proper conduct. Old-age pensioners are not expected to go to 'pop' concerts; they are expected to go to old-time dancing. But the general respect accorded to each age group is also a function of the various statuses which contribute to the overall judgement of social status. The status of adult implies a status of adult worker and the likelihood of being a parent. These statuses also carry with them expectations of the style of leisure appropriate for adult worker, and the rights to leisure for a parent. The status of child implies an overall expectation that he will grow up and that his leisure will contribute to (or at least not obstruct) this process. This leads us to a conclusion echoed elsewhere in this book, that leisure is best seen as related to other social activities. It is most easily analysed and understood when it is seen in the context of the overall pattern of social behaviour. The first of our contributions, from Elizabeth and John Child, looks at children and leisure and takes a broad cross-cultural view. In this they examine the existing theories of play and find them lacking in sociological perspective. For them the functions of play are related to the expectations which a society has of its children as children, and also what it will expect of them as adults. They distinguish four categories of play and examine their form and content in different societies. They conclude that in advanced societies like our own there is greater emphasis on creative and imaginative play than on physical play and games of skill, but the latter two categories of play exhibit considerable similarities across a range of societies.

The next of our contributors, Cyril Smith, examines an age group which has had a critical role to play in our interest in leisure: young people. He looks at three differing views about the process of adolescence, the perspectives of socialization, of adolescence as a period of transition, and of the youth culture, and then goes on to examine how of each of these may throw light on leisure of the young. He finds that none of these perspectives is sufficient by itself. He concludes by exploring the relationships between the leisure of the young and the leisure of other age groups.

Colin Bell and Patrick Healey take a much wider slice of the life span for their examination of the family and leisure, though they are particularly interested in the role relationships of husband and wife during the family-building and child-rearing stages. They are particularly concerned in achieving comparability of sociological treatment between the work and leisure of the married woman and man. To do this they look at the wife as a domestic worker and examine how the time available after necessary work is done might, subject to the norms and expectations of the conjugal relationship, allow for the development of leisure for the housewife. They find the non-traditional, democratic family structure conducive to the growth of such expectations.

In the last chapter in this part of the book, Amelia Harris and Stanley Parker look at the leisure of the elderly. They find that the quantity and quality of leisure varies widely within this category. The financial constraints of old age have their effect as does the growing infirmity with advancing years, but what also seems important, especially since it raises matters of retirement policy and education, is whether there is as yet a satisfying social framework established for this period of life. This seems especially relevant to the position of men on retirement, though perhaps the anxieties which are supposed to be attached to this change have been exaggerated. They conclude that leisure for the elderly should have a positive role in life and not be identified simply with loss of employment.

9 Children and leisure

Elizabeth and John Child

If, as Bell and Healey note in Chapter 11, sociologists have given little attention to the leisure activities of wives and mothers, they have been even less interested in the leisure of children up to the age of puberty. There is, indeed, some question as to whether we can usefully employ the concept of leisure at all for pre-school children, since time for them has not generally become institutionally divided between obligatory activity (at school) and non-obligatory activity. For school children the notion of leisure becomes more appropriate, although the choice of leisure pursuits is normally restricted by parents, by social legislation, and by the very limited amount of money they have to spend.

For pre-adolescent children, the term 'play' has normally been used to describe activities which there is no obligation to undertake and which serve as ends in themselves — what for other groups we would call 'leisure' (1). Psychologists have given more attention to play than have sociologists, and have been more concerned with it as an element in individual development than as a socially learned and culturally derived set of behaviours. Both psychologists and sociologists tend to agree that play is free and spontaneous and is not intended to achieve an immediate objective, although it does have a deeper meaning in regard to personal development and the socialization process.

In practice, the play and leisure of pre-adolescent children amount to much the same activity, since such children generally play in their leisure time. Children can be said to have leisure in contrast to their obligations to, say, attend school and do homework. Even though leisure is understood to include passive activities such as watching television, or even just taking a nap, some commentators have written of 'passive' as well as 'active' play and would include spectator activities within the ambit of play. We can proceed, then, with the working assumption that play is by far the greatest element in children's leisure, and that for practical purposes the two are virtually synonymous.

This chapter describes studies of children's leisure in Britain and elsewhere which, taken together, demonstrate the influence of social variables upon patterns of play activity. It will become apparent that existing theories of play, most of which employ a bio-psychological rationale, cannot readily explain these systematic social variations. A new framework of analysis is therefore required which incorporates both sociological and bio-psychological dimensions.

Theories of play

There are three broad types of theories about play: physiological, biological and psychological. The Surplus Energy Theory advanced by Friedrich Schiller and Herbert Spencer, and the Recreation Theory put forward by Lazarus and others are *physiologically* based. Schiller considered that animals played when they had surplus energy to use up. Spencer took this proposition further by arguing that play was typical of children and young animals high up the evolutionary scale. Parents provided for the basic needs of these young, whose energies had consequently to be expended on those purposeless activities which Spencer regarded as play. Lazarus saw play as meeting a person's need for recreation. According to this theory, when someone is tired he can paradoxically recuperate by expending energy in vigorous recreation. It is relatively easy to think of cases which refute both these physiological theories and they therefore fail to provide a satisfactory explanation even for individual variation in play behaviour (2).

Among the major *biological* theories of play are the Pre-Practice Play theory advanced by Karl Groos and the Recapitulation Theory put forward by Stanley Hall. Groos defined play as the 'generalized impulse' to practise those instincts necessary for survival in adult life. He considered that the higher species were born with undeveloped instincts and were granted a period of childhood in which to practise them. Therefore, in contrast to Spencer, Groos viewed play as highly purposeful. Hall wrote very much under the influence of Darwin's work and sought in evolutionary theory a causal explanation for children's play. The result was the somewhat tortuous Recapitulation Theory of play which, in short, argued that at each stage of development the child re-enacted the experiences of his race at a definite stage in its history. For example, Hall argued that the urge which children had to climb trees was recapitulating the ape stage in man's evolution. Hall's theory fails entirely to stand up to the test of empirical evidence, such as the fact that a child of two years will choose to play with a model of advanced technology such as a toy car. While Groos' theory may account in part for the popularity of, for instance, certain warlike and hunting games with small boys, there is no evidence to support his assumption that basic instincts mature in adulthood rather than earlier in life (3).

Sigmund Freud and Jean Piaget have advanced the most influential *psychological* explanations for children's play (4). Freud used play as a tool for clinical diagnosis of mental disorders and as a therapy for emotionally disturbed children. He considered that it had two main functions. The first and major function was the re-enactment of unpleasant events in order to master them. This was his theory of 'Repetition Compulsion'. The second reason he gave for play was 'Wish

Fulfilment' that is, the modification of events in play as one would have liked them to have happened in reality. Later writers, including Melanie Klein, Lowenfeld and Helanko, have similarly viewed play as tension-relieving, and appreciated its therapeutic value (5).

Piaget thought that play was similar in kind to other activities such as learning and imitation, and as such it shared with them the processes of accommodation and assimilation. He defined play as pure assimilation. Assimilation can generally be described as the organism's digestion and integration of materials and signals in order to make them part of its make-up; whereas accommodation is the prior stage of receiving information and signals from the external world and the adjustment necessary to make this reception possible. According to Piaget, when the two processes are in balance, intelligent adaptation occurs and the child is engaged in learning. When accommodation predominates over assimilation, imitation results, and when assimilation predominates over accommodation, play occurs. Piaget envisaged a behavioural continuum with play at one end and imitation at the other. As soon as an activity contains a preponderance of assimilation Piaget would call it a play activity, and regard it as increasingly 'ludic' the greater the imbalance of assimilation over accommodation.

While these more recent psychological theories may provide powerful explanations for an individual child's motivation to play and emotional attitude towards adults and other children in the play situation, they cannot cope with the systematic social variations in the forms of play behaviour which are found in practice. For example, a child from any social background may feel aggressive if thwarted, but it is observable that in a play situation the working-class child will tend to vent his aggression directly on other children, whereas a middle-class child may be more inclined either to suppress its manifestation or else to vent it on inanimate objects such as toys. An explanation for this type of difference cannot be sought in the psychological variable of aggression but must derive from an appreciation of different social-class norms of behaviour.

It is remarkable, then, that *sociological* analyses of play have been so rare. A few writers, such as Caillois, Huizinga and Kroeber, have recently adopted a more sociological approach, though this has been largely of a quasi-philosophical nature and has not been closely linked with empirical data. Kroeber and Huizinga both see an element of play as pervading many social activities, including religious ceremonies, legal proceedings and even war. Caillois and Huizinga disagree over the question whether play can be said to have preceded culture or whether it is derived from culture. In other words, are the forms of play among children to be regarded as universal or as socially determined? The following review of evidence will lead us towards the view that certain categories of play (most notably physical play) follow almost universal patterns, while other categories of play (most notably imaginative play) appear to be very largely a product of particular social environments (6).

The degree of cross-cultural variation

One can distinguish four broad categories of children's play: (a) imaginative play, (b) creative play, (c) physical play and (d) games of skill. Imaginative and creative play exhibit considerable differences between societies, and we will suggest that the explanation for these can be found primarily in different socialization requirements. On the other hand, physical play and games of skill exhibit considerable similarities across a range of societies.

1. Imaginative and creative play

Imaginative play may take the form of solitary make-believe or of dramatic role-playing in groups of children. Imaginative play is closely associated with the process of acculturation and therefore clearly bears the imprint of social factors. It would seem that in societies characterized by complex roles, imaginative play is correspondingly rich and widely indulged in, while in societies with simple structures, where the nature of roles is easily grasped through observation alone, it is a little used play form since it serves no great purpose for the child.

It has been observed that in traditional societies, where the pattern of life changes little between generations, and where children partici-pate directly in adult activities through being assigned work roles at a very early age, there is little, if any, imaginative play. In such cases, there is no strict division between the role of a child and that of an adult. Children have little need to copy adult activities in play because at an early age they engage in similar pursuits themselves.

In many sectors of British society, there would seem to be more ambiguity about the role of the mother than of the father, and (as is described later) girls have been found to engage more in dramatic role-playing than boys. Imaginative play appears rapidly to reach a peak of popularity around four years of age and remains popular for the next four years. While in Britain imaginative play does not appear to be the most popular type, in the Okinawan village of Taira it is. And again the factor of social complexity affords an explanation. In Taira life is particularly complex for children because they are usually bilingual, wear western clothes and yet think of themselves as Japanese. There is a great deal of dramatic role-playing among girls who act out their mother's household duties. This is stimulated by the dual nature of the mother's role, in which she is not only responsible for the running of the household, but is also an equal partner with her husband in agricultural work. Girls seldom act out the mother's agricultural role because they rarely see her at work in the fields. Boys, in contrast, indulge far less in dramatic role-playing because it is easier for them to understand the nature of their father's role which has only one traditional facet, that of bread-winner.

In short, the evidence suggests (a) that children will engage in more imaginative play the less they are able to participate in adult roles and (b) that the content of imaginative play will tend to be more varied when these adult roles are more complex.

In creative play the child expresses his creativity through the use of materials such as paper, crayons, paint and plasticine. Creative play depends on the ability of parents to provide their children with these necessary tools and only during this century has it become predominant in advanced societies. In less developed societies most parents cannot afford the necessary materials and under these circumstances creative play appears to be subsumed into forms of imaginative play.

2. Physical play and games and skill

There is often a remarkable similarity, as the Opies have found, in the type of physical play activities which can be found across societies (7). For example, games such as 'Crusts and Crumbs', 'Fox and Chickens', Blind Man's Buff', 'Hide-and-Seek', 'Tug of War', 'Leapfrog' and 'Stroke the Baby' are played in similar forms in a large number of countries and indeed go back in their origins some 2,000 years to the ancient Mediterranean world. However, although there are few cross-cultural differences in the *nature* of physical play activities, there is some difference in the *degree* to which children engage in physical play. In some societies it is the predominant type of play, while in others it is far less prominent. At least as important as cultural location, so far as physical play is concerned, is the sex difference, and we shall examine the situation in Britain in some detail later.

There is no hard and fast dividing line between physical play and games of skill. Games such as football, which are usually placed in the physical play category, require high levels of skill, while games such as hopscotch, juggling and marbles are distinguished merely by an increasing preponderance of the skilled over the physical element. At the physical end of this continuum, children may engage in forms of 'rough-and-tumble' play while at the skilled extreme one has games of dexterity or indeed of mental skill, such as chess. Apart from team games, games of skill occupy a minor place among British and American play activities, but enjoy a major role in many other societies.

The basic forms of many games of skill are similar throughout the world, and in some cases there is evidence to show how they have spread from one country to another. Hopscotch is of ancient origin and originally symbolized the labyrinth through which the initiate had to wander. In the game the child had to push a stone (symbolizing the soul) towards the exit of the labyrinth. With the growth of Christianity the layout was amended to the form of a basilica and the meaning given to moving the stone was now that of helping the soul to reach heaven. Thus, while there is a widespread similarity in the form of games of skill between societies, it is important to note that the substance and the meaning of their rules have become closely related to the traditions of particular cultures. The 'spirit of the game' reflects the prevailing values of a particular society – for example the phrase 'play to win' lacks a meaning outside competitive societies such as our own.

Explanations for cross-cultural variations

Only a few attempts have been made to account for cross-cultural variation in children's play patterns, and among the most interesting has been that of Roberts and Sutton-Smith. They have put forward a 'conflict-enculturation' hypothesis to account for cross-cultural variations in play (8). They suggest that people play games as an outlet for the personal inner conflicts which their particular type of child-rearing has precipitated. For example, in those societies which stress success as an important goal for the child, games of physical skill are prevalent. According to the 'conflict-enculturation' thesis, such games are played by children who are under pressure to achieve and who use simulated achievement in games to assuage their anxiety. In short, the basis of involvement in games is the need for relief from inner tensions which the socialization process has brought about.

It is interesting to note that Roberts and Sutton-Smith's mode of explanation refers to cross-cultural differences in social expectations and behaviour as the sources of corresponding differences in play patterns, but they refer to specifically psychological mechanisms in order to relate the two sets of social phenomena.

Play in Britain and America – variations within cultures

1. Sex differences

Many writers on children's play have noted the effect of sex differences. Some have highlighted the different activities enjoyed by boys and girls, while others have singled out their different ways of playing. Roberts and Sutton-Smith pointed to various links between child-rearing practices and the games children played. Combining the results of two studies, by Barry and Child and by Sears *et al.*, the Roberts and Sutton-Smith thesis is supported in the case of American children (9). In the United States greater emphasis is given to achievement in the upbringing of boys, and American schoolboys have been found to play more games of physical skill. On the other hand greater emphasis is placed on obedience in the upbringing of girls and they do, as Roberts and Sutton-Smith would predict, play more games of strategy.

A recent study in America by Rosenberg and Sutton-Smith has indicated that girls are increasingly coming to prefer what were formerly male play activities (10). Thus, traditionally male games such as baseball, soccer and camping do not now show significant differences between the sexes. This change over time does not represent so much a convergence between the play roles of the two sexes as an expansion in the scope of girls' leisure activities.

The senior author found in her own study of pre-school children's choice of play materials and equipment at Telford New Town that boys and girls agreed on the most and least popular items. Lego building blocks were a firm favourite equally for both sexes, probably because of the many uses to which they would be put. Chalking on blackboards and playing with sawdust were the least popular activities, presumably because both were regarded as inferior substitutes for painting or crayoning, and for playing with sand respectively.

Pre-school girls enjoyed non-vigorous physical play activities involving a fixed motion, such as swings and swing-boats, to a much greater extent than did boys. In contrast, boys' play preferences for physical play centred on more vigorous activities such as the climbing frame and push carts. These sex-related differences in physical play preferences were the most marked of any, as Table 1 illustrates. It is worth noting that mothers were not in attendance during the play sessions involved and that there was no direct adult encouragement for boys and girls to

Table 1 Pre-school children's play activities where boys' and girls' preferences are different, Telford New Town, Salop, 1968

The figures show the mean percentage engaging in each activity

Play activity	Boys	Girls	Level of confidence
Push carts	13·09	7·09	<·001
Climbing frame	7·72	4·01	<·005
Swing	0·56	4·61	<·0005
Swing boats	6·22	8·20	<·10
Painting	6·29	8·60	<·20

25 simultaneous observations were made for boys and girls at five-minute intervals during each of 33 mornings. Observations for each day were averaged.

select particular activities. So even at an early age girls do seem to be the gentler sex, though how far they have already been trained to this remains an open question.

A further study at Telford New Town attempted to trace the variation of play patterns with age while also recording differences between boys and girls. This study was not confined to pre-school children, but included children from the ages of three to twelve. It was found that more activities were confined to girls than to boys. It was girls almost exclusively who played with dolls and who did knitting, sewing and cooking. It was boys almost exclusively who played football and at cards. Boys tended to have a slightly wider variety of play activities, but most of these were variants of physical play. More marked was the tendency of children from both sexes to engage in a greater range of activities between the ages of five and eight, as the following figures show:

Average number of different play activities engaged in — Summer holiday period, Telford New Town, 1968

Age	Boys n = 132	Girls n = 112
3-4	10·7	9·8
5-8	18·6	17·2
9-12	15·0	14·1

These figures seem to suggest that children do engage in a very wide range of different leisure activities, but the provisions at Telford when the study was made were such that children had no less than 62 different activities to choose from.

2. Age differences

Although the popularity of different activities was found to vary according to the child's sex, the ages at which particular pursuits became popular remained similar for both sexes. Differences between the sexes emerge more clearly if we think in terms of the basic categories of play – physical (including games of skill), creative and imaginative – rather than in terms of specific activities. Girls engaged fairly heavily in all three basic types of play, though at different ages. When girls are about three years of age their play is mainly creative, with painting a favourite activity. During the following year, imaginative play reaches a peak of popularity for girls and it stays popular over the next four years, although it never becomes the most popular type of play. From four to seven years of age, girls enjoy all three forms of play, with creative play declining in popularity and physical play rising over this age range. After about six years, and throughout the rest of the age range up to twelve which was sampled, physical play dominates in girls' leisure activities.

In contrast, play among the boys was focused on physical activities. Throughout the whole age range from three to twelve years, boys took part in physical activities most of all. Although their level of interest in creative play over the age range approaches that of girls, this type of play never predominates, while boys were found to show very little interest in imaginative play. These findings must, however, be treated as provisional since the fact that the study was carried out during the summer may account for some of the emphasis on physical play.

As well as chronological age, children do of course differ in mental age; the relation between the two scales of age is measured in I.Q. scores. Several studies of 'gifted children', those with high I.Q.s, have produced similar results in regard to their play behaviour. This exhibits greater intellectual activity and variety, a preference for quieter and less competitive games, together with a greater tendency to take part in play that is imaginative and either solitary or with older children.

3. Social class differences
There is little unanimity among researchers who have studied the possible effects of social class on patterns of children's play, but some have found social class differences to be systematically and extensively associated with children's leisure activities.

Mary Stewart, in a study comparing the leisure pursuits of English grammar school and secondary modern children, found differences in their reading habits, cinema attendance, radio programme preferences, in the clubs and associations they belonged to and in their favourite activities outside school. She also found that grammar school children, the majority of whom came from middle-class backgrounds, were more likely to belong to Scouts, Guides and religious organizations (11).

The Newsons have also illustrated how class differences can lead to different types of play (12). They point out, in their study of four-year-old Nottingham children, that working-class children have in general less play space inside the home, more siblings to play with and greater competition for their mother's attention, than is the case with middle-class children. Four-year-old working-class children tended to display more overt aggression and this, the Newsons consider, may well be due to the fact that their mothers intervene little, if at all, in their quarrels with other children, encouraging them instead to fight their own battles. By contrast, middle-class four-year-olds are less likely to play in the streets than in their own houses or gardens. In fact they hardly ever venture outside their home ground unless accompanied by an adult. Their parents exercise some control in the selection of their playmates, arbitrate in their disputes and pass judgement on these.

4. Family differences

Baldwin studied the effects of home environment on nursery school behaviour (13). He found that a 'democratic home' encouraged children to participate in nursery school activities freely and actively. Self-assertion as well as creative and constructive behaviour was also more prominent among children from this kind of home. On the other hand, an 'indulgent home', in which the child was spoilt, appeared to have contrary effects. It tended to make the child physically apprehensive and inhibited the development of physical skills. Thirdly, an 'autocratic home' was likely to produce a quiet, well-behaved, non-resistant child, who was socially passive and also restricted in his curiosity, originality and imaginativeness.

5. Regional differences

We have already noted how markedly contrasting patterns of children's leisure are associated with different cultural settings, and we reach a similar conclusion when examining regional sub-cultures within any particular society. The way in which this regional dimension has been studied varies considerably.

The Opies, in their study of children's street games in Britain, have shown how children consistently pass on different regional traditions in their games. For example, 'Chain He' is an old favourite but names for it vary widely. In Helston it is called 'Stringing up'; in Northampton 'Altogether Tiggy'; in Sleaford 'Long Chain Tag'; in Sale 'Staggy in the Button Hole'; in Pontypool 'Chain a Wedding'; and in Swansea 'Cock Warren'. A wide variety of children's street games exhibit minor regional differences.

Holme and Massie's comparison of children's play in Elm Green, Stevenage New Town, and Heygate, Southwark, also illustrates contrasts between different areas (14). Elm Green is new, planned, medium-density and pedestrian-segregated. Heygate, in contrast, is old, unplanned and badly over-crowded. It was found that in Elm Green children's play tended to be individual, passive and home-oriented. Parents, rather than the peer group, tended to influence it and the children in general became involved in group activities more slowly than their contemporaries in Heygate. Heygate children tended to play away from home and in groups. Their play was more active and included more games of a traditional character. A factor explaining these differences in play between the two areas was probably the lack of an established sub-cultural tradition in Elm Green.

6. Differences in immediate play environment

However, Holme and Massie also concluded that an urban environment, such as Southwark, could restrict children's play because physical inconveniences, such as crowded streets and traffic, sometimes prevented it from occurring spontaneously. The restrictiveness of an urban environment is particularly evident if children live in high flats, since a child often has to make a considerable journey to the play area below. This is most damaging for pre-school children, since there is often little room indoors for them to play in and parents are unwilling to let them go outside on their own.

Johnson contrasted children's play in well and poorly equipped playgrounds. She found that in well-equipped playgrounds children's play was characterized by greater amounts of physical exercise and play with materials, together with less social exchange and undesirable behaviour. In poorly equipped playgrounds the converse applied (15).

A number of writers have studied the influence of adults in the child's immediate play environment. For instance Bishop, in a study of the effect of mothers playing with their three- to six-year-old children, found that direct interference, control and criticism of the child's play gave rise to non-cooperation or inhibition of play on the child's part (16). Lippitt and White, in their classic study of adult leaders in children's clubs, illustrated how children responded to different styles of leadership. They found how three different patterns of leadership behaviour — autocratic, democratic and *laissez-faire* — resulted in distinctive kinds of behaviour among children and that a characteristic emotional atmosphere developed in each club (17).

Thus the physical aspects of the immediate play environment (or its 'technology'), the type of adult personnel and other children can all affect the quality of play. To borrow a concept from organizational analysis, these factors can be said to comprise the playground 'socio-technical system'.

Conclusion

The more influential theories on children's play are limited to the functions of play for the individual child. Piaget's analysis is the most highly developed of this genre and relies upon a hypothesized interaction between predominant modes of play and stages of intellectual growth. Empirically, the differentiation of psychological from social variables associated with play is problematic. The psychological variable least 'contaminated' by social influence is probably intelligence in the very early years, though sociologists have demonstrated the dangers of social bias in the measures normally employed. The age-level where social variables would appear to have a restricted influence on play are the first two years of life during which play is characterized by sensory-motor activity.

A review of comparative research evidence has suggested that even the apparently universal biological variables of age and sex do at an early age have culturally specific social meanings attached to them. This social meaning in turn is translated into expectations as to how the child should play. The problem of treating age and sex simply as bio-psychological universals in the prediction of play lies in the different meanings attached to age and sex roles in different communities. In addition the category of social membership in which children are located – be this social, regional or class – operates powerfully in the socialization of children into pursuing particular patterns of play. Clearly, then, an adequate analysis of children's play, which we have taken as representing children's leisure as a whole, must take account of the interaction between psychological motivators to play and social influences on the forms of behaviour which ensue. In any given play situation, the immediate socio-technical environment of physical equipment, adult supervision and other children will, as we have seen, also help or hinder the successful performance of behaviour to which the child's personal and social make-up predisposes him.

The presence of social and socio-technical influences on play remind us that our children are in large measure a reflection of ourselves. In so far as man can choose to make his society a better place, he can enhance the development of his children. Children have a facility, when they are granted the opportunity, of imparting qualities of play into their acquisition of knowledge and understanding, so that new horizons are eagerly sought and enjoyed. This would seem to be leisure at its most creative and fulfilling. If as adults we have an obligation to assist children in their play, we also have an opportunity to enrich our own lives by learning from it.

References

1 For a further discussion see A. Giddens, 'Notes on the Concepts of Play and Leisure', *Sociological Review,* March 1964.

2 F. Schiller, *Essays, Aesthetical and Philosophical,* London, 1875; H. Spencer, *Principles of Psychology,* Williams and Norgate, 1855, vol. II, ch. IX; M. Lazarus, *Uber die Reize des Spiels,* Berlin, 1883.

3 K. Groos, *The Play of Man,* Heinemann, 1901; G. S. Hall, *Adolescence, Its Psychology,* New York, Appleton, 1920, vol. I, ch. III.

4 S. Freud, *Beyond the Pleasure Principle,* Hogarth Press, 1955, *Complete Works,* vol. 18; J. Piaget, *Play, Dreams and Imitation in Childhood,* Heinemann, 1951.

5 M. Klein, *Contributions to Psycho-analysis, 1921-1945,* Hogarth Press, 1948; M. Lowenfeld, *Play in Childhood,* Gollancz, 1935, ch. XI; R. Helanko, *Theoretical Aspects of Play and Socialisation,* Finland, Turku University Press, 1958.

6 R. Caillois, *Man, Play and Games,* Thames and Hudson, 1962; J. Huizinga, *Homo Ludens: A study of the play element in culture,* Routledge, 1949; A. L. Kroeber, *Anthropology,* New York, 1948.

7 I. and P. Opie, *Children's Games in Street and Playground,* Oxford University Press, 1969.

8 J. M. Roberts and B. Sutton-Smith, 'Child Training and Game Involvement', *Ethnology,* 1, 1962.

9 H. Barry and I. L. Child, 'A Cross-Cultural Survey of Some Sex Differences in Socialization', *Journal of Abnormal Social Psychology, 55,* 1957; R. R. Sears and others, *Patterns of Child-rearing,* New York, Harper & Row, 1957.

10 B. G. Rosenberg and B. Sutton-Smith, 'A Revised Conception of Masculine-Feminine Differences in Play Activities', *Journal of Genetic Psychology, 96,* 1960.

11 M. Stewart, 'The Leisure Activities of Grammar School Children', *British Journal of Education Psychology,* 20, 1970.

12 J. and E. Newson, *Four Years Old in an Urban Community,* Allen & Unwin, 1968.

13 A. L. Baldwin, 'Socialisation and the Parent-Child Relationship', *Child Development,* 19, 1948; A. L. Baldwin, 'The Effect of Home Environment on Nursery School Behaviour', *Child Development,* 20, 1949.

14 A. Holme and P. Massie, *Children's Play: A Study of Needs and Opportunities,* Michael Joseph, 1970.

15 M. W. Johnson, 'The Effect on Behaviour of Variation in the Amount of Play Equipment', *Child Development,* 6, 1935.

16 M. B. Bishop, 'Mother-Child Interaction and the Social Behaviour of Children', *Psychology Monographs,* 65, 1951.

17 R. Lippitt, 'An Experimental Study of the Effect of Democratic and Authoritarian Group Atmospheres', *University of Iowa Studies in Child Welfare,* 16, 1940; R. Lippitt and R. White, 'The "Social Climate" of Children's Groups', in R. G. Barker and others (eds.), *Child Behaviour and Development,* New York, McGraw-Hill, 1943.

10 Adolescence

Cyril S. Smith

Since there is much disagreement as to what constitutes the social process of adolescence, it will be useful to demarcate the ground to be covered in this chapter. It will be taken in crude but convenient terms to cover that age category between the ages of 11 and 25; the period in Britain between entry into secondary education and entry into the married state for most of the male population. Adolescence, in the sense in which we are to use it here, lasts longer for the middle classes. It is a process which is marked by a number of stages recognized by such lay and technical terms as 'pubescent', 'adolescent', 'teenager', 'young person', 'youth' and 'young adult', some of which correspond to changes in social status. Such changes, because of their link with autonomy and command over resources, are highly relevant to leisure patterns. We shall use the term 'young people' as a generic term in this chapter in preference to what might be regarded as a pejorative term, 'adolescent'.

This article is divided into three parts: the first analyses the process of adolescence, the second explores the relevance of that process to the leisure behaviour of young people, and the third suggests some relationships between the leisure of the young and the leisure of other age groups. The assumption underlying this approach is that the meaning of leisure usually becomes clearer when it is related to some other form of behaviour. For example, its significance to adults is usually clearer when related to behaviour at work. In adolescence it becomes clearer when related to the process of socialization, the occupation of certain transitional statuses and roles, and to the emergence of the youth culture.

One perspective which might be taken in analysing adolescence is to see it as a period of socialization during which the knowledge, attitudes and skills appropriate to certain adult roles are internalized. During this period the young person has to learn how to become an adult worker, to prepare himself for marriage, and to incorporate the minimum requirements of his role as a citizen. Underlying all of these roles is the fundamental demand that he give up being a child (and this may mean unlearning some behavioural responses) and learn how to make his own decisions. The way those decisions may be taken will differ if the person is male or female.

Another perspective is to see adolescence as a period marked by various transitions in status and in the occupation of certain temporary roles. The requirements of these statuses and roles do not have to be internalized to the same degree as those which are to be occupied in adulthood. On the other hand since they are being currently performed, rather than rehearsed, there are various sanctions and rewards attached to their proper performance which ensure some degree of conformity. The apprentice will behave like an apprentice although he is soon likely to forget what it was like once he becomes a skilled adult worker. Other, less well defined, roles summed up in such phrases as 'boys will be boys' permit a certain range of deviant behaviour which ceases to be acceptable at the end of adolescence. David Matza has called these the 'subterranean traditions' of youth (1).

A third perspective in analysing adolescence might be to challenge the assumptions of socialization which imply fitting the young into society, and rather to see youth as an autonomous influence within the culture which may conflict with the consensus of values among adults (and in particular those with professional responsibilities in training the young). Here it is relevant to note the emergence of youth cultures in modern industrial societies and to see these not as the sum of individual adaptations to the stresses of growing up, but rather as a cultural adaptation to a change in the social structure. Eisenstadt has suggested that youth cultures may have the function of bridging the gap between the particularistic and expressive influences of the family on the child, and the requirements of the adult to behave according to universal and instrumental criteria of the modern economy (2). These adaptations tend to be somewhat short-lived in content, though since any single generation of young people is in itself short they may survive several generations.

All or any of these three perspectives might throw some light on the process of adolescence in modern Britain, and all three also provide different approaches to the understanding of leisure in adolescence. The 'socialization' perspective indicates the way in which the rewards of leisure encourage growth but also the relevance of experience of an area of personal choice and freedom to major decisions about work and marriage. The 'transitional' perspective draws attention to the great differences in behaviour over this period and how those might be related to access to resources and the degrees of freedom attached to each successive status. The 'youth culture' perspective shows how the leisure situation, which is far less constrained and controlled by adults than other social situations, may generate values and behaviour which are in sharp conflict with those required in the home, the school or at work. Each of these three perspectives will need to be explored at greater length to draw out their implications for leisure.

When their children enter adolescence, parents face the obligation to let them choose their own friends, and since such friends may be enormously influential it is an important situation to accept. Whilst enlarging the child's area of autonomy, it does not alter his control over other resources for leisure and although he may be allowed pocket money this will not determine the pattern of his leisure activities very closely. This initial freedom in choice of friends takes on a new significance later as an interest in the opposite sex begins, though parents seem more willing to permit this new degree of freedom to their sons.

Encouragement for the young person to make his own decisions has become especially common in his choice of occupation, though for those who enter higher education, the decision may be considerably delayed. Such encouragement is not so necessary in his other economic role, that of consumer, where the parents in their own interests may wish to restrain consumption. Here the young person's expectations tend to move one step ahead of his own ability to satisfy them, with the discrepancy being especially marked in the year before leaving school (which may account for this being the peak year for delinquency). Consumer behaviour, especially in the early years of adolescence, tends to be undifferentiated and inclined to satisfy basic personal needs such as eating and smoking. Only later does it become more reciprocal or aimed at pleasing friends.

Encouragement for the young person to choose his own marriage partner is now almost universal in Britain, though mothers are still likely to help their daughters to be chosen. Appearance is often a critical factor in the choice of marriage partner and ways of improving it through dress, hairdressing and cosmetics are a major item of expenditure for the teenager (3). Despite the increased interest which boys take in their appearance, it is still true that girls spend substantially more. Preparing oneself for the occasion is, however, only half the story; it is equally important to be in the right place at the right time, and this means for most young people going out to pubs and clubs. It appears that once serious courting begins the young couple spend less time out of their homes (4).

Whereas most people have the expectation of earning their living and marrying, and therefore have some preparation for it, not everybody is expected to take part in governing their community. Training for civic roles therefore is at a minimum, often merely encouragement to give consent to other people making decisions, and to obey the law. The Youth Service, which has responsibility for caring for young people as members of the community, seldom interprets this role in political or even social terms. The voluntary organizations, which form numerically the most important part of the Service, are more concerned with moral

education, the ethics of personal relationships, than social education (5). The civic provision, on the other hand, seems more concerned
with amenity than community. It affords an occasion for meeting
friends, for listening to pop music or playing games. But both the
voluntary and civic provision have to effect a compromise between the
expectations of their members that their clubs and organizations are for
'fun' with the more 'serious' educational expectations of their leaders,
if they are not to lose their clientèle.

The second perspective which might provide a basis for understanding the pattern of leisure in adolescence is to see it as a period of
successive small shifts in status and role which are by their nature
temporary. The child becomes defined socially as adolescent on
entering the secondary-school system. He becomes a young worker on
leaving school or a student on leaving secondary for further or higher
education. Each of these improvements in status carries with it greater
command over resources and greater freedom of movement. The
process is paralleled by changes in legal status. Certain transitional roles
in leisure behaviour seem to be linked with membership of this age
group; member of a pop group or member of an audience, for example.
In none of these statuses and roles can it be said that much needs to be
internalized before the young person passes on to the next stage, and
this may help to explain why juvenile behaviour so often appears
uncertain, and the young person at a loss as to how he should behave.

The status of 'school child' dominates the early years of adolescence,
and parents are likely to control the leisure of their teenage children if
it interferes with their readiness for school next morning. Later on in
the secondary school phase parents are only likely to continue these
controls if the children are in selective education. For others they may
recognize that their children are getting older in ways that the school
would not distinguish. They may accept, for example, greater freedom
in dressing than the school would permit. There are now signs, however,
of a greater sensitivity to the adolescent's need for status on the part of
the schools. Some may allow pupils over 14 to attend youth clubs on
the school premises (6).

Although the overwhelming majority of young people finish school
at 16, a substantial number remain in full-time education and, though
there is no obvious change in their status unless, and until, they enter
further or higher education, their pattern of leisure differs significantly
from young workers. In terms of time available for relaxation, it is
likely to diminish with the pressures of competition for examination
success and for entry into higher education. Most weekday nights
during term time become absorbed by the demands of homework (7).

To remain in full-time education means to remain in a state of
penury, despite the fringe benefits attached to life in colleges and

universities. State grants, which are now increasingly looking like a state wage, are usually no more than a third of the comparable industrial wage at the same age, and although this may be supplemented by vacation employment, and by the concealed subsidies for some of living at home, it usually means a style of life visibly poorer by contrast with young workers. Much less is spent on keeping up appearances and on manufactured entertainment. Less will be spent on personal transport but probably more on foreign travel. Many more facilities for sport and recreation will, however, be available free of charge to students at their colleges.

Starting work full-time means that the young worker has much less time available for leisure. His working hours will closely resemble those of adults, though he is less likely to work shifts, and he is forbidden from working overnight until he is 18. He has to set off for work earlier than he did for school, and he returns home about two hours later, probably more fatigued than when he came back from school. With the five-day week his weekends will not be much affected, and if anything he will be better off than those school children who work part time on Saturdays, but his holidays will be much shorter. It cannot be said, however, that the loss of free time on entering work requires a change to a new pattern of leisure behaviour. When the new pattern does eventually emerge, it is likely to be a result of an increase in resources to satisfy developing, but not entirely new, needs.

Although starting work may mean less free time it does bring a sharp increase in income which makes it possible to exercise more choice in what to do with the free time left. Notwithstanding the practice in many industrial areas for young workers to 'tip-up' their wages to their mothers and to receive back their 'spends', their disposable income is likely to double (8). Those in manual occupations can expect to be earning the full adult wage at 18; usually about double the wage at which they started. They can now afford to buy more cigarettes, go to the cinema more than once a week and perhaps pay for their girlfriends, and they can increase their spending on their appearance. They can buy radios, record players, records and tape recorders. In a year or two they may begin to buy their own transport.

Another marked difference in status which cross-cuts the differences of school and work is that between male and female. Throughout adolescence there is a greater obligation on the girl to perform household duties; to share in the shopping, cooking and cleaning. Moreover, when she has completed these chores she will, especially in early adolescence, be much less free to move out of the home because of the supervision her parents will wish to exercise. Although these controls are much less strong than they were, many surveys have reported similar findings to those reported for Bury; that, of the sample of 14-18 year olds, 85 out of the 137 boys were at home two evenings or less in the week compared with 61 of the 132 girls (9). Such sex differences in behaviour tend, however, to become less marked in the later years of adolescence.

Despite the spread of equal pay in British industry, girls are still likely to earn substantially less than boys. This is partly a function of their concentration in certain lowly paid sectors of industry such as distribution, and partly of the occupations they follow. Patterns of expenditure also differ, with girls spending much more on their appearance, particularly on clothes and cosmetics, and boys much more on drink and cigarettes (10). Although it is likely that girls are greater consumers of the products of the teenage culture (they buy and listen to more music and they read more), boys are greater addicts of sport.

The changes in social status which have been discussed often mirror changes in the roles to which the young have access. A delay in the age at which they can start work will be reflected in the age at which they might be able to afford to marry and start a family. It is characteristic of modern societies to extend the period of education for their young. During this period of dependence before assumption of the full status of adult in work and marriage, it has also become characteristic for the young to be closely identified with the world of entertainment, as entertainers or the entertained, and more recently for them to be associated with protest. Indeed the two are closely linked since some entertainers have become leading figures in social protest. This leads on naturally to consider our third perspective on leisure and adolescence, that of the emergence of youth culture.

Youth cultures are not entirely new in industrial society, though they have become a more visible and acceptable part of the cultural scene since the 1950s (11). Wherever young people have gathered together, apart from adults, they have tended to develop their own style of life, and the marked segregation of boys during adolescence in traditional working-class communities produced the typically 'corner boy' culture. This segregation is now more common throughout all social classes, and moreover the pattern is shared by girls as well as boys. The expansion of the mass media has made it possible to achieve a symbolic unity of the young in one sense and, therefore, a segregation without the physical association which was previously necessary.

Youth cultures differ from their parent cultures in industrial societies by placing a far greater value on emotions than upon reason. Feelings are seen to be unique, spontaneous, free, honest and dramatic, whereas reason is associated with uniformity, calculation, control, concealment and routine. British youth culture shares these values, but in an environment notably hostile to them, not only because of the traditional British reserve, but also because of our settled ways of doing things. Although the expressive values of youth culture have relevance to a wide range of relationships, it is in the leisure situation where they are most appropriate, and where they are least likely to bring young people into conflict with adults. Indeed, in this situation, adults are prepared to be influenced by the young. It is in school, where effort may be suborned by identification with youth culture (as Sugarman's research clearly shows (12)), or in the work situation where appearance may affect job opportunities, that adults react most strongly against it.

Music is in many ways the central activity of the British youth culture from which many subsidiary activities flow, and this contrasts with the central importance of sport (or, as they term it, 'athletics') to the Americans. Indeed there is, as Emmett has shown with secondary-school children, some antipathy between the two (13). Those youngsters who are most 'with it' are least responsive to the school's sporting activities. Active interest in sport declines after leaving school, and the survey conducted for the Crowther Committee (1959) among National Servicemen showed that only one third (31%) continued to play team games in the three years after leaving school (14). This figure dips sharply in the twenties and is a bare handful after the age of thirty. Watching sport tends, however, to increase after leaving school and in the early decades of adulthood. It is the most popular choice of television programme among young men.

The emergence of youth culture has not only had implications for the leisure of young people, and for the commercial exploitation of this popular market, but it has also presented a more fundamental challenge to the nature of industrial society by stimulating the growth of the 'underground'. One hypothesis which might account for this development is that the failure of C.N.D. in the early 1960s led to a temporary withdrawal by the young from social concern into the private world of drug taking, but this in turn has also led (partly as a reaction to what was considered harsh police control over a harmless pastime) to a renewal of protest in many forms. Such protest has been especially concerned with race relations, but more recently also with the nostalgia for a simpler and purer way of life in the communes. It has increased the number of young people dropping out in order to seek a less competitive and more cooperative existence.

It is difficult in the absence of sound research to establish what effect the youth culture has had upon young people, and whether that effect continues into adulthood. It is equally difficult to establish whether the youth culture has changed the behaviour and attitudes of adults in our society. It has certainly made people more aware of generational differences and established certain forms of behaviour as especially youthful; to be 'with it' is a case in point. It has changed the character of 'pop' music and entertainment for adult audiences, especially on the radio. It has altered clothing and hairstyles for other age groups than teenagers. It has probably led to the wider use of marihuana among adults.

The impact of the leisure styles of the young upon their elders, however, should not be overestimated and the reciprocal influence in the other direction is considerably greater. Adults still form the larger part of the market for most forms of entertainment and it is only with their support that these remain economically viable. Adults still control the media and own the more expensive forms of receiving entertainment through the media. Changes in adult pastimes, such as for example the increase in gambling, have had many repercussions for the young.

Television may not be as popular with teenagers as with their parents but it is still the most popular pastime for them (15). Although they may watch television in youth clubs they are more likely to watch it at home in the company of other members of their families. The choice of programme to be watched has in some way to satisfy the various needs of the generations within the family, and the parents are likely to have the final say if there is a dispute. This is no longer true for radio, which has become the most powerful influence for disseminating pop culture to the young. A combination of technical innovation (the transistor) and a rising standard of living for the teenager has increased the ownership of radio receivers widely among adolescents. In the 1930s the age of one radio per family, no television and one sitting room (for the mass of the population), the radio programmes had to have family appeal. Now they can reach the adolescent without being filtered through the family and, with rising standards of house room, adolescents can enjoy their interests in private. Much the same situation is true of 'pop' records which have depended on the wider ownership of record players, and where the adolescent is again a dominant part of the market.

Little is known about how far young people share other aspects of the home-centred family life of their parents. They do not apparently contribute to the do-it-yourself movement of home improvement. They do not travel with their parents in the family car, although they may occasionally borrow it. They are much less likely than in the past to take their holidays with their parents. They go out more often, especially to go to the pubs which their parents have forsaken, and to the cinemas. They are more likely to go to dance halls. But they may find, if they live in small towns, that their cinemas and dance halls have been closed and converted to bingo halls for their mothers to use.

Although most of the comparisons which have been made between young people and other age groups have been with their parents, it is instructive to compare them with their younger brothers and sisters, and with their grandparents.

There is a sense in which it might be said that children do not have leisure because they do not work. Life in the primary school, especially with the modern activity-centred curriculum, resembles what they do when they are at home. Moreover, children do not have much free time because it is in the nature of being a child that freedom is limited, and in any case they lack the resources needed to turn free time into leisure. It is noticeable that there is relatively little commercial activity directed at the leisure of children, rather it is more concerned with the toys which parents buy for their play. Their freedom is within, in their imaginations.

Old age, it might be thought, clearly differs from youth in its patterns of leisure. As Harris and Parker show in chapter 12, it is still commonly associated with a superfluity of time and a poverty of resources, and often represents a past society's views on the merits of work and leisure. The disappearance of sexual drives and the loss of physical mobility are in sharp contrast with the vigour of youth. Yet there may, in the future, be increasingly some meaning in the conception of old age as a 'second childhood', or at least a second youth, if trends already evident in the U.S.A. are followed here. For some, old age is a period of affluence where personal interests can be expressed, and are no longer overshadowed by work.

In closing our survey of the patterns of leisure among the young it might be worth asking why there is often believed to be a special relationship between leisure and the behaviour of the young. It is clearly not a simple relationship which follows from the popular assumption that the young have more free time and money at their disposal, for among the young there are great differences in possession of these prerequisites for leisure. Some have a lot of time and very little money, and some have the reverse. What perhaps makes this hypothesis more meaningful is to ask why some groups try to establish this special relationship or act as though it were meaningful. It will then become clear that there is a definite commercial advantage in establishing this relationship in certain markets. It will also be clear that the State behaves as though it has a special responsibility for protecting itself from the risks of delinquency which occur in leisure, and also to protect the young from the risks of corruption.

Any enterprise which wants to expand its markets can do so by increasing the speed at which its products become obsolescent. Fashion, especially where it is associated with the steady throughput of one young generation after another, is a way of doing this. It has been characteristic of all the markets for products which the young consume: canned music, dress, cosmetics. But, more importantly, since they seldom provide more than a share of the total demand it has led the way to a shift in the attitudes of other age groups who consume the same products. Youth-inspired fashion has become an important way of keeping demand alive and rapidly changing (16). It would be naïve however to assume that commercial exploitation of the teenage consumer is the only form of exploitation. The entrepreneurs of the entertainment world, who may be working for large public corporations such as the B.B.C., may see their professional advancement by lifting the ratings for their programmes with the younger generation as the brand image.

The power of the young in the markets for leisure may be novel, but the State has long been aware of the dangers which the young face on the streets when they are at play. Although some have seen this as an opportunity for the State to provide satisfying recreation, others have seen it more as a way of keeping the young out of trouble. There is no question that it was the anticipated social problems of the Second World War which prompted the creation of the Youth Service, nor that its post-war boost by the Albermarle Committee came substantially out of the concern at the rising rates of juvenile delinquency (17). The State has only slowly begun to find its way to a more positive policy for leisure for youth, as for other age groups, and it has generally found it easier to proceed on the firm ground of sport and physical recreation.

Perhaps the last word on leisure and the young ought to come from those who see themselves as prophets of the young. The spokesmen for the 'Underground' see a new civilization emerging from the present ferment of ideas. It will be a return to the older Paradise where we lived in a land of plenty and our needs were simple. 'Like a child taking its first steps, members of the Underground are learning how to live in the future where work is rendered obsolete.

'They are relearning how to play.' (18)

References

1 D. Matza, 'Subterranean Traditions of Youth', *Annals of the American Academy of Political and Social Science*, November 1961, pp. 102-18.

2 S. N. Eisenstadt, *From Generation to Generation*, Routledge, 1956.

3 M. Abrams, 'Expenditure by Teenagers 1965', *Financial Times*, 28 January 1966.

4 C. S. Smith, *Young People at Leisure*, University of Manchester, 1966.

5 C. S. Smith, 'The Structure and Function of Voluntary Youth Movements in Great Britain', paper given at First International Convention of F.O.N.E.M.E. in 1968 in Milan and published in the collected papers of that Conference.

6 Youth Service Development Council, *Youth and Community Work in the 1970s*, H.M.S.O., 1969.

7 Government Social Survey, *Schools Council Enquiry 1, Young School Leavers*, H.M.S.O., 1968.

8 ibid, p. 141.

9 See for example the survey of Bury, C. S. Smith, op. cit., 1966.

10 M. Abrams, op. cit.

11 C. S. Smith, *Adolescence,* Longman, 1968.
12 B. Sugarman, 'Involvement in Youth Culture', *British Journal of Sociology,* vol. XVIII, no. 2, June 1967.
13 I. Emmett, *Youth and Leisure in an Urban Sprawl,* Manchester University Press, 1971.
14 *15-18, Report of the Central Advisory Council for Education – England,* (Crowther Committee Report), vol. I, 1959.
15 Government Social Survey, *Schools Council Enquiry 1, Young School Leavers,* H.M.S.O., 1968, p. 173.
16 P. Abrams, 'A Sociological Portrait: age and generation', *New Society,* 2 December 1971.
17 C. S. Smith, 'The Youth Service and Delinquency Prevention', *Howard Journal,* June 1966.
18 R. Neville, *Play Power,* Jonathan Cape, 1970, p. 273.

11 The family and leisure

Colin Bell and Patrick Healey

In the context of the ill-defined continuum from work to leisure, work usually means productive activity, taking place extra-domestically, within the economic system, for financial returns. To this is customarily added the statistically and culturally preponderant figure of the male as the worker, with the result that concern with leisure has traditionally been a concern with the time *men* spend off the job. We would argue that the sociology of leisure, such as it is, has been *over-concerned* with the non-work activities of men, and has relegated women to a subsidiary and residual category.

This issue is related to problems of definition surrounding women's domestic activities. While subsumed under the broad term *housework,* these seem to be regarded by both sociologists and popular opinion as being of a different order to activities engaged in within the wider economic system, that is, as not being comparable to work in the non-domestic sense of the word. This has led to a lack of concern for the work and non-work spheres of women. Attention should be focused on the question of whether this distinction can be made either for the woman with two jobs, one in a factory and the other at home, or for the full-time housewife and mother. Workers (male) are usually seen to operate within a situation of work-plus-leisure. Is it possible to locate women within a similar framework of family-plus-leisure?

In this chapter we present the outlines of an approach to the sociology of leisure and the family related to important concepts in family research, whereby leisure can be located within the framework of the family considered as a functioning unit in its most basic aspects. We believe that this must include, as an urgent consideration, the neglected area of leisure potentially available to the woman in a family. We are not primarily concerned, therefore, with what people may actually do with their leisure time, nor with whether or not the family *per se* may be regarded as a leisure activity. There is already a considerable body of literature which discusses this aspect of the question in some detail (1). Rather we are concerned to present a framework both for the definition of leisure in relation to marriage and the family, and for an assessment of its availability to husbands and wives.

Our approach is characterized by the definition of leisure in the negative (what it is not), considerations of domestic time budgeting (actual behaviour), and family norms (culture).

If we consider leisure as a function of work, we can see that, in the industrial sphere at least, structural factors were responsible for creating both leisure and the sociological concern with it. It has become a truism to say that leisure is a creation of the industrial system. By this is meant that increasing technical efficiency has progressively liberated the worker from the productive process. The shortening of the working day with maintained or increased production gave the worker the chance to support his family at a decent level, and have time for leisure. The onset of automation has created further opportunities for leisure, with the anticipation that eventually work will become a minor activity, taking up a tiny proportion of time. If and when this occurs, society may become dominated by leisure rather than work patterns.

Our aim is to use this kind of framework in the discussion of leisure and the family. Our primary objective is to achieve comparability of sociological treatment between the work and leisure of the married woman and man. We are concerned with the time that is available for leisure when certain activities, considered as economic contributions to the family, have been extracted. The elements extracted as not constituting leisure are (i) the extra-domestic job of the husband and wife (if any); (ii) domestic work of the wife and non-work-obligations of the husband. Non-work-obligation refers specifically to activities which are considered to be necessary contributions by the husband to family life, e.g. decorating the lounge, fetching coal, feeding the goldfish. Where a wife may be engaged solely in domestic work, this is considered as comparable to the husband's job, on the basis that it provides a service which would otherwise have to be supplied by paid agencies. It is, therefore, regarded as economically productive activity. Once this separation between work and leisure has been made for the housewife as for the 'worker', it no longer becomes relevant to talk of *housework* being somehow different from other jobs because it is pursued by women for reasons of love and service which give a particular kind of satisfaction. The issue of job-satisfaction becomes a separate one which can be considered on the same lines as that of any other worker.

Leisure and family structure

We take leisure to be activities freely entered into once the elements listed above have been accounted for. In the first instance this involves consideration of domestic time budgeting in order to see how much time is spent in non-leisure activities, and by whom it is spent. When this has been determined, the time available for leisure to each family will be known. Over a wide range of family types it emerges that *leisure is a direct function of family structure.* The family we refer to is the nuclear family (2), and by family structure we mean the conjugal role organization of the family and its relationship to its network of social relationships.

Sociology and conjugal roles

There are a number of theoretical and conceptual schemes within which the discussion of conjugal roles could fruitfully be treated (3). We shall consider it in the light of the most well-known, which is the work of Elizabeth Bott. In this, conjugal role playing was linked to social network structure (4).

Bott suggested two things. Firstly, that all marriages could be analysed structurally within a typology of conjugal roles that had three broad categories: joint, complementary and independent. Joint organization meant that, 'activities are carried out by husband and wife together, or the same activity is carried out by either parent at different times'. Complementary organization was when 'activities of husband and wife are different and separate but fitted together to form a whole'. And lastly, independent or segregated organization meant that 'activities are carried out by husband and wife without reference to one another' (5).

The second suggestion made by Bott was that these conjugal role arrangements were related directly to social network structures, which she ranked according to the degree of 'connectedness' they displayed. Connectedness was taken to refer to the density of social relations (6), the extent to which each member of the network has social relations with every other member, and in the second edition of her book Bott actually substitutes the term density for connectedness. Bott's central hypothesis took the form of the bald statement that: 'The degree of segregation in the role-relationships of husband and wife varies directly with the connectedness of the families' social network.' (7) Network structure was presented as an independent variable, and conjugal role playing as a dependent one.

With this basic, and very influential, framework in mind, we shall do two things — we shall use it for the discussion of leisure as a function of marital structure, and also make some critical remarks concerning it and its implications for the study of leisure.

The traditional and non-traditional marriage and leisure

In terms of social change, the segregated conjugal role family is usually regarded as undesirable, primordial or 'traditional'. The complementary role family is seen as a transitional type and the jointly organized family as the high point of democratic development, a microcosm of the free society, or 'non-traditional'. Presented simplistically, the argument runs that over time there has been a general move from the traditional to the non-traditional family but that at any one time the middle class will be found to be more non-traditional, i.e. have a more joint and less segregated family structure, than the working class.

The traditional marriage and leisure

One does not have to search far to discover the ideal type of traditional marriage in the literature of sociology (8). It is seen as based upon rigid sex-role segregation, with the wife and mother (almost inseparable roles) contained within the domestic and maternal spheres, and the husband concerned solely with extra-domestic economic and leisure activity. Segregated conjugal roles are a natural product of this absolute acceptance of the mutually exclusive worlds of 'men's work' and 'women's work'. The only meeting ground of husband and wife is in the bedroom, although even this only in the early days of marriage, with the woman never finding sexual satisfaction because of the insensitivity of the man and the lack of communication which characterizes their relationship. Power relations in this type of marriage are asymmetric, with a structure of paternalism ranging from benevolent to repressive. Only in the spheres of home and children does the woman exercise any authority, and even this can be viewed as delegated by the man rather than personal and freely contracted.

Personal autonomy is low in this type of marriage: individuals interact and define themselves and others on the basis of accepted role definitions. There is little status dissent (no questioning of established orders of being and doing) and an associated cognitive poverty. The world is seen as composed of 'natural' and 'unnatural' elements; the former being that which is done and the latter that which is not done, both in the sense of that which actually exists and that which is normatively required. All behaviour patterns are considered to be necessary in that they originate in essential qualities of nature, defined biologically as far as sex-roles are concerned. This view does not leave room for consideration that action might be contingent, deriving existence and validity from particular situations rather than from natural laws.

The patterns of leisure that this marriage type enforces are quite different for men and women. The fundamental sex-role segregation runs through all behaviour. The world of the man is extra-domestic, and within this world are contained all his interests and pursuits. His major reference group is composed of male friends of either occupational, kin or neighbouring acquaintances (or individuals who occupy all three roles simultaneously) and he associates with these in the local working men's club or pub. Primary allegiance is to this peer group and all leisure activities are carried out within it.

For the woman in this marriage, the kitchen is entirely her place, a place she occupies either alone, or in the company of children or female kin, usually her mother. All her time, whether she may view it as leisure or drudgery, is contained within the domestic situation or some variant of it. When she is not in her own home she is in that of female kin, and her children are ever present. The woman's life is determined by domesticity, and her leisure is contained in the same way. Individual or non-domestic leisure is precluded by the rigid organization of her life. No relationships that are not based on kinship or neighbouring are possible, and non-kin heterosexual contacts are absolutely excluded.

The full implications of this marriage type become apparent when the woman has, for purely financial reasons, to take on a job outside the family. She then participates in the economic support of the family, but her work is looked upon as subordinate to that of the man and she is still considered as the primary domestic worker. Because of the basic sex-role segregation that runs through family life, the man does not expect to participate in women's work. The extra-domestic work of the woman is viewed as an aberration of necessity and in no way decreases her domestic responsibility. It is at this point that considerations of 'family disorganization' associated with absentee mothers may occur. The working mother in a situation dominated by segregated sex-roles cannot cope adequately with work and home, and in the absence of changed attitudes and increased aid by the husband, the home and children may suffer. The move of the wife out of the home to a job may be a first step towards family change. It is a step away from the role segregation characterized by Parsons as instrumental/expressive, where the husband earns the money and the wife cares for the home (9). But it needs changes in male and family attitudes for change to succeed. The only alternative is for strains to be set up in the family, and 'symptoms' of 'disorganization' to emerge.

The traditional marriage is an integrated system based upon a useful division of labour, and in its way, within its context, it works. This is not to say it is desirable (or undesirable), but simply that it is *a* solution to problems of economic support and domestic arrangement. When the woman leaves the family to work this leads to a transitional phase when the equilibrium of the traditional family system is disrupted. One solution is for a regression to the traditional type of family, another is a move to a new type which will constitute another integrated system of interrelated and interlocking parts. (Integration here refers to the ability of the system to function without serious unintended consequences.)

All activity in the traditional family, including leisure, reflects the general structure of married life. The basic sex-role segregation means that, for the wife not employed extra-domestically, leisure is a domestic and unindividual affair, occurring within the home and virtually undifferentiated from the ordinary round of life. For the working wife, leisure in any form may be totally excluded by the pressure of commitments. Not able even to fulfil these commitments adequately for lack of time and energy, she finds leisure an inconceivable luxury. The husband, of course, does have the time for clearly distinguished leisure, because his responsibilities and work are confined to formal extra-domestic spheres. His working hours are after all frequently restricted by law. In a more fundamental sense, however, the man is no 'freer' than the woman. Both are contained within accepted definitions of family and inter-personal relations. There is little questioning of normative behavioural types, and neither partner has any great amount of personal 'autonomy', even though the work and leisure of the man are more varied than that of the woman. Married life can be seen as little more than the playing out of implications contained in the rigid definitions upon the basis of which marriage was contracted.

The non-traditional marriage and leisure

The non-traditional marriage and family is described empirically *par excellence* in the Rapoports' studies of the dual career family (10). The basic characteristic of this marriage type is the absence of rigid sex-role definitions. Marital partners relate to one another on the basis of individual personality, and consequently possess considerable personal autonomy. There is no rigid acceptance of cultural or sub-cultural definitions, for the only governing principle of behaviour is that persons should be free to express their individuality within the context of consideration for other family members. Domestic activity and leisure, as well as participation in the wider economic sphere, are therefore a matter of pragmatic accommodation to individual wishes, and marriage and family relationships are a creative, personal enterprise. The Rapoports write that 'there is a division of labour in relation to family functions that is distributed between the partners on an equal status basis' (11).

Jointness of conjugal organization, in the sense that activities are pursued together at some times and are interchangeable, is revealed in every aspect of the family organization. Equal opportunity is available to each partner to pursue individual and cooperative activities in work and leisure.

The distinction between activities which are shared and those considered interchangeable is an important one. Sharing may mean no more than that the husband, for a variety of reasons (such as an overburdened wife becoming shrewish or lack of a clean shirt on Monday morning), has agreed to aid the wife in what are considered to be her legitimate duties. This would be no more than the man helping in 'woman's work', and would indicate little movement away from traditional sex-roles. For the move from a traditional to a non-traditional family to be complete, there would have to occur a change in both norms and behaviour. If such a change in norms did not occur it could be supposed that apparent 'democratization' of family life would disappear if the situation that made it necessary were to change. Lack of consistency between changes in sex-role attitudes and family 'democratization' may account for reported inability to locate a constant orientation of conjugal role organization underlying every sphere of marital activity (12). Where traditional norms of sex-roles persist, true jointness of conjugal role-playing may only be demonstrated in spheres of family life which require little activity by the man, or little public exposure of the joint behaviour. In situations where some jointness may be necessary to family functioning (Bott's loose-knit networks), the continuing influence of traditional sex-norms may cause no consistent emphasis on joint or segregated behaviour, but a mixture of the two in both domestic and leisure spheres. For these reasons we would consider it necessary to distinguish between the joint marriage characterized by shared activities and the genuinely non-traditional marriage, in which activities are either pursued by both partners at the same time or are interchangeable. We would also suggest that the joint marriage with its continuation of sex-role segregation at a basic level is a much more common institution than the non-traditional marriage.

The jointly organized marriage releases the housewife for leisure. In this zero-sum game, increased leisure time available to the wife necessarily means less time available to the husband. The man in this situation occupies a position of work, plus family, plus leisure, while the woman moves into a situation of work plus possible non-domestic leisure. Joint organization does not create more time for the woman solely because of male participation in domestic work. A lessening of the burdens of wife and motherhood also occurs as a result of increased contraceptive effectiveness in jointly organized marriages, which allows both an absolute decrease of the task of bearing and caring for children, and a planning of childbirth according to individual preference. The crucial issue of personal autonomy occurs again here. Real joint marital organization does not simply make time available for leisure, especially women's leisure. It also supplies the structure of values which make individual leisure a part of the self-image of marital partners. Because it is associated with movement away from strict adherence to traditional attitudes, husband and wife become more able to exercise their autonomy and arrange their leisure in a personal way. The acceptance of traditional thought styles and forms of interaction gives way to a more open and creative life and leisure style. The non-traditional marriage with both husband and wife pursuing careers may carry this process one stage further by merging work and leisure. In this instance, such distinctions as that between what persons have to do and what they want to do, as well as that between home and workplace, may become as redundant as sex-role distinctions.

Networks

In the discussion so far, only the relationship between husband and wife and the bearing it has on attitudes and time available for leisure has been discussed. A second area is that of the parent-offspring relationship. As the participation of offspring in domestic affairs can only be presumed beyond a certain age, and as they, at least initially, will contribute nothing to the normative definitions underlying family structure, this area is not explored here. What is much more central is the relationship of the marital pair and their offspring to their social context, i.e. their social network.

Networks have been current in sociological discussion since Barnes' famous paper in 1954 (13). Bott applied the concept to the discussion of conjugal roles, and the relationship which she claimed existed between them seemed to indicate the existence of some kind of sociological law pointing to structural determinants of individual behaviour that could be conceptualized on a more manageable level than that of the total social system. The conjugal relationship is seen as a function of structures, but structures at a level intermediate between institutions and system.

Bott's claim that 'close-knit' networks would be associated with segregated roles, and loose-knit networks with joint roles, was based upon an assumption about the amount of support a family needed to derive from its environment in order to survive. In close-knit networks there is such a close association on all levels between the family and its friends, kin and neighbours, that the housewife receives a great deal of functional and emotional support. This support has the effect of rendering unnecessary the participation of the men in domestic affairs. In the loose-knit networks, however, lack of support makes joint organization necessary if the family is to survive as a viable unit.

This is applicable to our traditional-non-traditional scheme. The segregated traditional family might be expected to be found with a close-knit network, and the non-traditional with a loose-knit network. We find, however, that the situation is more complex than this. Bott's close-knit network is essentially what has otherwise been conceptualized as a working-class community where, as Fallding has pointed out, it is not so much a matter that a segregated family type is structurally possible, but rather that it is rendered necessary by a deep sex-role segregation that crosses the whole community (14). In this way, Bott tied the concept of the 'close-knit' networks to traditional family definitions, so that the significant element was not the structure of relationships (density) but the persons in the relationships and the norms governing their interaction.

When we consider the 'loose-knit' network two major related criticisms emerge. First, joint-conjugal roles are far from the only response to structural isolation of the family; the classic over-burdening and loneliness of the wife is an equally plausible and empirically real alternative. A degree of jointness may be called for in order to save the family from disruption caused by discontent of the wife, but real jointness and a non-traditional form involves normative change; that is, a move to a family based less on sex-role segregation. There is thus no more *necessary* relationship between loose-knit networks and joint roles than between close-knit networks and segregated roles. It all depends on the norms underlying the network. We consider that in making conjugal roles dependent on networks Bott was simply employing a manageable unit of analysis rather than the most valuable unit, which was class, and the normative systems derived from class (15).

Our second criticism is that the concept of the loose-knit network would appear to be an empirical absurdity. The situation in which a family knows lots of people, but none of them know one another, would appear not to exist. If it did, it would only be in the case of a family of constant, frequent and spectacular geographical mobility. Our research indicates that even highly mobile middle-class families do not exhibit a loose-knit network. Rather, they show a series of locally dense network clusters in various locations which may be loosely knit together into a whole. This means that each local cluster may be dense, but there may only be one common member of all the clusters – that is the one family that is the reference point of investigation. There is no doubt that some of these clusters are different from the close-knit networks described by Bott: they are more transient, change personnel over time (sometimes quite quickly), have a lower kin content (often nil) and tend to be heterogeneous in terms of background of personnel. However, these networks *are* dense and often supply considerable support for the family, and yet are associated with *joint* or non-traditional conjugal organization.

Network and leisure

In homogeneous working-class communities the social network is a vital element in the leisure activities of both husband and wife. Local activities with peers constitutes male leisure and variants of domestic activity with female kin the leisure of the woman. It is only because of such characteristics of communities as homogeneity, length of residence and the presence of kin that the woman has any discernible leisure in this type of family. As Young and Willmott have pointed out, when families of this kind move from a close-knit network, the person who loses most is the wife (16). Separated from her kin, with the tie with her mother at best attenuated and possibly broken, the loneliness of the wife can become acute. It is then that her subjection to the domestic scene is most obvious, for her traditional domestic relaxations are precluded. It must be stressed, though, that networks are a function of life-style which are a reflection of norms. The structure of leisure in traditional families will be a product of norms of sex-segregation. The network acts as a tight communication net for the reinforcement and perpetuation of norms. Norms about sex-roles, which may be traced to a class basis, are maintained by constant interaction within the community. Deviance, or experiment, is avoided because of traditional expectations and mechanisms of social control. Leisure patterns are thus a function of norms of behaviour, and these in turn are maintained by network structure.

In non-traditional families located in locally dense networks, there are norms conducive to the individual pursuit of leisure and family organization which ensure an equitable distribution of the scarce resource of time between husband and wife. In addition to these elements, the denseness of the network ensures that certain kinds of functional support, such as baby-minding, create even more free time for individual or joint leisure by husband and wife. Where the jointly organized family is in a genuinely loose-knit network with low density these increments of leisure time are not possible. It is in this situation that the question of conjugal role organization and the time it provides for leisure becomes most relevant. It must be stressed that it is only when family and network structure are accompanied by norms and values that support the wife's pursuit of leisure, especially leisure of an individual and non-familial kind, that networks become a variable in the availability of leisure. In other instances, they play a subordinate role, as a mechanism for norm maintenance, or a supplier of marginal support in the form of petty services.

Conclusion

We have attempted to demonstrate that leisure is a function of conjugal role organization, which in turn is produced by norms and expectations upon which family life is contracted and continues to be based. Norms and family structure have an interesting relationship to networks, which sustain norms and provide them with a context within which their implications are worked out. A consideration of leisure structurally, i.e. in terms of available time after necessary work is done, allows comparability between the activities of man as industrial and commercial worker, and woman as domestic worker, and avoids many inconsistencies and problems inherent in other approaches to leisure.

We have noted the often reported movement from traditional to democratic family structure (what Burgess called the development from institution to companionship marriage) (17). The growth of public services such as nurseries will help to free the woman for even further leisure as this change progresses. It will also create a social climate where change will be possible for both men and women. For this change to be complete not only must there be alterations in conjugal and domestic organization, but also in the sex-role norms underpinning the contemporary family.

Notes and References
1 See, for example, Kenneth Roberts, *Leisure,* Longmans, 1970: J. Dumazedier, *Toward a Society of Leisure,* Collier-Macmillan, 1967.
2 In a full analysis, of course, the role of what is usually called the extended family would also have to be examined in this context.
3 The two outstanding schema are probably the structural-functionalist and the interactionist. For a brief introduction to these see F. I. Nye and F. M. Berado, *Emerging Conceptual Frameworks in Family Analysis,* New York, Macmillan, 1966.
4 Elizabeth Bott, *Family and Social Network,* Tavistock, 1957.
5 ibid., p. 53.
6 J. A. Barnes, 'Networks and Political Process', in J. Clyde Mitchell, *Social Network in Urban Situations,* Manchester University Press, 1969.
7 Bott, op. cit., p. 59.
8 cf. Dennis, Henriques and Slaughter, *Coal is our Life,* Eyre & Spottiswoode, 1956; Young and Willmott, *Family and Kinship In East London,* Routledge, 1957; and the useful summaries of community studies in J. Klein, *Samples from English Cultures,* Routledge, 1965.
9 Talcott Parsons and Robert Bales, *Family, Socialization and Interaction Process,* Routledge, 1956.
10 Robert and Rhona Rapoport, *Dual-Career Families,* Penguin, 1971.
11 ibid., p. 7.
12 Lee Rainwater, *Family Design,* Chicago, Aldine, 1965.
13 J. A. Barnes, 'Class and Committees in a Norwegian Island Parish', *Human Relations,* 7, 1954.
14 H. Fallding, 'The Family and the Idea of the Cardinal Role', *Human Relations,* 14, 1961.
15 It is interesting to note that Bott's early work shows a class-oriented analysis ('The Concept of Class as a Reference Group', *Human Relations,* 7, 3, 1954). This changed to a network approach only after Barnes' article ('Class and Committees in a Norwegian Island Parish', *Human Relations,* 7, 1, 1954). See for example E. Bott, 'Urban Families, Conjugal Roles and Social Networks', *Human Relations,* 8, 4, 1955. Only in the central hypothesis of *Family and Social Network* (1957) was network structure accepted as an *exclusive* factor in conjugal role-playing rather than an *emphasis.* Even there it was constantly qualified in the rest of the book by reference to normative and personal factors of a class-based kind. Unfortunately, it has been the bold central hypothesis rather than the extensive qualifications that has exerted an influence in sociology. See Colin Bell, *Middle Class Families,* Routledge, 1969, and Patrick Healey, *Conjugal Roles and Social Networks: a Middle Class Case Study,* M.A. thesis, University of Essex, 1970.

16 Young and Willmott, op. cit.
17 Ernest Burgess and H. J. Lock, *The Family: From Institution to Companionship*, New York, American Book Co., 1953.

12 Leisure and the elderly

Amelia Harris and Stanley Parker

In this chapter we want to consider what leisure means to elderly people and to describe and evaluate some of the efforts made to provide for their leisure. Our initial concern is with the amount of free time elderly people have and with the question of how much of this can be regarded as true leisure. An examination of the attitudes of elderly people to the prospect and actuality of increased leisure after retirement is followed by a review of survey findings on how they do spend their time. The question of the aims and achievements of old people's clubs is important enough to deserve separate treatment. Finally, we look at the existing provisions made to prepare people for retirement and at the ways in which they can be helped to adjust to the change in roles and status which this implies.

How much leisure?

If one defines leisure as the time remaining after the necessary allocation of time to sleep, work, household chores and other functions of daily living, and also considers anyone aged 65+ as 'elderly', then one might well be forgiven for thinking of the elderly as having a great deal of leisure. But this assumes that nearly all men retire from active work at 65, and there is ample evidence that this is not so. In Britain half the men continue to work (sometimes reduced hours) for two years after 65, one in three men are still working at 70, and one in four at 75 (1).

An important distinction is between on the one hand the elderly who are in reasonable good health and living in their own homes or rooms, and on the other hand the elderly who are in some degree incapacitated or have to be looked after in an institution of some kind. The first group is in the majority, but the second group adds up to a sizeable minority. More than three quarters of the elderly have no, or only minimal, incapacity when assessed on a scale which takes into account personal care and the ability to perform certain physical tasks of normal daily living (2). But some 5% of the elderly are in residential homes or hospitals (3). Of those in private households, about 1%-2% are bedfast, and a number of local surveys show the proportion of housebound people of retirement age as falling within the range of 7%-11% (4).

Health and mobility have an important effect on both the amount of leisure and the quality of its enjoyment. For those in good health and able to move about freely, retirement can bring new opportunities to take up, or have more time for, a wide range of leisure pursuits. But for the elderly who are impaired the problem of 'filling' free time is partly solved in that things take longer to do anyway. A report on the handicapped and impaired showed that more than half of those who said they missed something as a result of being impaired gave answers that demonstrated a sense of deprivation in the ability to use leisure time (5). Elderly impaired men most frequently had to give up participating in sports and gardening; for elderly impaired women it was mainly handicrafts, walking and shopping (6). The report makes the important point that

> essential to a pleasant appreciation of leisure is the feeling of 'freedom', both freedom *from* and freedom *for*. To what extent does leisure for the old and the impaired mean freedom *from* the performance of roles that they enjoyed fulfilling and freedom *for* enforced idleness, at worst 'vegetation'?

The picture emerging from the sample of predominantly old impaired people was one of a population with above-average amounts of disposable time but frustrated physically, mentally, environmentally and financially from fully enjoying this extra free time.

Attitudes to increased leisure
How does the prospect of increased leisure appeal to those about to retire — is it something they look forward to or dread? The main difficulty in answering this question is that the gain in leisure is in most cases accompanied by a sharp drop in income. It is not easy to separate out the attitude towards having more time in which to do what one pleases — which, in theory at least, should be a positive attitude — from the feeling that this can only be achieved by losing income with which to maintain an accustomed standard of living.

A reasonable income is wanted, but so is a constructive use of time and the maintenance of a valued social life. A survey among manual workers, aged 55+ and still in employment, illustrates the point.

> Though money was an important reason for continuing at work, it rarely seems to be the sole or dominant reason . . . when older men apply for a job or ask to be retained, they tend to emphasise their income problems. It is an objective argument; distrust of leisure or fear of being cut off from the working community do not seem to them to be good reasons to put forward when approaching an employer for work (7).

It is common to ask about attitudes to retirement in advance, but perhaps it is more relevant to discover the retrospective views of men *after* their retirement. A sample of 50 Glasgow manual workers (admittedly not a representative sample, since they all belonged to clubs and were in other respects a well-adjusted group) were asked what advice they would give to someone at work who was shortly to retire. More than a quarter of them advised not giving up work at all, if that were possible; and over a third counselled the pursuit of some kind of activity, interest or hobby (8).

What do men say they enjoy in retirement? The main answers appear to be 'nothing' (42%) and 'rest' (41%) (9). 'Free time' and other answers account for the remaining 17%. There is some variation by class: more manual and service workers (45%) than white-collar workers (29%) were likely to say they enjoyed nothing in retirement. The question is, of course, open to more than one interpretation: those who said 'nothing' may have meant that there was no *special* thing about retirement that they enjoyed, or it might have been that retirement gave them no *new* source of enjoyment. In any event, very few retired persons claimed to miss the work itself (8% of white-collar workers and only 3% of manual workers). A majority (56%) missed 'nothing' about work, and the main thing missed was money (24%). However, findings such as these should not necessarily be taken at their face value, since it is not always easy for people to express in an interview situation their deeper feelings about what work meant to them. Perhaps the views of the Glasgow workers quoted above are more typical of those who have been forced to retire and thus change the work habits of a lifetime.

Below we shall discuss some of the features of pre-retirement courses which are available to prepare people for adjustment to a life without paid employment. Here it is relevant to note, in connection with attitudes to retirement, that these may well be strongly influenced by attendance at such courses. For example, a report of the St Helens Preparation for Retirement Committee suggests that 'the course had stimulated thought and influenced people to direct their energies to make for a happy retirement' (10). It was also found that experience of retirement tended to lead to a gradual process of adjustment. Six months after retirement opinion was equally divided between finding it enjoyable, or alternatively being bored, shocked or finding it very difficult to adjust. Two years after retirement most found themselves enjoying it, some reflecting on the days not being long enough. It is a sad thought that a minority who failed to adjust after retirement did not survive long.

How do they spend their time?

The problem of what to do with extra time available is one mainly facing retired persons, of whom the majority are men. Women may well find that retirement from their job or from responsibilities connected with their own children is filled to some extent by activities connected with their grandchildren. So far as leisure is concerned, some facilities are provided by local authorities, by voluntary effort, and by the catering of leisure industries for old people's needs. One of the chief provisions is for old people's clubs, which we shall consider in more detail below. Local councils sometimes provide special coach or minibus excursions for old people, while home visits organized by volunteers, which are usually with an ostensibly practical purpose such as cooking or cleaning, often have a sociable and consequently a leisure function. Since elderly people are often short of money, many forms of help consist of price concessions, usually during specified hours. Thus there are cheap fares between 9.30 a.m. and 4 p.m., and concessions at public baths. There is also some commercial price cutting for elderly people, for example cinema visits and hairdressing.

An important effect on activities is changed financial position. Some elderly people have to stop going out to places of entertainment or other events because they cannot afford it. Many of them use public libraries and museums as places to get warm or pass the time comfortably. According to the Government Social Survey report *Planning for Leisure,* the pattern of leisure of the elderly differs from that of younger people in several marked respects. Whether in full-time employment or not, men aged 61+ spend more time on gardening, while among the retired group park visits and walks increase sharply (11). Single women aged 61+ spend much more time on social activities than other women.

So far as sports and games are concerned, active participation by men and women after the age of 60 drops off in all events except bowls for men (12). Spectating, however, is a different matter: there is hardly any fall-off in attendance at soccer matches by men after 60, and in the cases of cricket and tennis there is actually a marked increase. With women, on the other hand, interest in sport declines sharply after 60: the only sports to attract more than 1% of elderly women as spectators are cricket and swimming.

A survey by the Pre-Retirement Association confirms the general finding about loss of activities and interests in old age, and offers some explanations of why this should be so (13). Comparing the life of the retired man with the middle-aged one, we are made aware of how much of his former activity is lost, and how little extra seems to be put in its place. Perhaps the need to assert some territorial rights at home is what drives men into the garden, for over half of them claimed gardening as a favourite spare-time activity. It is significant of the impact of a compulsory retirement policy that though the retired men were free to go out and about in the daytime, housebound activities claimed twice as much of their interests as outside ones. In contrast the men in the pre-retirement group, though going out daily to work, took a higher proportion of their pleasures outside the home.

The sub-group of elderly men who are impaired provide a further example of the effect of changed role-status at retirement on leisure pursuits. Ten per cent of such men, compared with only 6% of younger impaired men, said they spent some of their spare time on housework, cooking or looking after the family (14). Elderly women, however, showed a slight *decrease* in these activities, which indicates a shift in domestic roles between some elderly couples.

The pros and cons of clubs

At present there are more than seven thousand social clubs for elderly people in England and Wales. They vary a great deal in their scope and in the way they are run. Some are no more than weekly or monthly socials held in a church hall, with a Christmas party and summer outing thrown in for good measure. Others are quite elaborately equipped day centres. An increasing number of clubs are run by the old people themselves with their own officers and committee. In others, however, the old people sit passively while voluntary workers perform even the simplest tasks (15).

Most old people's clubs meet once a week or fortnight in borrowed or rented premises (16). The meeting is usually for two or three hours, mainly sitting and talking over a cup of tea, but sometimes with bingo or some other kind of entertainment. The clubs are mainly organized by voluntary groups – over a third by the R.W.V.S., and most of the rest by Old People's Welfare Committees, the National Federation of Old Age Pensioners Associations and the Red Cross. Many clubs are connected with a church or chapel, and there is usually a local authority subsidy. Some clubs are run direct by the local authority. Not infrequently the same volunteers may run several clubs in various parts of the town, so that any individual club is open for one afternoon a week only.

The clubs cater fairly well for the relatively more physically active among elderly people. But there is no standard procedure for visiting club members who are sick, and only a small minority of clubs have any transport for collecting members from their homes. The clubs are usually run on very small budgets, and they are discouraged from making serious recruiting drives for more members because they lack space in restricted premises.

Less than 7% of old people attend a club in any given week, and it has been estimated that only 15-20% of those entitled to use the clubs ever do so (17). The clubs are more popular with women than with men: old men attending clubs are mainly married men going with their wives. There is a strong social-class difference between clubs for old people and other clubs. More working-class people attend old people's clubs, and other types of clubs are more popular with the middle class. Taking Lewisham old people's clubs as an example, about 4% of social class I (professional) people were members, about 8% of classes II, III and IV, and 15% of class V (unskilled) (18).

Clubs specifically for old people are less popular with the elderly than are clubs unrestricted by age. This particularly applies to men, whose overall club attendance is greater than that of women. One reason for this is that working men's clubs are popular among men of all ages in the more industrial areas. In line with their frequent claim not to miss anything about work, few elderly people retain much contact with their fellow workers — even when they continue to live near the place of work. Tunstall believes that in this field Britain has much to learn from American companies and trade unions (19). A social club close to or within the company buildings would enable retired men to mix with their former fellow workers on familiar ground. Such clubs might help to overcome the fairly common resistance to the idea of going to clubs on the grounds that they are only for the lonely, the decrepit or the 'dodderers' who talk only about their ailments, their grievances and the past. Another point is that old people's clubs are usually purely social, whereas other types of club, for example local authority centres for the physically handicapped, also provide other services such as meals, bathing facilities and handicrafts. Perhaps old people's clubs would be more popular and useful if they could provide a wider range of such services.

The question of whether clubs — specifically for old people or not — are a good thing is part of a broader issue of whether active leisure is something to be encouraged in preference to passive leisure. While there is every reason to seek to provide more adequate facilities for those who wish to take part in club activities, it is questionable whether people who show no signs of needing more social contact should be under pressure to 'join in'. It is not demonstrable that club membership, and the methods of passing time that this implies, are preferable to allowing elderly people, if they wish, to experience pleasurable withdrawal to dwell on cherished memories.

Preparation for retirement

What should be done to prepare people for the normally quite sudden change from being fully employed to leading an alleged life of leisure in retirement? It seems increasingly taken for granted that some kind of preparation for retirement is necessary, and various bodies have from time to time launched a number of different schemes. Conferences about the problems of how to handle leisure in later life have led to the setting up of training courses for those about to retire. These courses deal with problems of finance, health and housing, and usually include lectures and discussions on the importance of developing new interests. In London, for instance, the Camden Council of Social Service held a well-attended course under the general title of 'Starting Life Again at 60' (20). Similar courses have been organized by universities, colleges and the Workers' Educational Association, and the B.B.C. frequently includes talks on this subject in its radio programmes.

The courses often depend on employers being interested enough in the first place to finance them, or to pay the fees of the worker and give him time off to attend the lectures. The success and continuation of the courses depends, too, on the interest of the workers themselves. Some of the proferred places have not been taken up, and this has led to a diminishing interest on the part of the companies concerned, so that a good many of the courses started in recent years have been discontinued. Furthermore, with a very few exceptions, there has been no attempt at assessment of the success of the courses in achieving their intended aims. Most of those who attend the courses are manual workers, many of whom class themselves as handymen who would continue to do work of some sort after retirement (21). Those employees who do not have the opportunity or desire to attend courses are sometimes provided with relevant literature. Thus the Civil Service has prepared a booklet entitled *Towards Retirement,* containing useful information about money, occupational and housing matters, as well as some rather paternalistic advice about maintaining a spirit of optimism, giving up smoking and not having imaginary illnesses.

Adjusting to role change

Although the question of leisure for the elderly should by no means be identified with the question of adjustment to retirement, there are substantial grounds for seeking to understand the changing content and functions of leisure in the context of changed role-status on retirement, particularly in the case of men. One of the most frequently quoted contributions to thinking in this area in recent years has been the 'disengagement theory' of Cumming and Henry. According to this theory

Ageing is an inevitable mutual withdrawal or disengagement resulting in decreased interaction between the ageing person and others in the social system to which he belongs. The process may be initiated by the individual or by others in the situation. The ageing person may withdraw more markedly from some classes of people while remaining relatively close to others. His withdrawal may be accompanied from the outset by an increased preoccupation with himself; certain institutions in society may make this withdrawal easy for him (22).

The theory has led to a large number of research studies, some of which support it and others refute it. It has been extensively criticized, chiefly on the grounds that there is no reason to suppose that its propositions apply outside contemporary United States culture. It has also been suggested that, though it may be an adequate description of ageing as experienced by many fairly healthy and economically secure old people, it is not acceptable as a picture of ageing among other important groups of old people, such as the poor, the housebound or the isolated (23). It seems more reasonable to agree with Crawford that, so far as Britain is concerned, the emphasis on social welfare for the elderly is not on 'withdrawal' but on continued participation in the social system (24). Retirement is consequently to be seen as a form of *imposed* withdrawal from a central life role which affects both husband and wife. Voluntary disengagement, in terms of anticipated withdrawal from social participation after retirement, is observable only in a small minority of people.

We need to appreciate the extent to which the 'disengagement' theory in particular, and the prevailing ideas about retirement in general, are class-based. It is significant that Crawford finds a *change* rather than a cessation of anticipated involvement after retirement by most groups. Middle-class men anticipated less interaction as friend and worker and more as leisure-time-user; working-class men felt the same, apart from substituting 'parent' for 'friend'. Middle-class women anticipated less interaction as worker and more as leisure-time-user; working-class women anticipated less interaction as neighbour and worker and more as parent (25). There is thus no question of 'disengagement' for most working-class women. Their lives have been embedded in an extended family and neighbourhood network, and they have probably never thought about separate activities or time called 'leisure'. But for other elderly women and most elderly men there is a real problem to be faced consequent upon the involuntary loss of one role and the difficulty of finding another. The strong expectations about leisure are often not realized. This prompts the question: should we, as well as preparing people for retirement and the loss of social life following loss of the job, also encourage them to develop another and more leisure-oriented social circle?

Conclusion

Both the quantity and quality of leisure for the elderly depend to a large extent on personal circumstances, especially finance, health and mobility. Although many men are glad to retire at the end of a long and often not very satisfying working life, a number of them have few resources to cope with a life without regular employment. Women generally experience a less sudden change at retirement age, which may partly account for their tendency to live longer. Patterns of leisure change with the advancing years, being restricted both by money and the physical activity required. Old people's clubs vie with all-age clubs to help occupy the time of the elderly; each type of club makes its own special appeal, but there is clearly much scope for better facilities. Attempts are made to prepare people for retirement, though the level of interest in, and therefore the duration of, such courses is somewhat unstable. One is left with the impression that elderly people who may need, consciously or unconsciously, more social and leisure facilities, training, encouragement and so on, are in practice often left to their own devices. There is the feeling that once people have left paid employment anything they do is likely to be of little importance, and that they have very little to look forward to. Yet retirement is surely something that one should experience as an enjoyable period of life (in so far as health allows) rather than a time of deprivation and diminished status. Leisure for the elderly should have a positive role in life, and not be identified simply with loss of employment.

Notes and References
1 E. Shanas and others, *Old People in Three Industrial Societies*, New York, Atherton Press, 1968, p. 292.
2 ibid., p. 27.
3 ibid., p. 21.
4 A. I. Harris, *Health and Welfare of Older People in Lewisham*, Government Social Survey, 1962, p. 7.
5 C. R. W. Smith, 'Leisure Activities of Impaired Persons', in A. I. Harris, *Handicapped and Impaired in Great Britain*, H.M.S.O., 1971, p. 93.
6 ibid., p. 205.
7 *Workers Nearing Retirement*, The Nuffield Foundation, 1963.
8 Unpublished report submitted to the Glasgow Retirement Council, 'Inquiry into Attitudes to Retirement', 1961, quoted in F. Le Gros Clark, *Work, Age and Leisure*, Michael Joseph, 1966, p. 118.
9 Shanas, op. cit., p. 330.
10 Unpublished report.
11 K. K. Sillitoe, *Planning for Leisure*, H.M.S.O., 1969, p. 42.
12 ibid., p. 239.
13 E. Hutchinson, *Learning and Leisure in Middle and Later Life*, The Pre-Retirement Association, 1970.
14 Smith, op. cit., p. 203.
15 M. Penelope Hall, *Social Services of England and Wales*, 2nd ed., Routledge, 1971.
16 J. Tunstall, *Old and Alone*, Routledge, 1966, p. 286.
17 E. T. Ashton, *People and Leisure*, Ginn, 1971, p. 64.
18 Harris, op. cit., p. 37.
19 Tunstall, op. cit., p. 297.

20 Ashton, op. cit., p. 62.
21 See, for example, the report on a course held by the Barking Pre-Retirement Group by C. Thelma Wilson, November 1966.
22 E. Cumming and W. E. Henry, *Growing Old,* New York, Basic Books, p. 14.
23 Tunstall, op. cit., p. 240.
24 M. P. Crawford, 'Retirement and Role-Playing', *Sociology,* May 1972.
25 ibid., p. 224.

Part 4

The leisure industries

Introduction

In the three previous parts of this book we have dealt very largely with leisure from the point of view of the individual. Whether focusing on leisure as an aspect of culture, on its relation to work, or on its manifestations at various stages of the life cycle, the major concern has been with what leisure means to people, rather than what it implies for social institutions. In the remaining two parts of the book we shall be shifting the emphasis in the other direction. We shall still be dealing with matters which ultimately — and sometimes immediately — concern the individual, but which stem initially from an institutional source in society external to the individual.

The 'leisure industries' consist of all those economic organizations which exist to supply the public with goods and services to use in the search for enjoyment of free time. Many of these organizations are commercial, which means that they are in business essentially to make a profit. But in other cases the organizations are public or quasi-public, that is, their main purpose is to meet the leisure needs of the population, though they may do so on an economic basis of charging prices to cover the whole or part of costs. In Britain the leisure industries are *primarily* commercial, but they may be examined more widely as economic organizations which interact with the various publics they seek to serve. In this way we can, for instance, treat commercial television alongside B.B.C., and the non-pecuniary aims of football organizations as well as the purely commercial aspects of the game.

Remarkably few leisure activities or experiences can be had without use of goods or services of some kind or other. The scope of the leisure industries is thus almost as wide as the range of leisure behaviour itself. The various branches of the leisure industry cover the provision of entertainment, hobby materials, sports goods and facilities, games, holidays, 'leisure wear' and so on, plus a considerable proportion of the output of other industries which is not wholly attributable to leisure, for example, motor vehicles and the mass media of communication. Some of these branches of the leisure industry themselves include a wide variety of types of provision which imply significant differences for the supplier–customer relationship. Thus one can purchase sociable entertainment as an individual (escort agencies), as part of a group (club show) or on a mass basis (television programme).

Philosophical questions enter into a consideration of the leisure industries in two main ways. One concerns the guiding principles of public provision for leisure and the type of professional ethics or ideology held by those working in non-profit leisure organizations. These matters will be dealt with in the final part of this book on planning and policies. Here we may look in more detail at another issue relating to the leisure industries: that of the pros and cons of the commercial provision of leisure facilities.

The debate about commercial entertainment mainly concerns the extent to which the providers of leisure facilities should define standards of better or worse, desirable or undesirable, and then select their offerings to the public in accordance with these standards. Critics of commercial entertainment assert that the leisure industries aim to make people passive spectators of 'the show' in preference to doing things themselves, and that the mass market operates to standardize the public's tastes and interests. On the other hand, the proponents of commercial entertainment refute these charges. They maintain that, in catering to a wide diversity of tastes, the leisure industries give genuine pleasure and satisfaction to millions of people without dictating what is good for them, and that many types of recreation and amusement, once enjoyed only by the rich, are now within the reach of almost everyone. To some extent the critics and defenders of commercial entertainment deliberately choose to talk about different things — the one to attack the most vulnerable features and the other to defend more general propositions with which it is hard to disagree.

The wide scope of the leisure industries makes it necessary to ask which are the most significant sociological dimensions to study, and points to the impossibility of doing justice to the subject in less than a whole volume. The articles we have chosen for inclusion in this part of the book are necessarily highly selective, although we believe that they are broadly representative of the whole field. Some topics have received more attention than others in books, articles and elsewhere, and these reflect special problems of economic provision, public policy or sociological interest. Accordingly these topics are dealt with or at least touched upon here. The first chapter provides a general and largely factual basis for those to follow. The mass media of communication clearly cannot be left out of any account of the leisure industries, however restricted. At the risk of offending the devotees of other sports, we have chosen to deal with football, mainly because the sociology of football has been relatively more developed. Two chapters are devoted to holidays, but these treat the subject from two quite different perspectives and between them offer a depth of coverage scarcely possible in a single chapter.

Several broad themes may be seen to link all or most of the chapters in this part of the volume. The first theme is that of the processes of communications in helping to determine the nature of social relationships. The producers of leisure goods and services communicate to their customers (via advertising and to a lesser extent public relations) the wares they have to offer; correspondingly, the customers communicate back to the producers (via actual sales and to a lesser extent other consumer reactions) their tastes and preferences. Critics dismiss the offerings of the mass media as trivial expressions of the lowest common denominator of taste, intellect and interest but, as James Curran and Jeremy Tunstall show, this is not how many of the audience see the process of communication. Rather, the audiences tend to see television watching, radio listening and newspaper reading as status-conferring activities, and in particular the news content of the media as keeping them in touch with what is going on in the world. In another vein, Stephen Edgell and David Jary point to the communication functions of football as sociability for spectators during the game and as a source of conversation during the week.

A second and closely linked theme running through these chapters is that of the nature of the relationship between producers and consumers of various leisure activities or spectacles. This is explicitly discussed in the chapter by Stanley Parker, both in terms of the controls imposed upon producers and consumers and of the trend towards smaller and more specialized markets for some leisure goods and services. With football the 'producers' embrace a wide range of roles from club directors, managers and other remote organizers of the game to the actual players with whom the spectators can feel at least some sense of visual collective identity. Pradeep Bandyopadhyay shows how the social organization of a holiday camp provides yet another example of the forms of producer–consumer relationship: when 'worker and customer meet' there are opportunities for at least some of the workers to meet customers on equal terms off the job, to manipulate the relationship, exercise powers of patronage, and so on.

A third theme is that of the symbolism which pervades many of the products and less tangible services of the leisure industry. Just as one part of the footwear industry sells not just shoes but 'pretty feet', so much of the leisure industry sells 'fun' and the appropriate images to accompany this. Commercial football offers spectators not only the thrills of the game but also shared experiences, values and emotionalism: it gives a sense of social integration with the team supported, it features the ritual of chantings and responses, and has been regarded as a surrogate or secular religion. Another form of symbolism is seen in Barry Newman's typology of holidays according to varieties of class consciousness. Although there is a tendency to convergence in the type of holiday taken, the typical working-class visit to a holiday camp represents a collective, highly organized and passive experience in keeping with dominant values in the sub-culture. At the other end of the scale is the motorized caravan or camping holiday, with its privatized, loosely organized and active features symbolizing a middle-class way of life.

The initial chapter by Parker discusses a number of topics related to the economics of providing for leisure. The growth of the leisure industries is seen as part of a general process of structural differentiation within society, whereby people's leisure needs are increasingly satisfied via the goods and services supplied by commercial and public organizations specifically set up for that purpose. It is extremely difficult to estimate how much money is spent on leisure in Britain, but such figures as are available suggest that leisure spending has increased in recent years, although not much faster than spending generally. Forecasts of leisure spending over the next decade or so point to increasing numbers of second homes, cars, television sets, etc. and more segmented rather than nationwide markets for leisure products. On the 'production' side, leisure provides employment for a great number of people in different capacities. The roles of those engaged in various branches of the entertainment industry, such as the professional footballer, the comedian and the strip-tease artist may be compared sociologically, and especially in terms of occupational sub-cultures.

The subsequent chapters consider in greater detail various aspects of particular leisure industries. Curran and Tunstall review research which shows that far more time – nearly 30 hours a week on average – is spent on television viewing, radio listening and on the other communications media than is spent on non-media recreational interests. They point out that many everyday activities, such as eating, talking, driving, homework and housework are carried out simultaneously with exposure to the media. The authors take issue with sweeping criticisms of television which dub it 'electronic innkeeper to the less active minds of society'. They maintain that such criticisms ignore both the actual findings of media research and the complexity and subtlety of relationships between audiences and programme content. They also believe that an integrated approach to the sociology of leisure and of the mass media is required – an approach which would relate the findings of empirical investigations to broad concerns of social theory. They indicate the sub-fields of sociology that could be related to media sociology: organizations and industry, work and occupations, social stratification, family and kinship, youth and age, education, knowledge and culture.

In their chapter on football, Edgell and Jary combine a partisan, and even eulogistic, view of the game with an approach rooted in sociological and socio-psychological theory. Their analysis falls into three major parts: the structure of the game itself, its symbolic significance for supporters, and the effects of crowds. They first examine the structural explanation of the origins and popularity of the game. This explanation asserts football's compatibility with man's biology in a given social context: it serves as a source of acceptable excitement in fundamentally unexciting societies in which violence is controlled and emotions are constrained. A different, but not necessarily alternative, explanation of football's appeal is the symbolic one, mentioned above. Finally, the authors examine the football audience as a crowd, and they dispute much of the 'crowd psychology' and 'mass society' analysis. They do not deny that football sometimes gives rise to violence, but they point out that it allows for many outlets short of actual violence and that some hostile outbursts have sources outside the game, such as religious or ethnic divisions. They dissociate themselves from the view that sport is a necessary evil and that watching sport is merely a safety valve or compensatory − it is no less real than the rest of life.

Newman's chapter on holidays and social class traces the origin and development of holidays from the Victorian prerogative of a minority to their 'percolation' down to lower strata, to the workers' struggle for paid holidays. He notes that the 'problem of leisure' is often seen by the middle class as a problem for the working class, and that underlying this is the view that the working class is unable to initiate action and can only receive experience passively. The author goes on to propose his own typology of holidays, based on the three dimensions outlined above. Combination of these dimensions produces eight types of holidays − from the highly organized, collective and passive holiday camp to the loosely organized, privatized and active motorized caravanning. The changes in popularity of certain kinds of holidays are noted, and these changes are related to class factors such as the increasing ability of manual workers to take types of holiday once identified as middle-class, and the emergence of the short-cruise liner as the 'middle-class holiday camp'. But the judgement of some kinds of holiday as 'mindless' is an example of moral attitudes which are also class-based.

Bandyopadhyay takes up and develops the theme of the social organization and functions of the holiday camp. Using an interactionist approach (which complements rather than opposes the previous analysis of Newman), he examines the roles of managers, staff and holidaymakers in the camp. He draws on previous sociological study of situations in which workers and customer meet, and shows that such interaction over a period of a week or more often makes for a developing 'career' in the relationship. He finds that the age groups are mostly kept separate in camp and that its culture is largely set and dominated by the young singles rather than by the families, by staff rather than by campers, and by individual expectations rather than by public roles. The camp social system itself is a situation in which many social control processes are not expected to operate and do not in fact operate, although the amount of promiscuity is probably not as great as is often imagined. Finally, the holiday camp may be seen as one kind of 'total institution' in which outside identities are obscured by appropriate forms of staff–inmate social relations. Although the analogy with such total institutions as prisons and mental hospitals is subject to many qualifications, it can clearly be used to throw light on this fascinating form of holiday institution.

13 The economics of leisure

Stanley Parker

Whatever else leisure may be said to be, it is in one sense big business and provides work for a lot of people. In this chapter I propose to discuss a number of topics related to the economics of providing for leisure. The starting point is a brief review of the extent and different aims of commercial and public provision in this field. This is followed by a look at the somewhat unsatisfactory data on expenditure on various forms of leisure goods and services. Then we consider the changes facing the leisure industries and the various restrictions on them, including relations between them and their customers. Finally, certain issues connected with employment in the leisure industries are reviewed.

Commercial and public provision

Until around the beginning of this century most people (or family units) were responsible for catering for their own leisure needs. As part of a general process of structural differentiation within society, a variety of organizations have grown up specifically to satisfy the public's leisure needs. When the members of a family are at home their main recreation is television viewing, and free time outside the home is often spent seeking entertainment or amusement provided by other branches of the leisure industry. Many of the organizations catering for leisure do so on a national, and even international, scale, and it is the emergence of these organizations that has been responsible for many of the changes in the way people spend their free time (1).

Many, but by no means all, leisure organizations are run as commercial, profit-making enterprises. Some of the bodies catering for leisure interests are owned and controlled by public authorities, for example the British Broadcasting Corporation. Local authorities provide many forms of recreation such as sports facilities, parks, museums and libraries. Taking a wider view of what constitutes leisure, we see that other, perhaps less obviously 'leisure', goods and services are provided either through the market or by public authorities. For example, the photography and cosmetics industries – both with a substantial but unquantifiable leisure content – have annual turnovers of some £100m. and £200m. respectively. In the public sector, the local authority expenditure on parks, pleasure grounds, etc. was £23m. in 1970 (£8m. in 1960) (2).

The public sector of the leisure industries consists of those enterprises which provide facilities on a 'cover costs' basis and those which work on a 'subsidize unprofitable minority interests' basis. Under the latter heading public money is used to help private organizations that would have difficulty in functioning as commercial enterprises, for example, opera, ballet and theatre companies. Such state patronage of certain leisure activities is a form of social control of the way leisure is spent, a subject to which we shall return later in this chapter. On the narrower question of economics, there are arguments for and against state and other public patronage of particular leisure activities. The spending of public money on subsidizing minority tastes such as opera and ballet can be criticized as endowing one section of the population with privileges at the expense of the remainder. Against this, it is argued that, without such subsidies, many leisure pursuits would be forced out of existence, and that such pursuits, which uphold cultural values, are as deserving of taxpayers' money as is education.

The growth of leisure expenditure

It is extremely difficult to make even an estimate of how much money is spent annually on all forms of leisure. Official British statistics on consumers' expenditure list two categories which unambiguously refer to leisure — 'miscellaneous recreational goods' and 'entertainment and recreational services' — but in 1970 these accounted for £718m. and £566m., or only 2·3% and 1·8% respectively of the total national expenditure (3). However, a number of other categories of expenditure obviously contain a leisure component. If we take only an arbitrary half of the expenditure on alcohol, tobacco, motor cars, radio and television, books, travel, catering and other services, and charge this to 'leisure', we get a further £5,150m., or about 16·5% of the total national expenditure. Added to the two entirely leisure categories this would amount to about 20·6% of total national expenditure. The completely arbitrary nature of the half in these 'quasi-leisure' expenditures must, however, be admitted and there is very little value in making such estimates except as a basis for comparisons over time.

In 1960 the corresponding proportions of national expenditure on 'miscellaneous recreational goods' and 'entertainment and recreational services' were 2·0% and 1·7% respectively. Except for a fall in the proportion of expenditure on cinema admissions, the 1970 proportions were slightly above these. The same holds good for the half-leisure expenditures estimated above — in 1960 these worked out at about 15·5%, against 16·5% in 1970. Thus it might be said that, during the most recent ten years for which figures were available at the time of writing, expenditure on leisure as a proportion of total expenditure rose only very slightly. Furthermore, we can pinpoint the major source of this increase: in 1960 expenditure on the purchase and running of motor cars and motor cycles was 6·0% of all expenditure; in 1970 it rose to 8·5%.

So far, most of the analysis has been in terms of *proportions* of all expenditure devoted to leisure. But we must not overlook the increase in the absolute amount of total consumers' expenditure, of which leisure has had slightly more than its fair share. In 1970 consumers' expenditure amounted to £23,396m. and in 1960 £18,445m. (both at 1963 prices). This represents an increase during the ten years of 27% in real purchasing power. It seems reasonable, then, to conclude that leisure spending has increased, but not appreciably greater than spending generally. If spending on some leisure pursuits has risen dramatically — for example, on bingo and recreational boats — then this has to some extent been at the expense of other pursuits, notably cinema-going. A similar pattern seems to be evident in America. According to Fisk, there is no evidence that 'total measured leisure' expenditures are expanding more rapidly than expenditures on all consumer goods in the U.S. (4).

Changes facing the leisure industries

Industry, it has been remarked, needs the consuming time of workers as much as it needs their producing time (5). A good deal of the output of industry (defined broadly to include service as well as manufacturing industries) is aimed at meeting leisure needs, and the more time and money consumers have to devote to leisure the better these industries will prosper. Indeed, as workers achieve higher incomes and more time off from work, their increasing expenditure on leisure in turn creates employment in the industries which produce the goods and services demanded. The leisure market as a whole is a growing and fairly predictable one, but within it the markets for particular leisure goods and services are more fickle and less predictable. An example in recent years has been the conversion of many cinemas into bingo halls as the demand for the one fell and for the other rose.

One particular change that could have far-reaching consequences for the leisure industries would be the extension of the four-day week among more firms. At present only a very few firms in Britain operate a four-day week, but their employees are reported to be generally well satisfied with the arrangement (6). Although the average length of the working week (including overtime) is falling more slowly than is often supposed (7), there will probably come a time when further reduction will be sought in the form of an extra day off rather than fewer working hours per day. One of the problems would then be that the leisure industries would be faced with an increasing demand to provide facilities outside 'normal' leisure hours (8). At present shift workers and four-day week people often spend their 'abnormal' leisure hours around the house or garden, but this could be because of lack of other amenities rather than from choice.

The pattern of leisure generally is changing, and two different types of influence on the direction of change are the growth in car ownership and a dissociation between social class membership and distinctive types of leisure activity. The Government Social Survey report on *Planning for Leisure* (9) shows that car ownership has an influence on leisure behaviour independent of social class: in all socio-economic groups people with cars were more likely to be club members, to participate in sports and games and to make excursions to the country or seaside than those without cars. The diminishing influence of class is also seen in the fact that leisure activities which used to be the preserve of particular classes are tending to broaden their appeal or to decline. Fox-hunting and dog racing, for example, are declining; pubs, golf and foreign travel are broadening their appeal.

Entrepreneurs in the leisure market are in some ways in a favourable, and in other ways an unfavourable, position. On the one hand the leisure market, as Brightbill remarks (10), is open-ended. There is a limit to the amount a person can eat or drink, and a high income makes no difference to this limit. But there seems to be no limit to how much people are prepared to spend for pleasure — the market is 'elastic'. On the other hand, there is so much opportunity for individual choice that total demand, influenced by fads and fashions fostered by the media, changes radically from year to year. This means that one leisure entrepreneur's profits may be at the expense of another's losses when both are in the same sector of the leisure industry or perhaps in different sectors (11).

Much market research effort has been devoted to trying to forecast the market for particular leisure goods and services. Morrell has carefully analysed the trends, and concludes that in the period to 1985 'the amount of spending power for leisure will probably rise on average by around 4% per annum in constant prices, that is, about 1½ times as fast as spending on necessities' (12). This would represent a proportionately higher rate of increase in leisure expenditure than we have seen in recent years, but in view of the elastic nature of the demand for leisure goods and services it seems not unreasonable to expect it. Some of the extra expenditure will, according to Morrell, go on such things as second homes, cars and television sets, hobby gadgets and books, outdoor sports equipment, eating out for pleasure, and more frequent and distant holidays abroad. He also suggests that leisure spending is likely to be spread in such a way that the markets for many products will not be nation-wide in the sense that every home will want to possess a particular item. He could have added that, unless something is done to equalize or redistribute incomes, many people will continue to be able to spend little or nothing on leisure.

Relations between leisure industries and consumers

The people who run the commercial leisure industries are, in the much-quoted phrase of Durant, 'business men actuated by business motives' (13). This does not mean that they are indifferent to the feelings of the customers or to the standards of leisure behaviour that they help to promote. But some entrepreneurs in all branches of industry say in words or deeds that they are in business 'only for the money'. In recognition of the unfortunate consequences of this attitude for the consuming public, the state and various consumer protection societies, and sometimes associations representing the industry or trade itself, have taken steps to see that certain minimum standards of business conduct are adhered to. The leisure industries are no exception to this process.

Despite claims about the growing permissiveness of our society, there is still social control of much leisure behaviour through restrictions imposed on producers, distributors and consumers. Control of sources of commercial entertainment and pleasure is exercised through legislation, regulation and supervision. The licensing laws prescribe the hours of drinking in pubs, the number of greyhound meetings per track is restricted to two a week, commercial television operates under a franchise-granting authority and so on. State censorship, however, has relaxed in recent years, and the cinema industry has for some time had its own form of voluntary censorship, largely in order to avoid the more costly alternative.

Various associations have sought to achieve or maintain what they regard as desirable standards in leisure behaviour. They have, for example, concerned themselves with keeping Sunday free of leisure activities, getting certain books and plays banned, and keeping children off the stage. Also, there has been much local government opposition to the extension of bingo and betting shop facilities. The activities of such bodies – or, for that matter, of individuals who seek the same ends – are, of course, highly controversial. One school of thought points to the demand for public protection against what is deemed unwholesome in leisure activity, a demand that mainly concerns commercial forms of leisure. But another school upholds the right of individuals to enjoy themselves in ways of their own choosing, provided that this does not interfere with the rights of others to do the same.

In view of the volatile market for particular leisure goods and services, some of the larger companies engaged in the leisure business are diversifying their activities in the expectation that they will be able to cash in on the demand for new leisure activities and cut their losses on the old. A spokesman for one of these firms said that earlier they were in the 'entertainment' business but now they regarded themselves as in the 'leisure' business. The significance of this change is that formerly the policy might be summed up as 'getting people into boxes' – cinemas, dance halls, ten-pin bowls, and so on. The current policy is to cater for people's leisure needs in a variety of surroundings – to rely less on captive audiences than on finding out what the people wanted and supplying them with it when and where it was wanted. This would mean the company possibly going into new fields of leisure provision such as sports, travel and hotels.

The attitudes and tastes of the customers have been changing, too. In the 1930s and 40s the entertainment industry provided for the 'dream outings' of the masses: visits to cinemas (many of them huge 'picture palaces'), glittering dance halls, meals and music at the London Corner Houses – in short, an evening of escapism in surroundings vastly different from those found in the average home. But there was no great discernment or variety in tastes; the fare offered was remarkably uniform. Films were technically primitive by today's standards and popular catering covered only a narrow range of dishes. In recent years, however, changes have taken place which have made the customers more critical and more demanding. The spread of car ownership has meant that people can go further afield in their leisure hours, although some of them show an almost pathological desire to breathe each other's exhaust fumes. Foreign travel has introduced increasing numbers of holidaymakers to different foods, drinks and forms of entertainment. Television, too, has played its part in widening tastes; it has shown how people in different countries live and (more importantly in this context) has stimulated desires to acquire the styles of life depicted in the commercials and in some of the programmes.

One important consequence of these changes is, as suggested in the earlier quotation from Morrell, a fragmenting of leisure spending and smaller and more specialized markets for some leisure goods and services. This trend can be seen in the cinema industry, which has been reorganizing to take account of the altered market. One large cinema chain is going to invest £10m. over a seven-year period to 1977 in building 'triple-theatres' – small cinemas showing three different feature films under one roof for audiences with different tastes. The holiday industry is also parcelling people into package tours and despatching them to ever more distant and exotic places. As one commentator said, with a touch of irony, Jumbo jets will whisk holidaymakers to India and East Africa; the Taj Mahal is no more than a plastic meal away; safaris are as accessible as the lions of Longleat.

Employment in the leisure industries

A substantial and growing proportion of the population is employed in one or other of the leisure industries. As with expenditure, figures for employment are not easy to arrive at, since the leisure/non-leisure boundary is not easy to define. There are official figures for persons employed in 'sport and other recreations' and 'betting' (both rising in the period 1960-70), 'catering and hotels' (fairly stable) and 'cinemas, theatre, radio, etc.' (falling slightly), but this is only part of the picture. People employed in providing materials for hobbies, in the holiday industry, a considerable part of travel, book production, the care of gardens and pets, and so on, should also be considered for inclusion. In the field of public enterprise those employed in running museums, parks and water areas are also in the domain of leisure.

It is not feasible to discuss the total range of occupations in the leisure industry, since some have been the subject of many studies while others have not been examined at all. We may, however, usefully review what has been concluded about a small number of typical occupations in this category (14).

The entertainment industry — and particularly the mass involvement in watching and supporting popular sports such as football — suggests that the role of the entertainer may be as important as it is varied. The professional footballer, the comedian, and the strip-tease artist are all work roles which share certain common features: (a) they give to the person performing them considerable scope for 'role style' or personalized performance, (b) the context in which they occur is a fairly 'loose' one and this fluidity itself is linked to the emergent nature of the work situation, (c) authority, with its attendant sanctions against stepping too far out of line, is likely to be asserted after the event when the 'performance' has finished and the public are not present, and (d) these occupations pose the dilemma of working to *make* others enjoy themselves, this dilemma being expressed through the strains inherent in playing a role which must closely match the expectations of the paying customers.

Certain skills, personal attributes and the exercise of specialized knowledge or techniques tend to knit occupational groups into fairly well defined sub-cultures. The role of the strip-tease artist is a good illustration of this process. The need both to excite the sexual phantasies of the customer or 'punter' and to maintain some sense of self-integrity result in the stripper having to learn how to handle the exacting demands of her occupation. A good stripper will enter into a kind of game with her audience, exciting their interest, provoking them to call to her in a ritualized way to 'take 'em off', while adhering to the norms regulating the degree of physical contact between stripper and audience.

The cohesiveness of an occupational sub-culture depends not only on the specialized skills of the role and the norms which regulate social relations in the work situation but also on admission and recognition strategies. In the case of the stripper these are minimal. A process of self-selection tends to occur and girls recognize the scope they have to perform in their own way. Authority is loosely exercised as long as the interest of the audience in the act is maintained. The general status of the stripper is low, not because the income is usually small but because it is regarded as a morally deviant occupation. This is but one occupation in the leisure industry whose members are said to be part of a deviant sub-culture, another example being the dance musicians studied by Becker (15).

Less deviant but often less financially rewarding is the role of the comedian. The village idiot and the strolling player are the historical forerunners of the professional comedian today. The clown in the circus and the 'patter merchant' both trade in humour. Success in finding new material is the main factor distinguishing the mediocre from the successful performer. The drive for originality and the idiosyncratic ability to make people laugh tend to preclude the development of a strong occupational sub-culture. Occupational skill is individualized and stylized and 'the act' becomes the basis for occupational status and economic reward. The tensions in the work role of the comedian are considerable. There is a desire among the audience to laugh both *at* and *with* the performer. The performance itself becomes a process of identity projection for both audience and comedian, and humour mediates the tension of working at making people laugh. Some comedians *are* in real life the kind of person around whom their act is woven, and this can create personal problems which sometimes result in premature death in tragic circumstances. The British Tony Hancock and the American Lenny Bruce are examples.

Professional football provides another instance of the way in which a public performance – in this case a collective one – constitutes the core of the occupational activity. As Edgell and Jary note in Chapter 15, the main attraction of football is the controlled tension between two sub-groups holding each other in balance. The flexible tension-balance that can make the game so exciting to spectators cannot be produced and maintained at just the right level if one side is very much stronger than the other. Also, there are a variety of roles in the game, each requiring different physical and psychological characteristics (for example, forwards tend to be more 'self-oriented' than defenders).

To be employed in one of the leisure industries may aid the process of upward social mobility, particularly if the occupational role is a public one giving employment also to many other 'backstage' workers.

Thus professional football has provided acceptance into the democratic fraternity of the entertainment world where performance counts and ethnic or social origin is hardly a handicap. In some cases, such as professional boxing, coming from a lower socio-economic background may be a positive advantage, since it has been said with some evidence that such people make the best fighters.

One important qualification is necessary to the statement that in the entertainment world performance counts. Films and television have given rise to the ·'star system', which means that a small group of entertainers are in continuous demand, while the services of others are comparatively little sought after. The star system produces extremely wide variations in the earnings of professionals possessing similar skills. Some actors are millionaires while others, with skills apparently little different, are out of work or under-employed and living in poverty. To a lesser extent, such disparities occur also in professional football, horse racing, golf and a number of other spectator sports.

Finally, employment in the leisure industries may be a 'bridging' occupation, that is, an occupation which provides, through work experience, the conditions and opportunities for movement from one occupation to another (16). Sometimes this mobility is more or less forced on an individual because of the short working life in some sports and branches of the entertainment industry. Thus athletes may become coaches, jockeys may become trainers, and film actors may become directors. Downward mobility may, on the other hand, also occur, as in the case of boxers who become 'punchy'.

The above considerations indicate that the study of employment in the leisure industries promises to be a rich field of further inquiry for the social scientist. It is a link between at least four concerns: the structure of the national economy, the source of income for employees, the rewards (other than income) which they may expect from a job in 'leisure', and the ways in which the paying customers can be provided with what they want.

Notes and References

1 These matters are discussed more fully in K. Roberts, *Leisure,* Longman, 1970, pp. 63-85.
2 *National Income and Expenditure.* H.M.S.O., 1971.
3 ibid.
4 G. Fisk, *Leisure Spending Behavior,* Philadelphia, University of Pennsylvania Press, 1963, p. 29.
5 R. Lynes, 'Time on Our Hands', *Harper's Magazine,* July 1958.
6 R. Miller, 'The Four-day Week', *Guardian,* 28 February 1972.
7 R. Boston, 'What Leisure?', *New Society,* 26 December 1968.
8 An associated problem is that of the erratic use of buildings and open spaces: some services for leisure, under-used most of the time, are saturated at peak times, causing discomfort and frustration.

9 K. K. Sillitoe, *Leisure and Planning,* H.M.S.O., 1969.

10 C. K. Brightbill, *The Challenge of Leisure,* New York, Prentice-Hall, 1963, p. 35.

11 In the record industry, new companies are constantly appearing on (and disappearing from) the scene, mainly because of the strong element of luck involved when signing up a relatively unknown artiste (John Graham in 'Sound of Leisure', *The Times,* 29 November 1968).

12 J. G. Morrell, *Business Forecasting for Finance and Industry,* Gower Press, 1969.

13 H. W. Durant, *The Problem of Leisure,* Routledge, 1938, p. 22.

14 The subsequent paragraphs are a condensed version of part of the chapter by S. R. Parker and M. A. Smith, 'Work and Leisure', in R. Dubin (ed.), *Handbook of Work, Organization, and Society,* New York, Rand McNally, 1973.

15 H. S. Becker, *Outsiders: Studies in the Sociology of Deviance,* New York, Free Press, 1963.

16 L. Broom and J. H. Smith, 'Bridging Occupations', *British Journal of Sociology,* December 1963.

14 Mass media and leisure*

James Curran and Jeremy Tunstall

Academic specialization within the social sciences has caused the study of the mass media as a leisure phenomenon to be neglected. Students of the mass media have become preoccupied with specialist areas of controversy within their own subject. Sociologists studying leisure have been content, in the main, to leave the mass media to their colleagues professionally engaged in research into the media. An academic apartheid has developed in which leisure and the mass media appear almost as two different entities.

The absurdity of this situation is illustrated by the need to rely upon unpublished market research data rather than upon academic studies in order to ascertain the importance of the mass media as a leisure pursuit. An attempt is made in this article to draw together some of the more accessible findings available in Britain. This evidence shows that the mass media dominate the leisure of the great majority of the adult population. Historical analysis of the data suggests, moreover, that the mass media's dominance of leisure is increasing rather than declining. This basic finding, so long disregarded by sociologists of leisure, underlines the need for an integrated research approach. A new sociology of leisure-and-the-mass-media has much to offer, and much to gain, from other fields of sociology and social science.

Mass media dominance of leisure

Unfortunately, no study is available which reconstructs in detail the way in which people in Britain spend their time on an average day. A number of time-budget studies have been carried out during the last decade, however, which provide some indication of the relative importance of the mass media as leisure activities.

The best known of these studies, the Government Social Survey's *Planning for Leisure,* is in some ways the most misleading (1). Although it reports that television viewing is the foremost leisure activity in Britain, it seriously underestimates the importance of the mass media in relation to other leisure pursuits. For example, items such as dress-making and sewing, regarded by many women as household chores,

* The authors wish to acknowledge the International Publishing Corporation's grant to the Open University for research into the British Press of which this essay is, in part, an incidental by-product.

were classified as 'crafts and hobbies'. Consequently, the proportion of women recreationally active in non-media pursuits was artificially inflated. More important, the method of measurement used in the survey was so rough and ready as to provide a totally unrealistic guide to the adult public's principal recreational interests. The results were based on respondents' self-rating of their most important single leisure activity, recalled retrospectively, in some instances for a period as long ago as six months before the interview. It is doubtful whether retrospective questioning of this sort, designed to meet budgetary requirements rather than satisfy the researchers' own high standards, can yield very meaningful results. The survey's principal value is the extensive and relatively precise data collected for outdoor and physical recreations. These data show that, by comparison with the mass media, outdoor recreations have a very small following. The majority of the adult population said that they never actively participated in any of the sixty-three principal outdoor and physical recreations during either the summer or winter season.

More comprehensive evidence is provided by an I.P.C. time-budget study in which respondents were questioned in detail about what they did in each half hour of the day on representative Sundays during the winter and summer (2). This study puts into true perspective the alleged growth of activities such as yachting, angling, pony-trekking and camping that has attracted so much journalistic comment. Only a cumulative total of 32% of respondents claimed to have engaged, on an average Sunday, in any form of non-media recreational activity, even though this was broadly defined to include the work-related activity of needlework as well as conventional recreations such as card-playing, gardening and going out for a walk. Indeed, the true proportion is likely to have been very much less than 32%, since the cumulative total was calculated by double counting all people who engaged in more than one non-media recreation during the course of the day. In striking contrast, 73% said that they watched television or listened to the radio and an aggregate total of 69% said that they did some sort of reading on a typical Sunday.

Even during Whitsun bank holiday, television viewing appears to have been the only recreational interest enjoyed by the majority of the adult population according to a simple retrospective survey commissioned by Beaverbrook Newspapers (3). A similar pattern of recreational activity emerges from the two time-budget studies, carried out by the B.B.C. and A.T.V. (4). Although both surveys relate to a seven-day period, they tabulate people's activities on a half-hourly rather than a daily or weekly basis. Yet even when the cumulative totals engaged in daily activities are calculated (and this inevitably means double counting the same people) the mass media emerge as the only daily source of recreation enjoyed by the majority of the adult population.

The evidence of the time-budget studies shows that the mass media dominate the leisure of a recreationally inactive public. Yet even these surveys seriously underestimate the total number of people who use the mass media. There is a tendency for respondents to omit mention of such activities as newspaper and magazine reading which may take up relatively little time in any single half-hour segment, but nevertheless absorb a significant amount of leisure time over the whole day. Radio listening and television viewing also tend to be understated, partly because these can be carried out simultaneously with other activities and partly because some respondents' spontaneous memory recall is distorted by normative attitudes hostile to the broadcasting media (5).

Evidence, derived primarily from continuous monitoring surveys, suggests that television, radio, and the newspaper press amount for approximately 30 hours per week of the total time available to the average adult in Britain (6). Yet, even this mean figure conceals the massive amount of time devoted by some sections of the population to the mass media, since demographic sub-groups vary significantly in their media intake. A B.B.C. survey in 1972 showed, for instance, that adults in the lowest social grade spent 45% more time watching television than adults in the highest social grade, while women not at work spent 72% more time listening to the radio than men not at work (7). Extensive unpublished data also suggest that people who are heavy users of one medium tend also to be heavy users of another medium (8). The mass media would appear to take up as much as two thirds or more of the total disposable time available to this minority of heavy users.

Even the most everyday activities, such as eating, talking, driving, homework and housework, are carried out simultaneously with exposure to the media. Associated with the growth of television viewing at the expense of the radio, however, the broadcasting media appear to have become increasingly a dominant rather than secondary activity. Unlike the radio, television viewing is usually either the only or the most important activity that people engage in when the television set is on (9).

Indeed, so great has been the impact of television that it would appear to have resulted in a reallocation of what is conventionally defined as 'leisure' and 'work' within the home. An early B.B.C. survey reported that housewives with a television set in the home spent substantially less time on cleaning, cooking, washing and sewing than did non-television-viewing housewives (10). Although the difference may reflect inherent differences in the samples of those possessing and not possessing a television set, every attempt was made in the survey to eliminate non-television influences by careful matched sampling. The finding that television reduced the time spent on household activities is entirely consistent with other evidence showing that the time devoted to household chores is highly elastic and is influenced by subjective orientations to the activity itself.

Such is the mass media dominance of leisure that such 'popular' activities as soccer, rugby league, racing, cricket, tennis and billiards are pursued primarily as recreations through the mass media (11). For instance, only 14% of people claiming to be 'interested' or 'very interested' in soccer stated that they played soccer in the last week. A slightly smaller proportion of this group (13%) said that they were members of a football club or association. Yet no less than 87% said that they regularly read about soccer matches in their newspaper and 98% said that they regularly watched soccer on television.

In short the mass media clearly dominate the total field of leisure activities. They are the only leisure interest pursued regularly by the majority of the adult population. A wide variety of leisure and work activities are accompanied simultaneously by exposure to the mass media. They represent the principal channel by which the majority of people participate in a wide range of hobbies and recreations. So powerful is the media dominance of leisure that subjective perception of leisure itself appears to have been modified by the introduction of television in the home. Above all, the mass media is the most time-consuming leisure interest amongst a recreationally inactive public.

Interesting dominance of the mass media

The empirical evidence on the effects of television viewing on other leisure activities is inconclusive and contradictory. Some survey investigations suggest that television viewing has displaced time previously devoted to other non-media recreational interests; others suggest that television viewing has stimulated interest in, and increased the time devoted to, new recreational pursuits. Still other surveys indicate that television viewing has had no impact at all on non-media leisure activities (12).

The explanation for this inconsistency lies in the methods used to measure the effect of television viewing on other non-media leisure pursuits. The standard research procedure has been to compare the behaviour of TV-owners and non-TV-owners, and to attribute the difference between the two samples to the impact of television. These differences may nevertheless reflect variables other than television viewing of which the most important are the inherent differences between the groups of viewers and non-viewers that are being studied. Indeed, possession of a television set, distinguishing regular viewers from non-viewers, is often symptomatic of more profound differences of attitude and behaviour. Although frequent attempts have been made to circumvent these methological problems by matched sampling techniques, it has been argued in detail elsewhere that the researchers concerned have failed, in practice, to eliminate non-television influences by the techniques that have been used and that their findings must be treated with extreme caution (13).

The same methological problems have vitiated empirical survey investigations into the effect of television on the other media. An alternative strategy for studying the impact of television is possible, however, since there exist sufficient historical data for the mass media, unlike other leisure activities, to establish in broad outline whether the expansion of the time devoted to television viewing has been accompanied by a decline in the time devoted to other media. Although a causal connection cannot be assumed between trends in the consumption of different media, it is possible by this method to discover whether the total time devoted to the mass media has increased since the introduction of television in Britain.

There has been a sharp fall in cinema admissions per annum from 1,585 million in 1945 to 501 million in 1960, and 193 million in 1970. This decline must nevertheless be put into perspective. Cinema-going has never been a major time consuming activity by comparison with other media. Average per capita cinema attendance per day was only 0·08 in 1945 and by 1970 it had fallen to 0·01. This decline does not represent a very substantial reduction, therefore, in the total time budgeted for the mass media.

Newspapers, unlike the cinema, are a major time-consuming activity. Approximately five hours a week are spent reading national and provincial newspapers by the average person over fifteen years old in Britain. Yet, contrary to the apocalyptic predictions of Marshall McLuhan and other media prophets, television viewing does not appear to have made major inroads into national newspaper reading. There is detailed evidence that national newspaper consumption as measured by the total number of square inches of newsprint purchased per capita, by personal expenditure on national newspapers as a percentage of total consumer spending, and by the percentage of newspaper items read, has increased since the introduction of television. During the same period, the total number of national newspaper readers has also grown steadily, although the size of the national newspaper audience has remained relatively static as a percentage of the adult population. Newspaper readership, which reached unprecedented proportions during the artificial conditions of the war and its immediate aftermath, has been maintained at the same high level ever since despite, or perhaps because of, the introduction of television. Indeed, thirty-five years after the first television programmes were broadcast from Crystal Palace in 1936, the national press reached, on average, an audience of 1·029 million more adults than did television (14). The difference is even greater when provincial evening newspaper readers, who do not read a national daily, are taken into account. In 1971 the average issue of a provincial evening or national newspaper was read by 4·807 million more people than watched television on an average day (15).

Nor does there appear to have been a very serious reduction in magazine reading. The post-war decline in gross magazine circulation does not signify a fall in real consumption. Indeed, national newspaper circulation also fell during the same period despite the fact that real consumption of national newspapers increased. Although people bought fewer newspapers per capita, they nevertheless paid more and read more in newspapers that were both larger and more expensive. Gross sales statistics are a very misleading index of consumption because the quantities that they measure are not constant over time. Since magazine prices and paging also rose during this period, gross circulation figures for magazines need to be treated with the same caution as they do for newspapers. Nor can the decline in magazine circulation be attributed to the effect of television viewing. The factors that were principally responsible for artificially depressing newspaper circulation during the same period — fewer publications and higher prices — also operated in the magazine industry. Further evidence is needed other than gross circulation figures in which so much faith has been misguidedly placed in the past. Continuous readership surveys, covering the two periods 1947-55 and 1956-67, show that the percentage of adults reading the four basic categories of magazine (general weekly, general monthly, women's weekly and women's monthly) declined only very slowly (16). Indeed, even in 1971 the average person over fifteen years of age read an average issue of no less than three magazines, and well over two thirds of the population read an average issue of at least one magazine.

Evidence for book reading, derived from periodic discontinuous surveys carried out during the last 25 years, is less reliable. While these data must be treated with caution, they do at least establish that book reading is an active interest only amongst a minority. Changes in the level of book consumption are unlikely, therefore, to influence very greatly mean figures for the total time accounted for by all the mass media. Indeed, approximately one third of the adult population appear not to have read a book during the previous twelve months throughout most of the post-war period (17). This admittedly imperfect evidence also suggests that there has not been a serious decline in book reading. The two most comparable surveys, both using the same definition of readership, are those carried out by the B.B.C. in 1955 and by I.P.C. in 1965. In 1955 27% said that they were currently reading a book, as compared with 26% who made the same claim ten years later.

The time devoted to record playing does not appear to have been significantly reduced. In fact, the number of people playing records and cassettes seems to have increased steadily during the television era. The proportion of households in Britain with record playing facilities rose from 38% in 1963 to 58% in 1969 (18).

The two most time consuming media, radio and television, are fortunately the ones for which most detailed information is available (19). Although radio listening has declined, this has been more than offset by the greatly increased time devoted to television viewing. The average person spent 7·7 fewer hours listening to the radio per week in 1971 than he did in 1948. This reduction was very much less, however, than the average net increase of 13·2 hours spent watching television during the same period. *Indeed, the total time devoted to both radio and television in 1971 was 44% more than it had been in 1948.*

In short the evidence strongly suggests that mass media dominance of leisure, which is such a striking feature of modern Britain, is increasing. There has been a very substantial increase in average per capita consumption of the broadcasting media, which account for more time than all the other media put together. The traditional print media, which account for a large part of the remaining time devoted to the mass media, have proved to be remarkably resilient. Only the cinema and theatre, representing a very small proportion of total media consumption, have suffered a serious decline. There seems little doubt, therefore, that the mass media occupy more time now than they did before the introduction of television.

Since there has been only a small reduction in the average number of hours worked in Britain during the post-war period, it is quite possible that the mass media have acquired an increased share of the average person's total disposable time. It cannot be inferred from this, however, that the mass media have displaced time that was previously devoted to recreational and social activity. If there has been a disproportionate increase in media time, it may well have been at the expense of 'sitting', 'resting' and 'doing nothing in particular' which time-budget studies suggest still account for a substantial amount of leisure time, as well as at the expense of household work activity. The large increase in mass media consumption does not necessarily denote, as we shall see, increased 'passivity' amongst the adult population.

Much of the existing research data relevant to the sociology of leisure is scattered about in a large number of *ad hoc* and descriptive surveys of the mass media audience. A further limitation is the élitist sub-cultural values which shape much not only of the academic but also of the commercial research. John P. Robinson scornfully concludes from his discovery that television viewing is the main recreational pursuit in twelve different countries: 'TV's major present role is that of electronic innkeeper to the less active minds of society' (20) Such expostulations all too frequently appended to — rather than derived from — media research are value-laden and simplistic; they entirely ignore the great complexity and subtlety of relationships between audience members and the medium of television and its programme content. Over a period of 40 years a small number of 'uses and gratification' studies have been published (21). Yet these demonstrate the importance of the mass media in gratifying audience dispositions and personality needs of which many media producers and academic researchers appear to be totally unaware.

Many media researchers, television producers and newspaper journalists cavalierly dismiss the offerings of the mass media as trivial expressions of the lowest common denominator of taste, intellect and even interest among the national audience. Most members of this audience, however, regard themselves as deriving prestige from at least some of their exposure to the mass media. Television is regarded as the most authoritative, trustworthy and informative source of news about current affairs, and respondents in a number of surveys have claimed to rely principally on television to know what is going on in the world. These *claims* in relation to television reflect a complex cluster of attitudes and some similar claims were made for radio listening as against newspapers before television was widely diffused. But newspaper reading is also regarded as a status-conferring activity. When asked how they felt after reading their newspaper, no less than 32% (a high figure for an open-ended question) spontaneously replied that they felt either 'better informed', 'more up to date', 'more interesting' or 'more enlightened'. The large majority of respondents in the same survey were contemptuous of non-readers of newspapers. In a sentence completion question, 'people who don't read daily papers' were described as 'dull', 'stupid', 'ignorant', 'illiterate', etc. by no less than 70% of the respondents (22). Contrary to the educated élite's predominant view of the mass media as trivializing and degrading, the majority of the audience regard exposure to the mass media as imparting not only information but also prestige.

There is substantial evidence that the mass media facilitate interpersonal communication. Not only do people conceive themselves to be more interesting after exposure to the media, but a number of unpublished surveys reveal the importance of the mass media as a subject of common conversational interest. Thus 70% of the respondents in the above-mentioned study agreed with the statement that 'I often talk with my friends about the things I read in the papers'.

An especially important series of surveys was carried out by Odhams in the late 1950s on the readership of the *Daily Herald*. While these unpublished findings are too rich and complex to be summarized here, the typical hard-core reader of the *Herald* emerged as an elderly, poor working man, with a strong sense of personal deprivation and highly critical of the values of a society that countenanced social injustice and an inequitable distribution of wealth and power. A large proportion of hard-core readers believed that people were not very concerned about what happened to the elderly and, indeed, were critical of other working people, in particular the young, who were thought superficial in outlook and lacking in commitment to the values and ideals of the Labour movement. What emerges clearly from these surveys is that the *Daily Herald* helped to create a group identity for hundreds of thousands of people who had a personal sense of deprivation and who felt that their interests had been overlooked and neglected by society at large. A multi-dimensional identification between readers and the newspaper, the way in which the paper's editorial content structured social reality, the readers' vivid perceptions both of the newspaper itself and of their fellow regular *Herald* readers combined to create a potent sense of fellowship centred upon devoted loyalty to a trade union newspaper.

Any categorization of the functions of the mass media as 'entertainment, information and education' is in danger of over-simplifying the variety, the complexity, and depth of meanings attached by different groups within the national audience to the use of the mass media. One aspect of the subjective meaning of the media is demonstrated by audience reaction to withdrawal. A number of studies have reported the strong sense of deprivation felt by respondents at the time of a newspaper strike or non-publication during national holidays (23). Nor is television deprivation experienced as trivial; Steiner reported evidence on what happened when the TV set broke down — nearly half of American families had the set repaired in one day, and two thirds had it repaired within three days.

Leisure and the mass media: separate development as social science fields

The empirical study of both the mass media and leisure first took place on large scale during the inter-war years in the United States. Although mass media consumption was already by the 1930s the dominant American leisure-time activity, these two social science fields had separate beginnings and have remained separate. This academic apartheid which, in our view, crippled the sociology of leisure and seriously weakened the sociology of the mass media, resulted partly from the existence of academic departments of journalism and communications within many American universities and partly because of the supply of research funds from radio and press market-research sources. Leisure research grew up in another quarter of the academic grove. Leisure researchers were predominantly interested in the 'constructive' uses of leisure – and their research funds mainly came from the worlds of education and outdoor recreation.

The sociology of leisure has not yet recovered from this isolation. Mass media research was, however, the beneficiary of Hitler's persecution of European Jews. Many brilliant Jewish refugee scholars in the United States, appalled at the uses to which the Nazis had put the mass media, set about studying the media in the States. Between 1935 and 1950 a high proportion of the most able American sociologists, political scientists and social psychologists at some time conducted empirical work on the mass media. Since about 1950, however, there has been a decline, relative to other fields of sociology, in the quality of mass media research – which has, once again, been left largely to the professors of journalism, communications and public relations.

Today there is an urgent need for the sociology of the mass media to be set in the context of the sociology of leisure. The sociology of leisure in its turn is a flabby, spineless creature unless it acknowledges that modern man's leisure is dominated and structured by the mass media. At present the sociologies both of the mass media and leisure have too few strengths and too many weaknesses in common. One prominent common weakness is the over-reliance of both 'fields' on random sample surveys; such surveys have many strengths but also artificially isolate individuals from the social context in which their leisure/mass media behaviour occurs. This over-reliance on random sample surveys is related to the fact that commercial market research – despite its many weaknesses – is a potent influence on both mass media and leisure research.

The situation is paradoxical. Academic researchers are aware that commercial data in these fields exist – and they are aware that the sheer scale alone of this data must make it superior in some ways (for instance in the analysis of trends over time). Oddly enough, however, at least in Britain few academics attempt to re-analyse this rich source of data.

An integrated approach to the sociology of leisure and the mass media is required

Harold Wilensky's Detroit research is an example of what can be gained from a combined study of leisure, life styles and mass media consumption (24). This research is one of the outstanding contributions both to the sociology of leisure and to the sociology of the mass media. Among the many virtues of this study is Wilensky's determination to relate his empirical investigations to broad concerns of social theory.

The greatest advances during the 1960s were made in fields of sociology where a vigorous interplay took place between theory and empirical research. Sociologists of the mass media and of leisure would be unwise not to follow these examples; but, since leisure and the mass media touch society at so many points, a number of other sub-fields in social science can be expected to contribute something. These include:

(a) The sociology of organizations and industry

The large commercial organizations in the mass media and leisure industry have been little studied. The perspectives of organizational sociology have much to offer here; both leisure and the mass media are studied too exclusively from the point of view of audiences and consumers. There is much to be gained from looking at these fields from the point of view of the producers. One noticeable aspect of these organizations (especially in Britain) is the overlap of the leisure and media industries. Despite, or perhaps partly because of, frequently expressed criticism of the 'commercialization' of leisure and the media, these leisure/media organizations retain a strong element of 'prestige' or non-profit goals.

Non-profit goals are especially noticeable in a substantial segment of the B.B.C.'s output, but commercial television companies also have a non-profit (licence-renewal) goal. News organizations have a non-revenue goal in certain areas (such as foreign correspondence), mixed goals in other areas (such as politics, aviation, education, labour), a sales revenue goal (e.g. football and crime news) and an advertising revenue goal (e.g. motoring and fashion news). The majority of journalists are hostile to the advertising revenue goal (25). The weight which has long been attached by British national newspapers to non-profit and non-revenue goals has repeatedly allowed new entrepreneurs to enter the field, and, by giving greater emphasis to the sales revenue goal, to achieve rapid financial success. Consequently, blandly to assume that leisure and media organizations are even *attempting* to maximize profit – as many sociologists and élite commentators do assume – is extremely misleading.

(b) The sociology of work and occupations

One survey has reported that reading the *Financial Times* on the journey to work is an important part of the stockbroker's or the investment analyst's intake of financial intelligence (26). But little systematic evidence exists about the substantial amounts of media consumption which occur at work – especially radio listening and the reading of newspapers purchased by fellow workers. This media consumption at work is of central importance for the whole question of 'leisure at work'.

Equally little is known about the media consumption and leisure behaviour of members of particular occupations. This is a serious gap in the large social science literature on particular occupations and professions. Analyses of patterns of general media consumption and leisure use, combined with consumption of specialized work-related media and other work-related leisure activity, would appear to offer rich possibilities for the study of occupational communities and ideologies, and for studies of professionalization and trade unionization.

(c) Social stratification

With a few exceptions, notably Harold Wilensky, sociologists studying stratification have largely ignored leisure and mass media consumption – despite the obvious importance of this consumption for such themes as class identification, class consciousness and 'privatization'. Stratification surveys typically include only a few clumsily-worded questions about leisure and the mass media – questions of a type which has conclusively been shown by follow-up studies to produce grossly misleading replies.

These weaknesses of academic stratification surveys are all the more regrettable in that the substantial quantities of *reliable* survey data on social class differences in leisure and media use which do exist have never been subjected to sophisticated sociological analysis. Especially important are the B.B.C., Joint Industrial Council for Television Advertising Research and J.I.C.N.R.S. surveys, which have repeatedly shown that the heaviest media usage is concentrated at the white-collar and skilled-manual levels of social class. Lowest media exposure is among the professional and managerial strata *and* among the elderly poor. Thus the latter, who have the most 'leisure' time available, expose themselves least to the media. But at the other end of the stratification system the strata from which the managers of media/leisure organizations, the communicators and the performers (including politicians) are drawn also expose themselves relatively little to the media. If, as Denis McQuail has suggested, (27) full membership of a modern society requires a substantial amount of media exposure, then the conclusion that not only our elderly poor, but also our educated elite are outsiders is of some importance.

(d) Sociology of family and kinship

Since so much leisure is spent, and mass media consumed, within the family context, family sociology has much to gain from, and to offer, these fields. Obviously suitable areas for such developments include life-cycle analysis, family network studies, and 'exchange' theories.

(e) Youth and age

Adolescents are much heavier users of minor media (radio, films, records) and much lighter users of majority media (television and newspapers) than the adult population. The connection between this media-use pattern, other adolescent leisure patterns and 'youth culture' in general has yet to be adequately explored and explained. But social gerontology also would gain from a closer integration with the sociology of leisure and the media. The central place attributed to television in the theory of 'disengagement' has, for instance, never been adequately tested (28).

(f) The sociology of education, knowledge and culture
The sociology of education has not yet taken full account of the high level of mass media consumption by children. But recent developments in the sociology of knowledge have perhaps the most to offer, and the most to gain from, an integrated sociology of leisure and the media. Berger's and Luckmann's call for a sociology of 'everything that passes for knowledge in society' is stimulating but lacks clear directions as to specific empirical projects that such new sociologists of knowledge might conduct (29). Despite Berger's and Luckmann's lack of explicit interest in the mass media, these media play a rather large part in the social construction of common-sense knowledge. At the communicator end of the communication flow, the management of appearances is nowhere carried on with more vigour than in television studios, which sometimes seem like a world invented by the dramaturgical sub-school of the symbolic interactionists.

*

These are only some examples of what sociology has to gain from, and can contribute to, an integrated sociology of leisure and mass media. At a time when a more confident and mature sociology is returning to many of the concerns of the founding fathers, it is perhaps well to remember that men like Marx, Veblen, Simmel and Weber — were they alive today — would surely have been concerned with a phenomenon which occupied such huge slabs of the waking hours of hundreds of millions of people as the mass media do today in industrial and industrializing societies.

Notes and References
1 K. Sillitoe, *Planning for Leisure,* H.M.S.O., 1969, p. 17. Unfortunately, the most misleading findings of the survey have been given a wider circulation by their publication in *Social Trends,* H.M.S.O., 1970, pp. 77-9, in which the researcher's own rigorous methodological qualifications have been omitted.
2 *How People Spend their Sundays,* I.P.C. Marketing and Research Services Department, 1968. All figures cited from this survey have been calculated as an average of summer and winter activities which are tabulated separately in the original I.P.C. survey report.

3 *How People Spend Whitsun,* Opinion Research Centre, 1971.

4 British Broadcasting Corporation, *The People's Activities,* 1965; *The Midlands Activities Survey,* A.T.V. Marketing and Research Services, 1970.

5 See Kent Geiger and R. Sokol, 'Social Norms in Television Watching', *American Journal of Sociology,* vol. 65, 1959; G. Steiner, *The People Look at Television,* New York, Knopf, 1963.

6 *Quarterly Audience Research Bulletins,* 1971. B.B.C. Audience Research Department and *Detailed Analysis of Time Spent Reading Sunday Papers on and After Sunday,* I.P.C. Marketing and Research Services Department, Ltd, 1963. *Reading Popular Sunday Papers and Reading and Viewing on Sunday,* I.P.C. Survey Report MS173, 1967.

7 B.B.C. Audience Research, *Survey of Listening and Viewing,* Weeks 6 and 7, 1972.

8 See, for instance, *Target Group Index Report 1971,* British Market Research Bureau Ltd; *Joint Industry Committee for National Readership Surveys* (J.I.C.N.R.S.) 1971, and *Institute of the Practitioners of Advertising National Readership Surveys,* 1968 (special computer print-out generously undertaken by I.P.C.).

9 See, for instance, *A Re-appraisal of Attention Value Ratings,* London Press Exchange Ltd (report), 1965; *Television in the Home,* Lintas Ltd (report), 1962; *The Midlands Activity Survey,* op. cit.

10 *Television Inquiry* (1950), B.B.C. Audience Research Department Report UR/51/192.

11 *Minority Publications Survey* (supplementary tables), I.P.C. Marketing and Research Services Dept, 1964.

12 The best summaries are contained in L. Bogart, *The Age of Television,* New York, Ungar, 1956; W. A. Belson, *The Impact of Television,* Crosby Lockwood, 1967.

13 J. Curran, 'The Impact of Television on the Audience for National Newspapers 1945-1968', in *Media Sociology,* ed. J. Tunstall, Constable, 1970.

14 Derived from J.I.C.N.R.S., 1971, special computer print-out generously undertaken by The Thomson Group and B.B.C. *Quarterly Audience Research Bulletins,* 1971.

15 Derived from J.I.C.N.R.S., 1971, special computer print-out kindly provided by the Evening Newspaper Advertising Bureau Ltd.

16 *Hulton Readership Surveys,* 1947-56, and *Institute of Practitioners in Advertising N.R.S.,* 1956-67 computer print-outs from a special run generously undertaken by I.P.C.

17 *Viewers, Viewing and Leisure,* B.B.C. Audience Research, 1955; *Book Reading Survey,* Gallup Poll Ltd, 1955; *Young Publishers Report,* 1959; *Report on Books and Book Reading Habits,* I.P.C. Report 1955; *Survey of Europe,* European Research Consultants Ltd, 1965.

18 Reader's Digest Survey cited in *Ownership of Records,* I.P.C. report MS 145, 1963; *A Survey of Europe Today,* Reader's Digest Association Ltd, 1970.

19 B.B.C. *Quarterly Audience Research Bulletins,* 1948.

20 J. P. Robinson, 'Television and Leisure Time', *Public Opinion Quarterly,* 1969.

21 The best summary of these is in 'The Social Origins of the Gratifications Associated with Television Viewing', J. G. Blumler *et al.,* unpublished mimeograph, Leeds Centre for Television Research.

22 *A Survey to Study Attitudes to Daily Newspapers,* Odhams Press, 1958.

23 For example, *Absence of Newspapers during Christmas 1966 – Consumer Reactions,* I.P.C. report MS, 1967.

24 H. L. Wilensky, 'Mass Society and Mass Culture: Interdependence or Independence?', *American Sociological Review,* vol. 29, April 1964.

25 J. Tunstall, *Journalists at Work,* Constable, 1971.

26 British Market Research Bureau, *The GEC Bid for AEI: A Report on Factors Affecting Investment Decisions,* J. Walter Thompson, 1968.

27 D. McQuail, *Towards a Sociology of Mass Communication,* Collier-Macmillan, 1969.

28 E. Cumming and W. E. Henry, *Growing Old: The Theory of Disengagement,* New York, Basic Books, 1962.

29 P. L. Berger and T. Luckmann, *The Social Construction of Reality,* Allen Lane The Penguin Press, 1967.

15 Football: a sociological eulogy

Stephen Edgell and David Jary

Football in Britain is . . . not just a sport people take to, like cricket
or tennis. It is built into the urban psyche. What happens on the
football field matters not in the way food matters, but as poetry
does to some people or alcohol to others; it engages the personality.
It has conflict and beauty, and when these two qualities are present
together . . . they represent much of what I understand to be art.
The people own this art . . . they cannot be fooled in it as they can
in other things.

Arthur Hopcraft, football journalist and writer (1)

Association football is not one leisure activity but many. Two or more
men or boys can play casual football. Twenty-two men and a modicum
of equipment, and formal football involving 'fixtures' and leagues is
possible. Each winter week almost a million men play football. And
football is watched, with a degree of audience participation, either in
small gatherings of players' friends and relatives or in the largest of
regular leisure crowds. There are more than two million regular
'supporters' of professional football, and the millions grow to include
nearly half the adult male population in a television audience watching
at least one televised game a week.

Football is by far the most popular team game and spectator sport in
Britain. According to the report of the Government Social Survey,
Planning for Leisure, one in three adult males play or watch football at
least once a month (2). Football bridges generations and classes.
Although age limits playing, spectating does not decline with age. And
remarkably, in a society in which there are wide differences in the levels
of participation between socio-economic status groups in most leisure
activities, and where one third of selective and private schools exclude
football from their curricula, there is little variation between social
classes in the incidence of football spectating. Nor is this merely a
British phenomenon. A German survey finds 'football far and away the
"favourite sport", and the sport which approximates most closely to
the index of the general population as far as its relationships to patterns
of social stratification is concerned' (3).

Football also enters leisure more indirectly as a major and salient topic in the conversation of fleeting encounters and in more prolonged sociability. Conversation and reflection is supported by a large literature, ranging from the factual to the fantastic. It is the sports pages of newspapers which most men read first, and football is pre-eminent on sports pages. Sport is frequently a central interest in leisure, and among life interests (in one survey at least) comes second only to the family, outranking work, religion and politics (4).

Professional football also has a huge symbolic significance. Most supporters of football are followers of a single team playing under a traditional name. Typically the supporter's team is representative of his place of birth, residence, or both. Names like Arsenal and Ipswich Town can, as they do for the present authors, command loyalty and become a source of individual location in wider society. This greatly heightens the intrinsic gratifications of the game. Many supporters' involvement with a football club is their most intense emotional involvement with any abstract idea of community or social movement. Nor is the size of a team's 'support' completely gauged even by the large support at the ground. Each team has many followers who, although they may rarely attend games, read and discuss its reported activities.

However, the enjoyment of professional football does not wholly depend upon the possession of particular loyalties. Many watch wholly or partly for the aesthetic enjoyment and the excitement of football's inherent dynamics and the skills of supreme players. And the game is also the basis of the football 'pools', a form of gambling blending football knowhow with chance, and offering the possibility of total escape from work with limited horizons to a life of choice and permanent leisure. Football is an 'industry' as well as a sport — but we will want to argue that at least at its central core it is an industry with other goals than *profit* maximization.

Although in the late 50s and early 60s there was some concern inside football that the simultaneous spread of television, the private car, the five-day working week, and the suburb far from the football ground would undermine football's popularity — and for a time attendances at games fell -- the tendency has now reversed. In its various forms football is *the* British game. And, as the recent World Cup competitions have emphasized, football is also the 'world game', and powerful enough to start a war between El Salvador and Honduras. It has been described as Britain's 'greatest export of all time' (5), for its international diffusion has been nearly universal. 400,000,000 people watched the final of the 1966 World Cup between England and West Germany on television. As Arthur Hopcraft says, football should 'compel examination'.

Yet the sociology of football is sparse. Partly this is because the country of sociology, the U.S.A., happens to be a country of little football. It also reflects the widespread neglect of leisure in sociology mentioned so frequently in this volume. Even where there has been social science treatment of football, the focus has been on its alleged pathologies rather than its joys. In this chapter we attempt to explain the phenomenal success of football among games and leisure activities. We do so in terms of the intrinsic character of the game, its defining structural composition; in terms of its symbolic significance for supporters and followers; and over and above all these, in terms of the emotions of crowds.

Structural explanation

Structurally, football is one of a large number of physical games involving a conventionalized and diluted inter-group fight. Undoubtedly elemental drives involving sociability, the hunt, territory, pecking-order and hierarchy are channelled and gratified in these games. The science of ethology may have important things to say to the sociologist of sport. We are more dubious, however, of the contribution of psycho-analysis (6). In either case, however, any *general* features of animal man that may help in explaining sport games will not automatically explain football; they do not explain why it is more popular than other sport games. After all, such games existed and were widespread in pre-industrial societies, yet many of them have been eliminated, and most others have remained localized. Most of them possessed a ready tendency to slip from mock to real fight and to threaten public order. Certainly this was true of the localized versions of football played in many parts of Britain. What, then, brought the standardization of some games, and why, of all those to be standardized, did association football gain the greatest hold over human imaginations?

Modern forms of inter-group games were formalized and in some cases invented in a revolution in games, which was a late concomitant of the industrial revolution, and occurred initially as a transfunction in the leisure of the Victorian middle-class, largely between 1860 and 1880 (7). The physical restriction of the urban environment played its part in this revolution. So did the formation of a national education system, and the uses made of Christianity within this. Sport had always been something to be controlled. From the time of the Protestant frost on 'Merrie England' it became a subject for 'moral suspicion'. With the public schools it became an *agent* of social control and socialization. More than a diversion, sport became a 'duty'; something that 'ought to be done', capable of improving moral as well as bodily stature, a source of beneficial intangibles of relevance far outside sporting domains, a source of 'team spirit', a 'sense of fair play', of 'learning to accept defeat'. All these and an anti-aphrodisiac too! McIntosh cites a survey of sport in Birmingham which shows these connections with agencies of moral control and improvement: over 20% of football and cricket clubs in Birmingham that were founded before 1880 were connected with the Church and Chapel (8). With the assistance of the railways, organized sport had rapidly diffused beyond the public schools to begin to touch the entire range of the middle classes.

With the introduction of the Saturday half-holiday the working classes also took to organized sport. Above all else they took to football. But not just playing it. Spectating also caught on. In industrial towns teams like Blackburn's Rovers had the audacity, first, to pay their players and then take on and defeat the might of the amateur South. This shook the structure and challenged the culture of Victorian sport. It has not been properly understood or fully accepted by some even today. But everywhere, it seemed, towns and teams followed the path of professionalism, and Saturday football watching gained its present niche in the national diary. Attendances at the Football Association Cup Final grew from well under 10,000 in the 1870s to well over 50,000 at the turn of the century. Names like Aston Villa, West Bromwich Albion, Wolverhampton Wanderers, and Blackburn Rovers had acquired their modern symbolic aura. Soon football became so much a part of accepted life as to be simply 'taken for granted'. But there were spectator sports before football. Prize-fighting and horse-racing for example have a longer history. And in the nineteenth century all the modern 'conflict' sport games started with roughly equal chances of development. Why football emerged supreme in Britain and became so widely diffused beyond it remains to be explained.

One possible explanation, since it rests on claims about the character of the fundamental structure and dynamics of the game, we will call the *structural explanation.* Basically this asserts football's compatability with man's biology, a compatability which is believed to be greater than that of other sports. Elias and Dunning, although perhaps not quite so specifically as we suggest, have proposed a version of such a structural explanation, in which football's dynamics are seen as particularly well-suited to engendering the endocrinal changes which constitute excitement (9). For Elias and Dunning, however, football's popularity as a source of excitement is culturally relative. Rather than something of more universal appeal, football is a form providing a level of excitement acceptable in today's 'civilized' and fundamentally 'un-exciting societies' in which violence is carefully controlled and emotionalism greatly constrained.

It is possible, however, to envisage forms of the 'structural' theory making a more *universal* claim. Games can be divided into intellectual or physical competitions; games of chance; games involving pretence;

and games producing vertigo (or similar physical sensations) (10). Although football falls mostly in the category of physical competition, it might be argued that it possesses elements of the other ingredients of games as well, for example, intellectual contest, chance and pretence. It could be contended that in each of these elements football has especially high appeal. Thus a stronger form of the structural theory might well assert that football comes nearest to *maximizing* the possible social and biological gratifications for games. It could be seen as providing, perhaps not the 'substitute' for earlier available excitements that Elias and Dunning want to make it but something *sui generis*; optimizing human gratification in a *universal* way. We next present evidence for such a view.

Like any game, football becomes a game by the establishing of rules in which the largely unordered real fight is replaced by a rule-ordered contest. This is always likely to be a source of restricted gratification. But football's rules are relatively unobtrusive. It avoids the 'rule-dominated' character of many inter-group games. Often sports are episodic, but football achieves virtually a continuous flow – even 'off the ball', a player is involved. Accordingly football easily achieves the total involvement of spectator and player. Moreover, although it effectively limits, it does not eliminate the excitement and the emotional release of the bodily contact aggression of the real fight. Yet, as the recent, much publicized, tightening of the restrictions upon it by football authorities shows well, physical force is not permitted to predominate over other physical sensations and physical skills, or over the use of intelligence. Nor are extremes of weight and height of overriding importance, as they are in so many games. A further distinctive characteristic of football is its balance between individual virtuosity and team domination. In addition, the game offers to players a variety of playing roles, heightening its subtlety and blend for player and watcher alike: each role requiring different physical and, as has been shown by Payne and Cooper (11), distinct psychological characteristics. Forwards are more 'self-oriented' than defenders; centre-halves are least self-oriented of all. 'Strikers', 'wingers', 'midfield players', 'sweepers', 'full backs' and goal-keepers, each category distinctive in role and ever-changing in interpretation, all allow for difference in aptitude and personality, and the enlargement of football's overall gratifications.

Beyond these factors individually, are the intellectually and aesthetically satisfying configurations which they make up, and the general richness and variation in pattern and style, which football's overall form allows. In all but the most one-sided of football games, there exists continual possibility of oscillation in the contest. Football's normal pattern involves possession and repossession of the ball; this allows continuous possibility of change from defence to attack. Margins of victory and defeat being usually small, football leaves great scope for 'chance' to increase the uncertainty of 'the result', adding to the general excitement of the game by exaggerating what is a vital part of the enjoyment of all contest sports. The way in which levels of action and excitement can build up as the time remaining for play grows less, and as action to change the result – if it is to be changed at all – becomes imperative, is perhaps shown in the timing of goals in League football. More goals are scored during the last ten minutes than during any previous ten-minute period of the game (12). The importance to football of maintaining what Elias and Dunning describe as a configuration of 'controlled tension' is reflected in adjustments which have been made to the rules of the game. There have been occasions in the history of football when defence has gradually dominated attack, threatening the balance of tension. This threat is seen in the number of goals per game in the First Division of the English Football League. Numbers fell from 4·5 in the year of the League's foundation, 1888, gradually, and with all the regularity of Durkheimian 'social currents', to reach around 2·5 per game in 1925 (13). At this point the 'offside' law was changed, making scoring easier, and goals per game increased to 3·7. By 1950 this average had again been reduced to 2·7, when fears for the spectator appeal of the game were again expressed. In the late fifties there was a recovery lasting for a number of years, but recently defence has again become ascendant, and with it has come renewed discussion. However these marginal problems with the dynamics and structure of football only serve to underline the game's fundamental structural strengths. In other sports rule adjustments are far more frequently necessary, and because they are so often necessary, are less effective.

Although admittedly our evidence stands in need of greater coordination, we hope we have given good reasons why a *universal* structural theory might be worth taking seriously. Were precise and additive measures of the gratifications of games possible, for most of the dimensions on which the structure and dynamics of games vary, football would score high. Its total gratifications could well come nearest to some biologically-based optimum for games. All other games appear to involve and to maximize fewer of the possible dimensions. Rugby, for example, allows more physical violence, sheer physique is more crucial, it has fewer roles, is noticeably more episodic, and its balance is tipped against individuality. Sports like tennis and golf are individual sports and their group forms are artificial, making them an unpromising basis for the establishment of the kind of communal loyalties which are so obvious in connection with football. That they possess other limitations of form in comparison with football needs no emphasis.

It is not surprising, then, that football has become so widely diffused, especially as there are still other of its structural features which have aided its rapid adoption wherever it has been introduced. Its simplicity gives it ready initial comprehensibility. In its simplest forms it requires no equipment other than a ball. It is affected relatively little by the vagaries of the weather. A game can be completed in under two hours. It is played on a play area which is large enough for many thousands to watch, yet is not too large or irregular in shape to undermine the intimacy of the crowd and the total visibility of the game. It could be, then, as Lawrence Kitchen has suggested, that football, along with modern science — so clearly a world-wide language and procedure — is a 'global idiom' (14).

Perhaps (a possible law?) once it is available football tends to establish itself in the face of other sporting activities, wherever it is introduced. Just as with science — a parallel might be drawn also with industrialism — it may be that it spreads by its capacity to optimize biological gratifications and social ends. A similar successful leisure 'imperialism' may be the triumph of jazz and 'rhythm and blues' forms in popular music. In football, as in all these parallels, we may be in the presence of what Parsons has called 'evolutionary universals' (15). Football would not then be the sublimated, substitutive, second-best kind of 'mimetic' gratification that Elias and Dunning and others imply. If football were, as they suggest, *merely a substitute* for more primeval (now socially controlled) violent excitements, surely sports like motor racing or wrestling would sweep the market. It is hard to believe that a populace reared on horror films and compulsory daily diets of televised war, a public that also constantly risks death in motor cars, lacks excitement to the extent Elias and Dunning's thesis would seem to require. We doubt whether their theory can really *explain* football's appeal, and that is why we propose the construction of an *evolutionary* alternative.

But what of the most obvious 'deviant case' in the coverage of an evolutionary theory, the failure of football to establish itself in the U.S.A.? In fact, this could be easily and reasonably handled by an 'auxiliary theory', that 'where other professional team-games are strongly established and culturally entrenched prior to football's professionalization, the spread of football is hindered.' Thus the 'deviation' of the U.S.A. would be explained by the cultural accident of professionalized baseball before the arrival of football, and later, the adoption by an influential section of higher education (i.e. Harvard and Yale) of an American version of Rugby football (16). Once institutionalized, these sports possessed an inertia and control over socialization into sport watching. The situation suggested is similar to that of American political parties. These, the first modern parties, are now amongst the most anachronistic, but their massive institutionalization and symbolic associations preserve them. How exactly similar institutionalization has preserved American forms of sport will be clearer when we have examined the symbolic heightening of football, to which we now turn.

The symbolic explanation

Structural explanations of football explain its appeal both to players and spectators. But of course there is also the familiar symbolic addition to the basic structure of the game, the loyalties, the culture, the symbolic accretions that, added to the game, make it also an 'industry'.

We must now examine in what way these 'symbolic' factors 'explain' modern football. It must be stressed at once that any explanation will not be an autonomous explanation, but will be dependent upon (and therefore also supportive of) the structural theory. For if it were not for football's fundamental superiority of structure, other sports than football would possess its extent of symbolic associations — football's massive symbolic accretion is what the structural theory 'predicts'.

Symbolic addition to football begins whenever a team has a 'history' and particularly when it gains an audience or an external public; a public which need not actually be physically present at the match. Frankenberg, in his study of a village football team in North Wales, shows the familiar situation which a team game, far more easily than individual sport, creates. 'The honour of the village and its place in the outside world were at stake in every game and in the day-to-day conduct of the club.' (17) Such symbolic overtones as these heighten the gratifications and general responses, not only of the spectators, but also of players. And when the audience becomes a 'crowd', as in professional football, to these is added the 'psychology of the crowd'. Football expands from a private inter-group game to become, what many see as, a kind of theatre or surrogate religion. A team's supporters become members of communities of shared experience, values, and above all, shared emotionalism. They become members of a 'sub-culture'.

Supporting a football team brings not just a sense of social integration but an *actual* sociability. Not just for the duration of a game but in the week between, it is a source of conversational escape and sustainer of friendship and family ties. As well as providing integration, football also brings 'differentiation' from other groups. In today's fashionable jargon, it 'labels' men, but in a way which men find pleasurable. With this labelling comes 'ranking'. Especially is this ranking elaborated in football. In all grades of the sport teams are ranked into positions within leagues, and a kind of social mobility between higher and lower leagues exists. In comparison with the complexity, the imprecisions and relative permanence of the rankings of everyday life, football's rankings are clear-cut but always subject to change. Each game holds promise of change for the better. Each season begins in hope as a rebirth in which all teams in a division start equally ranked. Rankings can be enjoyed vicariously and dispensed with when the emotional going gets tough. Of course ranks are a feature allowed by other sports; they are a source of the higher levels of interest in the sports, rather than the political, pages of the press. But football's rankings are more significant for more followers than the rankings of other sports. They are, especially for the working class, an extension of group and individual status and identity. And there exists substantial reason for the supporter's identification with his team. Supporters like Liverpool's 'kop' are acknowledged by their players actually to contribute to their team's performance by their capacity to raise the psychological atmosphere of the game. And the conspicuous success of the 'home team' in league football is indication that this effect exists at most grounds.

Besides these psychic contributions which supporters make, the supporters also alter the quality of the team performance by financial contributions, made in entrance fees and via a continuous chain of fund-raising projects. Chief of the financial supporters are the directors of football clubs, who may contribute thousands of pounds. As everybody knows, well-supported, wealthy clubs can buy star players from clubs less fortunate. It is this aspect of football which is often labelled — and misunderstood — as commercialism. But football is not a straightforward branch of the entertainment industry; in Britain it is not run for profit (18). Though football clubs are limited companies, few ever declare dividends. Football pool promoters and magazine proprietors may exploit its appeal but, however much their efforts help to raise football's symbolic appeal, they little affect the game's dynamics on the actual field of play.

The role of big finance in football is best seen as part of the sum total of the sports contest that football is. It is used to raise the level of team performance or — in the case of poorer clubs — to preserve a team's existence. In this football contrasts with professional wrestling, with speedway racing, with American baseball, as well as with many other spectator sports. Wrestling, as it is seen by the sociologist Stone (19), has passed from being a sport to official classification (in Texas) as 'burlesque'. It is, says Stone, a modern 'passion' play in which wrestlers with often several carefully managed identities literally 'dramatize' good and evil for their socially disadvantaged audience (mainly the young and old, with females outnumbering males 2 : 1). Stone denies that wrestling simply 'cons' its public, but in depicting wrestling as a form of epic theatre run strictly for profit he enables us to highlight how far football is from being that kind of commercially staged event. Football does not 'rig' results as wrestling does in the blatant pursuit of financial advantage. (Spectacular exceptions like the Sheffield Wednesday affair, by the attention they attract, only prove the rule.) Football teams do not normally move callously from location to location in the search of greater profit, as do speedway teams in Britain and baseball teams in America. In the typology of professional sport football stands at one end, far removed from the sports like wrestling which inhabit the other. Football clubs maximize their rankings, not their profits: finance is a means to that end.

However, the power of the purse does mean that in general the best 'supported' teams are also the best teams, and that these are to be found in the largest centres of population. But even here there is no simple correlation; a further indication of the symbolic aspect. In conurbations there are to be found rich and high-ranking clubs, with capacious grounds, alongside poorer clubs, drained of support by the more powerful symbolic appeal of their larger neighbours. There also exist large population centres, like Bristol, lacking a First Division team, while centres of limited population, like Burnley or Ipswich, can sometimes sustain First Division teams. More usually, however, the lot of teams in a small population centre is a vicious circle of low population and low symbolism.

Further illustration of the power of symbolism in football is that teams undergoing a dramatic change in rank within the League do not immediately gain or lose support in direct proportion to their change of ranking. Clubs such as Aston Villa, in their period in the Third Division, may continue to attract higher than average 'gates' for their division and for their ranking within it. It seems that people are socialized into support for a football team over a period of years. The club name, its colours, its ground ensure a continuity of support when honoured players have departed the field and the team contains those who have never played in the higher levels of the game. Teams as highly successful as the recent Leeds United may nevertheless lack support because preceding years of mediocrity have prevented a steady process of socialization into football watching. Nor is this continuity simply a matter of 'home' support. Visiting teams like Manchester United, even when no longer in a high position in the First Division, or teams like Aston Villa and Preston North End, relegated from the First to Third Division, still attract larger crowds than their divisional average, not because they always have a different quality of players, but because their names have associations with previous fame and excitements.

The importance of a legacy of associations in yielding support for football clubs allows us to notice how well our auxiliary theory for football's weak American diffusion fits our overall theory once the symbolic dimension is added. Socialization into playing football is heavily affected by the strength of professional sports within any area. Professional football's massive symbolic loading in Britain brings to amateur or casual football 'pretence' and fantasy. With the end of most restrictions on players' pay, and especially since the publicity of the last two World Cup Competitions, the leading footballer is more than ever before a larger-than-life figure. Amateur footballers borrow the names and styles of dress and play of famous clubs and emulate the mannerisms of leading players. This element of pretence has been part of football's enjoyment since the advent of the professional game. It is the lack of it in America which we believe to be the reason for its failure, despite costly promoting, to spread in America. Football without an established professional layer is faced with a vicious circle. Until there is a large football playing public, local players of quality will not emerge to attract spectators to any emerging professional game. Until there is an established professional game few local players of quality will emerge.

Football as a surrogate religion, as an instrument of political response and control, and as a 'crowd phenomenon'

There are other sociological theories of football and modern sport about which we are less certain or which apply but little to the British scene. Nonetheless some mention must be made of these. If what they claim is true, most of these constitute enlargements of the symbolic explanation. None of them says anything to contradict the structural theory. They can be divided into:
(a) claims that sport is a form of religion,
(b) claims that sport can be an agency of social control,
(c) an analysis of football support as the protest of the socially underprivileged,
(d) suggestions that sport watching in large crowds provides opportunities for 'collective behaviour'.

Let us take first the claim that it is a surrogate or secular religion. There are some plausible analogies. Grounds can certainly possess the aura of a church. Arthur Hopcraft expresses a common feeling when he says 'Whenever I arrive at any football ground, or merely pass close to one when it is silent, I experience a unique alerting of the senses. The movement evokes my past in an instantaneous rapport which is more certain, more secret, than memory.' That so many professional players who write biographies – unrealistic as a *genre* as these may sometimes be – report a similar sense of awe on entering grounds, bears testimony of the 'religious' quality. Ritual and ceremony are other analogies. Football has chantings and 'responses'. Above all, however, there is football's capacity to 'integrate'. The sense of membership that a partisan crowd can engender is an aspect of this. But it might be thought to lack the eschatological and ethical dimensions perhaps required to justify the label 'religion'. However, while discussing the functions of the Coronation, Young and Shils have argued (using Durkheim) that even these elements can be present in sport (20). They maintain that the ceremonial and celebration of the Coronation upheld and reaffirmed the 'moral values which constitute society', and remarked on the sense of 'uplift' and 'inspiration' which some people reported themselves feeling. This, drawing upon Durkheim, they saw as 'religious'. They also believed that the famous cricket test match 'stand' between Watson and Bailey aroused a comparable, also 'religious', response. They would undoubtedly have similarly regarded the Wembley World Cup Final of 1966. A fuller argument for football as religion, then, might stress not only its function in providing integration with a particular group or nation, but also its capacity to generate a wider, more universal sense of shared humanity and 'the ultimate'.

Something akin to these religious functions is also involved in the sources of sport effects that get labelled 'political'. Thus Ian Taylor argues that Mexico and Brazil provide instances of countries where football has the effect (and is deliberately used to have that effect) of helping to unify and control deeply divided societies – the involvement of industrial companies in the ownership of football clubs in these countries is no accident (21). A second article of Taylor's deals with football violence and sees this as based on the protest of a class. Taylor's case is that increased football violence is the result of working-class football supporters – especially an unemployed and underprivileged 'rump' of these – who resent the threat to working-class culture posed by increased middle-class involvement with the game (22).

Another theory of football violence sees it as emanating from the psychology peculiar to the crowd. When they avoid seduction by the appeal of Freudian interpretations, official and semi-official reports on crowd violence in football favour this theory (23). Sociological social psychology has long recognized distinctions between groups, audiences and crowds. By 'crowd' social scientists have usually meant something more than merely a large group. Crowds exist when there is a possibility of 'collective behaviour', which is defined as 'that form of group behaviour which emerges and develops in *undefined* emotional situations; it is marked by a process of interaction in which impulses and moods are aroused, spread, organized and mobilized on specific objects for action' (24). Rather than fully intended, the outcomes of collective behaviour evince great unpredictability. The original theorists of crowd phenomena, Le Bon and MacDougall (25), saw ever present in crowds great risk to social conventions: crowds were liberators of base and destructive emotions. Ever since, the study of the crowd has mostly been by social scientists fearful of the prospect of a 'mass society' dominated by the tastes and opinions of the lower classes. What have been seen as crucial to the effects of crowds are disinhibitory forces stemming from their size and the physical proximity they allow.

It is easy to see why versions of such theories should have appealed to those responsible for or concerned with the maintenance of social order. Proven 'pathologies' of the football crowds would easily lend support to legal restrictions. But we dispute any great relevance of collective behaviour theory to the understanding of most football crowds. As we see it, football crowds are rarely crowds in the full socio-psychological sense. Proximity there is. Moods and impulses are aroused and are spread. But there is a great element of social design and predictability in the football crowd. Football crowd behaviour tends to be highly ritualized rather than 'undefined'. Its forms of disinhibitory behaviour seem better regarded as institutionalized and mild forms of 'saturnalia'. Sacred songs become profane. The referee, the team manager and anyone in authority can be verbally assaulted with a virtual immunity from retaliation. There is opportunity for catharsis and therapy. The Harrington Report on Soccer Hooliganism mentions a psychiatric patient

> who suffers with chronic anxiety, tension, and phobias, who said when he visited the local ground 'All my fears disappeared and I found I could argue with no inhibition whatsoever.' ... being a football spectator gave him a feeling of freedom from inner tension and anxieties.

Thus the net social effects of the football crowd – if one wants to see them in the context of 'social control', and we don't particularly – seem functional rather than not. Moreover, the effect is not merely this therapeutic form. The generation of mood and impulse is far more often a source of extended enjoyment, further enlarging the effects of structure and the sense of community basic to the game, than it is a source of uncontrolled behaviour.

It would be pointless of course to assert that football crowds never take on the form of outright collective behaviour. Although he does not apply his model to football specifically, Smelser's analysis of the collective behaviour of the 'hostile outburst' (26) describes the process involved. 'Deprivation', in a situation with opportunity for the expression of ideas, needs only a 'precipitating factor' to trigger off an outburst. But we reiterate that such outbursts are few in number. We certainly dispute that football violence is a central feature of the British game. We doubt whether there is a *specific* football violence worthy of study. The sources of violence seem largely exogenous to the game, lying deep in religious, ethnic or class divisions. As we see it, much football violence is violence for which football is almost accidentally the publicly visible and highly policed location. It is for these reasons that we find ourselves unconvinced by Taylor's suggestion that violence can be interpreted as a highly specific protest against football's loss of class exclusivity.

Future research

Certainly, football violence does not merit the lion's share of the attention of research interest in football that it gets. Even the recent attempts at elimination of violence from the field of play were widely misunderstood as a moral crusade rather than, correctly, as an attempt to adjust a threatened imbalance in the structural pleasures of the game. Focus on violence removes the main attention from where it should be, on the exploration of the positive qualities of the game. If what we claim about the 'superiority' of football is true, better study of football could have wide implications for our knowledge of the functions of sport and leisure as a whole. It could tell us central things about Man. As we said, many aspects of the evolutionary theory proposed stand in need of 'pointing' in cross-cultural research – for example, some separation of features of football that are universal or only general to all industrial societies, or specific to one or a few, including a better test of how far football is a response to the constraints of civilized societies. Besides greater study of the general gratifications from football play, it would be interesting to have a typology of supporters. And how are football supporters sociologically or psychologically different from those who never watch football? Are they less or more active in other areas of leisure? By how much do local 'partisans' exceed in number the less partisan (perhaps more cosmopolitan) 'aesthetes'? What are the detailed patterns of socialization into football, and their relationship to kinship and friendship networks? Why do more men watch and follow spectator sports than women? (27) When do supporters stop following football? We hope such research will be undertaken. As Britain's leading game, football's sociology deserves to be better known.

Concluding remarks

We have suggested explanations of football's popularity. We end by stating the wider relation of our view of football to two of the prevailing popular 'sociological' views on sport in general. The first of these is Lorenz's contention that sport, particularly international sport, is a 'safety valve' (28). The second, typified by Goodhart and Chataway (29), and widespread, is that 'the growing passion for spectator sport may be seen as a sad commentary on the inadequacy of the societies we have created'. Goodhart and Chataway feel that 'it is only because millions of people are not effectively involved in the communities in which they live and work that they identify themselves so passionately with the participants in some sporting ritual'. Each view appears to regard sport as a 'necessary evil'. Though there may be something in the safety valve idea, we do not feel it takes analysis very far. From what we have said it will be clear already that we reject whole-heartedly any idea that watching sport is merely 'compensatory' (30). We find such ideas a depressing failure of imagination — related perhaps to a failure to escape the grasp of the secularized Protestant work ethic and its undervaluation of leisure for its own sake. The experience of spectating — especially football — is more than a compensation and is no less real than the rest of life. It is time that it received its full and proper valuation.

Notes and References

1 *The Football Man, People and Passions in Soccer,* Collins, 1966.
2 K. K. Sillitoe, *Planning for Leisure,* H.M.S.O., 1969, and *The Report of the Committee on Football* (The Chester Report), H.M.S.O., 1968. The age and sex distribution tables in the survey seem to indicate that women's domestic roles and their general socialization mitigate against widespread attendance and participation in sport.
3 See the essay by G. Lüschen in E. Dunning (ed.), *The Sociology of Sport,* Cass, 1971.
4 J. P. Robinson, article in *International Review of Sport Sociology,* vol. 2, no. 2, Unesco, 1967.
5 P. Goodhart and C. Chataway, *War without Weapons,* W. H. Allen, 1968.
6 See articles in G. H. Sage (ed.), *Sport and American Society,* Reading, Mass., Addison-Wesley, 1970, especially section 8. Compare these with some plainly ludicrous psychoanalytic theories in A. Nathan (ed.), *Sport and Society,* Bowes and Bowes, 1958.
7 E. Dunning, 'The Development of Modern Football', and N. Elias and E. Dunning, 'Folk Football in Medieval Britain', in Dunning, op. cit. See also A. Giddens, 'Sport and Society in Contemporary England', M.A. thesis, University of London, 1961, and P. C. McIntosh, *Sport in Society,* Watts, 1963.
8 D. D. Molyneux, 'The Development of Physical Recreation in the Birmingham District 1871-92', unpublished thesis, University of Birmingham, 1957.
9 N. Elias and E. Dunning, 'The Quest for Excitement in Unexciting Societies', paper presented to the British Sociological Association conference, April 1967, and 'Dynamics of Group Sports with Special Reference to Football', *British Journal of Sociology,* Dec. 1966.
10 See article by R. Caillois in Sage, op. cit., and the discussion in McIntosh, op. cit.
11 R. Payne and R. Cooper, 'Psychology and the Good Footballer', *New Society,* 14 July 1966.
12 'When Are Most Goals Scored?', article in the *Football Association Year Book 1961-2.* Possibly, however, this fails to adequately allow for 'injury time' added to this final period.
13 'Is League Football Growing More Defensive?', article in *Football Association Year Book 1965-6.*

14 See 'The Contenders', *The Listener,* 27 October 1966.

15 Talcott Parsons, 'Evolutionary Universals in Society', *American Sociological Review,* vol. 29, no. 3, June 1964.

16 For some indirect support for this view see D. Riesman and R. Denney in Dunning, op. cit.

17 R. Frankenberg, *Village on the Border: A Study of Religion, Politics and Football in a North Wales Community,* Cohen and West, 1957.

18 *The Football Industry,* Political and Economic Planning Report, nos. 324-5, and *English Professional Football,* P.E.P., no. 496, 1966.

19 G. P. Stone, 'Wrestling – the Great American Passion Play' in Dunning, op. cit. Stone looks at American wrestling, but there is no reason to think, at least in those aspects of Stone's work we have used, that Britain is different.

20 M. Young and E. Shils, 'The Meaning of the Coronation', *Sociological Review,* vol. 1, no. 2, 1953. See also É. Durkheim, *The Elementary Forms of the Religious Life,* New York, Collier Books 1961; Allen and Unwin, 1968.

21 I. Taylor, 'Social Control through Sport', paper read to the British Sociological Association conference, April 1971.

22 I. Taylor, ' "Football Mad": a Speculative Sociology of Football Hooliganism', in Dunning, op. cit.

23 J. A. Harrington and others, *Soccer Hooliganism,* Bristol, John Wright, 1968, and *Crowd Behaviour at Football Matches,* H.M.S.O., 1969.

24 H. Blumer, 'Collective Behaviour', in *A Dictionary of the Social Sciences,* ed. J. Gould and W. L. Kolb, Tavistock, 1964.

25 See R. Brown, *Social Psychology,* New York, Free Press, 1965, and D. Martindale, *Nature and Types of Sociological Theory,* Routledge, 1964, for useful brief summaries of the literature.

26 N. J. Smelser, *Theory of Collective Behaviour,* Routledge, 1962.

27 See McIntosh, op. cit., pp. 128-33 for suggested biological determinants of the sex distribution of sporting interests and activities. There are also the ethology-based speculations that male and group sports activities derive from hunting and the like. See Desmond Morris, *The Naked Ape,* Jonathan Cape, 1967, and Lionel Tiger, *Men in Groups,* Thomas and Nelson, 1969.

28 Konrad Lorenz, *On Aggression,* Methuen, 1966.

29 Goodhart and Chataway, op. cit.

30 We do not dispute that football has some *elements* of 'compensation'. Supporting a team gives the opportunity critically to discuss its style, tactics, skill and prospects, a degree of thoughtfulness which may be rare in other spheres of life. But we reject the suggestion that it is compensatory in the sense that it would necessarily be replaced if 'better' were possible.

16 Holidays and social class

Barrie Newman

The British Tourist Authority has estimated that 40·25 million holidays were taken by the British people in 1970. Of these holidays, 34·5 million were taken in Britain and 5·75 million abroad. The estimated expenditure of holidaymakers was given as £1,260 million (it rose to £1,440 million in 1971). These findings are based upon the B.T.A.'s definition of a holiday of 'four nights or more away from home'. It may be necessary to refer to such an accepted measure when considering holidays in a general sense. But such definitions ignore considerations of how the time is used and the kinds of choices people make in deciding between alternative uses of time. The figures need to be accompanied by some explanation of what holidays mean to people and what factors shape the meanings they attach to their use of time.

What kinds of expectation do people have of their holiday experience? How do these expectations relate to their general ideas about leisure? 'Leisure is not merely neutral time involving neutral activity.' (1) It is the pursuit by people of what they enjoy. To what extent is this process shaped by the social context or by such factors as type of work, family and community? What part do these influences play in shaping the choice by people of what they enjoy? In general, then, there is a need to explore beyond the rather bald statistical definition of the holiday; to examine the subjective and normative influences which have moulded, and still do mould, this traditional but rapidly changing institution.

The origin and development of the holiday

In industrial society leisure may be a meaningful concept only when related to work. Although the origins and nature of leisure are to be found in the restriction of spontaneous activities and the beginnings of enforced labour, the process by which holidays gradually became universal for workers in Britain cannot be traced by a mere recitation of dates and of reforms.

With mechanization, with the onset of the Industrial Revolution, workers were increasingly 'subdued to toil', and this was reflected in longer and longer work days and more working weeks. The Industrial Revolution destroyed traditional, pre-industrial patterns of leisure. Such was the 'break' that the new patterns of leisure, and particularly the holiday, were themselves a 'creation of industrialism'. As Tom Burns observes, social life outside the work situation has not *re*-emerged; it has been created afresh, in forms which are themselves the creatures of industrialism (2).

During the early stages of industrial capitalism the coercion and social tyranny of the 'inhuman use of human beings' was dominant. It was only in the mid nineteenth century that work for the industrial workers began to be limited to regular hours, leaving a daily margin of time for leisure and gradually an increasing amount of holidays. As a regular feature of society, however, holidays may be said to have 'percolated' down to the lower strata. The earliest records of holidays in Britain reflect a concern with a return to native and physical health, in particular with 'taking the waters'. Spa towns such as Bath and Tunbridge Wells were the main holiday resorts of the eighteenth century, their popularity remaining unchallenged until the emergence of seaside towns. A belief in the curative powers of salt water grew, and this, together with the royal patronage of such towns as Brighton, established the vogue of holidaymaking by the sea. It was at such seaside towns that the taking of holidays was emulated by, and became the accepted habit of, the middle class. It became the norm for middle-class families and gradually those considered marginally middle-class or 'lower' middle-class to spend a number of days away from home at the seaside.

As the middle class came to embrace the desirability of more and more travel, larger numbers of the lower middle class, who hitherto had spent very little time in this way, found themselves faced by small but not unimportant outlays on transport fares, not merely to and from their place of employment but elsewhere on leisure occasions, on excursions and, especially, for the purpose of their annual holiday (3). In this process clear and dominant views emerged as to the acceptable standards and types of holidays. These views were based upon the emulation of the leisured class.

For the majority of workers, however, paid holidays remained uncommon (4). At a time when Ruskin and Morris were popularizing their views of work as a creative process (5), work for the majority remained a curse. Holidays were a prerogative of a minority, of those who had a formal education and a 'sense of responsibility', who were considered able to manage large amounts of leisure time. The belief persisted among this minority that leisure for the majority, where it existed, needed to be controlled and, where granted, needed to be introduced in a very gradual way. Extensive leisure and holidays among the masses were often believed to encourage activities considered both dangerous and associated with degeneracy or, at best, to entail a 'frivolous dissipation of time' (6).

It is not surprising, then, that even in the 1930s less than two million workers had paid holidays. There were public holidays (7) which, with the spread of railways, enabled many manual workers to go on a day's trip to the seaside, but it was not until 1938 and the Holidays with Pay Act that a framework was provided for a major extension in collective and voluntary agreements for paid holidays. The length of time it took to recognize the important link between the holiday and the health and morale of the work force is difficult to explain. Whatever the reason, however, it is clear that with the growth of 'welfare capitalism' there was a change over time from a 'burn-up policy' whereby workers were used up in the same way as machines and then scrapped, to the 'maintenance policy' where greater value was placed upon 'social capital' and where holidays were seen as a form of investment in workers (8). As the Amulree Report (9) pointed out, the evidence tends to show that the need for holidays arose partly from questions of health and efficiency and the abatement of industrial fatigue.

The way in which the holiday has been studied reflects this dominant concern with the holiday as a compensation for and recuperation from work. A 'maintenance policy' is in the long run far more efficient than a 'burn-up' approach. As an extension of the analysis of the needs of industry, leisure itself has been viewed as a 'problem', as a question of social control rather than the free exercise of choice.

Holidays and social class

There is a sense in which the discussion of social class and its relation to the holiday is a historical question. To some extent it is reasonable to claim that the social justification offered for leisure in general and the holiday in particular is class-based. The labouring classes who formed the manpower of early capitalism had to be controlled. They had to submit to discipline and learn the virtue of ceaseless labour. The leisure of such workers was correspondingly dissipative, aggressive and cumulative — they had to be reminded of their 'station'. The only rights they had were to subsistence, disease and early death. The 'proper' use of time and resources was in self-improvement and hence the holiday was the reward for diligence.

The middle class thus came to see the holiday as a reward for effort expended. It is very doubtful whether the working class believed in this combination of individualism and puritanism. Early holiday patterns, for example those of the Lancashire cotton workers on their 'wakes week' holidays to Blackpool, had a collective quality, with a premium on 'having a good time'. B. M. Spinley, in her study of Paddington, noted that typically 'the preferred form of holiday to take is a trip by coach to Southend with many stops on the way to have a drink, the day at Southend going from pub to pub, and then a similar trip home again' (10).

The pattern, however, has changed with the expansion of leisure time and leisure interests, greater affluence and the fragmentation of work. The more clear-cut connection between type of holiday and social class is giving way to a more complex situation. Some would claim that the analysis of leisure in terms of class is redundant. We are moving towards a 'leisure democracy' (11) in which the main differences in types of leisure are said to be not class-based but attributable to the existence of a number of small 'taste publics'. Although there is no doubt some truth in this, as a generalization it seems a questionable proposition, if only because of the differential access to leisure opportunities that class-based income allows.

The claim that we are moving towards a leisure democracy may be assessed by looking at two issues: (a) the evidence for types of class consciousness, and (b) the relation of class consciousness to the type of holiday people choose and what they expect to result from their choice. This two-step analysis has some dangers. It assumes that 'class consciousness' is a viable concept. Perhaps it would be safer just to refer to the patterning of attitudes. However, it may be claimed that there is a sufficient literature on class to warrant use of the concept, even though it is contentious. It is also doubtful whether there is any clear relation between class, as a crude economic category centred on occupation and income, and the types of behaviour people engage in. Clearly, occupation and income influence people's opportunities for choice and thus limit their behaviour, but this is not quite the same claim.

Perhaps the greatest danger is in assuming that any one model of society is itself sufficient to explain variations in individual behaviour. Conflict models and integration models pose quite different theories of stratification and, without entering into this debate, it would seem reasonable to claim that both agree on one basic issue: that an individual's perspective of social reality, his view of the social world, may well be related to the level of investment he believes he has in the existing economic and social organization of society.

1. Class consciousness

Marx originally claimed that class consciousness was a direct outcome of the division of labour. The proletariat were without property and the means of production – thus they were without power. Alienation was a symptom of the disease called capitalism. Men were exploited, and being aware of this exploitation was itself the basis of class consciousness. The bourgeoisie were not alienated – they were the exploiters, and class consciousness for them was in recognizing their own interests and defending them.

The Marxian model has been refined in many ways – from Weber to Blauner. The history of the concept of class consciousness is too diverse to enable any useful summary to be made for the purpose of this discussion. However, a few relevant points may be extracted. Class consciousness is considered to depend on the denial of power to one group and its monopoly by another. This consciousness is seen to be reinforced both through the social relationships of work and the central values and life choices of culture. The working class is thus characterized by a *dichotomous* view of the social structure in terms of 'us' and 'them'. They share a work situation and a market situation which supports this view. Being insecure in the labour market reinforces the desire for collectivity and the class basis of social relationships both within work and outside it. Working-class culture, centred on immediacy, hedonism and collectivism, provides a total framework of meaning according to which social and economic choices are made.

The middle class is said to differ on all these points. Its members possess a *unitary* view of social reality. Society is a hierarchy, a career ladder, and differences in opportunity are a result in variation in effort, merit and commitment. Their typical work situation is far less conducive to collectivism, and relative security in the labour market makes such collectivity unnecessary. Professional and managerial work has high status, and this is reinforced by the kind of culture and life styles of the middle class. The central values are those of deferred gratification and individualism, and the fabric of social relationships consists in acting out these values through status and income choices.

These two views of the social world are not without refinement. Much effort has been expended in describing and analysing the relation between the elements *within* class and the possible variations in class consciousness which may be produced by the social structure (12). One important issue is how far class perceptions result in the existing social and economic order being regarded as 'legitimate' or 'illegitimate'. How far that order is accepted as right and just is the basic question. Ford and her colleagues have suggested that working-class consciousness may take four forms (13). Those who reject the existing social and economic order as illegitimate tend to adopt a dichotomous power view – an 'us' and 'them' model of reality. If this order is regarded as legitimate then a 'deference' view may result – 'they' have a right to rule and own and make the major decisions, and inequality is part of the natural order of things. On the other hand, the working class may to some extent have adopted a middle-class view of the world – they may see society in terms of a hierarchy or ladder. If they do and they regard this as legitimate, they will have a 'prestige' model – if not, an 'instrumental-collective' view.

Typology of class consciousness

Perception of the shape of the class structure	Evaluation of the legitimacy of class structure	
	Illegitimate	Legitimate
Dichotomy	power models	deference models
Hierarchy	instrumental-collective models	prestige models

These variations are important for several reasons. They enable us to avoid the rather simplistic view that working-class consciousness is homogeneous. They suggest that there is an association between the ongoing world of social relationships and the behavioural choices people make. And they have the merit of helping us to see that the attempt to link social class with one kind of behaviour choice — the holiday — is not a simple task.

2. Types of holiday

The B.T.A. published one table in 1970 of holidaymaking by socio-economic group, and although the data are not very helpfully presented it may be calculated that only about 20% of the highest (AB) socio-economic group did not take a holiday in 1970, compared with about half of the lowest (DE) group (14). Other socio-economic groups (C1 and C2) were intermediate between these extremes. Another notable finding is the extent to which the taking of a second or subsequent holiday is class-based: the AB group (14% of the population) took 56% of these holidays. Thus we have a solid statistical basis for saying that the propensity to take a holiday varies directly with social class, measured by the market research categories used by the B.T.A.

To go beyond this purely statistical analysis we need to develop an assessment of type of holiday along dimensions which reflect class-related views of the social world. These dimensions include the following: a 'collective' or 'privatized' orientation to the holiday experience; how organized the holiday is; and whether participants take an active or passive part in the process. These dimensions may be useful in analysing holiday patterns and how they are changing, and from them it may be possible to develop a typology. If these dimensions are discussed in relation to social class then some of the influential factors may become clear.

The working-class holiday is often characterized by a high degree of organization, collective orientation and passivity (15). The holiday camp is a good example. As suggested by Bandyopadhyay in the following chapter, the camp organizes and administers a holiday for a large number of people, feeding, housing and entertaining them. Camp life is highly structured, with an emphasis on entertainment. A complex of programmes is offered, with shows, sports, competitions, dances and games. The holiday centres on these entertainments, the food being mass-produced and the chalets regarded as sleeping units, out of which the guests have to be coaxed as much as possible. The holiday camp is the industrialized holiday *par excellence*. It is popularly held that holiday camps have a highly passive clientèle consisting of people who are chivvied, admonished, encouraged and cajoled into 'having a go' in the competitions and sports and into generally contributing to the fun atmosphere.

It has recently been reported, however, that the more highly organized, large-scale holiday camp has become less popular, while the more informal, self-catering, more family-centred type of holiday has increased in popularity. Holidaymakers, once happy with the smiling regimentation of the large holiday camp, now prefer, it seems, a greater variety of choice. In recognition of this, the larger holiday camps are providing self-catering and more individual choice. The newer holiday camp projects are much smaller, village-type camps with an emphasis on 'interest' holidays catering for specific hobbies such as fishing. In the main, loosely organized, active, but collective-oriented holidays are envisaged for the future.

The growth of package tours provides another instructive example. Holidays abroad are obviously linked to changes in transportation and the relative cheapness of flying by charter. Clarksons, a major tour operator in Britain, said they had carried 500,000 people on holiday in 1970 and estimated a figure of 700,000 in 1971. In a recent review of types of package holidays, Brenda Jones emphasized the order, speed and routinization of these tours. The coach became 'our cave for the next eleven days, the holidaymakers venturing out to look at the Italians rather than to mingle with them'. There is a quality of uniformity and routinization and, in the case of tours moving from one place to the next and in viewing buildings, a relatively high degree of activity.

At the other extreme is the loosely organized, privatized and active kind of holiday. An illustration of this is camping. In 1971 a slightly larger proportion of holidaymakers went camping in Britain than went to holiday camps. Camping is seen as a means by which the holidaymaker and his family can cater for themselves, can seek isolation and retire briefly from the stresses and strains of mass society. This kind of holiday is a means of self-expression, a form of ego-expansion in which the cares and limitations of everyday work are temporarily forgotten. It is a middle-class type of holiday, exemplified by the motorized caravan – the Volkswagen or Dormobile. Rayner Banham describes the camping van as the intellectual carriage which has an adaptability to the rapidly changing modes of bourgeois-intellectual life – camping holidays in Calabria with three children under five and other forms of higher masochism (16).

More detailed studies of camping holidays have been carried out in the U.S.A. and have established a social-class relation with the different types of camping holiday. The Outdoor Recreation Resources Review Commission report (17) found that camping was largely a preserve of the higher socio-economic groups. A crucial distinction arises, however, between wilderness camping and caravan holidays. Stones and Traves found that those campers who preferred a more solitary existence in the wilderness seldom came from dead-end jobs, and tended to be recruited from the professions (18). The desire for and realization of a more direct contact with nature would seem to be related to 'ego-expansion' where a more direct involvement with nature necessitates the exercise of initiative and skill. Etzkorn found that trailer campers or caravan people tended to be skilled manual foremen and those in the more routinized non-manual occupations (19). Among the more important conclusions is that trailer campers valued the social resources on the camping sites as much as the natural resources.

Such holidaymakers are perhaps less concerned with activity and the degree of control over the environment than with the opportunity to control more directly where they go, what they do, and with whom. Trailer caravan holidays exhibit the characteristics of a low degree of organization, passivity and privatization, which would seem to fit the instrumental-collective category. Holidays here afford an opportunity for joint planning and action within the domestic group, providing an important integrative mechanism in terms of greater choice and organizational complexity, of brochures to be looked at, travel arrangements to be made, choice of accommodation and activities. The emphasis Bott (20) places on loose networks and the greater possibility of spouses sharing leisure pursuits, and the home-centredness of many workers may be reflected in the privatized, loosely organized yet passive holiday.

If these dimensions are useful in discussing and analysing types of holiday, then perhaps it would help further to present them in the form of a typology:

Typology of holidays

Type of orientation	Degree of organization		Participant involvement
	High	Low	
Collective	Holiday camp	Relatives	Passive
	Package tour	'Interest' holiday camps	Active
Privatized	Hotels	Trailer caravan	Passive
	Sailing schools	Motorized caravan/camping	Active

Conclusion

Leisure and the holiday are increasingly seen as characteristics of contemporary industrial society. Non-work time has been freed from nineteenth-century puritanical notions of sin and waste, only to be replaced in the early twentieth century by the notion that leisure is time to be used constructively. There had to be a good reason for spending time in certain ways, a socially justifiable reason, because one's own preferences were not held to be reason enough.

Changes in transportation have produced demands for holidays of new and different kinds, the mobile touring holiday having grown in popularity at the expense of the more static holiday resort. Although there is now a greater choice of what to do and where to go, holidays for many of the working class are still highly organized. Willmott quotes a motor mechanic of eighteen who described his annual holiday thus:

> When we go on holiday we go to a holiday camp on Canvey Island — my brothers, their wives, Mum and Dad, my Uncle Joe and his wife, Aunt Flo and her husband who live in Hackney Road, Aunt Jean who lives in Cambridge Heath Road, and Aunt Margaret from Bishop's Way. There are only twenty-two of us this year. We're going to Dymchurch near Folkestone. We're going in a big Dormobile and we'll have four chalets and a caravan (21).

Changes are taking place in holiday behaviour, however. Working-class people are today more able to select a type of holiday that approximates a pattern once identified as exclusively middle-class. The second holiday is still largely a middle-class privilege, but increasingly manual workers are able to take more than one holiday a year, one to be spent with relatives, the other abroad or at a resort in Britain.

Although there is little direct evidence on the role of holidays in the new residential areas such as Greenleighs, it is fairly clear that holidays have increasingly become a means by which extra-domestic kin are re-united for a week or more at a time. And this applies to both working-class and middle-class families. Collective camping holidays of the type cited above could well be seen as indicators of the degree of effectiveness of links between kin and the quality of kin relationships.

These considerations are not restricted to the working class. Firth and his colleagues, for example, estimated that only 25-30% of their middle-class informants avoided kin when they went on holidays or chose the place of their holidays irrespective of kin considerations (22). For the majority, kin were usually involved in holiday plans, particularly in subsidiary holidays. The family cycle is also an important consideration here. In the family-building stage, kin may often 'relieve' parents of children, enabling parents to have holidays on their own. Again, this may well be related to the salary structure of many middle-class career patterns in which holidays for all the family may be too much of an economic burden. The degree to which holidays are spent with kin, and the type of holiday, for example camping as opposed to hotel, may vary according to the family stage.

Given that there is a quality of uniformity and routine about many holidays, it is important to note that such holidays are not limited to the working class. Hotels, traditionally the preserve of the middle class, have never been content merely to provide bed and board. They have, in different degrees and qualities, catered for a range of interests and needs. The proud boast of many of the leading European hotels is that the guest need never leave the hotel during his stay and still experience a wide and varied programme of events. This is an important factor in the emergence of the 'middle-class holiday camp', the liners which are engaged in short cruises of ten or eleven days in the Mediterranean. Here the keynote is routine uniformity and passivity.

It would be sociologically satisfying to suggest that there is a convergence occurring in terms of the social class basis of holidays. But this would be rather too sweeping. It may be safer to say that class differences are not as clear-cut as they once were, with the tendency for consumption patterns to form the basis of life styles. To some extent the routinization of work that was once seen as typical only of manual labour is being extended by the mechanization of the white-collar world. Certainly there seems to be some degree of convergence with regard to market situation and job security which may affect the financial ability to take holidays of various kinds. And yet there are differences in holiday patterns, and these appear to centre upon how far people want to enjoy themselves in their own way or prefer everything 'laid on' for them. This may reflect a fundamental difference in outlook stemming not so much from class as from cultural values.

Notes and References

1 B. Berger, 'The Sociology of Leisure', in E. O. Smigel (ed.), *Work and Leisure,* New Haven, College and University Press, 1963, p. 26.

2 See Chapter 3.

3 J. A. Banks, *Prosperity and Parenthood,* Routledge, 1954, p. 94.

4 The first instance of paid holidays for manual workers came in 1884 when Brunner-Mond gave their employees an annual week's holiday with pay.

5 J. Cohen, 'The Ideas of Work and Play', *British Journal of Sociology,* December 1953.

6 ibid.

7 Bank Holiday Acts, 1872 and 1875.

8 R. Glasser, *Leisure: Penalty or Prize?,* Macmillan, 1970.

9 Cmd. 5724, 1938.

10 B. M. Spinley, *The Deprived and the Privileged,* Routledge, 1953, p. 53.

11 K. Roberts, *Leisure,* Longman, 1970.

12 D. Lockwood, 'Sources of Variation in Working-Class Images of Society', *Sociological Review,* 1965; J. Goldthorpe and D. Lockwood, 'Affluence and the British Class Structure', *Sociological Review,* 1963.

13 J. Ford *et al.,* 'Functional Autonomy, Role Distance and Social Class', *British Journal of Sociology,* December 1967.

14 *The British on Holiday,* 1971. The report in 1972 contains few equivalent statistics.

15 Walking, climbing and swimming – all relatively low on organization, collective orientation and passivity – were shown by an Opinion Research Centre poll to be substantially less popular with working-class than with middle-class holidaymakers (*Sunday Times,* 28 May 1972).

16 'In the Van of Progress', *New Society,* 30 April 1970.

17 *Outdoor Recreation for America,* U.S. Government Printing Office, 1962.

18 G. Stones and M. Traves, 'Camping in the Wilderness', in E. Larrabee and R. Meyersohn (eds.), *Mass Leisure,* Glencoe, Free Press, 1958.

19 K. P. Etzkorn, 'Leisure and Camping', *Sociology and Social Research,* October 1964.

20 E. Bott, *Family and Social Network,* Tavistock, 1957.

21 P. Willmott, *Adolescent Boys of East London,* Routledge, 1966, p. 70.

22 R. Firth and others, *Families and their Relatives,* Routledge, 1970.

17 The holiday camp

Pradeep Bandyopadhyay

Holiday camps are both numerous and popular in England. They constitute an important category among the different types of holiday accommodation available (1). I shall deal with the sociological aspects of the holiday camp, the patterns of social interaction, roles and experiences, although these are not confined to the one institution. They may also be found in cruises or, on a much smaller scale, in hunting lodges or plush hotels at seaside resorts. Thus although the holiday camp by and large is avoided by middle-class holidaymakers, there are types of vacation enjoyed by the middle classes which, from a sociological point of view, may be comparable.

The camp holiday is usually one week, but about a fifth of the people in the camp I studied return or stay on for a second week. It is more usual for those taking a two-week camp holiday to go back to work after the first week (usually in June) and then return for a second week in the peak period of July-August. Among a lot of families the second week is still used either for visits to relatives or for work on the house and hobbies: building cupboards, a boat, gardening, etc.

The social organization of a holiday camp

From an organizational point of view, the holiday camp consists of three categories of people whose orientations toward and expectations of the camp are different: the *managers,* who are full-year salaried employees and many of whom have shares or other proprietary rights in the camp; the *staff,* who are seasonal employees on weekly wages and who expect to benefit from the camp facilities without much expenditure and whose utilization of the camp and its social or 'fun' opportunities is limited by their work roles; and the *campers* themselves, who have paid for a week's holiday, hold more or less specific expectations about what holiday enjoyment involves, accept that to get the best out of the camp vacation money will have to be spent, expect service, and have uses of time quite different from the workaday routine of the rest of the year.

The division of functions within the camp is both an indication of what campers expect of a successful holiday and also of the extent to which a camp is a relatively autonomous society. The latter depends for some functions on the larger society within which it is located, but also provides equivalents within its boundaries for other functions. The *contrast* between the social experiences and roles a camp offers and those available in 'normal' society, and at the same time the symbiotic *interdependence* between what the camp offers and what is 'taken for granted' in the larger society is an interesting problem for sociological analysis.

The managerial functions are connected with entertainments, bars, catering, the dining hall; overall control is in the hands of the camp manager with an assistant and a personal secretary. Besides the areas of concern of each of the managers, there are other areas under supervisors responsible directly to the camp manager or to the accountants or the office manager. These include *chalets*, involving the chalet office and chalet maids and porters; *security*, involving the security guards, night patrols and the lost property office; the *shops*, with the shop assistants and stocks; the *café*, which functions as a snack-bar during the early mornings, afternoons and evenings, with the staff on rotating shifts; and the *nursery*, with its staff who enable parents to be free from looking after babies and infants.

A number of issues arise when the holiday camp, as an organization, is compared and contrasted with other social institutions. The holiday camp, from a formal organizational point of view, belongs to the group of organizations that are *economic* in the sense of involving exchange of services and/or goods between buyers and sellers. However, compared to most other economic organizations, the holiday camp is different in a number of ways that will be considered below.

Lack of bureaucracy

The holiday camp does not exchange definable, 'objectified' and discrete items for which money is both necessary and (at least usually) sufficient; but rather it offers possible happenings not usually available, the relaxation of conventional social controls, the avoidance of certain roles and the availability of certain others, the exclusion of onerous or undesired work, and – especially for women and older retired people – the escape from domestic chores and routines. All of this greatly widens the range and kinds of relationships available to members of a family, couples, groups or pairs of adults or adolescents.

The major consequence, organizationally, of what is sought from the holiday camp is the much greater uncertainty about 'production, distribution and consumption'. No standardization of services and attitudes ever reaches the precision of saleable goods. The management cannot easily routinize or bureaucratize, or use statistical sampling for quality control. Social interaction in general, and managerial directives and decisions in particular, are much more *ad hoc* and situationally determined: innovation, alteration and change are accepted as unavoidable and as occupational hazards. This affects all staff and campers more or less, and especially the managers, entertainers, hostesses and dining and dance-hall attendants. The services of the staff and their functions are continually changing in quality, partly owing to their own state of mind and health but also owing to the variability of the audiences' or clients' expectations. Their services are usually very specific personal ones and are located in social situations rather than connected with images of the 'average consumer' or of a large mass audience where a great many individual variations may cancel each other out.

Certain regular patterns and types emerge, but there are also the exceptional cases or 'crises' that call for new or unusual processes of coping or manipulation. These cases are sociologically most interesting, since they throw into clearer relief the regularities and the taken-for-granted set of responses and expectations. Further, the lack of bureaucracy allows for interactions between managers and other staff not otherwise available; thus there are processes of loyalty, phased promotions that are situationally rather than bureaucratically determined, and forms of antagonism in changing power relations.

Face-to-face interaction

The holiday camp is an instance of those organizations where clients and 'producers' are face-to-face through the entire process of exchange and interdependence. William Foote Whyte laid special emphasis on this aspect of the organization of the restaurant industry. In relating his studies of the restaurant as a particular type of 'service industry' to the then developing study of behaviour in the social systems of factories and corporations, he remarked:

> When worker and customer meet, in the service industry, that relationship adds a new dimension to the pattern of human relations in industry. When the customer takes an active part in business activity, the whole organization must be adjusted to his behaviour (2).

In that study Whyte went on, in the tradition of the 'human relations school', to explore the contexts in which waitresses cry or break down, the relations between tipping and self-esteem, and the emotional rather than economic significance of waitress-customer interactions. He noted how the chance occurrence of one unpleasant incident with a customer may so throw a waitress off balance that she loses her normal capacity to cope with other customers – producing a chain of unpleasant interactions which she may define as a 'bad day', or as failure on her part to successfully perform her role.

In the holiday camp, the customers are face-to-face with those serving not just for a brief hour or two but over a whole week, and the interactions naturally involve much more than the exchange of definable services. The relations between staff and camper may move from phase to phase of a pattern, thus providing a 'career' in the camp experiences of certain campers or staff (3). Opportunities for this sort of dynamic, developing interaction between camper and staff are not equally available to all staff or all campers, and this feeds back into the social system of the camp as an indicator of prestige and status. Further, the process of staff-camper interactions is a varying one depending on a number of factors: (a) the *structural position* of staff, (b) the *expectations* about relationships that staff or different campers may hold, (c) the *times* when a particular member of staff can seek out and sustain an interaction or situation with campers, and (d) the extent to which the situation is under the *control* of the initial participants (for in public gatherings one has to manipulate a situation so as to include or exclude others who may be nearby or who may want to enter into the situation (4)).

For example, the kitchen porter can have virtually no opportunities to initiate interactions with campers during his work shift. He is physically removed most of the time, and when he is near campers during work he bears signs which inhibit interaction: wearing overalls, carrying a bin of waste food or hurrying to a destination where even willing campers may not follow or accompany him. Waiters and waitresses, by contrast, are required by their work to meet and interact with campers in groups at dining tables. They have the opportunity to favour certain campers – for example, by bringing in an extra helping or by sustaining conversation during slack periods – and thus initiate relationships that can be continued and canalized in certain preferred directions during the evenings or during time off.

Dining-hall supervisors have these opportunities to an even greater extent. Their role *requires* conversing with campers and introducing those at table to each other, and breaking any embarrassing silences that may occur, looking into complaints and joking with campers. They exercise extensive powers of patronage: extra helpings, delivering sandwiches to campers after hours, altering seating arrangements through exchanges, and so on. Their opportunity to invite selected campers for a drink, to a film or to dance is considerable. The public definition of their role is such that any such invitation will not be taken amiss and very rarely refused. Since generally supervisors are not tipped, campers are unable to offer monetary rewards for services rendered; social exchange will require accepting an invitation to drink or, at the least, sustaining a conversation initiated by a supervisor.

The position of the entertainers illustrates these aspects even better. They have high prestige and social status both by managerial definition and by the responses of the campers. In camp they perform the same occupational role as outside; by and large they belong to a union and are contracted out to the camp by external agencies. These factors serve to set them apart from other categories of staff, and they make efforts to convey this distinction to campers and to maintain the higher status accorded to them. Their roles require them to interact with campers in certain expected ways. Since there are only about 40 entertainers for some 2,000 campers, many of the expectations of campers about possible encounters with entertainers are only hopes.

Campers' expectations of entertainers relate to quality of performance, clothes, appearance and facial expression – the always smiling, gay, coquettish dancer or hostess, the tense facial gestures of a drummer, the slightly cool and distant look of musicians during a recess, denoting both unavailability for casual interaction and their difference from other categories of staff. Musicians or dancers tend to keep company with attractive or high-status members of the opposite sex, whether campers or fellow-staff. Thus it is expected that the dancers or hostesses be the 'girl-friends' of one of the musicians or campers, and not of a waiter. Similarly, if there is any attractive single woman among the campers it is widely expected that she will keep steady company, if at all, with a high-status or 'glamour' person: one of the musicians, a soccer star, a comedian or a particularly attractive and distinctive camper.

The expectations of campers also have to do with getting dates with a musician or dancer, the possibility of a romance (sometimes to show off and boast about), or getting noticed by a musician or singer when it comes to requests. Competition between campers of the same sex over such expectations may be strong, involving as it does also the relations between members of staff or between a returnee camper and newcomers.

This introduction of continuous, direct interaction of customer and 'producer' gives customers a high degree of control over the social organization of the camp and the work roles of staff. It has already been noted that bureaucratic operations are almost impossible, and that even repetitive performances on the part of staff are altered and influenced by different groups of campers. But camper control can go even beyond this: to actually influence promotions, careers and success of entertainers or comperes, and even dismissals. For example, in the evenings virtually all non-working staff are on the dance floor, in the cafe or at the bar, dressed for the evening (and often in the latest youthful styles). They then have the opportunity to do just what the campers do and get acquainted with many campers. At the little tables surrounding the bar and the singers they entertain campers with songs and jokes and even dress up and perform comic skits. If these are particularly popular with campers, the latter request appearances on stage for the member of staff – kitchen porter or waitress or whatever – who has so entertained them. These appearances can be kept up one or two nights a week over several weeks, at the end of which, if a vacancy among the regular entertainers occurs, the person involved is given the available job by the management, with the approval of the campers (5).

In some instances the camp managers may allow a member of staff to perform his adopted role without change of official job – this is more economical, since entertainers' fees are considerably higher. In such cases the possibility of a career develops: the person involved may seek to return the following season as a hostess or a comic. Returnee staff are sought by managers because the more a career can be offered, the better the performance of the staff and the less the chances of a sudden departure.

Seasonal staff

Another aspect of the social organization of the camp is its seasonal nature. The camp society exists only during the summer months, almost all of the staff being employed only during the season from May to September. This means a very restricted population for recruitment purposes: those with steady employment and with careers dependent upon length of service, and most of those with families, are unlikely to quit their regular jobs for a season in camp.

The camp recruitment is thus confined to a largely self-selected category of workers who are geographically mobile, hold unsteady jobs and are not hampered from moving from one occupation and place to another. A very large proportion of camp staff are consequently young or, if old, single with little or no family attachment. They have usually been in other occupations with a high labour turnover: in catering, nannying, maritime or construction work. Most are unskilled, used to living with strangers, and have usually developed the combination of casual openness to social intercourse and sharp suspicion and unsentimentality that life in mobile occupations requires. They feel little sense of loyalty towards the organization that employs them and have few career hopes. Their commitment is wholly instrumental. Wages can nearly all be saved (board and lodging is free) and campers can be 'conned' into providing drinks, snacks, petting and sex – and even money and a job at the end of the season.

There are few hesitations to leave if a more desirable alternative presents itself. Staff 'elope' with members of the opposite sex, to work in bars in the nearby seaside resort, or to go elsewhere. This aspect of seasonal employment also inhibits routinization and formalization of the camp and contributes to uncertainty. It allows staff, like campers, a greater scope to manipulate their work situation than is available in factory or office employment. For example, while the convention is that those guilty of physical violence, drunkenness or molesting campers are to be immediately dismissed, the actual distribution of dismissals is associated with slack periods and periods when students are available for employment (July-August), and are rare when the camp is full and the employment exchange fails to direct job-seekers to the camp. This allows the shrewder staff to play the demands of the job and their after-work behaviour differently under the various circumstances. Kitchen staff would take food, and even sell it; barmen would drink on the house or take an excessively large tip if a camper offered it. Groups of staff also have considerable scope to manipulate the entire camp services. Bars are often crowded by staff out of uniform and campers kept waiting for drinks – thus prompting campers to try to remain with a particular barman or maid and to offer tips to ensure favoured treatment.

These kinds of manipulative opportunity available to staff encourage 'conning' and exploitative relations with campers. Almost all staff have a low opinion and total disrespect of the bulk of campers. They are 'suckers', paying so much money to get just what the staff were getting for almost free; and so easy to cadge drinks from, eager to spice the holiday with a 'romance', crying out to be cheated. Those who were admired or respected among campers were those who demonstrated special skills on musical instruments or in acrobatic dancing, etc., or those who were deemed to be showing courage or moral rectitude – for example, an English woman with a blind Indian husband who quietly did everything to make his stay enjoyable, or the many families who wheeled around a disabled or paralysed member.

Age categories are kept separate in camp. Infants and children are all members of a 'cub club' and are taken off to playgrounds or skating rinks under the supervision of camp 'uncles' and 'aunts' who keep the children occupied and separate from their parents at times other than meal times. Parents can, of course, keep their children company on the grass or around the swimming pools. Adolescents are separated, without supervision and by culturally distinctive activities. Thus a separate dance-hall and attached bar and snack bar provides only beat and rock music with amplifiers, and lights are dimmed for 'teen dancing' and dating. There are television rooms and a variety of indoor games. This ensures separation of adolescents and adults through their different interests. Dress in the teen places allows great variety: from jeans and T-shirts to the latest 'mod' elegance.

Among the grown-ups the atmosphere of a large evening pub combined with Mecca-type dance-hall prevails. Men wear suits or blazers and are well-groomed, and the women are in dresses associated in working-class homes with evening wear: glittering and gaudy dresses and cheap but twinkling jewellery are a common sight. The older teenagers, and especially the teenage staff, shift from one domain to the other along with the evening and the mood. The 'lads and lasses' among staff invariably belong to little groups, ranging from just two or three to a dozen of their peers, who often come to the camp for work together. They usually set the pace early in the evening at the teen dance-hall.

The dances do not require couples, although towards the late evening couples emerge among those who did not start out on a date. The various groups – now sorted out into couples – move over to the main dance-hall to capture the floor from the elderly couples dancing older, slow dances. Most of the evening is over, and the band quickens tempo and becomes youthful and the younger campers and staff 'cha cha cha' and 'shake' while the older couples, usually married, drift to the walls to watch. The culture of the holiday camp is largely set and dominated by the young singles rather than the families, by staff rather than by campers, and by individual expectations rather than by the public roles.

Sexual and familial conduct

Finally, we may consider the relation between sexual and familial conduct and the camp social system. There are two aspects to this: the patterns of behaviour *within* marital and familial units (whether any particular forms are taboo or not) and those *outside* of marital or familial units. Since the vacation for campers consists of social situations and roles different from those surrounding work, home and everyday associations, the role relations and identities *within* the family alter too. The removal of children, the absence of work routines and domestic chores, the absence of local neighbourhood friends and kin, and the removal from daily or weekend leisure-time locations (e.g. the local pub, the garden, the cafe or the working men's club) leads to a situation where husband and wife, and in some cases one or both parents of either, spend almost all their waking hours together. A typical response from a husband was:

> The best thing about a holiday camp is that it is a holiday for the wife. When we went camping or stayed with relations it was not much of a change for her, was it? Now we are really together, none of us has to work, and we can do things together. I dance with her every evening. She is a woman, you know!

A postman expressed the same view, and added:

> To me it's very important to be with my wife and to give her a holiday. I was offered a job last year, more pay, more prospects, but

it meant going away some weekends. I could not take it: she would be lonely. The weekend with the family is what I love. So, here I am still a postman, but it is happier.

The wives' responses to a week in camp emphasized the same points, but many of them compared the vacation in camp to having another honeymoon. A typical comment was this from the wife of a clerk in a dry-cleaning establishment, who worked in a biscuit factory herself:

I like holiday camps. It is like having a second honeymoon. Arthur and I went to a little place in Wales when we were married. This is the only time I am with him for everything. This morning we had breakfast together — I have never had bacon and eggs with him in the whole year. We have such different hours: I just barely see him before tea, and then I usually have the children to look after.

I have quoted these statements because they were frequently expressed, and showed little individual variation. It is believed that births in Rio de Janeiro show a peak about nine months after the carnival — a similar phenomenon may well occur among couples at holiday camps! However, in an age of widespread use of contraceptive pills any inquiry, even if undertaken, is unlikely to prove the point. Yet this 'second honeymoon' experience is well known to the camp managers and has been the major way in which the character and culture of holiday camps have changed in the last two decades.

Formerly, the camps were often just dormitories receiving busloads of young men and women from the mills, mines and factories during wakes weeks or similar breaks in the work routines. The emphasis was on exhausting physical sports: soccer and wrestling mostly, and boisterous drinking and dancing in the evenings. Campers showed a far smaller age-range than today. In the last decade, however, the major category among campers has been married couples with children. This family orientation is reflected in the replacement of dormitory-type residences with two, three or four person 'chalets', and common wash and bathrooms are gradually disappearing. Tables in the cafe, the bar and the lounges are small and obviously meant for families or small groups. The dining halls no longer have the cafeteria or refectory atmosphere, and multiple sittings in the same hall are declining.

Although a majority still come by railway or coach, a growing minority arrive in cars. Collective dances like the hokey-cokey are still immensely popular, and collective singing is still encouraged by the entertainments staff as a means of inducing social interaction among strangers. Nevertheless, older campers who recall camp experiences in earlier decades are unanimous in noting the change from the crowds of 'lads and lasses' of the wakes weeks.

One of the persistent stereotypes about life in holiday camps is that a great deal of sexual promiscuity prevails. This belief, and the expectations it gives rise to, are shared by many of the staff and single campers. This creates a society within the camp where a fairly large number of people expect to engage in sexual relations with others. The norms and conventions of the wider society in the regulation of sexual relations generally do not apply, unless voluntarily adhered to.

Many social control processes do not operate in camp. The 'significant others' surrounding one at home, neighbourhood and workplace are able to exercise control through approval, disapproval, gossip, ostracism and so on. In the camp one is surrounded by strangers and newly-met peers who can have no claims to control over one's behaviour. Further, sexual partners are not in everyday proximity: real addresses out of camp are often hidden. There is a heightened consciousness of the time cycle: the phases of the relationship have to be covered within a week where campers are involved. Conventional routines and timetables customary in boy-girl relations have to be dispensed with. Availability, degree of commitment and expectations about termination have to be communicated early and the nature of the liaison defined.

With regard to sexual availability the common distinction is between those who will engage in sexual relations and thus complete the dating cycle fairly quickly and without obligations, and those who will not. The vocabulary of such classification passed on from older staff to new arrivals or campers in the camp studied includes 'cows', 'untouchables', 'loners', 'taken', etc. The girls freely available at the cost of a drink in a pub or wine-lodge or merely on invitation (usually at the fish and chip shop after midnight) are 'cows'. They are considered 'common', and few male staff wish to commit themselves for more than a night or two to sexual relations with 'cows'. They go from male to male in a particular group of 'lads' or between several such groups. This ensures that the 'cows' involved cannot establish any claim to exclusiveness. The 'untouchables' are social isolates unavailable for sexual relations, either because they have steady boy friends or are complying in camp with the traditional norms governing pre-marital sexual conduct. Such compliance usually leads to social isolation, restriction of relations to one or two members of the same sex, and in some cases to withdrawal from the camp.

However, unlike the externally-held stereotype, sexual behaviour in camp is neither promiscuous for the most part nor a 'free-love' situation. As Nelson Foote observed of American University students who rush to Sweden in the summer to acquire 'experience' in a 'free-love society', most are soon disappointed and realize that, even when sex is play, there are rules of the game (6).

Holiday camps as total institutions

It is pertinent to see whether holiday camps relate to the model of total institutions proposed by Goffman and much developed since then (7). In the traditional models of total institutions, such as prisons and mental hospitals, there are certain dominant features. The interacting population is divided into two categories, the staff and the inmates. The latter are administratively and coercively controlled by the former. Their outside identities are stripped away in ritualized ways, and the staff then proceed to provide new subordinate interactions and identity. In doing so, inmates develop an 'underlife' – a counter-culture – not visible to staff but cementing inmate social relations and setting at a distance the institutional process of control.

If total institutions are to be much more, in a sociological sense, than places where strangers eat, drink, interact and sleep together, then this aspect of identity-alteration and tight control is essential. The totality implied is one of control; from the staff viewpoint, as little scope as possible must be left for failure of the control processes. From an inmate viewpoint, social distancing and defensive interactions with a supportive counter-culture must be developed. From existing knowledge a typology of total institutions sharing some characteristics but differing in others is emerging. Mode of entry, kind and degree of structural conflict, presence and visibility of an underlife, extent of staff control over identities, the destruction or enhancement of social and self-esteem, pleasurability or otherwise of imposed or optional activities – these are some of the variables in such a typology.

The attempt to treat holiday camps as total institutions is an extreme example of applying such a typology. Entry is voluntary; staff and campers are not structurally prone to conflict; they mutually exploit each other, with the campers being, for structural and temporal reasons, more vulnerable. Instead of rituals of degradation and loss of esteem, there are processes of elevation of status and roles; instead of imposed unpleasant work routines there are optional pleasurable 'fun' or play situations. Instead of maximizing organizational control over inmates, the campers are enabled to manipulate the organizational machinery within the limits of organizational survival and economic profitability; instead of an underlife exclusive of staff, the involvement of staff is essential to the culture of a holiday camp. One could elaborate each of these features, and others.

The point, however, is that either we confine the concept of 'total institution' to institutions requiring rigorous control of inmates by a staff or hierarchy, or the concept should not imply the control and lack of choice that it does. The holiday camp cannot exercise a high degree of control over campers: the latter choose to exploit the options offered to realize expectations about enjoyment, relaxation and vacationing. The relations between campers and staff involve play elements and strategic interaction and communication for transient but pleasurable ends. The social exchanges are usually mutually advantageous. Few power-conferring obligations result.

Finally, successful role playing in a holiday camp is both undertaken and possible because of its limited duration. Vacations and vacation roles must come to an end and become memories, if the present function of annual vacations is to continue. That is to say, present forms of the vacation are reciprocally related to present urban and work life. With the transformation of work life and community and urban living, the present institutional forms of leisure and vacations may also be altered. Patterns of social interaction and the cultural features of holiday camps are not necessarily intimations of social life in the possible future society of leisure.

Notes and References

1 The British Tourist Authority's publication *The British on Holiday* (1971) states that the proportion of the adult population taking a holiday away from home has risen from five in ten in 1951 to approximately six in ten during the years 1962-70. It shows that, of those going away from home on holiday 3% in 1951 were in holiday camps. The percentage rose to four in 1955 and has remained around six from 1963 to 1970.

2 W. F. Whyte (ed.), *Industry and Society*, New York, McGraw-Hill, 1946, p. 123. More detailed analysis will be found in Whyte, *Human Relations in the Restaurant Industry*, New York, McGraw-Hill, 1948.

3 The concept of 'career' in the analysis of social processes has been developed and used by Erving Goffman and Howard S. Becker, among others. cf. E. Goffman, *Asylums*, New York, Doubleday, 1961, and H. S. Becker, *Outsiders*, New York, Free Press, 1963.

4 The analysis of social interaction in public places owes much to the pioneering effort of E. Goffman, *Behaviour in Public Places*, New York, Free Press, 1963.

5 The opportunity to demonstrate entertainment talent is given to staff every week when the regular entertainment staff have an evening off.

6 Nelson Foote, 'Sex as Play', in R. Meyersohn and E. Larrabee, eds., *Mass Leisure*, New York, Free Press, 1960.

7 The basic work is E. Goffman, *Asylums*, op. cit. Vilhelm Aubert has contributed interesting developments to the theory in *The Hidden Society*, Totawa, N.J., Bedminster Press, 1965.

Part 5

Education, planning and policies

Introduction

It cannot be said that leisure has as yet become an important issue of public policy in Britain. It figures little in the party manifestoes and is not expressed in the main organization of the business of government. It has no specific profession organized to advance its interests and it is seldom stated as a primary objective in discussion of areas of relevant social policy such as education. It is still almost impossible to make an accurate assessment of public expenditure in this field. Having said all this, one does not have to look very far to see evidence of the State controlling hours of work, or to detect signs of what the law permits in one's own time, or to sense the hidden hand of government behind the television screen. There may be no single policy for leisure in Britain today, but there are a great many separate indications of the expectations which govern the behaviour of the individual citizen in this sphere of his life, and the pressures which may legitimately be brought to bear upon him during leisure time. In this introduction we shall examine the public responsibilities which have been assumed by the State and other organs acting on behalf of the State, and the issues which have been provoked by such an assumption of responsibility. We shall examine further the shift from the negative regulation of behaviour to a more positive concept of support for leisure in making available public funds and guiding the public educational system.

We shall need to examine firstly the issues which have made leisure a matter for public intervention, and as might be expected the security of the State has always been a central issue. 'Bread and circuses' may have been replaced by 'Mr Kipling's cakes and TV' but the hard facts of keeping the people happy can never be far removed from the mind of those who govern. In the nineteenth century, as Burns has indicated in Part 1 of this book, the government under pressure from the factory owners was inclined to break this first rule of government and insist on the virtues of hard work, thrift and austerity. But it not only found the consumption of alcohol and gambling difficult to control, but eventually it had to concede the legitimacy of leisure in the Ten Hours Act. Since then the successive achievement of the six- and the five-day week, and the parallel achievement of holidays with pay, have been more the result of trade union activity than of the efforts of political parties. Nevertheless, the role of the State as a 'good employer', whether in the Civil Service or the nationalized industries, must not be disregarded in accounting for this trend.

The State has not only had to interest itself in leisure to keep the workers happy but it has also chosen to concern itself with its effect on public morals. Some people have odd ways of finding pleasure which other people find offensive and public opinion has been especially sensitive about exposing children to adult pleasures. To these ends the State has sought to censor the activities of artists, and restrict the range of sports and recreation which the public can enjoy. Sometimes it has embodied these controls in law (though the implementation of these by the police and the courts has varied in effort) and sometimes it has relied upon somebody else to do its job, such as in the cinema where the industry does it through the British Board of Film Censors, or in television where it is exercised by public corporations. It is clear, however, that we are now living in a period where public opinion has swung markedly against State control of private morals.

At a time when State control is losing favour with respect to the traditional pastimes associated with sex, drink and sport, it is interesting to see new public controls being urged for the physical environment. For some time certain areas around the large cities have been protected as 'green belts', but now closer supervision is being urged over the pollution of our air, and of our rivers and sea.

The role of the State in the field of leisure must not, however, be seen as an entirely negative one of telling people what they must not do. It has also increasingly assumed an educational function to encourage what is creative and healthy, sometimes by an explicitly didactic approach in formal education and at other times by subsidies, or by facilitating what people want to do. The issues which underlie this activity, and to which we will return in our conclusions, are how far the State can leave it to the market to provide what is needed (especially where that market is monopolistically organized); secondly if the State is to intervene how is it to be decided what is best for the public?; and thirdly, if it means spending public money how is the priority which is to be assigned to leisure to be rated against other claims on the community such as the relief of poverty?

The educational function is most clearly seen and most legitimately organized where it concerns the young, though our contributors are sceptical about the success of our schools in preparing the young for leisure. They place much more emphasis on the strategic role of the institutions of Further Education such as the Youth Service and Adult Education. Simpson is even uncertain about the democratic assumption that everyone is capable of the highest and would like educationalists to go for more modest objectives of helping people enjoy the pleasures of entertaining their friends and getting the best out of what commerce provides. Jary goes further in arguing that liberal adult education does not have to be instrumental, or even in the narrow sense 'educational'; it offers an opportunity for social contact and for people to be themselves.

It would be a narrow view of education to see it as confined to organized learning situations, and though we may not wish to see the B.B.C. in quite the heroic terms which Lord Reith had in mind, it is clear that whether intended or not, the mass media contribute greatly to the education of the nation. This implicit understanding has become an explicit element of the public discussion of control of the mass media. Those who argue for commercial radio or television cannot succeed in their arguments without reference to the provision they will make for 'prestige' programmes or for current affairs.

Education for the better enjoyment of life is no new development in British education (one thinks of the universities in the eighteenth century), but as yet it has been seldom related specifically to leisure needs of the masses. The Youth Service and Liberal Adult Education have been more explicit about this than have other sectors of education. State support for the production and consumption of leisure activities is very recent. Support for physical recreation extends back only to 1937 (and then was more concerned with preparing the young for war than with the immediate pleasures of sport). Support for the arts was restricted before the last War to support for museums and galleries. Support for tourism tended to be a by-product of some other government policy such as to reduce unemployment in rural areas. It was not until the 1960s that any substantial increase in public resources was made available for sport, the arts and tourism.

Sport and the arts are the main contenders for government subsidies, and both are administered within the Department of Education and Science though in separate branches of that ministry. Sport seems to do better under Conservative governments and the arts under Labour, though sport is a far more democratic pastime than the arts. Both are organized under independent councils to spend public money and they get similar amounts, currently about £4 million. Both also receive subventions from local authorities, though here the spending on sport and physical recreation far exceeds that spent on the arts. There are, however, no reliable figures to show the amounts.

The Wolfenden Committee report on *Sport in Britain* in 1960 marked a watershed in public interest in sport, and led to the appointment of a minister in 1962 to coordinate government aid to sport. The rapid growth of spectator sports in the 1960s with the widespread ownership of television, and the issues of national pride which have been fostered by international competitions such as the World Cup and the Olympics, have made politicians very sensitive to criticisms that Britain does not do enough for its athletes and sportsmen. Gambling has grown rapidly but it contributes little to sport considering how much it gets from it. If comparisons are made with other countries, expenditure on sport in Britain by the State is still small; the West Germans began a fifteen-year expansion programme in 1960 to cost £586 million. It is likely that public expenditure will grow considerably, especially as it may serve the purposes of those who wish to promote interaction with Europe.

Art is far more difficult to patronize than is sport. It is easier to live with when it is dead. Subventions to museums and galleries (which go back to the 1840s), concert houses and theatres, are less controversial than is support for the living artist. Moreover, despite the radical social commitment of some artists, especially those associated with the theatre, the notion of art is still widely regarded as élitist. Visiting art galleries, attending concerts, going to the theatre are regarded as middle-class interests, especially associated with living in London, and the South. Jennie Lee, as Minister for the Arts in the Labour Government, did something to dispel this view but it still has a very strong hold in the provinces and among working people. With this situation and with its concern for more pressing social priorities, it is unlikely that a future Labour Government will expand expenditure greatly in this field. The present Conservative Government has made it clear that money for development must largely come from entrance charges to museums and galleries.

The future of tourism in Britain as it affects the native population is, as Michael Dower suggests, uncertain. The number of people taking holidays at home has remained fairly static as the numbers taking holidays abroad has shot up. The primary concern of successive governments with tourism has been economic and particularly with the supply of foreign exchange so that when balance of payments difficulties have threatened holidays abroad were restricted and incentives were given to attract foreign tourists here. The Development of Tourism Act of 1969 sharply increased public expenditure by instituting substantial loans and grants for hotel building. This economic aim has also encouraged the growth of tourist facilities and road building in remote rural areas, where there is the added economic advantage of reducing unemployment and regional subsidies.

We shall, by way of conclusion, return to the three issues which seem to underlie the public debate about leisure. How far can it be left to the market to organize its supply? Who is to decide what people shall be offered? And what priority can be given to leisure within the overall framework of social policy? With regard to the first of these, it is clear that the public likes to organize its own leisure and prefers, where it can, to buy what it wants. It is also clear, on the other hand, that no government is prepared to allow commercial interests just to sell what they think the public will buy. A strong body of public opinion, notably among the educationalists, would like to see the government take a positive role in offering what they think the public needs. They stress what they think is the exploitive tendency of business to get quick profits. They further stress the lack of real competition in important areas of entertainment such as the cinema and commercial television because of the cost of, and restrictions on, entry into this field. They point to the slow response which business has made to people's leisure needs and its indifference to areas which appear unprofitable. This point of view has been ably expressed by Raymond Williams, but it would be unrealistic to suggest that at the present time it is generally shared. Despite a Labour Government for six years of the last decade, the commercialization of leisure made relatively more progress than did the social policies for leisure.

The role of the market in the provision for leisure is related closely to the second issue of who is to decide what people shall be offered, for it is often assumed that the alternative to the market is the bureaucracy, aided by government committees, and guided by the Minister. Here the criticism derives not only from the dislike of being told what to do by bureaucrats, but there is an added doubt about the élitist assumptions of these officials. In Williams' view, the answer to this situation lies in the control over the product by the producer, and where this is not possible by public ownership and the licensing of facilities to the producers. Although there is little sign of this happening it does resonate with a certain groundswell of public opinion about participation and workers' control. It has, of course, not been without its problems in the socialist countries of Eastern Europe where there are differences of view among the producers about what should be produced, but this seems to have been a creative situation for them, especially in the cinema.

The question as to the priority to be assigned to leisure in the overall framework of social policy takes two forms; the first being to find a balance between employment and leisure, and the second to assess the worth of the competing claim which leisure makes on public expenditure. In considering the first of these, we have to try to reconcile certain inconsistencies in government policy. There are enormous pressures to achieve greater productivity and economic growth but these are associated with higher rates of unemployment, premature retirement from the labour force, and delayed entry into it. The higher rates of unemployment spring from the frictions of more rapid economic change, the retirement of the elderly, from the belief about a decline in their productivity, and the delayed entry of the young because of the belief in the higher economic output which comes from extended training. It is clear that the young would like to begin work earlier and some of the elderly to continue working later, yet they have to concede these claims in order to satisfy the achievement of greater productivity and higher earnings for those who still work. Thus some people have more leisure than they want and very little money to spend on it, and other people have much higher incomes and long working hours.

The second aspect of the question about priorities is to ask what priority can be afforded to the 'good life' when some people are struggling to survive in bad housing and on low incomes. So far these debates have been kept apart from each other but, where we have brought them together, it has been difficult to make progress. For example, would the money to be spent by the National Gallery on a Titian be better spent on several hundred houses? Despite these difficulties, the debate on public expenditure is being widened all the time to include more issues, to relate those issues to each other, and to ask who benefits from decisions and who is to pay for them. We are already beginning to accept that former luxuries (some of which mean more interesting and enjoyable leisure) are part of the basic standard of living which all should enjoy in modern Britain, and we also accept that we must do more to equalize access to the amenities the community provides. We have not, however, so far united our interest in the Arts, Sport, Recreation and Education into a coherent policy for leisure which would make our Governments as interested in the way we spend our leisure as they are in the way we earn it.

Not all of our contributors would necessarily agree that we need a synoptic policy for leisure, and in any case they approach the problem from different perspectives. Jary takes an interesting area for discussion. Education has always been responsive to the needs of the economy, and no more so than at the present time. Adult education has in many ways reflected the ideology and purposes of full-time education. Part of it has been directly vocational and most of it has had a strong flavour of self-improvement, or seen from the point of view of those providing it, it was intended to reduce social inequality. It is not to be enjoyed. Jary argues – and in this he finds support from his own research – that those who attend evening classes go for different reasons. They see them as ways of expressing themselves, of finding friends and having fun. He concludes, in the light of the debate about the cultural revolution, that such purposes are not only legitimate, and therefore should not be regarded as secondary or be hidden, but that they point the direction for education for the future.

Simpson, who has a background in non-vocational Further Education, reaches similar conclusions by a different route. He argues that formal education has never been successful in confronting the problems raised by leisure. He puts this down partly to the *de haut en bas* tradition of educationalists and partly to the fact that people do not want to be organized in their leisure time. They prefer to buy what they want and the educationalist is suspicious of the commercial exploitation of such preferences. He argues that education should help people acquire the skills they need to get social prestige and to make and sustain friendships. He adds, however, that this must not be done at the expense of the cultivation of our inner selves.

Raymond Williams is also interested in education and particularly in education to meet the needs of young people and adults. But for him the problems of leisure should not be treated apart from the broader issues of building a socialist society. In the field of the arts and communications he sees certain cultural forms which assert social distinction, to keep the people and particularly the young in their place. The central fact about the institutions which maintain these forms is that they are in the hands of speculators, and education by itself can make little progress until that situation is changed. But Williams does not wish to see the speculators replaced by bureaucrats acting on behalf of the State. He would like to see the means of the communication in the hands of the artists and the producers, either in their ownership or leased from the community.

Weddell shares Williams' view about bureaucracy but in looking at broadcasting policy he does not see the answer to the present situation in giving more power to the producers. He favours a more community-oriented policy in which the Government should abandon its past role of regulative restriction in favour of a more dynamic intervention. Already governments have, as a result of the competition induced by commercial television, had to relax their tacit controls over the hours of broadcasting. He would now like governments to take advantage of the technological innovations which make it possible to broadcast more cheaply, both in the production and reception of programmes, to devolve the rights to broadcast much more widely to local community groups. The Government must be prepared to accept a wider range of views but also to moderate between the inevitably competing claims upon the still scarce resources.

In the last of our contributions examining policies for leisure the emphasis is less on intellectual and social values, and more on physical needs. Dower looks at physical recreation and examines the increasing demands which it will make on our scarce resources, and especially the scarce resource of space. He finds that already with relatively low standards of provision demands are difficult to satisfy. In daily reach of home there needs to be open space for hockey, swimming, sports halls and adult education. At the weekend there is a rapidly rising demand for golf and water sports, and for access to countryside. Though the pressures of our own population migrating for their annual holidays are felt more and more in other countries, we are hosts to a vast army of foreign tourists. More and more hotels and transport will be needed to accommodate them. Dower thinks that these problems are manageable if we observe four principles: an imaginative use of resources, skilful management, a planned integration of tourist needs with the needs of the countryside, and lastly a partnership between those who provide for recreational needs to stimulate initiative but avoid duplication.

The five contributions chosen for this part of the book do not exhaust all aspects of public policies about leisure. More might have been said about censorship since it remains an issue of some public concern. Something might have been said about the future of the working week, or the working year, or the working life. All are likely to become of more importance, and the return of mass unemployment has made people more conscious of the fact that work may be a scarce value in future that will have to be rationed more carefully. It will be easier to ration if people are more willing to accept leisure. However, the line must be drawn somewhere and the selection of topics for this volume reflects present concerns, and what we know about them. There has perhaps always been a tendency in the field of leisure to run ahead of ourselves. Some bridges are best crossed when we come to them.

18 Evenings at the ivory tower: liberal adult education

David Jary

I am aware of what is going on in the world but I do not yet get a chance to discuss with other people these problems. I hope to do this at the class.

I am seeking insights into man's relationships with man . . . the study of existing patterns and future trends.

Another attraction is the possibility of meeting a kindred spirit, an eligible man, who shares common interests.

The words are those of students in non-vocational adult education classes talking about their reasons for attending their courses (1). In any winter week in Britain one in every twenty-five adults will spend one of their evenings at a local college or university attending a non-vocational adult class. Over a longer period a much larger proportion, possibly in excess of 30% (2), will attend a class. Adult education is a considerable leisure-time activity. In terms of numbers of participants and their regularity of commitment it is roughly on a par with the watching of professional association football. Yet, when even a glance at the quotations above suggests the importance of intrinsic gratifications, adult education is too often analysed as *education* producing extrinsic effects rather than as *leisure* yielding immediate gratifications. Adult education often fails to live up to narrow educational criteria employed in evaluating it. But as leisure it may perform functions for which no other forms of leisure are a substitute. This chapter describes and explains adult education, giving special attention to its under-emphasized aspects as leisure and play, and argues that the under-valuation of leisure functions is a typical, even growing, feature of general educational thought. Although important in its own right, adult education will also serve as a case study in educational and leisure purposes.

The shape and goals of liberal adult education
We shall be analysing in detail only a part of adult education, the sector specializing in the provision of courses in academic subjects at or near

university level. Usually this is referred to as Liberal Adult Education. While the Local Education Authorities provide the bulk of classes in adult education, those in liberal academic subjects are mainly, and often jointly, provided by two organizations, a voluntary body — the evocatively named Workers' Educational Association — and the Extra-Mural Departments of universities. Annual enrolments in their courses are around 200,000. In many ways liberal adult education exists at one end of an extreme typology of adult education. Of all adult education liberal adult education presents perhaps the highest psychological barriers to participation and its course content is demanding. For an evening its students enter the ivory towers of academic subjects and confront the fundamental and potentially transforming issues these subjects raise.

It might seem simple to ask the organizations of liberal adult education what their students are striving for, but organizations' views of their goals are notoriously poor indicators of actual results. There is in any case a particular reason for not accepting their views about the functions of adult education for, in response to what has been called their great 'institutional insecurity' (3), the adult education organizations' own claims for their purposes have been grandiloquent rather than descriptive. Nevertheless, these claims must be our starting point. Much of the distinctive style and content to be found running through the claims of liberal adult educationalists can be traced to the founding father of contemporary adult education, Albert Mansbridge, who started the W.E.A. in 1903 to encourage universities to provide classes for those denied opportunity of full-time higher education. Writing soon after the W.E.A.'s first decade, Mansbridge saw its classes as

> incontestably proving that the workers of England . . . are alive and responsive to the finer creations of the mind and spirit . . . [possessing a] divine spark which the slightest breeze will fan into flame, lighting up with joy unspeakable the way of knowledge (4).

His conception of the W.E.A.'s goal was dualistic; it would bring individual development and social harmony. He looked to the liaison of the universities and the W.E.A. to help bring workers more fully into the political life of the community. Mansbridge's mixture of individual and social functions has remained the core of adult education's public expressions of purpose.

There have been other organizations some with less consensual, even revolutionary, goals (5) but it was the W.E.A.'s work that attracted government financial support. In one of the early reports about adult education which Hobhouse and Headlam made to the Board of Education, they described the W.E.A. as accustom[ing] the student to the ideal of work familiar at a university ... aimed not so much at filling the mind of the student with facts and theories as at calling forth his own individuality ... [and at enabling him] to distinguish between what may be called a matter of fact and what is certainly a matter of opinion (6).

This kind of report led to the W.E.A. and the universities receiving public funds in support of their adult education work. The organizations also won the sympathy and the time (as class tutors and guides) of numbers of very eminent academics (7).

Although there was room in Mansbridge's view of adult education for individual enjoyment, this was usually accompanied by a puritanical alter ego, by a tendency to deep mistrust of immediate pleasures, and a preference for obviously 'self-developing' and 'socially purposive' forms of adult education. That this remains the basic ingredient of liberal adult education's idea of itself can be illustrated by a recent policy document of the W.E.A., which states

Adult education has a positive role and it seeks to encourage informed discussion and study of the problems facing society in the belief that it is vital to the health of the democracy. It seeks to develop *serious and sustained* study (8).

Education for social purpose continues as the core ideology. Any suggestion that leisure *primarily* for its own sake may have priority over other purposes is likely to be attacked by the movement's spokesmen. Certainly it will be handled with caution. One telling tract states that adult education 'is liable to be regarded ... as a resort of those who are casually seeking diversion for their leisure time.' Instead its author wished to see it 'as an essential expression for those who would enjoy their lives to the full and *shoulder their responsibility* as persons and citizens', claiming that the goals of adult education should be to produce a 'sense of values and the self-discipline of the people' (9).

Without denying that these ideologies have had *some* effect on the shape of adult education, my central argument will be that, *contrary to its ideologies,* liberal adult education is primarily a leisure-centred activity. Rather than 'sustained study' or 'social purposiveness', informal teaching methods, extensive class participation and particularly lengthy discussion periods are a typical feature of its classes. Many classes seem centred on immediate gratifications, even – dare I say it – on 'fun'. The actuality of what, in adult education, is sometimes weightily referred to as the 'grand tradition' of earnest study, is often a group obviously enjoying an admittedly rather different from everyday intellectual interaction, but with obvious wider social purposes little evident. Although classes are usually organized around subjects like

English literature, history or sociology, these subjects are treated in a very different manner from their treatment in undergraduate education. They are mined for their general relatedness to life, and above all for their personal relevance. They are used as promptings for generalized reflection and discussion. But rather than education with a core of sustained private study, the heart and life of the whole activity of liberal adult education is the immediate pleasure of the class.

My conclusion is that this leisure-centredness of liberal adult education ought not to be hidden or apologized for; it should be recognized and its gratifications elaborated. This will not be to accept that liberal adult education is an 'irrelevant casual diversion'. Far from it, liberal adult education will be seen as a highly distinctive form of leisure. That such leisure functions are often missed or played down indicates the strength of the forces at work in sociology, in adult education, and in society at large, against taking leisure seriously.

Sociological theories of adult education and leisure

Perhaps the most systematic attempt to outline the main functions of adult education is that of Floud and Halsey, although they admit that their suggestion is little more than a preliminary framework (10). They divide adult education's functions into five. There are 'remedial' and 'mobilizing' functions, involving processes of *occupational and political differentiation* – i.e. equipping people to occupy specialist 'roles' – which the institutions of full-time education did not, but might have performed. There are 'assimilative' functions, where integration is the focus. Again these *might* have been performed by full-time institutions. Floud and Halsey see the contact which British liberal adult education provided with university 'élite culture' as an assimilative function. Only their final two functions, referred to as 'compensatory' and 'recreative' are continuous leisure functions. However, since compensatory education is seen by them as arising from the emotional and intellectual deprivations associated with narrow and routinized work, and because their recreative function remains an unexplicated residual category, Floud and Halsey's schema must be regarded as biased towards extrinsic effects, and limited in its treatment of adult education as leisure. This we must remedy by utilizing general theories of leisure.

Sociologists, like Dumazedier and Giddens, have provided basic conceptual distinctions (11). 'Obligatory' leisure activities (e.g. church-going, lawn-cutting) and 'instrumental activities' (into which remedial adult education clearly falls) must be distinguished from leisure in its 'pure' forms. Pure leisure occurs when obligation and *extrinsic* instrumentality are absent and when only more immediate affectivity and *intrinsic* leisure gratifications are involved. But the absence of extrinsic instrumentality does not imply what Floud and Halsey's schema might suggest, that leisure functions cannot be further specified. Much non-obligatory leisure is spent in purely 'restorative' relaxation, but some leisure has more ramifying implications. 'Play', for example, is often distinguished from restorative leisure by its latent potentialities for personal transformation. It is just these play aspects of adult education as leisure that are often neglected. At least two sets of play elements seem likely to be involved. First there are affiliative needs for physical contact and for other forms of intimacy and interaction. Secondly, there are needs for self-esteem, self-consistency and an ordered world view.

If, as in animal play, there was a direct functional relationship between play and organic and societal survival, it would be a simple matter to move from the above analysis to an adjustment of Floud and Halsey's functional schema. However, because this is not so, their stress on assimilation and integration – with its neglect of human creativity – misses the individuation of 'identity' and enlargement of self that human play and therefore adult education can provide. Their category of compensatory education, which gets closest to capturing these effects of education, nevertheless finally remains shackled within a perspective assuming a norm in which 'central life interests' are in work. It suggests that adult education is needed only to satisfy groups who are deprived of more normal gratifications, mainly from work. Neither this category nor Floud and Halsey's recreative category can adequately elaborate adult education as leisure, *sui generis*. I suggest that liberal adult education as leisure provides for two overlapping kinds of play. These are:

(a) sociability – interaction primarily for its own sake and
(b) self-expansive play, involving self-display, self-expression and self-insight, but stopping short of (or in addition to) Floud and Halsey's extrinsic functions.

Sociability, as I will use it here, is (approximately) Simmel's term. All social activity involves sociability, but sometimes, as at parties, sociability 'exists for its own sake and for the sake of a fascination, which in its own liberation from [social] ties, it diffuses'. Simmel actually refers to this as a 'play form'. It need have 'no extrinsic results', and 'entirely depends upon the personalities among whom it occurs'. Thus on the whole it grows freely, but it must always avoid (a risk it always faces) breaking down into the 'naturalism' of basic drives. Although it is not seen by Simmel to possess extrinsic purposes, sociability is not without seriousness and it does have wider effects, for it involves play with serious aspects of life. Simmel sees in it a capacity for transferring the 'seriousness and tragic to a symbolic shadowy play form', which reveals reality obliquely. He also suggests that it is 'the more serious person who derives from sociability a feeling of liberation and relief' and that he does 'so because he enjoys [in sociability] . . . a concentration and exchange of effects that present all the tasks and all the seriousness of life in a sublimation and at the same time dilution' (12).

The liberal adult education class can be best considered as providing a *specific* form of sociability situation. The *class* is the centre of liberal adult education far more than it is in almost any other form of education. Members of classes demand precisely the mixture of structure and flexibility required for successful sociability; gratification through conversation is pursued in a way that is typical of sociability – many an adult education tutor has come to grief in failing to notice that. We noted that the typical subject-matters of liberal adult education are the social sciences and the humanities. These contain the topics of human concern and dilemma which are the same stuff of more spontaneous sociability situations. Automatically raised are the serious and tragic sides of man. But the presence of a tutor and a subject focus takes the sociability of the adult class beyond the 'usual'. Moreover, as we will later see, its students may well be just those kinds of people for whom Simmel felt sociability yielded most. Finally, as well as people well known to each other – 'familiars' as Potter calls them – the liberal adult education class also brings contacts with 'casuals', whom Potter regards as a creative ingredient of sociability situations contributing 'insight' and 'fresh' behaviour (13).

Sociability is also involved in our second form of play, the self-expansive. Riesman and Watson regard sociability as having 'a special contribution to make both to the development of unique individual identities and the development of shared norms and identities which facilitate social integration.' (14) But the development of identity and the development and display of self are not *only* found in sociability. In liberal adult education they can stem from the more formal exchange of orthodox teacher-student roles as well as from reading, thought and creative expression connected with the class, rather than from sociability as such.

Social recruitment

Unfortunately research on all kinds of adult education has been by survey method and little related to explicit functional discussions (15). The information most frequently yielded by these surveys is about the age, sex, marital status and occupation of participants. In all types of non-vocational adult education the majority and, it seems, an ever-increasing proportion of students, are female. (The actual ratio in liberal adult education in 1968 was 2 : 1.) In general the unmarried have higher rates of participation, and the married with young children, who have the lowest quantities of pure leisure time, lower than average rates. The proportion of students from manual occupations has fallen over the years until today it stands at around 20%: scarcely remedial.

The low support from manual workers has been the source of much soul-searching by liberal adult educationalists. Most sociological studies of working-class leisure reveal a predominance of recuperative activities, often closely connected with kinship, locality, and perhaps work groups. Adult education, as a specialized individual activity, normally housed in urban centre institutions, is markedly incongruent with working-class life. If entered into, it is capable of creating tensions in relationships with family and friends and dissatisfaction with work. There are several studies, notably one by Trenaman, showing the 'reinforcing' character of education (16). Attitudes towards education established in schools either inhibit or encourage further involvement.

In general the more educated a person the more he continues to seek education. It certainly could be argued that liberal adult education does remarkably well in recruiting working-class students. Especially does it do so in those courses which it arranges in conjunction with industrial firms and trades unions — courses which incidentally *do* display clear extrinsic purposes (17). It is also true that adult education's own usual modes of recording the occupations of its students — with its separate entries for housewives, the retired, etc. — tends to underestimate the extent of working-class participation (18). Furthermore, much of the 'middle-class' enrolment, at least in the classes the W.E.A. provides if not so clearly in university provided classes, would appear to be concentrated in the lower rather than the upper reaches of that class. In all this, the W.E.A.'s name and ideology may be a valuable property.

In arguing above that adult education would be better seen as leisure, it is not my intention to argue for it to drop all its remedial concerns. What I am arguing against are attempts to hide the manifest fact that it is not *mainly* an agency of remedial education, and against the great feelings of guilt about its remedial failure which periodically sweep adult education (19). My argument against such guilt feelings must rest on further elaboration of my sketch of the positive qualities of the leisure-oriented adult education class and student.

The purposes of liberal adult education students

Broad analyses of social recruitment give little guidance on the precise motivations and gratifications of the students. Precisely because social class, and especially education, explain differential participation in a whole range of leisure activities, general characteristics of socio-economic status groups and occupational categories fail to explain particular activities which involve only a minority of *any* socio-economic group. A more direct analysis of motivations and gratifications is required, and other research may be of assistance here (20).

The *Adequacy of Provision* survey examined the whole range of adult education and found that one sixth of the students saw themselves as most interested in 'personal contact within the class', one half in 'self-development' for its own sake, and a few who regarded their adult education as 'merely recreational'. All these responses would seem to constitute intrinsic rather than extrinsic purposes. At the other extreme, only 10% mentioned 'work-related' motivations, and a somewhat smaller percentage 'family relatedness'. In relation to liberal adult education primacy of leisure was even more striking. 'Self-development' (around 70%), and 'social contacts through the class' (nearly 20%) far outweigh instrumental orientations, although family, work or community-relatedness are mentioned by a few.

A more sophisticated American inquiry by James Davis of one kind of American liberal adult education – the Great Books Programme – confirms this picture (21). Davis's methodology involved him in the cluster analysis of participants' selections from a check-list of twenty-four reasons for joining the programme. The analysis yielded four clusters. The first consisted of predominantly vocational items –28% of respondents checked one or more of these items by Davis. Next the analysis suggested a 'self-help' cluster, from which 51% chose at least one item. In it were brought together items concerned with improving taste and gaining self-confidence with people of higher intellectual background, and reading skills. It was Davis's opinion that this cluster included the most superficial of the motives, a concern with the externals of social status, for example. The third cluster, 'content', involved deeper intellectual and abstract concerns and a desire for self-insight, rather than gimmicks. In Davis's opinion, this cluster, from which 68% selected one or more item, came closest to the official ideology of the programmes. Finally, the analysis gave a cluster which Davis labelled 'cosmopolitanism'. It was made up of the items 'escaping the intellectual narrowness of my community', 'talking with people who have more intellectual interests than my usual friends', and 'meeting people who are quite different from me'. This had the highest check-rate, 71% checking one or more items.

There is much in the **Great Books** survey that supports the outline of liberal adult education advanced in this chapter. The links can be made explicit by way of Table 1, categorizing forms of adult education. Where it is not self-explanatory, its content is explained earlier in the chapter.

Table 1

Societal functions	Individual needs – primacy of extrinsic instrumental	Individual needs – primacy of intrinsic play
Differentiation–Individuation	1 Remedial–Mobilizing	3 Self-expansive
Integration	2 Assimilative	4 Sociability

The categories of Table 1 correspond to Davis's categories as follows:

1. *remedial mobilizing*: 'stepping stone': items involve 'increasing ability to carry out my job through intellectual training or group discussion', yet making friends *per se* did not correlate highly with the cluster.

2. *assimilative*: 'self-help': items concerned with improving taste and gaining confidence, but perhaps concerned with the veneer rather than the substance of status.

3. *self-expansive*: 'content': items display depth of concern with the 'basic issues of life' and gaining self-insight.

4. *sociability*: 'cosmopolitanism': items stressing opportunities to meet people with a wider range of interests than usual friends.

A survey of my own can be used to provide further confirmation and illustration of the leisure character of liberal adult education. The survey was part of an attempt to assess the motives of students in liberal adult education classes in sociology and social psychology. The following distribution of orientations was found:

3	clearly self-expansive	10%	
4	clearly sociability	15%	80%
3 & 4	a combination of the two *(including a clear sub-category of 15% seeking solution to a specific personal problem)*	55%	
1	vocational *plus 5% with clear social purpose*	15%	20%

10% of the respondents were placed in category 3 because they showed a definite and serious interest in a subject and little or no concern with the social interaction of the class. Another 15% who gave heavy emphasis to the attractions of sociability offered by the adult class, but had little concern with anything wider. The classification of a further

15% who said that they were seeking help in handling *personal problems* is more difficult. Such orientations have sometimes been seen as threatening educational purposes. Where social science is the subject, this need not be the case. A few brief examples of students' reasons for attending classes will illustrate this claim.

> To reduce time spent in a less than happy home . . . shy, inhibited bachelor suffering from extreme social isolation of adolescence.

> My personality is best described in an article 'The Swing from Science', I am a 'converger' . . . but I am at a complete loss when dealing with people . . . I wonder should I divorce my wife.

> I do not like myself as a teacher. I want to learn enough to change my ways or my job.

With attitudes and expectations such as these, there is scope for self-insight to emerge both from the course content and from social interaction in the class.

By far the largest category of responses were the 40% who mentioned the sociability of the class but also stressed a broader band of interests and concerns, in people and society. While their very attendance at a class indicates their willingness to be at least a little more disciplined in their thought and talk about social life, they are not strikingly more focused on purposes extrinsic to leisure than people in more diffuse sociability situations. It is a serious discussion of things in general, coupled with some feeling of self-expansion that they seek from adult education. Again some brief quotations will convey something of this:

> Interested [because I read] semi-sociological works like Richard Hoggart, *Uses of Literacy* . . . now see the subject wider . . . feel that I am getting a deeper understanding of problems and more tolerance.

> I don't necessarily expect the course to provide answers to problems but to give clearer understanding.

> In old age one tends to become censorious, and sociology should broaden one's perspectives.

> As a technologist I consider that the social sciences have more relevance to present-day problems than natural science and technology.

In my survey 80% of liberal adult education students in social science showed little or no vocational purpose and few signs of the specific 'social purposes'. For the remaining 20%, however, these purposes were present. Fifteen per cent claimed a vocational purpose and 5% indicated a specific social purpose. None of these sought adult education for a remedial or mobilizing function. Adult education thus seems to provide an opportunity for reflection, self-expansion and sociability.

But do these personal statements of private purposes correspond to actual effects or functions? Earlier we concluded that an analysis of the socio-economic status of participants alone brought little insight to understanding the motives in adult education. But now the motivational analysis makes possible a reformulated occupational analysis, in which *specific* occupations rather than broader groupings of occupations are considered.

The idea of an opposition pattern of work and leisure (one of three suggested by Parker (22)) fits well what we earlier saw as the obstacles existing to working-class participation in liberal adult education. But it is Parker's idea of extension of work into leisure which is especially relevant. Gould's discovery that there are large differences in the levels of adult education participation *within* socio-economic groups (teachers and social workers and service occupations for example are over-represented; business and commerce under-represented) can be related to Parker's terms (23). Although exclusively vocational purposes are not revealed by surveys, we do find some general vocational connectedness. Certain occupations, like social work and teaching, are especially compatible with the kinds of play and sociability which liberal adult education provides.

A useful analogy exhibiting this kind of compatability of work and leisure can be made with those who are active in social movements (24). Parkin shows that the support for movements like C.N.D. comes from the highly educated, but that there is a strong tendency for certain occupations, in particular the 'welfare and creative professions', to be heavily over-represented in C.N.D. and movements like it. Parkin's view is that it is not merely a matter of certain occupations producing leisure orientations, but that the occupations are themselves chosen by the activists as compatible with a whole style of life. Parkin outlines this style as involving an interest in the dynamics of interpersonal relationships, an ethical sensitivity and concern, and a relative lack of interest in economic goals. Parkin sees higher education as making a vital contribution to the formation of the integrated occupation and leisure style of the middle-class radical.

A similar life style may support liberal adult education. While it is unlikely that liberal adult education is as decisive as full-time education in creating styles (and certainly, as Bochel and others have shown, and consistent with what we earlier argued, it is relatively less associated with *specific* political activism (25)), there would seem strong parallels between the kinds of ethical sensitivity and interests mentioned by Parkin and the characteristics of liberal adult education students. At the very least, adult education participation appears to grow from a larger style of leisure. A kind of 'cultural activism' pervades its clientèle. Several studies, including my own, find students making a differentially large use of libraries, theatres, 'quality' newspapers and the like, and a much smaller than average usage of the *mass* media. Many students might fairly be described in terms similar to Riesman's notion of the inside dopester (26). While he takes little part in active politics, the inside dopester knows 'a great deal about what other people are doing and thinking in the important "great issue" spheres of life, goes to great lengths to keep from looking and feeling like an uninformed outsider'. He is 'politically cosmopolitan rather than parochial'. He is sensitive, flexible in social situations, and although morally concerned, he does not 'moralize'.

Types of liberal adult education class

It is not my intention to argue that every liberal adult education class is dominated by intrinsic leisure rather than by extrinsic goals. Nor would I wish to claim that a 'serious' sociability pervades all classes. There are clear exceptions to both patterns. Particular classes reflect the styles of their membership. We can construct the following provisional *ideal* typology of classes:

	Strong, clear motives Individual recruitment City-centre location	Weaker motives Collective (i.e. industry-based or communal) recruitment Suburban or smalltown location
Preponderance of occupational relatedness; social science emphasis	Extension	Specific
More general social science and far greater arts and humanities emphasis	General	Discursive

The 'extension' type (we are employing this term in Parker's, rather than the adult education administrator's, sense) and the 'general' type are those in which are to be found the kind of sociability, self-expansion purposes and life and leisure styles we outlined. The other two are contrasted exceptions to our suggested pattern. 'Discursive' classes, because they are based upon pre-existing groups, lack strong subject motives and contain students who would not enter adult education but for group pressure upon them, and consequently have little of the styles of those recruited individually. The frequent choice of local history as a subject in small-centre classes can be seen as a device for moulding a viable class from locality interests when other strong common interests are lacking. Another solution in those circumstances is for a class to develop as a coterie revolving around a particular tutor's weekly performance, a state of affairs labelled 'spell-binding' inside the adult education profession.

Liberal adult education for what?

Tyrrell Burgess has recently asserted that the W.E.A. provides 'ornamental knowledge mainly to middle-class people' (27). I hope I have demonstrated that his verdict should not be accepted. His error would seem to be that if liberal adult education does not attract the working class, then it is merely a 'casual diversion'. But there is more reason for quoting Burgess's views than the remarks he directs at the W.E.A. His remarks can be seen as part of a currently modish, general philosophy of educational provision; a view which also finds the Open University wanting. Since it, like adult education, caters for those already possessing considerable educational advantage, it is seen as 'rather short on egalitarian purpose'. This view has also encouraged the expansion of full-time education in vocationally-oriented polytechnics rather than in universities. George Brosan puts this case bluntly — 'the main task of the system of higher education outside the universities is to deal with the matching sector, i.e. to provide a basis of manpower that the universities have not provided.' (28) His message is clear. Occupational differentiation, economic, mobilizing and remedial goals must be uppermost; the universities have failed; polytechnics must provide something different. These more general debates about tertiary education and leisure provision are very relevant to my thesis about liberal adult education and to current policy issues.

Some of the best liberal adult education has occupational relatedness but it is to do with occupational play rather than with the occupation *per se*; liberal adult education provides a sociability and an opportunity for self-development especially suited to particular roles. Occupational relatedness there may be, but participation is far from confined to a narrow band of occupations; individual life and leisure styles are the crucial causes and effects of participation in liberal adult education. Liberal adult education sometimes performs mobilizing and remedial functions. Doubtless it also has political repercussions and implications for social control, but these are not the individual purposes at its core; nor are they superior to such purposes. A recent policy survey of American tertiary education went so far as to argue that we have entered an era of 'cultural revolution'. 'More people are now seeking vocations or life styles outside the Horatio Alger syndrome than ever before . . . Higher education is built on the work ethic and we are now shifting to a more sensate culture.' (29) In such an age, when personal liberation and ethical exploration is becoming a watchword, and with the competitive work ethic questioned from many sides and now by 'ecologists', surely Brosan's and Burgess's assessment of adult education can't be right, either for adult education or for higher education as a whole.

Notes and References

1 The quotations are from a sample of social science adult students in fifteen W.E.A. and extra-mural classes which I made in Lancashire, Yorkshire and Cheshire in the winter of 1967-8. I record my gratitude to all the respondents, tutors and organizations involved.

2 These estimates are derived from the recent survey, *Adequacy of Provision*, published by the National Institute of Adult Education, March 1970.

3 Burton R. Clark, *The Marginality of Adult Education*, Chicago Center for the Study of Liberal Education for Adults, 1958, and *Adult Education in Transition*, Berkeley, University of California Press, 1956.

4 Albert Mansbridge, *University Tutorial Classes*, Longmans, 1913, pp. 2-3.

5 The most important was the National Council of Labour Colleges. For general historical accounts of adult education see T. Kelly, *A Short History of Adult Education* in Great Britain, and J. F. C. Harrison, *Learning and Living, 1790-1960*, Routledge, 1961.

6 Mansbridge, op. cit., p. 145.

7 That men like R. H. Tawney have been involved shows that, although it has usually involved commitments to peaceful rather than revolutionary change, support for liberal adult education far from represents support for the *status quo*.

8 *Unfinished Business,* a W.E.A. Policy Statement, 1970, p. 3, my italics.

9 Mabel Tylecote, *The Future of Adult Education*, Fabian Society, 1960, p. 1, my italics.

10 Jean Floud and A. H. Halsey, 'The Sociology of Education', *Current Sociology*, vol. VII, no. 3, 1958.

11 A. Giddens, 'Notes on the Concept of Play and Leisure', *Sociological Review*, March 1964; J. Dumazedier, *Toward a Society of Leisure*, Collier-Macmillan, 1967.

12 Georg Simmel, *The Sociology of Georg Simmel*, ed. Kurt H. Wolff, Glencoe, Free Press, 1950, pp. 41-57.

13 Robert J. Potter, 'Friends, Familiars and Strangers as they Converse at Parties' mentioned in P. E. Hammond, *Sociologists at Work*, New York, Basic Books, 1964, p. 238.

14 Hammond, op. cit., ch. 10, D. Riesman and J. Watson, 'The Sociability Project', p. 237.

15 e.g. W. E. Styler, *Who Were the Students?* National Institute of Adult Education, 1950, or *Aspects of Adult Education*, W.E.A., 1960.

16 J. Trenaman, 'Education in the Adult Population', *Adult Education,* vol. 34, 1962.

17 See A. H. Thornton and F. J. Bayliss, *Adult Education in the Industrial Community,* National Institute of Adult Education 1965, for one discussion of these.

18 Because of this some of the analyses of the social class participation made by analysts of adult education seem to have greatly miscalculated the proportions. For example see R. Pahl's *Adult Education in a Free Society,* New Orbits Group, 1962.

19 A recent bout can be read in *W.E.A. News,* Sept. 1971 and Jan. 1972.

20 W. E. Styler, 'The Motives of Adult Students', *Adult Education,* vol. 23, 1950.

21 J. A. Davis, *Great Books and Small Groups,* Glencoe, Free Press, 1961.

22 S. R. Parker, *The Future of Work and Leisure,* MacGibbon and Kee, 1971.

23 J. D. Gould, *The Recruitment of Adult Students,* Vaughan College Papers, no. 5, University of Leicester, no date.

24 Frank Parkin, *Middle Class Radicalism,* University of Manchester Press, 1968.

25 John Bochel, 'The Recruitment of Local Councillors', *Political Studies,* vol. 14.

26 David Riesman and others, *The Lonely Crowd,* New York, Doubleday, 1953, especially pp. 210-15.

27 Tyrrell Burgess, 'The Open University', *New Society,* 27 April 1972.

28 See George Brosan, in Brosan and others, *Patterns and Policies in Higher Education,* Pelican, 1971. Eric Robinson, in *The New Polytechnics,* Turnstile Press, 1968, voices similar arguments to Brosan and to Burgess.

29 The Carnegie Commission on Higher Education, *New Students and New Places,* 1971, p. 3.

19 Education for leisure[1]

James Simpson

Dangers and difficulties beset the concept education for leisure. In the first place, it may be translated into an emotive blur-phrase with which we can simply re-package any existing curriculum so that the same basic medicine, as with prescriptions like 'education for life', or 'for citizenship' or 'for democracy', can persist without much consideration of its effectiveness. A new rationale is found – a change in the vocabulary of educationalists without, necessarily, much change in the practice of educators. As such it has serious contemporary rivals in 'education for maturity' or 'adjustments'.

The second danger is a little harder to define and arises from that curious kitchen-sink *narodnichestvo* which nowadays prompts many of us to suspect our own predilections as prim and bourgeois, and induces us to ascribe almost moral force to mass behaviour-patterns as revealed by sociological surveys, grounding an educational philosophy, almost, on consumer research. This has many merits and is a salutary check on such assumptions as that paella belongs to an ethically higher order of things than fish-fingers. If pushed too far, however, it can abolish any real dialogue in education for leisure, reducing it to the facilitation of mass trends which are often dictated by irresponsible interests.

Surely educationists ought to be able to assert personal values based on the notion of more and less fulfilling activities, or on that of enlarging people's range of experience and choice. They can still be alive to the limitations, for mass application in 1966, of leisure patterns that have prevailed among élite classes – of the sort portrayed with considerable continuity from Jane Austen or Charlotte Yonge to Alison Uttley. It may not be without significance that so many of these pictures are by woman or that a woman – the late Dr Macalister Brew – was among the foremost apologists of an education for mass leisure based largely on the assumption that élite *mores* should be diffused.

The third danger lies in an over-simplification whereby education is called upon to solve a 'problem of leisure' which consists in the appearance or threat of large quantities of non-work time created by automation and hanging heavy on the recipients. There may not be such a problem, and if there is, it is by no means so easily defined. It is true that since 1860 the average industrial worker has gained 1,500 hours a year of non-work time, and at each stage of this increase some public concern has been expressed about the social and moral consequences.

Shortly after the 1914 war, for example, the International Labour Office studied the 'problem' set up by the eight-hour-day types of legislation and expressed concern at the possibilities of mass drunkenness, debauchery and *ennui*. These dire results do not seem to have followed, and none of the contemporary surveys today gives us a picture of people complaining that they have nothing to do — except for certain small categories of teenagers and pensioners. Overtime, the second job, the great increase in the married woman labour force, and the time necessarily given to academic and vocational education, may, in fact, have reduced the national annual quantity of leisure. And to fill it there is a vastly multiplied range of leisure activities brought by technology and affluence within the reach of the average citizen.

Educationists who plead the new problem of leisure as an urgent reason for the development of this or that in the curriculum cannot point to the horrors of blank time. Rather they are expressing, whether they are frank about it or not, their disappointment with the way ('trivial', 'escapist', 'stultifying', 'unconstructive') that people use their time. Anyone, of course, is entitled to make such judgements but if he is pressing for anything which involves the expenditure of our effort and resources he must convince us that some improvement in the use of leisure is necessary for specific aspects of the welfare and happiness of people individually and as a community. And he must indicate means whereby, in a free society, this improvement can be made — the sort of water from which, and the sort of setting in which, the horse will in fact drink. Otherwise we shall be no further ahead.

Widening horizons

The present position seems to be that the schools and various establishments of further and higher education devote a considerable amount of their time to education which, whatever other purposes it also serves, should enrich leisure by widening horizons of interest and enjoyment, sharpening perception and discrimination, and leading towards that thing — is it a quality of mind or an accumulation of knowledge and skills? — which is known as 'cultivation'. The effects of mass leisure are, however, in the opinion of well-placed observers, disappointing. Some time ago, for example, Jack Longland suggested, at an N.U.T. conference on popular culture, that the influence of thousands of hours in the schools given to the arts and crafts and to physical and cultural development was only very partially discernible in post-school leisure interests. It would, on the other hand, be a pity to be discouraged too soon. It is a matter of experience that there has been a small but steady increase in those who have been permanently won over to 'higher values' by the work of the schools, and this will have a cumulative effect if we are patient, although the Newsom Report has identified a substantial section of pupils among whom this kind of development is rare and unlikely. Is it possible to do more? If so how? On what social and ethical grounds is there any special urgency at present for making the attempt? It is not suggested that the following considerations provide answers but that they may help towards a clearer definition of the questions.

Studies of the nature of leisure do not offer unmixed encouragement to educators. In less industrialized and specialized societies no very clear line is drawn between work and play or relaxation, and much of work is enveloped in ritual or in domestic informality. Until quite recently in our own type of society leisure, except as a period of recuperation from work, was the preserve of a minority. To think of training for mass leisure would have been pointless, although the lack of such training became painfully clear during the unexpected period of enforced mass leisure at the time of the great industrial depression, when the sense of aimlessness was more noticeable perhaps than malnutrition. Leisure for most people, as a separate block of time of significant dimension, is a product of the tertiary stage of industrialization. It seems to have led to some widespread change of attitude towards work – from a view of work as a desirable chief life-interest and as a moral end in itself to seeing it primarily as a means to personal life – the unavoidable sub-structure of leisure.

A number of thinkers from the Greeks to Piaget have expressed the view, put concisely by Schiller, that 'only in play is man fully human' and they have recommended an educational strategy based on this. Until recently, however, the inescapable economic condition of mankind has provided a soil that is refractory for the germination of such an idea, except for a privileged leisured class. A more protestant ethic has, accordingly, prevailed in education. Has technological advance altered all this? If so it might seem that golden vistas of personal development for millions were opening up before the educators' eyes. Some of the early diagnosticians of the ultimate effects of industrialization thought so. Marx, Engels and Proudhon envisaged a future in which emancipated workers would devote themselves to public affairs, astronomy and general cultivation. Only in limited measure has this type of expectation been fulfilled and, in so far as we are able to judge, even in countries where there is encouragement to the point of pressure, response to the sort of provision made in palaces and parks of culture and recreation has been far from reassuring. The very nature of leisure (the word is derived from *licere*) implies that much of it will be self-organized or, by extension, satisfied through customer-purveyor relationships.

Social change

It is perhaps only realistic to try and identify some of the needs of *homo conurbanus* which he seeks to assuage in leisure particularly those which emerge from high-density living in the mid-sixties, and particularly those with which it might be thought, *prima facie,* education could help. Many of these needs have been so documented by academic studies, reputable surveys or reports like Albemarle and Newsom, that it is sufficient only to recall them briefly. Perhaps the most frequently mentioned is loneliness – the sense of isolation and lack of identity. It is odd that, as we become more densely populated, there is so much reference to the need for meaningful human contact, as opposed to the lonely togetherness of the crowded tube train or cinema. A good deal has been written about it, notably Riesman's Lonely Crowd. A study made here states flatly that

> Loneliness among all age groups is the disease at the heart of our honeycomb society. The number of lonely people in Britain has been rising over the past twenty years and is an alarming iceberg of social malaise in a country which becomes more impersonal as mobility grows.

Shifts in population, the break-up of the extended family, new housing, the re-siting of industry, mass and passive entertainment, are among factors that have steadily diminished that group life which is the soil of mental health, where people can be persons and not merely faceless consumers, producers, viewers, passengers – units in somebody else's social engineering. Some indication of this may be given by the enhanced prestige of marriage and the nuclear family as the sole reality, the front door providing the only gateway from the anonymity of outside relationships into life as a real person. Yet we are assured that there are in-built psychological reasons why family life is bound to be an insufficient substitute for less emotionally charged groups. Allied to this and also to the increasing complexity, specialism, and professionalism, of modern life is a sense of impotence – often manifested as apathy – in influencing let alone controlling social environment, in finding a place for giving any significant service to individuals to the community.

New processes have tended to reduce, for many workers, including domestic workers, the demands which their job makes on personal skill, strength, technical mastery, initiative and creativity. This is true whatever classification – skilled, semi-skilled or unskilled, or even professional – is allocated to the job.

Leisure pursuits and interests have acquired much greater importance in the lives of many, and it is in these often, rather than in their work nowadays, that they seek to find status and identity. Technical progress has opened up to a broad mass of people the chance of a personal life in non-work time, and it has made available to them a profusion of desirable possessions and activities the mastery of which often demands considerable skill which they wish to learn. Few, however, translate their wish into fact and one clearly emerging problem of affluence is under-usage – the fact that so many people continue to mill round a restricted orbit in pursuits that make minimal demands on their personalities.

The sheer volume and intensity of advertisement – which seems to reflect some in-built need in our type of economy for demand to run somewhat ahead of expanding production – and, indeed, the rich profusion of entirely new materials and apparatus for personal life, constitute a formidable problem for many. Already consumer education has been identified as a valuable element in the schools and further education establishments. It is not entirely a matter of choosing between products. Admass pressures can lead to dependence on an endless and widening stream of things to buy as a solution to all the needs, difficulties and frustrations of life, so that new-won leisure has to be lost again in an attempt to gain extra money – by extra paid work – a process which is likely to be self-defeating and can lead to uneasy industrial relations. For this reason the cultivation of inner or independent sources of satisfaction might be seen as having social importance.

Our society is increasingly ordered. A larger and larger area of our lives is removed from chance, from hazard, or capricious individualism. It is subjected to an order which is manifestly just, well-planned and benevolent – an order which, we cannot deny, we have ourselves democratically created. It shepherds us into our proper traffic lanes and places us in clearly appropriate categories in various types of school or job, mental hospitals, or university, from the municipal maternity ward to the municipal crematorium. It is all sensible and just and leaves little room for causes that could hallow any expressions of human aggressiveness in embattled solidarity against oppressors within or foes without. The international scene too, is increasingly subjected to the rule of law, or the balance of terror. It may not be without significance that the World Health Organization has noted that countries with a high crime rate have a low mental illness rate. Undoubtedly, one of the real success stories of our Youth Service has been the type of adventurous activity associated loosely with the name 'Outward Bound'; but it has a minority appeal and, indeed, it seems difficult to relate to the kind of life that most of us lead, this strange world of orienteering, slalom, tods, cliff rescue, mountain rescue, sea rescue, cave rescue, sheep rescue, and so on.

A feature of our epoch to which it might be supposed education has a contribution to make is the intensified difficulty in communication between the elder and the young. Some of the factors at work have been sufficiently stressed — affluent emancipated youth, courted by the labour market, wooed by salesmen who build up teenage pursuits, fashions and language to something splendid and separate, the high point of life — salesmen who are irresponsibly indifferent to the fate of ex-teenagers. Less attention has been paid to another side of the picture — that among adults there is increased health, wealth and longevity. There is indeed a good deal of jealousy between the generations.

Educational contribution
Whether or not it is susceptible of any educational alleviation there is undoubtedly some malaise arising from widespread changes that are taking place in people's scales of values, and there is much confusion about which forms of conduct and what personal qualities are worth while. It has been observed that in many sections of the community, at all levels, a certain moral and social giddiness has arisen from the disappearance of those clear standards and signposts which were, not so long ago, provided by religious faith or the behaviour ideals set by higher social classes. It is a question of course how far education can be the creator of an ideology or how far it must work within a datum in this report. The prevailing view seems to be that education should put people in the position of 'forging out their own values'. Much of the nature of personal life, of leisure, will depend upon the type of standards and values which predominate at any given time — upon the patterns of ideal behaviour, and this includes recreation and relaxation, that are considered to be desirable, whether the label is 'more refined', 'nobler', 'more with-it', or 'more fun'.

If this is the sort of area of social and educational leisure-need that we must consider, what prospects are there of making a serious contribution through the work of the schools and colleges, and later through voluntarily undertaken further education? The pabulum that we have provided for many years now — the liberal and social studies (humanities and sciences) the arts and crafts, the physical skills — represents a distilled tradition of wisdom and it has been constantly increased and refreshed as a result of recent thinking and discovery. The techniques for its presentation and assimilation have themselves become a science. The diet has in the past few decades been enlarged by the addition of means whereby suitable attitudes and dispositions may be fostered in the young — means which are inherent in the curriculum and not merely its by-product of social training and corporate life. In so far as there has been a failure to provide the answer to leisure problems one may reasonably ask why this wisdom and these attitudes have proved inadequate.

Undoubtedly beneath all the prize-day tributes paid to education for 'life', 'maturity', and so on, those elements in education predominate which assist in replenishing and increasing the nation's stock of knowledge and skill for self-maintenance in a competitive world. While one may question the relevance today of some of the elements of this knowledge and skill that are still highly regarded, it could scarcely be said that the time seems ripe for making education for leisure central rather than peripheral. But even in the fringe — and it is by no means a negligible fringe — a certain mixture of austerity, academicism and high culture tends to prevail — a legacy perhaps of Calvinism and a public educational system which for much of its history was inspired by the conception of civilizing the masses *de haut en bas*. As a result a certain hierarchy of priority appears to operate with considerable force in educational circles, whereby esteem is given in descending order to vocational education (and this includes academic and liberal subjects leading to examinations), other work which could conceivably pay a career dividend (e.g. Spanish or economics voluntarily taken by an adult student), high culture (which pre-supposes some initial intellectual equipment), the creative arts, physical fitness, and lastly education for sheer diversion of an innocuous kind, diversions which are active and rural being placed higher than those which are passive and urban.

Leisure surveys

The resulting mixture in education that bears on leisure often contrasts sharply with what most surveys of mass leisure patterns indicate to be the facts in a mainly urban society. These surveys vary, but if one allows for some noticeable difference between those dealing with adults and those with youth, it would not be unjust to find some consensus along the following lines. Heading the list by far comes casual, informal, human intercourse — domestic and outside the home, and including all the ascents, plateaux and declines of courtship, love, friendship and family affections. After this obvious element pride of place goes to the mass media (mainly television and radio). Surprisingly, however, this place is almost shared by a group of active and creative utilitarian interests that centre on the home — adaptation, extension, decoration, embellishment, purchasing, planning, gardening, dress, cookery.

Those interests are heavily governed by commercial advertisement, have a strong note of social advancement — although the keynote is modernity rather than gentility — and depend largely upon the use of commercially-produced materials, kits and tools that are rarely seen in the schools (foam rubber, fibre-glass, small power-tools). Close behind comes active outdoor interests. These increasingly centre on the car and include car maintenance — but also the expeditions, trips, picnics, travels, and holidays whether by car or public transport and also active participation in sports, games, coursing, fishing, camping, skating, swimming, bowling, water pursuits – again very much affected by the latest forms of commercially-advertised gear and dress. Recreational and social activities of a more structured kind follow – the dances, parties, meetings in clubs and pubs, visits to cinemas, spectatorship at games and other events. Reading books invariably occupies a surprisingly high place but almost none of the surveys gives any clue as to the content of reading, and it must be remembered that nowadays, for a majority of people, the word 'book' covers magazines and comics. These are the chief categories and they occupy at least twice as large a percentage as the next in order – hobbies such as collecting, crosswords, pets – and gambling. After that we have only fragmentary distribution and it is somewhere here that we find, variously placed, some reflection of our educational striving – the interest in nature, the less utilitarian crafts, amateur drama and music-making, the theatre, concerts, and other forms of high culture including a maintained interest in liberal or social studies, or the active exercise of democratic citizen responsibilities. In general, as one of the surveyors, Brian Groombridge, points out, 'Popular culture in Britain is a domestic culture centring on the home and garden and linked to the world outside by the car and TV.'

One might add that it is a culture dependent in large measure upon the commercial provision of commodities and facilities, and it is here too that one may discern in much educational thinking and practice a traditional suspicion or contempt which leaves these goods and facilities out of account. There are of course notable exceptions but there is often little disposition in educational practice to take cognizance of non-educational television programmes, of the significance in children's lives of pop discs, of the admass-induced conspicuous spending which is one of the notable mass pressures of our time and has been called 'the wall-to-wall dynamic', although, among the young, clothes predominate as the concrete symbol.

Educational provision is slow to recognize the new rhythms of living that have appeared in the two-income family with its effect on the timing, tempo and content of leisure. The nourishing soup or pudding that needs careful preparation, the stitchcraft that lends itself to endurance and repair are, for many, as irrelevant as the concept of thrift in an age when the economy thrives on rapid, throwaway consumption and confident credit-buying. Nor is enough note taken of what appear to be, in the case of many people, something like in-built limitations. In one study of life on a council estate there was noted an almost universal aversion from serious music, to the point, apparently, of genuine physical pain. A similar sense of nausea in the presence of large arrays of books, as in a library, was noted by another. Most teachers of history have encountered a certain number of pupils for whom the past, in itself and in any shape or form, is nauseous.

The central difficulty about a programme of leisure education seems to be that as educationists we have not all in our hearts resolved a dilemma which is thrust upon us with increasing clarity as we try harder. We cling to the notion that everyone is capable of the highest (a highest about the nature of which we have little doubt), or at least capable of some stage on the road towards it, and that, at heart, they long for these heights and will be the better for their progress upwards, however painfully it has been made. It is as if mankind were strung out along the trail towards some golden west of attainment, some toiling manfully, some in breakdown postures, but all yearning onwards – 'Culture or bust'. It is this sort of thinking which underlies many of the attempts to use popular culture, as the surveys show it to us, as a 'starting point' – something to educate from and not for. Education through the popular arts is not infrequently a disguised form of changing the popular arts by critical analysis – a process, in film, for example, of weaning away from Goldfinger to the works of Fellini. It is not surprising that the intrinsic difficulties of doing this restrict its effectiveness to a minority. And yet, as educators, are we not dedicated to some such process in respect of all our pupils, not merely some? Could we be content to educate a minority away from popular culture and the rest for the enjoyment of it? Is not any dualism of aim and standard repugnant to us? It is by no means a new problem. Years ago Matthew Arnold, as an educator, joined issue with Tolstoy when he wrote, 'At present I can contribute to nothing which raises me externally above others, which separates me from them. I cannot any longer recognize any quality beyond the quality of man. I cannot seek a culture which separates me from men.' Tolstoy's words are surely moving, but can we take them less critically now than Arnold did?

But is this dilemma fundamental? Is it not being resolved by the passage of time? Many readers of this chapter, like the writer, may admit that in their leisure they habitually enjoy some of the elements listed high in the surveys mentioned earlier. Enjoyment of some parts of both popular and high culture commonly co-exist today. We can surely educate for both if we are so minded, and the process will be effective in so far as we take popular culture seriously in all its facets.

Acquisition of skills

There may be room, too, in educational establishments for greater awareness of the increasing wish of adults to use their leisure to better their situation in life in a new way – not through further vocational or academic learning that leads to advancement in, or change of career, but through the acquisition of skills and *mores* and possessions that confer social prestige. It would, perhaps, be a useful exercise for those who frame curricula in the schools to consider the change, in the last twenty years, in the programme of adult education classes provided by L.E.A.s, and the increasing part played in it by classes in flower-arrangement, skiing, sub-aqua interests, stock-market operations, fly-fishing, antique-buying, party-giving, the use of light in interior decoration, gastronomy and so on. The 'gracious living' motif is, also, increasingly represented in the Youth Service. Yet, although there are many exceptions, the leisure interests opened up by the schools are not usually presented in ways that associate them with this powerful tendency. Recently a sub-section of the Cultural Committee of the Council of Europe has identified a general trend in member countries as policies of *éducation permanente* — life-long education based on the need, in a time of high-tempo social change, for regular refresher courses throughout life, as much in matters of personal and social, as in vocational life. Involved in this, explicitly, is the need in the schools for a basic education in these personal and social matters which takes cognizance of, and works in liaison with, what is being done in the post-school years.

Perhaps, in the long run, one of the most fertile fields for developing education for leisure is indicated by the supreme place occupied in leisure-usage as we know it by human relationships and intercourse. Much can be done, and is done, as a preparation or effective personal life in this respect through well-established subjects of the curriculum, particularly English. In addition, the increasing use of group work in learning situations is likely to convey some knowledge of the mechanics and inherent benefits of group-life and of the attitudes and techniques which enable people to join, form and be valued and useful in groups in various ways and roles. On the other hand, to include this vast field in the curriculum in a more formal or direct way presents a formidable difficulty — one more of those difficulties in which the whole topic of leisure education abounds. Some of them have been sketchily outlined here. Around them all lies a question which is not one for educationists as such. How far are we at present wise to place a particular stress in education upon preparation for leisure? It is a question that would lead us into economics.

Reference
1 First published in 'Trends in Education', January 1967.

20 Shaping cultural institutions[1]

Raymond Williams

The extension of culture has to be considered within the real social content of our economic and political life. My studies of the growth of particular cultural institutions showed a real expansion, which of course is continuing, but showed also the extent to which this was affected or determined by other facts in the society. In the 1960s, the rate of growth seems promising, and we are busy with plans to maintain and increase it. Yet here, very clearly, is a major contradiction easily overlooked by following a simple rising graph, for while real art and argument are being more widely enjoyed, the distribution of a bewildering variety of bad art and bad argument is increasing even more rapidly. We are reaching the point where the contradiction between these different lines and rates of growth is serious and inescapable, yet even those who see this situation feel particularly uncertain about what can be done.

We must look first at a particular and local contradiction which can quickly confuse any such discussion. If someone proposes ways of extending good art and argument, and of diminishing their worst counterparts, someone else usually answers that we mustn't be snobs: that football, after all, is as good as chess; that jazz is a real musical form; that gardening and homemaking are also important. Who exactly is someone like this arguing with, since it is usually obvious that he is not really arguing with the man to whom he replies? Unfortunately he is arguing with actual people and a familiar way of feeling. It is true that certain cultural forms have been used as a way of asserting social distinction, and that much wholesale condemnation of new forms has been a way of demonstrating the inferiority of those two groups who have regularly to be put in their (lower) place: the masses and the young. This habit has to be resisted, but there is equal danger in a popular form of demagogy which, by the use of selective examples, succeeds in avoiding the problem of bad culture altogether. Can we agree, perhaps, before passing to the more difficult questions, that football is indeed a wonderful game, that jazz is a real musical form and that gardening and homemaking are indeed important? Can we also agree, though, that the horror-film, the rape-novel, the Sunday strip-paper and the latest Tin-Pan drool are not exactly in the same world, and that the nice magazine romance, the manly adventure story (straight to the point of the jaw) and the pretty, clever television advertisement are not in it either? The argument against these things, and the immense profits gained by their calculated dissemination, cannot afford to be confused by the collateral point that a good living culture is various and changing, that the need for sport and entertainment is as real as the need for art, and that the public display of 'taste', as a form of social distinction, is merely vulgar.

In a rapidly changing and therefore confused society, in which cultural forms will in any case change but in which little is done by way of education to deepen and refine the capacity for significant response, we have to learn forms of action as well as methods of criticism.

Two parallel efforts are necessary: on the one hand the maximum encouragement of artists who are seriously trying to create new forms or do significant work in traditional forms; on the other hand, the steady offering and discussion of this work, including real criticism and therefore its distinction at least from calculated and indifferent manipulation. It would be wrong to say that these efforts are not being made: some help, though still inadequate, is being given to the arts; some responsible offering and discussion is publicly underwritten. These policies fall within the evolutionary conception: a steady encouragement of elements of valuable growth. But while supporting them, and certainly wishing to see them extended, I find it difficult to feel that they go to the root of the problem. For it is usually not recognized that inferior and destructive elements are being much more actively propagated: that more is spent, for example, on advertising a new soap, and imprinting a jingle attached to it, than on supporting an orchestra or a picture gallery; and that in launching two new magazines, one trying to do a serious new job, the other simply competing to capture a share of a known popular market, the ratio of comparative investment is ludicrous, for hardly anything is behind the former, while huge sums of money are poured out on the latter.

The condition of cultural growth must be that varying elements are at least equally available, and that new and unfamiliar things must be offered steadily over a long period, if they are to have a reasonable chance of acceptance. Policies of this degree of responsibility seem impossible in our present cultural organization. The encouragement of valuable elements is restricted to what is little more than a defensive holding operation, which of course is better than nothing but which is hardly likely to make any general change. The rest of the field is left to the market, and not even to the free play of the market, for the amounts of capital involved in financing our major cultural institutions restrict entry to a comparatively few powerful groups, so that both production and distribution are effectively in very few hands. The serious new magazine referred to, usually the result of a major voluntary effort by a group of dedicated people, is unlikely to be even available for buying, in the sense of lying ready on the average bookstall where somebody might try it, while the new commercial magazine will be so widely displayed that it can hardly be avoided. It is then stupid and even vicious, when it is clear that no real competition exists, to use the evidence of immediate results as proof of the unalterable vulgarity of the public. Instead of the ritual indignation and despair at the cultural condition of 'the masses' (now increasingly uttered even by their supposed friends) it is necessary to break through to the central fact that most of our cultural institutions are in the hands of speculators, interested not in the health and growth of the society, but in the quick profits that can be made by exploiting inexperience. True, under attack, these speculators, or some of them, will concede limited policies of a different kind, which they significantly call 'prestige'; that is to say, enough to preserve a limited public respectability so that they will be allowed to continue to operate. But the real question is whether a society can afford to leave its cultural apparatus in such irresponsible hands.

Now I think many people feel the strength of this question, but feel even more strongly the difficulties of any possible alternative. Steady and particular encouragement, in the obvious limited fields, is quite widely approved, but any attempt to tackle the whole situation runs into major difficulties. For it is obvious that the amount of capital and effort required, to make any substantial change, can come only from public sources, and to this there are two objections. The first is the question whether such resources are really available, on the scale required. This goes back to the difficulty discussed earlier [in *The Long Revolution*]: that we find it almost impossible to conceive the financing of social policy out of the social product, and have never learned a system of accounting which would make this possible or even visible. For it is true, of course, that the present investment comes from the society and economy as a whole. The supply of advertising money (the contemporary equivalent of manna) can only come in the end from us, as workers and buyers, though it is now routed through channels that give control of this social capital to very limited groups. If we can realize that we are paying for the existing cultural system, by one kind of organization of the economy, we need not be frightened by the scale of resources required, since that organization is in fact subject to change. We should be much clearer about these cultural questions if we saw them as a consequence of a basically capitalist organization, and I at least know no better reason for capitalism to be ended. It is significant that the liveliest revolt against the existing system, particularly among the new young generation, is in precisely these cultural terms.

But then the second objection is deeply involved with this point. What is the alternative to capitalism? Socialism. What is a socialist culture? State control. There are many good liberals, and many anxious socialists, who draw back if this is the prospect. Better even the speculators, they say, than the inevitable horde of bureaucrats, official bodies, and quite probably censorship.

This difficulty has a representative significance. It is not only in cultural questions, but in the whole area of thinking about change in our society, that this knot is tied. Here is the deepest difficulty in the whole development of our democracy: that we seem reduced to a choice between speculator and bureaucrat, and while we do not like the speculator, the bureaucrat is not exactly inviting either. In such a situation, energy is sapped, hope weakens, and of course the present compromise between the speculators and the bureaucrats remains unchallenged.

Democratic policies are made by open discussion and open voting. In relatively small bodies, contact between members and policies can be close, though even here some responsibility for decisions will be passed to elected representatives rather than to members as a whole, and where much administrative work is necessary will also be passed to officials. The principle of the official in a democratic organization is quite clear: he administers within an elected policy, and is responsible to the membership for his actions. The practice, we all know, can be otherwise, but given an adequate constitution and genuine equality of membership it is still the best and most responsible system known.

There are strong arguments for the national organization of the means of cultural exchange, but the persistent danger, even in a democratic country, is that too large an organization becomes rigid and in a sense impenetrable. Any adequate cultural organization must be open, flexible and committed to genuine variety of expression. It would seem simple to say that the best people to run the various cultural organizations are those who use them for the production of their own work, for here is the deepest and most practical interest in keeping the organization flexible and open. Yet it is equally clear that the actual producers of cultural work cannot, from their own resources, command the ownership of any but the simplest means. Where indeed they can do so, no change is necessary. But in the press, in broadcasting and television, in the cinema and theatre it is obvious that this simple cooperative ownership is impossible. This ought not then to mean, however, that the control of these expensive means should be made available to the highest bidder, especially when he is not even particularly interested in the actual work but mainly in its financial possibilities. The signs are, in contemporary Britain, that this worst of all arrangements is becoming normal, with a dominant policy criterion of profit and with the producers turned into employees within this emphasis. In press and television this is especially the case, and powerful interests are working to extend the same system to broadcasting. It is urgent to define the alternative principle, which I think can only be that when the producers cannot themselves own the means of their work, these must be owned by the community in trust for the producers, and an administration set up which is capable of maintaining this trust. The difficulties here are obvious, but all administration and constitution-making in fact proceed from an emphasis of what is desirable, and I believe that if we can agree that this end is desirable, no society is better qualified from experience to devise adequate practical methods.

In the drama, for example, it would be possible for most theatres to be publicly owned, preferably by local authorities though perhaps with a small national network in addition, and then licensed to companies of actors. It would then be possible for these companies, through open regional and national organizations which they would be free to join or not as they decided, to pursue reasonably long-term policies on the guarantee that a particular production would go to a series of theatres, when financially necessary. Similar arrangements could be made, through permanent and regular liaison, with the broadcasting and television services. The advantages to the drama of permanent companies creating their own varying traditions, in a context of adequate professional security, would undoubtedly be great: almost all the good work we now have in the theatre comes from such companies, which are left, though, to struggle on as best they can with the hope of being eventually hired by the speculators who control the big national theatres. If we are serious about freedom in the arts, we can give it, in this way, to actual artists.

In the cinema, a related system is possible. As things now are, the makers of films are almost wholly in the hands of the distributors, who decide by certain crude tests, whether a film is worth making before it is made. This is the freedom of the artist which our liberals so complacently defend. It is clear that the number of cinemas is in any case going to decline. The opportunity this presents of a sensible reorganization ought not to be missed. The cinemas should become publicly owned and vested in an independent public authority. There should be at least two or three circuits, including one specialized circuit, to ensure alternatives. Production should be in the hands of independent permanent companies, which as in the case of the theatre would have to satisfy the public authority of their professional competence. Public money should then be made available to these companies, for the making of films which would be guaranteed exhibition on one of the circuits. The more independent companies there are the better, and it would be encouraging to see some links between some of these and the theatre companies already referred to. A possible organization of the independent authority would be joint representation between officers appointed by and responsible to Parliament and representatives elected by the permanent companies.

In the case of books, we already have a good range of independent publishers, though the pressures on them to surrender independent policies are severe. A rapid process of amalgamation (often retaining apparently independent imprints) is already under way, and new kinds of owner, often little concerned with literature, are becoming more common. With high costs, and the wide opportunities of the 'paperback revolution', it seems that a stage has been reached very similar to that in newspapers at the turn of the century. The quantitative thinking that can follow from such a system would be disastrous to publishing, past a certain point, and I think the time has come for an inquiry into the facts of recent changes and possible courses of action.

Meanwhile it is of vital importance that publishers who pursue, as now, responsible and therefore varying policies should be given all possible help. This can probably best be done in the now chaotic field of distribution. It is a standing disgrace that there should be hundreds of towns without anything that can be called a decent bookshop. The good independent bookseller performs an especially valuable service, but unless he is lucky in his locality he will often go under. The existing chain shops apply to books and periodicals simple tests of quantity: below a certain figure they do not consider particular items worth handling. Is this any kind of freedom, or free availability? I think we could set up a Books Council, representative on the one hand of publishers, booksellers and authors, on the other hand of Parliament, which would have the duty of ensuring the continued independence of publication, and at the same time the best possible distribution of books and periodicals here and overseas. The pressure to reduce publications to a limited number of standard items, easily sold in quantity, should be resisted as a matter of public policy. Such a Council could review existing bookselling arrangements, and wherever it found (as it would now widely find) that the real range of books and periodicals is not offered, it would have power to establish and guarantee independent enterprises committed to the policy outlined. It is very odd that we have accepted this principle, in the public library service, for the borrowing of books, but are still so far short of it in offering books that readers can buy and keep.

In the case of newspapers and magazines, we have to deal with a situation in which control is passing into fewer and fewer hands, within a policy dedicated not to the quality of newspapers and magazines but to their profitability. The criterion of profitability is being raised to absurd levels, in which for example a daily newspaper may have to cease publication if less than a million people buy it, and in which a steady decline in the number of newspapers and magazines seems assured. Again, is this freedom, or free availability? The quality of newspapers is unlikely to be raised either by exhortation or censorship. Experience in all other fields suggests that standards in a profession rise when they are in the control of members of that profession. Such professional responsibility is now virtually impossible, as a permanent and consistent policy, since the whole organization of the press (like the organization of the cinema and the theatre) creates a different atmosphere, in which standards are set by the controllers, on an estimate of likely profit, and the actual producers instead of feeling a common responsibility to their work are encouraged, in far too many cases, to compete with each other in supplying a predetermined article. Personal standards will always vary, but it is a poor society which creates institutions that give success to the least scrupulous and the least concerned. Any attempt to reform these institutions, though, is met with prolonged abuse and misrepresentation. Obviously we do not want a state-owned press, but I think we have reached the point where we need a new Press Council, including public and elected journalist representatives, charged with the maintenance and extension of genuinely independent newspapers and magazines (2). We need in particular to ensure the survival of local newspapers, and I think it is essential that these should become locally owned and managed, as very few of them now are. There are serious objections to involving local authorities in the ownership of local newspapers, though in certain cases this might be done.

More generally, the guarantee of independence, and any necessary provision of capital, should be accepted as a public service at national level, through a press Council including, as defined, journalist representatives. The same public service principle should be applied to magazines, on terms guaranteeing independence to professionally recognized editorial bodies. With experience, this principle could be extended to the national press. I do not see why the editorial bodies of any newspaper or magazine should not be free, by their own democratic decision, to apply to such a Press Council to be recognized as an independent enterprise, which would then be guaranteed freedom from any external private financial control. The terms on which this recognition and support would be granted would be the producers' own definition of policy. There might be cases when the Council, including public and professional representatives, would be unwilling to underwrite a particular policy proposed, but in such cases we should be no worse off than we are now: such a policy could be tried on the market, or financed much as now, for of course there can be no question of any newspaper or magazine being forbidden to publish. I think that with experience and goodwill a majority of professionally responsible independent papers could be built up, and even if we did not achieve a majority, we should at least have ensured that no newspaper or magazine could be killed by a financial organization indifferent to quality and interested only in immediate profit. Reform can only come from within, in such a field, if it is publicly supported.

In broadcasting and television we see an imperfect but still generally responsible public authority, the B.B.C., powerfully challenged by new kinds of organization. It is obvious, as these services extend, that we need the continual extension of choice, but it is doubtful if we shall get this, on any responsible basis, if we construe independence as the possession of working capital from elsewhere (mainly, as now, from advertising). There might well be two or more public authorities owning the technical means of distribution, but the same principle holds as before: policy can be generally defined by the public authorities, but the provision of actual work must be in the hands of the real producers. Practical networks exist, and their wide use is clearly desirable, but what one would like to see serving them is a variety of independent groups, with genuine local affiliations and alternative policies. The existing programme companies, in commercial television, are hardly ever of this kind, but are essentially a congeries of financial interests employing the real producers. It should be a matter of public policy to encourage the formation of professional companies to whom the technical means of distribution would be made available by the public authorities. The core of such groups would be the professional broadcasting and television producers, who would work out means of association with other professional companies in the theatre, the cinema and the press, with orchestras and other similar institutions of their region, and preferably with wider local organizations, including education committees and the great voluntary societies. In this way the dangers both of a central monopoly and of simple surrender to the speculators could be avoided.

I am very much aware, in putting forward these outline proposals, that much remains to be done, in detailed planning and in improvement, by discussion between all those with relevant experience. I do not suppose that any of these measures of reorganization would be easy, but I do claim, emphatically, that we can envisage a cultural organization which would greatly extend the freedom of the cultural producers, by the sensible application of public resources to cut out their present dependence on dominant but essentially functionless financial groups, and by forms of contract which while preserving responsibility in the spending of public money would give the producers control over their actual work. This is surely a hopeful way forward, and constitutions can in fact always be devised if there is substantial agreement on principles.

The matter is now urgent, for while some liberals still shy away from reform in the name of the freedom of the artist, or argue that culture in any case can never be organized (the spirit bloweth where it listeth), a very rapid reorganization of a different kind is in fact going on, with the area of real ownership and independence shrinking in every part of our culture, and seeming certain to continue to do so. I must plainly ask such liberals what they are really defending, for there seems little in common between the freedom they value and the actual freedom described recently by an owner of a television service and a great chain of newspapers as 'a licence to print your own money'. We have reached a crisis in which freedom and independence can only be saved if they are publicly assured and guaranteed, and the ways I propose seem a working basis for this, taking care as they do to avoid or minimize the real dangers of bureaucracy and state control.

Would the quality of our cultural life be improved by such measures? I feel certain that it would, in the real energies that would be released, but I am not thinking in terms of any overnight transformation. I say only that the channels would be more open, that the pressure for quick profit would be lifted, and that a more genuine range of choices would be made available. My whole case about social change is, moreover, that the interdependence of elements which I described as a matter of theory is an argument for conceiving change on the widest possible front: the changes in emphasis in our economy, in our ordinary working relationships, in our democratic institutions, and in education are all relevant to cultural change in this explicit field.

Notes and References
1 First published in *The Long Revolution,* Chatto and Windus, 1961, and published in Pelican Books, 1965, pp. 363-74.
2 The Press Council has now been changed, to include lay representatives, and there is an attempt, through the Monopolies Commission, to find ways of investigating and controlling mergers. These are welcome improvements but fall short of the policy argued here.

21 Scale, access and social control in broadcasting

George Weddell

Broadcasting has been defined earlier in this volume as one of the mass media which exert a dominating influence on the use of leisure in British society today. We are told by the audience researchers that the average citizen spends between fourteen and twenty-one hours a week in front of his television set alone. His use of the audible wallpaper supplied by sound radio accompanies a large proportion of what remains of his waking hours. The time spent on viewing television represents a large slice out of the leisure portion of most people's time budget. What this viewing does for them has been the subject of a good deal of conjecture, and of some carefully structured research. If Robert Silvey was right in asserting that 'television viewing is a form of play' (1), then the control and the structure of the providing agencies of this substantial input of leisure 'activity' come to be of some interest to social planners and policy makers.

Broadcasting structure: the classical model
Asa Briggs, in the third volume of his history of the B.B.C. (2) illustrates the strength which the country derived from the existence of a unified and nationwide radio service. Indeed, although the major part of that book deals with attempts to use external broadcasting as a weapon of psychological warfare, it is unlikely that the humdrum, sober and steady coverage of the war effort by the home services made a better contribution to the winning of the war than the expensive and fanciful 'black' and 'white' stations which broadcast overseas.

Although broadcasting has lost a good deal of the unifying and directive role which it played during those years, the coalescence of the evening's viewing round the main news bulletin on television on either channel still provides a common knowledge base for the majority of the population, with the concomitant effects on the formation of attitudes and of world view. On the whole people continue to look on the broadcasting services as something reliable and 'given'. They tend to credit the broadcast news with greater reliability than news from other sources. On the content, form or scheduling of programmes generally they do not want to have much influence. If one were able to take the view that broadcasting supply is of the same order as the water or gas supplies which are piped into the home this situation would be satisfactory. One would merely have to exercise a negative control so as to prevent any deterioration below a given standard of quality of a uniform product.

But broadcasting is neither that sort of product, nor is it uniform. Hence regulative quality control will not meet the case. The consumer of broadcasting makes much more diverse demands on his broadcasting services than on his water or his gas supply. The community as represented by its political institutions has specific views about the function of broadcasting. Not least, broadcasting was modelled by one particularly strong-minded man: John Reith. He used the concept of trusteeship for the national interest to develop a model of broadcasting structure which in essentials persists to this day (3). Owing to its inherent qualities and to the institutional and conceptual viscosity which causes public policy to lag behind the march of ideas and events, traces of it will linger long after consensus has ceased to be a motivating element in British broadcasting.

At present the classical model continues to dominate broadcasting structure, whether in the B.B.C. or in Independent Television. The broadcasters proceed on the assumption that their role is a didactic one; that their influence is pervasive; and that the mission of broadcasting has to be exercised with only qualified reliance on participatory devices, since these are both inadequate and misleading. Competition has hastened the development of checks on audience size. But these checks are pursued more because of their political and economical significance than from an interest in the audience itself. Hence the willingness, shared by advertisers and politicians, to rely on figures which bear little if any relationship to the impact of a particular programme.

These characteristics of the classical model: blanket coverage of a relatively undifferentiated audience and uni-directional broadcasting with a minimum of feedback mechanism, determine a third characteristic. This is the relationship of broadcasting to the prevailing socio-political orthodoxies. Given the rigidity of the model, it is not surprising that it allows of only marginal divergences from the accepted social and political norms. If access to broadcasting is strictly limited, it is essential that those who have access should, most of the time, reflect in their views the views of the majority in so far as these can be ascertained. Or, if the views of the majority are uncertain, the position maintained by the broadcasters must reflect whatever orthodoxies of the past have not yet been challenged beyond recall. This reflection must be more precise in the explicit treatment of controversial themes than in their implicit treatment. Thus a discussion on abortion has to be balanced; the treatment of the same theme in dramatic terms can be more *ex parte*.

The same considerations apply to political impartiality. Balance here is enforced more rigidly because of the vested interest in broadcasting of the ultimate controllers of broadcasting: the politicians. It is interesting to observe the unanimity with which both Government and Opposition, while disagreeing on everything else, unite in their determination to keep the broadcasters on a short lead. Marginal relaxations occur from time to time. The Scottish and Welsh nationalists have succeeded in achieving an element of access; the bargaining position of the Liberal Party fluctuates in response to its successes at the polls; the application of 'the right to reply' is extended to ministerial, as well as to party political broadcasts. But essentially the structure established in 1927 stands little altered.

Pound for pound this broadcasting structure yet provides the country with one of the best all-round television services in the world. Given the limitation which technical considerations place on access, the Reithian model has much to commend it. Few if any countries labouring under similar limitations of air space have succeeded in developing structures which provide much more satisfactory solutions. The North American pattern of commercial provision with a minimum of public control can boast a wider spread of channels; but this is vitiated by the conformism induced by unrestricted competition. Seven different Westerns on seven channels at the same time do not solve the problem of choice. Those countries, such as France, which regard their broadcasting systems as an integral part of the governmental information services thereby reduce the status of broadcasting to an agency of the government. Those, like Germany, which regard broadcasting as essentially a matter for regional devolution suffer, like Independent Television, from the over-capitalization inherent in servicing a single transmission channel from several distinct production units.

None of the examples cited so far display in their practices any attempt to meet the needs of a multi-cultural society within a limited airspace. The Dutch National Broadcasting Foundation and its related institutions furnish an example of a more imaginative approach to the solution of the problem. Here the statutory framework allows for contributions to the network by any political, religious or cultural group in the community which can attract the support of a sufficient number of paid-up members. Programmes reflecting the values and interests of six or eight such groups are currently included in the programmes of Dutch television. Together they take up about 45% of the programme schedule; the remainder is provided by the Broadcasting Foundation itself. The Dutch system has also found a way of avoiding over-capitalization by giving access to central production facilities provided by the Foundation to all accredited-interest groups (4).

It is unlikely that within the limitations of the classical model in

Britain new solutions of significance will be found. Certainly it is unlikely that they will be sought by the controllers of the broadcasting organizations themselves. The Actonian dictum about power operates here as elsewhere. Broadcasting organizations assume the status of estates of the realm and come to adopt a role identity which casts them as residual guardians of constitutional freedoms. To a greater extent than other public bodies they appear to be subject to a self-defining tendency which inhibits objective socio-political analysis. Thus the economics of scale which are thought to be appropriate to some forms of industrial and commercial undertaking are indiscriminately applied to broadcasting.

> We are moving into a period when larger and larger units are being formed in the world outside broadcasting, with power being accumulated in a shrinking number of centres. Is that the moment to weaken the capacity of the B.B.C. to resist and to be seen to be capable of resisting pressure? (5).

Lord Hill's question becomes the Director General's affirmation:

> If the strength of a public institution is reduced, its capacity for good as well as its capacity for harm is reduced . . . The structure of broadcasting in Britain will be found to be the right structure for the 1980s just as it has been for the 60s and the 70s (6).

The structure of broadcasting in Britain provides for the control of the executive staff of the broadcasting services, on behalf of the community at large, by governing bodies appointed as trustees of the public interest. The quotation from Lord Hill demonstrates how difficult it has become for the governors of the B.B.C. (or the members of the I.T.A. for that matter) to retain the detachment essential to the proper performance of this function. Their domestication to the interests of their respective organizations vitiates their independence to such an extent that they become little more than their spokesmen and uncritical advocates.

The search for new patterns

The need for structural reform is demonstrated by the inability of the broadcasters to see their operations in terms other than the interests of their own organizations. If reform will not come from within, it will have to come from without. But reform in which direction? There has been a good deal of criticism of the structure of broadcasting from broadcasters outside the corridors of power; there has been criticism by politicians; there has been criticism by moralists. But there has been little positive work on alternative patterns. Largely this has been due to the difficulty of bringing about greater flexibility within a television transmission system limited to three channels. The proposal to allocate the fourth channel gave rise to some interesting ideas for its use from people who realized that this would be the last opportunity to inject an element of variety into the pattern of television until the evacuation of the V.H.F. channels in the early 1980s makes possible their use for additional U.H.F. services.

The objectives of the reformers vary. There are those who want to give more power to the people. The objective of securing participation by the users of a broadcasting service in its management and content is, of course, a variation on the classical model. Lord Reith believed that, in an indirect sense, this was the objective of the Corporation as he created it. As long as the people are content to regard the conventional democratic structures as adequate for the expression of their needs and interests, a model related to these structures is likely to command assent. It is the growth of extra-parliamentary forms of participation and 'consumer' representation in many sectors of life which finds a parallel in the demands for consumer participation in broadcasting.

The demands for participation range from comparatively modest suggestions for the involvement of particular sections of the community in particular programme decisions to the wholesale handing over of any further television channels to community groups in local areas. An example of the former is the provision, presumably on the existing national services, of

> participatory programmes ... intended to promote social participation ... They work by addressing people in terms which they understand, on issues which they really care about and which they have in some way shared in selecting. The programmes are supported by specially contrived arrangements at the reception end for ensuring that a representative core of the audience may assimilate and evaluate the information received; and they are related in some way to the political and social instruments through which citizen viewers may press the conclusions at which they have arrived (7).

Variations on this theme have been practised on the B.B.C. and I.T.V. for many years, particularly in the educational output. But they have always been subject to the editorial control of the organization concerned. This seems to be an essential condition if coherence and responsibility are to be maintained on the national channels.

A different, and more promising proposal was put forward by the TV 4 Campaign which was active in 1971 and 1972 to promote discussion about the possible uses of a fourth television channel. The Campaign proposed that advantage should be taken of the smaller coverage areas of U.H.F. transmitters in order to create a series of genuinely local television stations owned by 'any group which is either non-profit making or willing to have its ability to distribute profits statutorily limited' (8). Since such stations would have only limited coverage it is thought that problems of impartiality and balance would be reduced. The stations would be licensed by a central authority whose hearings would be open to the public. A third proposal has been put forward by the Association of Broadcasting Staff, for the creation of a National Television Foundation. Such a Foundation

> would become a freelance within the British television industry, opening up a fresh source of production and encouragement for new ideas, some of them with high audiences, some of them with small ... The N.T.F. would have to prove itself in terms of its catholicity and not in terms of immediately recognizable balance as this word is applied in the existing services (9).

These schemes, good as they are in many respects, do not wholly carry conviction or hold out a promise that the last state will be substantially better than the first. One cannot escape the impression that what is really sought is more power for the producers at the expense of the 'controllers' of broadcasting. Whether or not the audiences will be better served remains an open question.

The new wave of devolution

The two main obstacles to the more effective participation of the users of broadcasting media in their control and in the production of programmes have been the limitation of access and the firm central control arrangements which were thought to be made necessary by this. Although the Government's role in the classical pattern of broadcasting is generally thought to be confined to the exercise of reserve powers, successive Governments have in fact intervened much more positively. As is indicated in the introduction to this part of the book, the absence of a coherent policy on leisure has not prevented Governments from taking measures reflecting firmly held views about how the people should, or should not, spend their leisure hours.

The history of the control of the hours during which radio and television programmes are allowed to be broadcast serves as an interesting example. While there was a monopoly of broadcasting this issue rarely caused friction between Government and the broadcasters, both because of the broadcasters' strongly held views about what was good for their listeners and because resources were limited. Until the outbreak of the Second World War it was unthinkable that broadcasting should begin except with the daily service at 10.15 a.m. (10). The service still survives at the same time, now surrounded by hours of programmes on either side. It was not until 1932 that continuous broadcasting was introduced on Saturdays between noon and midnight.

The 'closed period' between 6.15 and 8.0 p.m. on Sundays, intended to avoid interference with evening church services, began to be filled with religious programmes on radio in 1933; it persisted in television (with an element of attenuation to 7.25 p.m.) until the early 1950s. And the release of this time to the unfettered control of the broadcasters came about only in 1972 as a by-product of the total abolition of control over broadcasting hours by the Minister of Posts and Telecommunications.

Whereas radio hours could be controlled by means of a gentleman's agreement between the B.B.C. and the Government, the introduction of competition in television transferred the onus to the Government alone. Since advertising time is related to broadcasting time, more programmes bring the commercial television companies, within reason, more income as well as causing more expenditure. Since B.B.C. income is unrelated to broadcasting hours, and programmes cost money, more hours merely make it more difficult for the Corporation to balance its budget. Hence Government intervention between 1954 and 1972 was concerned both to maintain parity of hours between the competitors and to prevent television from affecting what were thought to be time-honoured socio-cultural behaviour patterns. It was thought that on the whole people should not be tempted to watch television during normal working hours. Hence the restriction of television transmissions to about eight hours a day (i.e. afternoon and evening). It was thought that children should be put to bed after the Children's Hour. Hence the 'toddlers' truce' between 6.00 and 7.0 p.m. which persisted for some years after the introduction of competition. It was thought that no one would go to evening services if there were competition from television. Hence the 'closed period' between 6.15 and 7.25 on Sunday evenings.

On the other hand certain types of programme were to be encouraged. School programmes, religious programmes, adult education programmes, programmes in Welsh. So these programmes were exempted from the restriction on hours. In this way the Government intervened not only negatively, but quite directly and positively in the content and pattern of television programmes. As late as December 1966 a Government White Paper asserted that

> In the Government's view, the amount of broadcasting will remain a matter of sufficient social importance to require that the Postmaster General should continue to hold and exercise his powers of control. Nor do the Government consider that any general increase in broadcasting hours will be justified for the present. They do not, however, rule out the possibility of more time for education programmes (11).

Barely five years later the whole set of rules was abolished without so much as a passing reference to the socio-cultural implications. The Central Religious Advisory Council, which is used by both the B.B.C. and the I.T.A. as a point of reference on religious broadcasting, had spent a good deal of time over the last few years considering the implications of a possible modification of the 'closed period'. Suddenly it found that it had nothing left to argue about.

But on the whole the move was right, for two reasons. Responsibility for the shape and content of the national broadcasting services is vested in the governors of the B.B.C. and the members of the I.T.A. As long as the Minister concerned exercised direct control over important areas of programme policy, this responsibility was little more than a façade. Now it will become apparent whether the broadcasting governors are capable of putting their role as trustees for the public interest first.

The second reason is the conformity of this move with the general trend for greater devolution in the mass media. I have argued the case for devolution elsewhere in some detail (12). Since 1968 the case, which then appeared sufficiently outrageous to the broadcasters to justify a virtual boycott of its discussion on the air, has become an accepted orthodoxy of thought about the future of broadcasting. Pressure for greater access to the media has come mainly from broadcasters themselves, as already indicated. But there is also a groundswell of demand from a wide range of citizens. It seems that we are about to experience a second Gutenberg revolution; this time in the broadcasting media. Jean d'Arcy has compared the communicators in the national broadcasting organizations with the medieval monks on whom, before the introduction of the printing press, the transmission of information depended. It may well be that results comparable to the cataclysms of the Reformation and the Enlightenment will follow on the technological revolution which makes possible the multi-channel and multi-directional communications systems of tomorrow.

Among the developments in communications technology which may be expected in the 1970s are the 'wired city' on which Post Office engineers have been working for some years. The new towns of Washington, Irvine, Craigavon and Milton Keynes are, or will be, wired for broadband sound and vision transmission into individual homes. Transmission systems into schools and educational institutions already exist in London, Plymouth, Glasgow and Hull. In addition the commercial wired radio and television companies which, up to now, have been prevented by law from transmitting any but the open-circuit services of the B.B.C. and I.T.V. are about to launch their first 'community television' service, which the Minister of Posts and Telecommunications has licensed in Greenwich.

The arrival of the video-cassette, much heralded and long delayed, now also seems to be imminent. People will be able to buy their favourite Western and watch it twice nightly as easily as at present they can acquire their own copy of the 'Top of the Pops'. Their dependence on carefully regulated open-circuit transmissions will lessen dramatically as a result of these developments.

At the same time as the range of reception facilities broadens, access to production facilities is becoming progressively easier. Radio, which used to be thought of as an expensive medium, is now one of the cheapest of the mass media. Television is yet regarded as out of the financial range of all but powerful national organizations. The high-cost image has, indeed, been fostered by the broadcasters, as in earlier years a similar myth was fostered by the film industry. It was not until the new wave of independent producers showed that excellence is not dependent only on financial resources that standards of judgement began to change. As a result the traditional film industry is dead, but film as an art form is very much alive.

It is to be hoped that the broadcasting empires will not go the way of Hollywood; that they will read the signs of the times and avoid a situation in which they will price themselves out of the market. A good broadcast standard V.T.R. machine at present costs about £60,000. The smaller and less sophisticated V.T.R. machines now coming onto the market cost about £500. The picture produced by the latter may only be 75% as good, but it is provided by a machine costing less than 1% of the cost of the former. Technical quality is an important criterion in all art forms. It is desirable in mass communications. But what is the use of exacting the last ounce of technical excellence if this is done at the cost of the vitality of the community?

Half a century after radio services opened, they have been allowed to return to their origins in the local community. The idea of *local* television may take as long to be realized. But there is no reason why it should. Independent Television showed that regional stations, modest by accepted B.B.C. standards, could be viable and make a contribution to the life of their areas.

> The smallest mainland television station on the I.T.V. network, Border Television, has an equipment asset value ... of around £400,000. Before it becomes fully equipped for local live colour to the I.T.A.'s exacting engineering standards, it will have spent another £150,000 ... You could equip a similar station for infinitely less, using X so-called closed circuit equipment. You could do it in black and white (for £45,000) or in colour (for £86,000) ... Television is only expensive if you care to make it so. And if you really *care* about television, and your viewers ... you can make it extremely inexpensive. And still (so we believe) infinitely more effective, relevant and useful (13).

This type of approach fills many professional broadcasters with horror. They fear the abandonment of some of the highest television standards in the world in favour of low-quality self-indulgent programmes produced by semi-professionals for each other. But this need not happen if we determine to apply the right mixture of freedom and public control to developments in broadcasting.

Broadcasting as a public concern

If broadcasting in the 1980s is to enrich the leisure hours of its viewers and listeners; if they are to participate more fully in determining what is offered; and if they are to have a chance to 'have a go' themselves; then this can, paradoxically, be done only by Government intervention. Planning for freedom is not a contradiction in this context. Government must have the courage of its convictions and plan in terms of dynamic intervention instead of regulative restriction.

There are some signs that this change of attitude may be beginning to occur. The Greenwich Cablevision decision may be a straw in the wind. But a total reversal of attitude is needed. Since Government intervention in broadcasting derived originally from the wish to control and regulate the use of airspace it has persistently been regarded as mainly technical in import. The Postmaster General remained the Minister responsible until the creation of the Ministry of Posts and Telecommunications. And the title of that Ministry gives no hint that decisions of grave socio-cultural importance ought to be made within its walls.

The case for a more social-policy-oriented Minister to take charge of broadcasting has been made, and refused, since broadcasting proper began. Lord Reith himself

> would have preferred control over the B.B.C.'s operations . . . to be exercised not by the Postmaster General but by a senior Minister like the Lord President of the Council . . . he did not like major decisions to be taken by Post Office officials who might be well equipped to deal with technical matters but knew little of the problems of programme building (14).

But nothing came of it. And the most recent Committee on Broadcasting under Sir Harry Pilkington reduced the argument *ad absurdum* by concluding that

> If a Minister's express responsibility were for the social aspects of broadcasting, he would address himself — and be expected to address himself — to the content of programmes. The effect must be to lessen the broadcasting authorities' independence of the Government. Under the present arrangement, the Postmaster General's responsibilities derive almost incidentally from his responsibilities for its technical aspects (15).

What is wanted in the new communications era is not, of course, Government control of programmes. The arguments against this set out earlier in this chapter are conclusive. But for Government to contract out of a forward-looking and sociologically aware interest in the structure of broadcasting would be fatal. We need to maintain and to strengthen the best of our national services. They must continue to set standards of technical excellence and, if possible, of artistic and professional achievement. But alongside *some* national and regional services of this kind there must now be made room for a growing diversity of other broadcasting facilities. These will serve sub-regional, area and local communities, special interest groups and specialist services. Some will broadcast over the air, others by cable. Some will be in sound only, others in sound and vision.

The role of Government in this development will be to facilitate technical provision, to ensure basic standards, to moderate between claimants for access. Most important, Government will need to form a view of the role of these developments in the spectrum of community-oriented social policies which it has now begun to pursue. Broadcasting developments need to be related to policies for regional development, policies for urban aid and community development, policies for the encouragement of participation in planning, and policies for industrial relocation and expansion. They must have regard to the more obvious questions of maintaining a healthy press and a viable broadcasting structure at national level now that nationwide coverage has been all but achieved. Decisions will be taken, whether by omission or by commission. Hence Government will bear the responsibility. It would be fortunate both for Government and for the people if it were exercised with foresight and imagination. In this way the people might be set free to shape the use of their major leisure time occupation in the future more creatively than in the past.

Notes and References
1 R. J. Silvey, 'Because it's Free', *Contrast,* Spring 1962, p. 213.
2 A. Briggs, *War of Words,* Oxford University Press, 1970.
3 See Lord Reith, 'Façade of Public Corporations' in *The Times,* 29 March 1966.
4 See Marcel van Dam, 'The Dutch System of Broadcasting' in *Proceedings of the Fourth Symposium on Broadcasting Policy,* Manchester University Department of Extra-mural Studies, 1972.
5 Lord Hill, 'The Broadcaster's World' in *B.B.C. Record,* April 1970, p. 12.
6 From a speech to Foreign Press Association, quoted in *The Times,* 6 April 1972.
7 B. Groombridge, *Television and the People,* Penguin, 1972, p. 240.
8 *Opportunities for the Fourth Channel,* The TV 4 Campaign, 1972, p. 7.
9 From a letter dated December 1971 from Mr T. Rhys, the General Secretary of the A.B.S., to the Minister of Posts and Telecommunications.
10 See A. Briggs, *The Golden Age of Wireless,* Oxford University Press, 1965, pp. 24-6.
11 *Broadcasting* (Cmnd. 3169), H.M.S.O., December 1966, para. 47.

12 See E. G. Weddell, *Broadcasting and Public Policy,* Michael Joseph, 1968, pp. 301 ff.

13 *Opportunities for the Fourth Channel,* op. cit.

14 A. Briggs, op. cit., p. 421.

15 *Report of the Committee on Broadcasting 1960,* (Cmnd. 1753), H.M.S.O., 1962, p. 116, para. 386.

22 Planning for leisure

Michael Dower

'Planning' and 'leisure' — the two words may go ill together. Should not our leisure be spontaneous, unplanned, free from the trammels which beset our working lives? Can we not go where whim takes us, to fish, to sail, to picnic or to court in the grass?

Alas, often we can't — or not without planning. The demands for leisure activity described in this book have broadly outstripped the facilities available to them. We are caught short — short of space in our homes, space in our towns, space in our countryside — space designed and managed for modern leisure. If nearly 60 million people are to gain that expansion of life which leisure can give, within this tight island, there must be planning in their name — unobtrusive planning, let us hope, but deliberated, widespread and continuing.

In this chapter, I want to sketch out the physical facilities we need. I group them at three scales — logical, regional, national — which are a bit arbitrary but which relate to our three main sorts of leisure, namely free time during the day, the weekend, and the annual holiday. I shall then suggest four principles of planning and management.

Space at local scale

The bulk of our leisure is spent in or near the home. Thus our houses are the core of our stock of leisure space — and a pretty rotten core at that. The faults in our housing are, of course, more basic than their inadequacy for leisure. Des Wilson, who founded Shelter, has pointed out that one million British people live in housing too old, damp, cramped and ill-equipped even to be called homes. Priorities in housing must lie with the meeting of basic needs. But a developed nation can reasonably expect its housing to be fit also for leisure.

What does this mean? Mainly space, privacy, warmth and light. With 91% of British households now owning television sets (1), the main living-room has gained a new importance — as a mini-cinema. There must be space in the living-room for that purpose and for the at-home entertaining which has also grown since the war. There must be space elsewhere in the house for the homework, hobbies and record-players of the younger generation: and there must be heating throughout the house, and reasonable sound-proofing between the different rooms. As for space outside the home, demands are gradually changing but not decreasing. The coal-house is replaced by the fuel-oil tank, the vegetable patch by the lawn. But space is needed for parking and tinkering with the car (51% of British households now own at least one (2)); for the lawn and flower garden; for children's play equipment and pets; for garages and workshops; for the growing number of caravans and boats.

The impulse towards more space in and around the home is shown by the great spontaneous exodus from towns to suburbs over the last century, a movement still in full flood. Material from the Political and Economic Planning study of *Urban Growth*, shortly to be published, shows that most of those who have already moved out one step — from the terrace or flat in town to the semi-detached suburban house — would like to make the further move into a detached 'rural' house. This is a mass impulse which many planners have neither recognized nor understood; and which many architects (themselves living in spacious Victorian homes with ample gardens) do not satisfy in the housing they design. Thus our national leisure-at-home is inhibited not only by an inherited stock of cramped terrace houses and early suburbs but also by a restricted supply of building land, with resulting high land prices and high densities, and by the insistence of architects on terrace housing and blocks of flats. I plead not for sprawl, but for flexible, private, warm and sound-proofed housing, reasonably spacious inside and out.

Beyond the home, but still at local scale, our stock of leisure facilities is generally far from adequate, particularly in the cities. Until recently, the officially accepted standards of open space and playing-fields were those of an acreage-per-1,000-population basis, proposed by the National Playing-Fields Association in 1924: and most of our cities were well below the standard. *Planning for Sport* (3), published in 1968 by the Sports Council, shifted the emphasis onto the intensive and flexible use of green space: the creation of hard all-weather surfaces for hockey, soccer and other sports; the provision of modern changing-rooms and toilets and of social facilities such as bars, lounges and club-rooms for family use; and the fact that outdoor leisure space must increasingly be complemented by modern indoor features such as sports halls and swimming pools.

With this emphasis, the gaps become obvious. The All England Women's Hockey Association, for example, published in 1969 (4) a scathing indictment of the grounds on which they had to play — often badly-maintained, closed early, lacking floodlights, with no heat or light in the changing-rooms and nowhere to make tea after the match. As a direct response to this report, the Sports Council persuaded the Government to sponsor, in the borough of Blackburn, a pilot project to examine all existing recreation facilities and see how, by small improvements, they could be made more fit for modern leisure: we shall see what happens!

Antiquity also affects our swimming pools. *Planning for Sport* records that, out of 744 public indoor swimming-pools in use in Britain in 1968, 434 were built before 1914; and states that many of these old pools fall short of modern standards, are costly to maintain and impossible to renovate, and should be replaced as soon as possible. Further work by the Sports Council has shown that, to reach acceptable standards of swimming-pool provision by 1981, we may need to scrap a quarter of our existing pools and build 500 new public indoor pools.

The other major indoor facility – the sports hall or sports centre – is more recently introduced. The Sportcentre at Harlow New Town, opened in May 1964, blazed the trail. Centred on a main sports hall measuring 100 ft x 120 ft by 30 ft high, with small halls around, it provides well-lit indoor space for badminton, basketball, fencing and many other sports, plus clubrooms and a large refreshment room. It is used intensively, seven days a week, fourteen hours a day. Since 1964, over 30 further indoor sport centres have been built in Britain: but, on the Sports Council's reckoning that one such centre is needed for any town with a population between 40 and 90 thousand, and a further centre for each added 50,000 of population, 30 centres is a mere first lap in a marathon of building. To meet this standard, we probably need nearly 1,000 new sports centres in Britain to meet the needs of our expected 1981 population.

Homes, swimming-pools and sports centres may provide the spine of our local leisure provision. But many other facilities are needed for the full life – play-spaces, adventure playgrounds, pre-school play-groups, youth clubs, adult education centres, arts centres and many others. The last twenty years have seen widespread pioneering in many of these fields, not only in new buildings like the Midlands Arts Centre at Cannon Hill Park, Birmingham, but in the imaginative use of existing buildings. The latter is well illustrated by the warm response among the people of North Devon to the wide variety of events – plays, music, music-hall, poetry, folk-singing, exhibitions and 'happenings' – organized in the town and village halls, churches, pubs and other places of the region by the Beaford Arts Centre.

Space at regional scale

Active weekend leisure has become a major fact for people – and planners – since the war. One third of all workers now have a clear two-day weekend: and the number of those who work on Saturdays is steadily falling. Indeed, for a growing number of people the weekend does not necessarily fall on Saturday and Sunday. Workers at Jersey Airport, for example, now do 12-hour shifts of work followed by 36 hours of leisure, with their work alternating between a night-shift basis and a day-shift basis on a fortnightly rota. Elsewhere, automation in industry is leading to new work and leisure patterns, such as seven days on followed by four days off.

Whatever the pattern, these growing slabs of weekly (as opposed to daily) leisure — when combined also with fatter pay packets and growing car-ownership or other mobility — allow people to get away from home and to use leisure space on a regional scale. This has led, for example, to the great growth of interest in golf and in water sports — two activities which make heavy demands in terms of space. The Golf Foundation reckons that the numbers of golfers in Britain doubled between 1954 and 1967 (5), a rate of growth which tallies with figures from elsewhere and appears to be continuing. If this growth continues, it appears from Sports Council figures that we shall need by 1981 over 500 new 18-hole golf courses in Britain: since each such course requires about 110 acres of land, and a capital cost (excluding the land) of about £80,000, the implications for planning are clearly large.

Water sports raise problems of similar magnitude. The last decade has seen a five-fold increase in those who sail for pleasure, and formidable increases in demand for power-boating, water-skiing, canoeing, sub-aqua diving and other water sports. There are reckoned to be over 3 million anglers in this country (6). Now Britain is not as rich in inland water, or even in sheltered coastal water, as many other countries. Only the Lake District and parts of Scotland and Northern Ireland contain large natural waters. But we have many usable rivers, and a growing heritage of man-made waters — the Broads, created by peat-digging six centuries ago; the intricate system of canals; and, growing year by year in area, the reservoirs and the 'wet' gravel pits and open-cast coal pits.

Except for the river Thames, the Broads, and some coastal estuaries like the Hamble, few of these waters are as fully developed for recreation as they could be. Less than half of our reservoirs are open to leisure use, even for angling (7), despite the growing acceptance in the water-supply profession that such use can be fully compatible with water-purity standards. The management of many rivers is so complex that no one has a clear responsibility for encouraging their use for leisure. But the pace of creative planning in this field has increased recently, notable examples being the switch in emphasis towards recreation in the work of the British Waterways Board; the pressure from Government towards the recreational use of reservoirs; and the major schemes for use of wet gravel pits, as in the Lee Valley Regional Park and the Cotswold Water Park. *The Planning of the Coastline* (8), published by the Countryside Commission, recommends the creation of a series of regional parks, both inland and on the coast, with a strong emphasis on water sport. Chichester Harbour, which already has quite severe congestion of sailing craft, is proposed as the first such park.

Bigger still, however, than the demands for golf and water sport are those of simple family recreation by car. More than half the families in Britain now own cars: for them, leisure is not limited to places they can reach on foot or by train, bus or tram. They have an untiring horse, a mobile room, with space for children, dogs, carry-cots, camping kit, picnic table, lilo, hamper and all – a home away from home. People with cars see their relatives twice as often as those without, and get into the countryside far more often. Their main demand is for road-space and attractive places to stop and relax. This demand for road-space is a growing problem for planners. Already in South London, weekend leisure traffic now exceeds weekday traffic on some main roads. The next decade will see growing concern with rural traffic management, as a counterpoint to the urban traffic management of the 1960s.

Space for the weekend motorist to stop and relax also demands creative planning. The intricate and long-settled countryside of Britain has many features to attract and serve the visitor – pubs, churches, roadside verges, village greens and common lands among them. When visitors were few in number, there was room for all – indeed landowners often turned a blind eye to trespass. But as numbers have grown to thousands and tens of thousands, much of the obvious open land has become over-run, many lay-bys soiled, common land eroded, and barbed-wire and 'keep out' notices bespatter the Green Belt.

In the mid-1960s, it became clear that widespread positive provision of leisure space in the countryside was needed – hence the Government's White Paper on *Leisure in the Countryside* (9) and the subsequent provision in the *Countryside Act 1968* (10). The most important powers in the Act are for the provision, by local authorities, of Country Parks and picnic sites – that is, areas specifically designed for informal public recreation – with 75% Government grant; and for Government grant towards similar provision by non-public bodies such as the National Trust. These powers, which came into effect in August 1968, have already led to over one hundred proposals by local authorities for new country parks and almost as many proposals for picnic sites; and the first grants towards private schemes have already been paid.

Space at national scale

The third main call which leisure makes on planning is the annual holiday, and particularly the holiday away from home – that is, tourism.

Tourism in Britain has two main elements – holidaymaking by British people within this country, and visits by foreigners. Total holidaymaking by British people grew steadily from 1950 to 1960, but was roughly constant at 35 to 36 million holidays a year during the decade up to 1970. Of these, about 5 million holidays a year were spent abroad, leaving 30 to 31 million holidays (defined as four nights or more spent away from home) per year in Britain.

The future prospects for British holidaymaking are frankly uncertain. Rises in population, in average income, car ownership, paid holidays and in numbers of school and university students and retired people over the last decade, have *not*, until 1971, produced any increase in the number of holidays. One may guess that people preferred to spend time and money on, in and from the home rather than face the cost, traffic and other uncertainties of a holiday away. As incomes and other factors rise further in the future, we *may* see another swing upwards in holidaymaking. It has been estimated that total British holiday trips within Britain might rise to about 40 million in 1980 (11). My own view is that such growth is unlikely to occur unless major improvements are made to the communications to and within our holiday regions, and to the accommodation and facilities available.

Visits by foreigners to Britain (including those for business and similar purposes as well as holidays) have been rising sharply since the war, from 203,000 in 1946 to 1·7 million in 1960 and over 5 million in 1970. The figure is expected to rise to at least 10 million in 1975; and heavy promotion, plus falling group travel costs, should ensure that it continues to rise thereafter.

Tourism on this scale has major economic significance to the country – hence the heavy financial support from the Government over the last decade for the tourist promotion work of the British Travel Association. But it also makes very heavy calls on accommodation and facilities; and it was the growing inadequacy of these which led to the Development of Tourism Act 1969. This Act replaced the British Travel Association by the British Tourist Authority; set up three National Tourist Boards for England, Wales and Scotland with a prime concern for tourist facilities within each country; provided for a limited period of Government grants and loans for hotel building; and set the framework for further work in planning for tourism.

The most immediate effect of the Act has been a rapid growth in hotel building, extension and improvement. Thus, within a year of coming into existence, the English Tourist Board alone had, by October 1970, received applications for statutory 20% grants towards £148 million-worth of hotel building or extension, which would add over 33,600 hotel beds before March 1973 – as compared with only 26,500 new hotel beds built in the whole of Britain in the decade up to 1966 (12). Nearly half of these 33,600 beds will be in London, serving mainly the foreign visitors who flock to the capital city. British holiday-makers need a wider distribution and variety of accommodation, ranging from the traditional 'with-catering' forms such as hotels, guest houses and cottages, through 'all-in' holiday camps, to the more informal 'self-catering' types such as holiday flats, chalets, caravans and camp sites. Since the war, there has been a marked increase in the proportion of holidays by British holidaymakers spent in the higher grades of hotels, in holiday camps and in most of the 'self-catering' types, with a decrease in that spent in the lower grades of hotels and in guest houses (13).

The changes in demand have been reflected in the trends of accommodation, with a strong swing towards self-catering types, particularly in some of the remote regions. In the South-West, for example, 41% of the 643,000 beds in the whole region are now of self-catering type (14). Their build-up has caused a number of problems – the scenic impact of camping and caravan sites, particularly on the coast; danger to public health, for example through overnight camping beside main tourist routes; threats to the economy of the older resorts as the traditional 'static' resort holiday gives way increasingly to the mobile holiday permitted by the car; and, most recently, the impact upon rural areas of the growing demand for 'second homes'. In *The Planning of the Coastline* (15), the Countryside Commission recommend the planning and promotion of holiday areas around revitalized resorts; and the creation of new resorts and holiday villages with a wide variety of accommodation and of recreation facilities.

Accommodation is not the only need: almost more fundamental are the attractions and facilities. Visitors are drawn to an area because they can see things, do things, they want to see and do. Expressed in economic terms, these are the 'products' they want to buy; and an area which wants such customers must know the products it can offer in a competitive world.

There are perhaps five main types of effective attraction, each presenting a main appeal to different markets. *First,* the traditional one of sun and sea, still a strong draw for British people who do not want to travel far on holiday, but not a serious magnet for overseas visitors: an asset to be safeguarded and developed, but not a universal attraction. *Second,* scenic driving by car or coach, a major interest since car-ownership became widespread, still a novelty and favourite holiday or weekend activity for millions, but likely to decline somewhat in future as the novelty wears off and road congestion gets worse. *Third,* sight-seeing, that is, visiting historic houses, castles, battle-fields, monuments, gardens, wild life parks, beauty spots, the homes and graves of ancestors; a real growth sector, still rooted in curiosity, but with a growing search for real understanding and information; popular among foreign visitors; presenting a challenge to the managers of manifold key features in each region. *Fourth,* active sports, no longer just for the squire with his shot-gun or the local poacher with his gaff, but for hundreds or thousands in fishing, sailing, canoeing, skiing, pony trekking, walking and climbing; demanding space, clubhouses, stables, equipment, approach roads. *Last,* educational activity, from field studies in botany to summer schools of art, language courses, conferences, National Trust cruises, children's summer camps; a growing market not confined to the summer season; requiring imagination to launch and run.

Together, these attractions make a clear-cut physical demand. They require limited areas of land and water in sole or dominant use for recreation, such as golf courses, beach access areas, historic sites or the country parks for which the Countryside Acts provide; a system of routes to link these, mainly roads, rights of way and waterways; and the secondary or sporadic use of areas of moor, wood or farmland for walking, riding, picnicking, shooting and so on. But they also increasingly demand the skilled conservation of resources and of heritage. Thus the angler must have pure water and healthy fish, the naturalist needs the osprey, others need the historical site and the scenery itself. This does not imply 'no change'; but it is a growing factor in the planning and management of land.

In addition to accommodation and attractions, the holiday-maker needs communications and services. I have mentioned the swing, in holiday transport, towards the car. Nationally, 67% of main holidays and 70% of second holidays by British people at home are taken by car (16). For holidays to remote regions, the proportion is even higher, for example 80% for visitors to Devon and Cornwall (17). In these regions, with little public transport, the car is clearly needed by most visitors, both to get there and to get around. Thus, good roads to and within the regions are vital – roads able to cope in many areas with a sudden doubling, or more, of the local car population in the summer; and, in places such as Aviemore, with year-round recreational traffic. Local life and traffic can adjust a bit, but it cannot disappear: visitors are tolerant of road congestion, but only to a certain point. In many areas, the inadequacy of roads is becoming a serious impediment to the growth of recreation and tourism, and road improvements a major item of cost to cater for them, as was well shown by the report on the Cairngorms area (18).

Visitors who do *not* have cars, of course, need a combination of private and public transport, which may be readily available in populous regions and main resorts, but is by no means always so in the remoter regions. The decline of rural bus and railway services since the war is a real drawback. One could wish that the policy of social subsidy had come earlier and done more to slow down the Beeching-type process of closure. The private railway lines such as the Ffestiniog and the Dart Valley Railway show something of the potential and imaginative flair which is needed.

The remoter regions, in particular, must increasingly gear their communications to the needs of the visitor – and use him to help to sustain and improve the year-round infrastructure for their residents. This is true also of services – water, sewerage, refuse disposal, hospitals, rescue services, police, information centres, garages, shops, toilets, roadside rest areas – inadequacy in any one of which may spoil the visitor's holiday and damage the reputation of the area. Such services have to be paid for (sometimes, as with water supply, to an extent much above local needs): but they help to earn the income from tourism, and, if skilfully planned, can form part of the year-round social structure of the area.

Four principles of planning for leisure

Having described some of the reasons why planning for leisure is needed at the local, regional and national scale, may I now suggest four principles which should guide such planning.

First, the imaginative use and adaptation of resources. Britain is a long-settled country, densely populated, largely in private hands, full of historic buildings and structures. Unlike the United States, we do not have large areas of uncommitted public land which we can devote to meeting the needs of leisure. With us, leisure must find its place on a land surface already largely pre-empted by other use – hence the need for imagination. I remember visiting a disused pump house of the Metropolitan Water Board at Stratford, East London, with Lord (then Sir John) Hunt, the mountaineer. We were working on the ideas which led to the Lea Valley Regional Park. 'Could the tall chimney of the pump-house be used for climbing practice?' I asked Sir John. 'Indeed it could,' said he, 'and the inside of the chimney could be used for pot-holing.'

This approach can extend to resources of all kinds. Canals, after their workaday past, can be turned into waterways for cruising, canoeing and angling; their towpaths into routes for walking and nature study; their warehouses into museums, hostels and field study centres. Disused railways can become private steam railways, bridlepaths or cycle-tracks. Disused gravel pits can become water-sport centres or be landscaped as the setting for water-side restaurants. Open-cast coal workings can be sculpted to form lakes, stadia and artificial ski-slopes. Disused engine-houses, maltings and dock warehouses can become arts centres, opera-houses and studios – witness the Roundhouse at Camden Town, the Maltings at Snape, the new use of St Katherine's Dock.

This subtle use of resources can permit leisure to be woven into the fabric of town and country without serious impact upon the major existing activities. Until recently, the major rural activities of farming and forestry have been more concerned to protect themselves from the impact of leisure — in terms of litter, fires, vandalism and traffic — than to consider any possible benefit they might gain from leisure or give to it. But interest in such positive benefit is now growing.

Thus my second principle is the integration of leisure in the countryside. A well-established aspect of this is the farm holiday, already an important source of income to many farmers and of holiday enjoyment to town families. The recent report on *Tourism and the Cornish Farmer* (19), for example, has shown that some 18% of all farmers in Cornwall now take in holidaymakers; that at least a further 20% would do so if they had space or time; and that gross receipts from visitors amount to more than a quarter of their net income for a majority of farmers concerned. Of course, many of the small dairy farms in Cornwall, near to the attractions of the coast, have both the need, the space and the opportunity for this type of trade. The two-room crofter's house in the Hebrides, or the remote hill farm in the Pennines or Wales, may seem less suited to the purpose. But, even in such areas, growth in farm holidays could be encouraged by extensions and chalet building of the type grant-aided in parts of Ireland; by conversion of farm buildings or layout of caravan and camp sites; by opening of tea-rooms and craft workshops; and also by creating attractions.

Thus the farmers, individually or in groups, could exploit or create opportunities for riding, shooting, fishing, nature study, even for educational use of the farming process and of the countryside. Action of this type, including game management and creation of farm ponds, has converted thousands of American farms into largely recreational enterprises; is the subject of current experimental projects by the Countryside Commission in the Lake District and Snowdonia; and deserves substantial thought here at a time of growing economic uncertainty for much of our marginal agriculture.

In forestry, too, leisure is growing in importance as a factor in forest planning and management. The Forestry Commission is already catering for public use, for example in its Forest Parks, school forests and camp sites. Now the Countryside Act (20) has given the Commission a specific brief for recreation, including powers to plant new forests for amenity purposes. We are likely to see in the State sector at least, not the actual multiple use of forest land, but the increasing use of forests as the setting and shelter for recreation, from camping to watching deer, picnicking to rally driving.

This sort of integration of leisure in the countryside has not only a physical and an economic importance – but also a social one in a predominantly urban nation. We all, as townsmen, look to the land for our food, timber, water, minerals, power and leisure: but for all of these, except leisure, we let others dig them for us. We do not go and get our own food, but we do go to the countryside for our leisure – and thus it brings us into direct contact with the land and, uniquely, gives us the chance to understand what the countryside is. Hence it reduces the dangerous ignorance which still persists between town and country. Moreover, this direct contact focuses the interest of townsmen on the countryside and on its conservation. When they see the beauty, the history, the wildlife, suddenly these things are not only there but they are important. There are votes in them, there is money being paid in entry subscriptions to conserve them, there are hands to help in physical work, and there are the hearts and voices of town dwellers legitimately urging change, or the control of change, in the countryside.

The third principle is the need for skilful management. It is not enough to create youth clubs, sports halls, country parks or water-sport centres. They must be managed. This goes way beyond the obvious things like cutting grass or stopping horse-play in swimming-pools. It may mean adapting, and then maintaining, a park, a lake or a forest to a level of use far greater than it would naturally sustain. It may mean directing people away from fragile areas to tough ones, preventing vandalism, reducing fire risks, checking pollution. Perhaps most tricky, it means finding ways to balance the use of land against its capacity – that is, the level at which the resource is not damaged by the users, and the user's enjoyment is not reduced by overcrowding. The two most obvious ways to control use – by congestion or by price – are rarely acceptable. Congestion wastes time, money and temper: price control acts against the less wealthy. We must find more positive methods – creation of a fair and accessible choice of places to go; sound design so that people need not constantly move about; sensible systems of circulation and traffic management – and, serving all of these, more and better information and education.

On the latter point – information – we are not well equipped. We have among the best maps in the world. But we have no Michelin Guide, no standard pattern of information about places to enjoy, no skilful use of news media to spread the load of recreation. Let me give an American example. The Huron-Clinton Authority at Detroit knows the capacity of each of its regional parks, element by element – beaches, for example, can take twenty-five people an acre, golf courses ten, nature study areas three. The car parks are fitted to this capacity, with overspill space onto grass areas for peak crowds; and the roads are fitted to the peak traffic. The flow of cars to each park is checked. The parks are linked together by telephone and to the radio wavelength of the police. When one park is full, this fact is broadcast and people are encouraged to go to one which is not.

Could not our new local radio stations do more of this? Could we not have consumers' guides to the leisure facilities of each region, a sort of 'Leisure Which?' Could we not have centres in each rural area like that at Brockhole in the Lake District or the Landmark Centre at Carrbridge in Inverness-shire, where the visitor can go and see what the area can offer?

The last principle is partnership. Effective planning for leisure must involve a host of people — public and private, corporate and individual. Public bodies must be involved because many resources suitable for leisure — for example forests, canals, reservoirs and school buildings — are in their hands; because they control the roads and other basic services; because some leisure facilities (at present prices, anyway) are uneconomic for private enterprise to provide, swimming-pools being a key example. But public bodies should also be ready to encourage private action, for example by landowners in opening their historic houses and grounds to the public; by gravel companies in creating water-sport areas; by voluntary trusts and clubs in building sports facilities. This partnership already exists, by grace of British pragmatism and common sense: we must continue to develop it.

Notes and References

1 *Family Expenditure Survey 1970,* H.M.S.O., 1971.
2 ibid.
3 *Planning for Sport,* Sports Council, 1968.
4 *Facilities for Women's Hockey,* All England Women's Hockey Association, 1968.
5 *Planning for Sport,* Sports Council, 1968.
6 *Digest of Recreation Statistics,* Countryside Commission, 1970.
7 *Amenity Use of Reservoirs Survey,* British Waterworks Association, 1969.
8 *The Planning of the Coastline,* Countryside Commission, H.M.S.O., 1970.
9 *Leisure in the Countryside,* H.M.S.O., 1966.
10 Countryside Act, 1968, H.M.S.O.
11 *Coastal Recreation and Holidays,* Countryside Commission, H.M.S.O., 1969.
12 *Investment in Hotels and Catering,* Hotel and Catering Economic Development Committee, H.M.S.O., 1968.
13 *Digest of Tourist Statistics,* British Travel Association, 1969.
14 *A Study of Tourist and Holiday Facilities in South West England,* Miles-Kelcey Ltd, Consultants for British Travel Association, 1969.
15 *The Planning of the Coastline,* Countryside Commission, H.M.S.O., 1970.
16 *Digest of Tourist Statistics,* British Travel Association, 1969.
17 *The Holiday Industry of Devon and Cornwall,* F. M. M. Lewes and others, University of Exeter, 1969.
18 *Cairngorm Area*; Report of the Technical Group on the Cairngorm Area of the Eastern Highlands of Scotland, Scottish Development Dept., H.M.S.O., 1967.
19 *Tourism and the Cornish Farmer,* E. T. Davies, Department of Economics, University of Exeter, 1969.
20 The Countryside Act, H.M.S.O., 1968.

Index of names